POST OFFICE CLERK-CARRIER

E.P. Steinberg

MACMILLAN
U.S.A.

Eighteenth Edition

Macmillan General Reference
A Prentice Hall/Macmillan Company
15 Columbus Circle
New York, NY 10023

An Arco Book

MACMILLAN is a registered trademark of Macmillan, Inc.
ARCO is a registered trademark of Prentice-Hall, Inc.

Library of Congress Cataloging-in-Publication Data

Steinberg, Eve P.
Post office clerk-carrier / E.P. Steinberg
        p.   cm.
ISBN: 0-671-79974-6
1. Postal service—United States—Employees. 2. Postal service—
United States—Letter carriers. 3. Postal service—United States—
Examinations, questions, etc. I. Title.
HE6499.S75   1993   92-45150
383'.145'076—dc20   CIP

Manufactured in the United States of America

10 9 8 7 6 5 4 3 2

CONTENTS

INTRODUCTION

HOW TO USE THIS BOOK

The Postal Service examination for Clerk-Carrier may be the most important exam you ever take. It can be your ticket to a rewarding career that offers good pay, excellent working conditions and a secure future. The very things that make the job appealing to you, though, make it appealing to many others too, and often hundreds of applicants compete for a single job opening. The only way to get the job you seek is to earn the highest possible score on the Clerk-Carrier exam. That's where this book can help. If you follow its advice and take advantage of the training and practice it offers, you will be well prepared to earn high scores on the postal exam and a spot near the top of the list of eligibles for jobs with the postal service.

Ideally, you should start your preparation two or three months before the exam. That gives you plenty of time to complete all of the Model Exams, and to decide on and practice the memory scheme that works best for you. If you begin early enough, you will be able to leave a few days between each Model Exam so that your memory of one sorting scheme does not interfere with your memorizing of another scheme. No matter how much time you have, start *now*. Work your way through the entire book, and give it all the time and attention you possibly can.

Read the first two chapters. Chapter One describes the job of the clerk and the carrier and presents the many advantages of working for the postal service. It gives you the encouragement you need to do your very best. Chapter Two tells you how to apply for a job with the postal service and what kind of exam you will have to take.

Next, take the Diagnostic Exam to discover where you stand at this moment. Choose a quiet, well-lighted spot for your work. Clear away all distractions from your desk or tabletop. Bring two sharpened pencils with erasers and a stop watch or kitchen timer to your work area. Tear out the answer sheet for the Diagnostic Exam, start the timer, read the directions and begin the Address Checking Test. Work quickly and accurately. When the time is up, draw a line under the last question you answered and under its answer space. Later on you may want to go back and answer the remaining questions just for the extra practice.

Follow the directions for timing and taking the Memory for Addresses Test. This test provides three sets of practice questions to help you memorize the sorting scheme. You are to answer all the practice questions. When you determine your score, however, count only the last set of questions, which is headed "Memory for Addresses Test." After you have completed the Diagnostic Exam, check your answers against the correct answers at the end of the exam. Following the correct answers you will find instructions for analyzing your errors on the Address Checking Test. Follow these instructions and learn what kinds of errors you made most often. If you understand the type of error you are most likely to make, you will be able to avoid that type of error on future tests.

Calculate your score on the score sheet provided, considering only those questions you answered within the time limit. You will notice that the scoring instructions for the two parts of the exam are different. Follow the instructions for each separate part in calculating your score. Then look at the Self-Evaluation Chart to see how well you did.

Do not be discouraged by low scores on the Diagnostic Exam. You still have plenty of time to improve your scores with the instruction and practice that follow.

The next two chapters contain concrete advice about the techniques for answering postal exam questions quickly and accurately. Read these chapters carefully and follow through on all suggestions before taking the remaining Model Exams. It's a good idea to come back to these chapters between exams or just before the actual exam to refresh yourself on ways to improve your scores.

Leaving ample time between them, take the remaining Model Exams just the way you took the Preliminary Exam. Time yourself accurately and score yourself honestly. Analyze the errors you made on each Address Checking Test so that you can try to avoid making the same mistakes in the future. After you complete each Model Exam, fill in the Graph to check your progress and locate your score on the Self-Evaluation Chart to see how your ranking improves.

As a final step, read and study the final chapter in the book, "How to Answer Number Series Questions." Although this kind of question is *not* usually part of the Clerk-Carrier exam, it *is* usually included in the exam for Letter Sorting Machine Operator. Once you establish your eligibility for Clerk-Carrier, you may also wish to qualify for Letter Sorting Machine Operator, and then you will need to know how to solve number series problems.

By the time you have completed this book, you should be well prepared for the Clerk-Carrier exam. These few final suggestions should help you do your best on the big day:

- Get a good night's sleep.
- Get up in time to eat breakfast and do whatever you have to do to insure that you are fully alert.
- Dress comfortably.
- Allow yourself plenty of time to get to the exam.
- Remember to bring your admission card and identification that has your picture or your signature.
- Choose a comfortable seat that is as free as possible from drafts, noise and traffic.
- Follow the directions of the test administrator. If you don't understand what you are to do, *ask questions*.
- Take a deep breath, relax and resolve to do your best. Your preparation and practice should pay off in high scores on the exam.

WORKING FOR
THE POST OFFICE

The United States Postal Service is an independent agency of the Federal Government. As such, employees of the Postal Service are federal employees who enjoy the benefits offered by the government. These benefits include an automatic raise at least once a year, regular cost of living adjustments, liberal paid vacation and sick leave, life insurance, hospitalization, and the opportunity to join a credit union. At the same time, the operation of the Postal Service is businesslike and independent of politics. A postal worker's job is secure even though administrations may change. An examination system is used to fill vacancies. The examination system provides opportunities for those who are able and motivated to enter the Postal Service and to move within it.

Since postal employment is so popular, entry is very competitive. In most areas the Clerk-Carrier Exam is administered only once every three years. The resulting list is used to fill vacancies as they occur in the next three years. An individual who has been employed by the Postal Service for at least a year may ask to take the exam for any position and, if properly qualified, may fill a vacancy ahead of a person whose name is on the regular list. (The supervisor may or may not grant the request to take a special exam to fill a vacancy, but most supervisors readily grant such permission to employees with good performance records who have served an adequate period in their current positions.) It is even possible to change careers within the Postal Service. A custodian, for instance, might take the Clerk-Carrier Exam; a stenographer might choose to become a letter sorting machine operator; or a mail handler might take an exam to enter personnel work. If the exam for the precise position that you want will not be administered for some time, it might be worthwhile to take the exam for another position in hopes of entering the Postal Service and then moving from within.

One very common "instant progression" within the Postal Service is that from clerk-carrier, a salary level 5 position, to letter sorting machine (LSM) operator, a salary level 6 position. Anyone who qualifies as a clerk-carrier is automatically offered the opportunity to take the LSM Exam. The advantages of becoming an LSM operator include not only the higher salary, but also the increased employment possibilities. The field is expanding, and there are far more openings for LSM operators than there are for clerks or carriers. In fact, unless you really do not want to operate a letter sorting machine, it is wise to apply from the outset for all three positions—Clerk, Carrier and LSM operator. The more lists you can get your name on, the better your chances of landing a postal job.

Salaries, hours, and some other working conditions as well are subject to frequent change. The postal workers have a very effective union that bargains for them and gains increasingly better conditions. At the time of your employment, you should make your own inquiry as to salary, hours, and other conditions as they apply to you. Job descriptions and requirements are less subject to change. In the next few pages we quote job descriptions as provided by the government.

POSTAL CLERKS

People are most familiar with the window clerk who sits behind the counter in post office lobbies selling stamps or accepting parcel post. However, the majority of postal clerks are distribution clerks who sort incoming and outgoing mail in workrooms. Only in a small post office does a clerk do both kinds of work.

When mail arrives at the post office it is dumped on long tables where distribution clerks and mail handlers separate it into groups of letters, parcel post, and magazines and newspapers. Clerks feed letters into stamp-canceling machines and cancel the rest by hand. The mail is then taken to other sections of the post office to be sorted by destination. Clerks first separate the mail into primary destination categories: mail for the local area, for each nearby state, for groups of distant states, and for some of the largest cities. This primary distribution is followed by one or more secondary distributions. For example, local mail is combined with mail coming in from other cities and is sorted according to street and number. In post offices with electronic mail-sorting machines, clerks simply push a button, corresponding to the letter's destination, and the letter drops into the proper slot.

The clerks at post office windows provide a variety of services in addition to selling stamps and money orders. They weigh packages to determine postage and check to see if their size, shape, and condition are satisfactory for mailing. Clerks also register and insure mail and answer questions about postage rates, mailing restrictions, and other postal matters. Occasionally they may help a customer file a claim for a damaged package. In large post offices a window clerk may provide only one or two of these services and be called a registry, stamp, or money order clerk.

TRAINING AND ADVANCEMENT

Postal clerks must be at least 18 years old and pass a two-part written examination. The first part tests reading accuracy by asking the applicant to compare pairs of addresses and indicate which are identical. The second part tests ability to memorize mail distribution systems.

Applicants who work with an electronic sorting machine must pass a special examination which includes a machine aptitude test. They must pass a physical examination and may be asked to show that they can lift and handle mail sacks weighing up to 70 pounds.

Applicants should apply at the post office where they wish to work because each post office keeps a separate list of those who have passed the examination. Applicants' names are listed in order of their scores. Five extra points are added to the score of an honorably discharged veteran, and 10 extra points to the score of a veteran wounded in combat or disabled. Disabled veterans who have a compensable, service-connected disability of 10 percent or more are placed at the top of the list. When a vacancy occurs, the appointing officer chooses one of the top three applicants; the rest of the names remain on the list for future appointments.

New clerks are trained on the job. Most clerks begin with simple tasks to learn regional groupings of states, cities, and ZIP codes. To help clerks learn these groups, many post offices offer classroom instruction.

A good memory, good coordination, and the ability to read rapidly and accurately are important.

Distribution clerks work closely with other clerks, frequently under the tension and strain of meeting mailing deadlines. Window clerks must be tactful when dealing with the public, especially when answering questions or receiving complaints.

EMPLOYMENT OUTLOOK

Employment of postal clerks is expected to grow slowly through the mid-1990s. Most openings will occur when clerks retire or transfer to other occupations.

Although the amount of mail post offices handle is expected to grow as both population and the number of businesses grow, modernization of post offices and installation of new equipment will increase the amount of mail each clerk can handle. For example, machines which semiautomatically mark destination codes on envelopes are rapidly being incorporated. These codes can be read by computer-controlled letter-sorting machines which automatically drop each letter into the proper slot for its destination. With this system, clerks read addresses only once, at the time they are coded, instead of several times, as they now do. Eventually this equipment will be installed in all large post offices.

Working conditions of clerks differ according to the specific work assignments and the amount and kind of labor-saving machinery in the post office. In small post offices clerks must carry heavy mail sacks from one part of the building to another and sort the mail by hand. In large post offices, chutes and conveyors move the mail and much of the sorting is done by machine. In either case, clerks are on their feet most of the time, reaching for sacks of mail, placing packages and bundles into sacks while sorting, and walking around the workroom.

Distribution clerks may become bored with the routine of sorting mail unless they enjoy trying to improve their speed and accuracy. They also may have to work at night, because most large post offices process mail around the clock.

A window clerk, on the other hand, has a greater variety of duties, has frequent contact with the public, generally has a less strenuous job, and never has to work a night shift.

MAIL CARRIERS

NATURE OF THE WORK

Most mail carriers travel planned routes delivering and collecting mail. Carriers start work at the post office early in the morning, where they spend a few hours arranging their mail for delivery, readdressing letters to be forwarded, and taking care of other details.

A carrier typically covers the route on foot, toting a heavy load of mail in a satchel or pushing it in a cart. In outlying suburban areas where houses are far apart, a car or small truck is sometimes needed to deliver mail. Residential carriers cover their routes only once a day, but carriers assigned a business district may make two trips or more. Deliveries are made house-to-house except in large buildings, such as apartment houses, which have all the mailboxes on the first floor.

Besides making deliveries, carriers collect c.o.d. fees and obtain signed receipts for registered and sometimes for insured mail. If a customer is not home the carrier leaves a notice that tells where special mail is being held. Carriers also pick up letters to be mailed.

After completing their routes, carriers return to the post office with mail gathered from street collection boxes and homes. They may separate letters and parcels so that stamps can be canceled easily, and they turn in the receipts and money collected during the day.

Many carriers have more specialized duties than those just described. Some deliver only parcel post. Others collect mail from street boxes and office mail chutes. Rural carriers provide a wide variety of postal services. In addition to delivering and picking up mail, they sell stamps and money orders, and accept parcels and letters to be registered or insured.

All carriers answer customers' questions about postal regulations and service and provide change-of-address cards and other postal forms when requested.

OTHER QUALIFICATIONS

Mail carriers must be at least 18 years old and pass a two-part written examination. The first part tests clerical accuracy by asking the applicant to compare pairs of addresses and indicate which are identical. The second part tests ability to memorize mail distribution systems.

Applicants must have a driver's license and pass a road test if the job involves driving. They also must pass a physical examination and may be asked to show that they can lift and handle mail sacks weighing up to 70 pounds. Applicants who have had health conditions that might interfere with work must have a special review to determine their eligibility.

Applicants should apply at the post office where they wish to work because each post office keeps a separate list of those who have passed the examination. Applicant's names are listed in order of their scores. Five extra points are added to the score of an honorably discharged veteran and 10 extra points to the score of a veteran wounded in combat or disabled. Disabled veterans who have a compensable, service-connected disability of 10 percent or more are placed at the top of the list. When a vacancy occurs, the appointing officer chooses one of the top three applicants; the rest of the names remain on the list to be considered for future openings.

EMPLOYMENT OUTLOOK

Employment of mail carriers is expected to change very little through the mid-1990s. Although the amount of mail may increase along with growth in population and business activity, more efficient delivery of mail should limit the need for additional carriers. Most job openings will result from the need to replace experienced carriers who retire, or transfer to other occupations. Openings will be concentrated in metropolitan areas.

WORKING CONDITIONS

Most carriers begin work early in the morning, in some cases as early as 6 a.m., if they have routes in the business district. Carriers spend most of their time outdoors in all kinds of weather, walking from house to house with their heavy mailbags. Even those who drive must walk when making deliveries, and must lift heavy sacks of parcel post when loading their vehicles.

The job, however, has its advantages. Carriers who begin work early in the morning are through by early afternoon. They are also free to work at their own pace as long as they cover their routes within a certain period of time. Moreover, full-time postal employees have more job security than workers in most other industries.

OCCUPATIONS IN THE POSTAL SERVICE

The U.S. Postal Service handles billions of pieces of mail a year, including letters, magazines, and parcels. Close to a million workers are required to process and deliver this mail. The vast majority of Postal Service jobs are open to workers with 4 years of high school or less. The work is steady. Some of the jobs, such as mail carrier, offer a good deal of personal freedom. Other jobs, however, are more closely supervised and more routine.

WHO WORKS FOR THE POSTAL SERVICE?

Most people are familiar with the duties of the mail carrier and the post office window clerk. Yet few are aware of the many different tasks required in processing mail and of the variety of occupations in the Postal Service.

At all hours of the day and night, a steady stream of letters, packages, magazines, and papers moves through the typical large post office. Mail carriers have collected some of this mail from neighborhood mailboxes; some has been trucked in from surrounding towns or from the airport. When a truck arrives at the post office, mail handlers unload the mail. Postal clerks then sort it according to destination. After being sorted, outgoing mail is loaded into trucks for delivery to the airport or nearby towns. Local mail is left for carriers to deliver the next morning.

To keep buildings and equipment clean and in good working order, the Postal Service employs a variety of service and maintenance workers, including janitors, laborers, truck mechanics, electricians, carpenters, and painters. Some workers specialize in repairing machines that process mail.

Postal inspectors audit the operations of post offices to see that they are run efficiently, that funds are spent properly, and that postal laws and regulations are observed. They also prevent and detect crimes such as theft, forgery, and fraud involving use of the mail.

Postmasters and supervisors are responsible for the day-to-day operation of the post office, for hiring and promoting employees, and for setting up work schedules.

The Postal Service also contracts with private businesses to transport mail. There are more than 12,500 of these "Star" route contracts. Most "Star" route carriers use trucks to haul mail, but in some remote areas horses or boats are used instead.

Almost 85 percent of all postal workers are in jobs directly related to processing and delivering mail. This group includes postal clerks, mail carriers, mail handlers, and truck drivers. Postmasters and supervisors make up nearly 10 percent of total employment and maintenance workers about 4 percent. The remainder includes such workers as postal inspectors, guards, personnel workers, and secretaries.

WHERE ARE THE JOBS?

The Postal Service operates more than 41,000 installations. Most are post offices, but some serve special purposes such as handling payroll records or supplying equipment.

Although every community receives mail service, employment is concentrated in large metropolitan areas. Post offices in cities such as New York, Chicago, and Los Angeles employ a great number of workers because they not only process huge amounts of mail for their own populations but also serve as mail processing points for the smaller communities that surround them. These large city post offices have sophisticated machines for sorting the mail. In these post offices, distribution clerks who have qualified as machine operators quickly scan addresses and send letters on their way automatically by pushing the proper button. These clerks must be able to read addresses quickly and accurately, must be able to memorize codes and sorting schemes and must demonstrate machine aptitude by their performance on the Number Series part of the exam.

TRAINING, OTHER QUALIFICATIONS, AND ADVANCEMENT

An applicant for a Postal Service job must pass an examination and meet minimum age requirements. Generally, the minimum age is 18 years, but a high school graduate may begin work at 16 years if the job is not hazardous and does not require use of a motor vehicle. Many Postal Service jobs do not require formal education or special training. Applicants for these jobs are hired on the basis of their examination scores.

Applicants should apply at the post office where they wish to work and take the entrance examination for the job they want. Examinations for most jobs include a written test. A physical examination is required as well. Applicants for jobs that require strength and stamina are sometimes given a special test. For example, mail handlers must be able to lift mail sacks weighing up to 70 pounds. The names of applicants who pass the examinations are placed on a list in the order of their scores. Separate eligibility lists are maintained for each post office. Five extra points are added to the score of an honorably discharged veteran and 10 extra points to the score of a veteran wounded in combat or disabled. Disabled veterans who have a compensable, service-connected disability of 10 percent or more are placed at the top of the eligibility list. When a job opens, the appointing officer chooses one of the top three applicants. Others are left on the list so that they can be considered for future openings.

New employees are trained either on the job by supervisors and other experienced employees or in local training centers. Training ranges from a few days to several months, depending on the job. For example, mail handlers and mechanics' helpers can learn their jobs in a relatively short time. Postal inspectors, on the other hand, need months of training.

Advancement opportunities are available for most postal workers because there is a management commitment to provide career development. Also, employees can get preferred assignments, such as the day shift or a more desirable delivery route, as their seniority increases. When an opening occurs, employees may submit written requests, called "bids," for assignment to the vacancy. The bidder who meets the qualifications and has the most seniority gets the job.

In addition, postal workers can advance to better paying positions by learning new skills. Training programs are available for low-skilled workers who wish to become technicians or mechanics.

Applicants for supervisory jobs must pass an examination. Additional requirements for promotion may include training or education, a satisfactory work record, and appropriate personal characteristics such as leadership ability. If the leading candidates are equally qualified, length of service also is considered.

Although opportunities for promotion to supervisory positions in smaller post offices are limited, workers may apply for vacancies in a larger post office and thus increase their chances.

EMPLOYMENT OUTLOOK

Employment in the Postal Service is expected to grow more slowly than the average for all industries through the mid-1990s. Mechanization of mail processing and more efficient delivery should allow the Postal Service to handle increasing amounts of mail without corresponding increases in employment. Nevertheless, thousands of job openings will result as workers retire or transfer to other fields.

EARNINGS AND WORKING CONDITIONS

Postal Service employees are paid under several separate pay schedules depending upon the duties of the job and the knowledge, experience, or skill required. For example, there are separate schedules for production workers such as clerks and mail handlers, for rural carriers, for postal managers, and for postal executives. In all pay schedules, except that of executives, employees receive periodic "step" increases up to a specified maximum if their job performance is satisfactory.

The conditions that follow are subject to collective bargaining and may well be different by the time you are employed by the Postal Service.

Full-time employees work an 8-hour day, 5 days a week. Both full-time and part-time employees who work more than 8 hours a day or 40 hours a week receive overtime pay of one and one-half times their hourly rates. In addition, pay is higher for those on the night shift.

Postal employees earn 13 days of annual leave (vacation) during each of their first 3 years of service, including prior Federal civilian and military service; 20 days each year for 3 to 15 years of service; and 26 days after 15 years. In addition, they earn 13 days of paid sick leave a year regardless of length of service.

Other benefits include retirement and survivorship annuities, free group life insurance, and optional participation in health insurance programs supported in part by the Postal Service.

Most post office buildings are clean and well-lighted, but some of the older ones are not. The Postal Service is in the process of replacing and remodeling its outmoded buildings, and conditions are expected to improve.

Most postal workers are members of unions and are covered by a national agreement between the Postal Service and the unions.

For a detailed description of 13 more Postal Service jobs, how to qualify for them, sample questions, and model exams for practice, purchase Arco's *Postal Exams Handbook*.

APPLYING FOR
POSTAL POSITIONS

The Post Office Clerk-Carrier Exam is not a regularly scheduled exam given on the same date all over the country. Rather, the Clerk-Carrier Exam is separately scheduled in each postal geographic area. An area may comprise a number of states or, in densely populated regions, may consist of only a portion of one county. The frequency of administration also varies, though generally the exam is offered every two or three years.

When an exam is about to open in a postal area, the postal examiner for the area sends notices to all the post offices serviced by that area. The examiner also places ads in local newspapers and commercials over local radio stations. State employment offices receive and post copies of the announcement, and Civil Service newspapers carry the information as well. The announcement that you can pick up at your post office looks like this:

The Opportunity: Applications are now being accepted, and examinations will be given to establish a register of eligibles or to expand the current register of eligibles from which future clerk and carrier vacancies in this Post Office will be filled. All interested persons who meet the requirements described in this announcement are urged to apply.

Qualification Requirements: No experience is required. All applicants will be required to take a written examination designed to test aptitude for learning and performing the duties of the position. The test will consist of 2 parts: (1) Address Checking, (2) Memory for Addresses. The test and completion of the forms will require approximately 1½ hours.

Duties: Clerks work indoors. Clerks have to handle sacks of mail weighing as much as 70 pounds. They sort mail and distribute it by using a complicated scheme which must be memorized. Some clerks work at a public counter or window doing such jobs as selling stamps and weighing parcels and are personally responsible for all money and stamps. Clerks may be on their feet all day. They also have to stretch, reach, and throw mail. Assignments to preferred positions, such as window clerks, typist and stenographic positions, etc., are filled by open bid and reassignment of the senior qualified clerk.

Carriers have to collect and deliver mail. Some carriers walk, other carriers drive. Carriers must be out in all kinds of weather. Almost all carriers have to carry mail bags on their shoulders; loads weigh as much as 35 pounds. Carriers sometimes have to load and unload sacks of mail weighing as much as 70 pounds.

The duties of newly appointed clerks and carriers are at times interchangeable. As representatives of the Postal Service, they must maintain pleasant and effective public relations with patrons and others, requiring general familiarity with postal laws, regulations, and procedures commonly used.

Employees may be assigned to work in places exposed to public view. Their appearance influences the general public's confidence and attitude toward the entire

Postal Service.

Employees appointed under this standard are, therefore, expected to maintain neat and proper personal attire and grooming appropriate to conducting public business, including the wearing of a uniform when required.

Carrier Positions Requiring Driving: Before eligibles may be appointed to carrier positions which require driving, they must demonstrate a safe driving record and must pass the Road Test to show they can safely drive a vehicle of the type used on the job.

Eligibles who fail to qualify in the Road Test will not be given the test again in the same group of hires. Those who fail the test a second time will not again be considered as a result of the same examination for appointment to a position that requires driving.

A valid driver's license from the state in which this post office is located must be presented at the time of appointment. Persons who do not have the license will not be appointed but their names will be restored to the register. They may not again be considered for carrier positions until they have obtained the required driver's license. After hire, individuals must also be able to obtain the required type of Government operator's permit.

Physical Requirements: Applicants must be physically able to perform the duties described elsewhere in this announcement. Any physical condition which would cause the applicant to be a hazard to himself or to others will be disqualifying for appointment.

The distant vision for clerk and carrier positions not involving driving duties must test at least 20/30 (Snellen) in one eye, glasses permitted, and applicants generally must be able to hear ordinary conversation with or without a hearing aid, but some clerk positions may be filled by the deaf.

For carrier positions which require driving, applicants must have at least 20/30 (Snellen) in one eye and 20/50 (Snellen) in the other with or without a corrective device for unlimited operation of motor vehicles. Hearing must be at least 15/20 with or without a hearing aid.

A physical examination will be required before appointment.

Age Requirement: The general age requirement is 18 years or 16 years for high school graduates, except for those for whom age limits are waived. For carrier positions which require driving, applicants must be 18 years of age or over. In general, there is no maximum age limit.

Citizenship: All applicants must be citizens of or owe allegiance to the United States of America or have been granted permanent resident alien status in the United States.

Salary: Results from collective bargaining.

Consideration: Consideration to fill these positions will be made of the highest eligibles on the register who are available.

How to Apply: Submit application Form 2479-AB to the postmaster of this office or place designated by him.

Opening date for application: _____

                                 Month   Day   Year

Closing date for application: _____

Month   Day   Year

Written Examination: Applicants will be notified of date, time, and place of examination and will be sent sample questions.

POST OFFICE JOBS OFFER:

Job Security	Liberal Retirement	Cash for Suggestions
Paid Vacations	Sick Leave with Pay	Promotion Opportunities
On the Job Training	Low Cost Life Insurance	Paid Holidays
	Low Cost Health Insurance	

Ask for an application card at your local post office. The card is bright yellow and in two sections joined at a perforation. Do NOT separate the two sections. The section on the left is called the Application Card, that on the right the Admission Card. Instructions for filling out both sections are printed on the back of the card. Follow these directions precisely, and carefully fill out both sections of the card. Hand in or mail the completed application as instructed.

The application and admission card look like this:

(We have had to separate the sections to fit the book page. You must not separate the sections.)

(Front)

(Back)

APPLICATION CARD

Name *(Last, First, Middle Initials)*

Address *(House/Apt. No. & Street)*

City, State, ZIP Code

Birthdate *(Month, Date, Year)*

Do Not Write In This Space

Telephone Number | Today's Date

Title of Examination

Post Office Applied For

PS Form 2479-A, April 1983

Instructions to Applicants

Furnish all the information requested on these cards. The attached card will be returned to you with sample questions and necessary instructions, including the time and place of the written test.

TYPEWRITE OR PRINT IN INK. DO NOT SEPARATE THESE CARDS. FOLD ONLY AT PERFORATION.

Mail or Take This Form—Both Parts—to The Postmaster of the Post Office Where You Wish to Be Employed.

PS Form 2479-A, April 1983 *(Reverse)*

✿U.S. G.P.O. 1983-655-793

(Front)

ADMISSION CARD

Title of Examination	Social Security No.	Do Not Write In This Space

Date of Birth	Today's Date	Post Office Applied For

If you have performed active duty in the Armed Forces of the United States and were separated under honorable conditions indicate periods of service

From *(Mo., Day, Yr.)* _____ to *(Mo., Day, Yr.)* _____

DO YOU CLAIM VETERAN PREFERENCE?   NO   YES IF YES, BASED ON

☐ (1) Active duty in the Armed Forces of the U.S. during World War I or the period December 7, 1941, through July 1, 1955, (2) More than 180 consecutive days of active duty (other than for training) in the Armed Forces of the U.S. any part of which occurred between Jan. 31, 1955 and Oct. 14, 1976, or (3) Award of a campaign badge or service medal

☐ Your status as (1) a disabled veteran or a veteran who was awarded the purple heart for wounds or injuries received in action, (2) a veteran's widow who has not remarried, (3) the wife of an ex serviceman who has a service connected disability which disqualifies him for civil service appointment, or (4) the widowed, divorced or separated mother of an ex-service son or daughter who died in action or who is totally and permanently disabled

Print or Type Your Name and Address →	Name *(First, Middle, Last)*
	Address *(House, Apt. No. & Street)*
	City, State, ZIP Code *(ZIP Code must be included!)*

This card will be returned to you. Bring it, along with personal identification bearing your picture or description, with you when you report for the test. ID's will be checked, and a fingerprint or signature specimen may be required.

PS Form **2479-B,** April 1983

(Back)

Final Eligibility in This Examination is Subject to Suitability Determination

The collection of information on this form is authorized by 39 U.S.C. 401.1001; completion of this form is voluntary. This information will be used to determine qualification, suitability, and availability of applicants for USPS employment, and may be disclosed to relevant Federal Agencies regarding eligibility and suitability for employment, law enforcement activities when there is an indication of a potential violation of law, in connection with private relief legislation (to Office of Management and Budget); to a congressional office at your request, to a labor organization as required by the NLRA, and where pertinent, in a legal proceeding to which the Postal Service is a party. If this information is not provided, you may not receive full consideration for a position.

Disclosure by you of your Social Security Number (SSN) is mandatory to obtain the services, benefits, or processes that you are seeking. Solicitation of the SSN by the United States Postal Service is authorized under provisions of Executive Order 9397, dated November 22, 1943. The information gathered through the use of the number will be used only as necessary in authorized personnel administration processes.

PS Form 2479-B, April 1983 *(Reverse)*

Applicant	Fingerprint
Make no marks on this side of the card unless so instructed by examiner.	
Signature of Applicant	

Political Recommendations Prohibited

The law (39 U.S. Code 1002) prohibits political and certain other recommendations for appointments, promotions, assignments, transfers, or designations of persons in the Postal Service. Statements relating solely to character and residence are permitted, but every other kind of statement or recommendation is prohibited unless it either is requested by the Postal Service and consists solely of an evaluation of the work performance, ability, aptitude, and general qualifications of an individual or is requested by a Government representative investigating the individual's loyalty, suitability, and character. Anyone who requests or solicits a prohibited statement or recommendation is subject to disqualification from the Postal Service and anyone in the Postal Service who accepts such a statement may be suspended or removed from office.

Have You Answered All Questions on the Reverse of This Form?

You will be notified by mail when the examination date, time and place are set. You will receive instructions as to where and when to report for the exam. You will also receive the admission card portion of the application card. Be sure to bring the admission card with you when you report for the exam. Along with the admission card and exam information, you will receive sample questions such as these:

UNITED STATES POSTAL SERVICE

SAMPLE QUESTIONS

The questions that follow are like the ones you will take in the test. Study them carefully. This will give you practice with the different kinds of questions and show you how to mark your answers.

Address Checking Test

In this test you will have to decide whether two addresses are alike or different. If the two addresses are exactly *Alike* in every way, darken space Ⓐ for the question. If the two addresses are *Different* in any way, darken space Ⓓ for the question.

Mark your answers to these sample questions on the Sample Answer Sheet at the right.

1 . . . 2134 S 20th St   2134 S 20th St

Since the two addresses are exactly alike, mark Ⓐ for question 1 on the Sample Answer Sheet.

Sample Answer Sheet
1 Ⓐ Ⓓ
2 Ⓐ Ⓓ
3 Ⓐ Ⓓ
4 Ⓐ Ⓓ
5 Ⓐ Ⓓ

2 . . . 4608 N Warnock St   4806 N Warnock St
3 . . . 1202 W Girard Dr   1202 W Girard Rd
4 . . . Chappaqua NY 10514   Chappaqua NY 10514
5 . . . 2207 Markland Ave   2207 Markham Ave

The answers to samples 2 to 5 are: 2D, 3D, 4A, and 5D.

Memory for Addresses Test

In this test you will have to memorize the locations (A, B, C, D, or E) of twenty-five addresses shown in five boxes, such as those below. For example, "Sardis" is in Box C, "5200–5799 West" is in Box B, etc. (The addresses in the actual test are, of course, different.)

A	B	C	D	E
4700–5599 Table Lismore 4800–5199 West Hesper 5500–6399 Blake	6800–6999 Table Kelford 5200–5799 West Musella 4800–5499 Blake	5600–6499 Table Joel 3200–3499 West Sardis 6400–7299 Blake	6500–6799 Table Tatum 3500–4299 West Porter 4300–4799 Blake	4400–4699 Table Ruskin 4300–4799 West Somers 7300–7499 Blake

Study the locations of the addresses for five minutes. As you study, sound them to yourself. Then cover the boxes and try to answer the questions below. Mark your answers for each question by darkening the space as was done for questions 1 and 2.

1. Musella
2. 4300–4799 Blake
3. 4700–5599 Table
4. Tatum

5. 5500–6399 Blake
6. Hesper
7. Kelford
8. Somers

9. 6400–7299 Blake
10. Joel
11. 5500–6399 Blake
12. 5200–5799 West

13. Porter
14. 7300–7499 Blake

Sample Answer Sheet

1 Ⓐ ● Ⓒ Ⓓ Ⓔ		8 Ⓐ Ⓑ Ⓒ Ⓓ Ⓔ
2 Ⓐ Ⓑ Ⓒ ● Ⓔ		9 Ⓐ Ⓑ Ⓒ Ⓓ Ⓔ
3 Ⓐ Ⓑ Ⓒ Ⓓ Ⓔ		10 Ⓐ Ⓑ Ⓒ Ⓓ Ⓔ
4 Ⓐ Ⓑ Ⓒ Ⓓ Ⓔ		11 Ⓐ Ⓑ Ⓒ Ⓓ Ⓔ
5 Ⓐ Ⓑ Ⓒ Ⓓ Ⓔ		12 Ⓐ Ⓑ Ⓒ Ⓓ Ⓔ
6 Ⓐ Ⓑ Ⓒ Ⓓ Ⓔ		13 Ⓐ Ⓑ Ⓒ Ⓓ Ⓔ
7 Ⓐ Ⓑ Ⓒ Ⓓ Ⓔ		14 Ⓐ Ⓑ Ⓒ Ⓓ Ⓔ

The correct answers for questions 3 to 14 are: 3A, 4D, 5A, 6A, 7B, 8E, 9C, 10C, 11A, 12B, 13D, and 14E.

By the time you receive the sample questions, you should be well through this book. Receipt of these samples will reassure you that the book is preparing you correctly for the Clerk-Carrier Exam.

On examination day, allow the test itself to be the main attraction of the day. Do not squeeze it in between other activities. Arrive rested, relaxed, and on time. In fact, leave ample time for traffic tie-ups or other potentially nerve-wracking complications.

In the examination room, the test administrator will hand out forms for you to fill out. He or she will give you the instructions that you must follow in taking the examination. You will also receive and do practice questions similar to those that follow. The administrator will not go over the practice questions with you, but will answer any questions you may have.

ADDRESS CHECKING TEST

DESCRIPTION OF THE TEST
AND PRACTICE QUESTIONS

Every member of the postal work force is responsible for seeing that every letter reaches the right address. If one worker makes an error in reading an address, it can cause a serious delay in getting the letter to where it is supposed to go.

Can you spot whether or not two addresses are alike or different? It is as easy as that. But how fast can you do it accurately? Look at the sample questions below. Each question consists of a pair of addresses such as this:

762 W 18th St   762 W 18th St   ●Ⓓ
  Are they Alike or Different? They are exactly Alike.
9486 Hillsdale Rd   9489 Hill Rd   Ⓐ●
  Alike or Different? They are Different. Do you see why?
1242 Regal St   1242 Regel St   ⒶⒹ
  Alike or Different?

Remember that this test measures both speed and accuracy. So work as fast as you can without making any mistakes.

Starting now, if the two addresses are ALIKE darken space Ⓐ. If the two addresses are DIFFERENT in any way darken space Ⓓ. Answer every question.

1 . . . 239 Windell Ave   239 Windell Ave   1. ⒶⒹ
          Alike or Different? Alike. Mark space Ⓐ for question 1.
2 . . . 4667 Edgeworth Rd   4677 Edgeworth Rd   2. ⒶⒹ
          Alike or Different? Different. Mark Space Ⓓ for question 2.
3 . . . 2661 Kennel St SE   2661 Kennel St SW   3. ⒶⒹ
4 . . . 3709 Columbine St   3707 Columbine St   4. ⒶⒹ
5 . . . 969 W 14th St NW   969 W 14th St NW   5. ⒶⒹ
6 . . . 4439 Frederick Pkwy   4439 Frederick Pkwy   6. ⒶⒹ
7 . . . 77 Summers St   77 Summers St   7. ⒶⒹ
8 . . . 828 N Franklin Pl   828 S Franklin Pl   8. ⒶⒹ

Check your answers with the correct answers. If you have any wrong answers, be sure you see why.

CORRECT ANSWERS TO THE PRACTICE QUESTIONS

1. A   2. D   3. D   4. D   5. A   6. A   7. A   8. D

MEMORY FOR ADDRESSES TEST

DESCRIPTION OF THE TEST
AND PRACTICE QUESTIONS

All clerks in the post office have to learn a scheme during their training period. Clerks use the scheme to sort the mail to where it is going. They must have good memories in order to learn the scheme. Carriers also need good memories.

In this test you will be given 25 addresses to remember. The addresses are divided into five groups. Each group of five addresses is in a box such as those below. Each box has a letter—A, B, C, D, or E. You will have to learn which letter goes with each address. You will be given time to study during the examination.

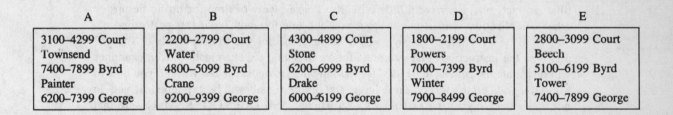

A	B	C	D	E
3100–4299 Court	2200–2799 Court	4300–4899 Court	1800–2199 Court	2800–3099 Court
Townsend	Water	Stone	Powers	Beech
7400–7899 Byrd	4800–5099 Byrd	6200–6999 Byrd	7000–7399 Byrd	5100–6199 Byrd
Painter	Crane	Drake	Winter	Tower
6200–7399 George	9200–9399 George	6000–6199 George	7900–8499 George	7400–7899 George

The next few questions show you how the questions look. Try to mark the letter of the box in which each item is found without looking at the boxes. At the actual exam you will not be able to see the boxes, but you will have been given more time to memorize.

1. 6200–6999 Byrd   1. Ⓐ Ⓑ ● Ⓓ Ⓔ
   This item is in box C, so Ⓒ is darkened for you.
2. Winter   2. Ⓐ Ⓑ Ⓒ ● Ⓔ
   This item is in box D, so Ⓓ is darkened for you.
3. 9200–9399 George   3. Ⓐ ● Ⓒ Ⓓ Ⓔ
   This item is in box B, so darken Ⓑ on the answer strip.
4. 3100–4299 Court   4. Ⓐ Ⓑ Ⓒ Ⓓ Ⓔ
5. Stone   5. Ⓐ Ⓑ Ⓒ Ⓓ Ⓔ
6. Tower   6. Ⓐ Ⓑ Ⓒ Ⓓ Ⓔ
7. 5100–6199 Byrd   7. Ⓐ Ⓑ Ⓒ Ⓓ Ⓔ
8. 6200–7399 George   8. Ⓐ Ⓑ Ⓒ Ⓓ Ⓔ
9. 2200–2799 Court   9. Ⓐ Ⓑ Ⓒ Ⓓ Ⓔ
10. Drake   10. Ⓐ Ⓑ Ⓒ Ⓓ Ⓔ

CORRECT ANSWERS TO THE MEMORY FOR ADDRESSES PRACTICE QUESTIONS

1.C	6. E
2.D	7. E
3.B	8. A
4.A	9. B
5.C	10. C

By the time you receive the sample questions, you should be well along in your studies. Compare the sample questions with the question styles detailed in this book. This comparison should reassure you that this book is preparing you correctly for the Clerk-Carrier exam. Continue preparing yourself for the exam so that you complete the book at least a week before the actual examination. You want to take your exam with a clear head so that you can memorize box locations without interference from any previous memorization.

ON EXAMINATION DAY

On the examination day assigned to you, allow the test itself to be the main attraction of the day. Do not squeeze it in between other activities. Arrive rested, relaxed, and on time. In fact, plan to arrive a little bit early. Leave plenty of time for traffic tie-ups or other complications which might upset you and interfere with your test performance.

In the test room the examiner will hand out forms for you to fill out. He or she will give you the instructions that you must follow in taking the examination. The examiner will distribute the pencils to be used for marking the answer sheet and will tell you how to fill in the grids on the forms. Time limits and timing signals will be explained. If you do not understand any of the examiner's instructions, ASK QUESTIONS. Make sure that you know exactly what to do.

During the testing session you will answer both sample questions and actual test questions. You will see the answers to the sample questions. You will not be given the answers to the actual test questions, even after the test is over.

At the examination, you must follow instructions exactly. Use only the Postal Service pencils issued to you. Fill in the grids on the forms carefully and accurately. Filling in the wrong grid may lead to loss of veterans' credits to which you may be entitled or to an incorrect address for your test results. Do not begin until you are told to begin. Stop as soon as the examiner tells you to stop. Do not turn pages until you are told to. Do not go back to parts you have already completed. Any infraction of the rules is considered cheating. If you cheat, your test paper will not be scored, and you will not be eligible for appointment.

USING THE ANSWER SHEET

The answer sheet for your postal exam is machine scored. You cannot give any explanations to the machine, so you must fill out the answer sheet clearly and correctly.

1. Blacken your answer space firmly and completely. ● is the only correct way to mark the answer sheet. ◑, ⊗, ⊘, and ∅ are all unacceptable. The machine might not read them at all.
2. Mark only one answer for each question. If you mark more than one answer you will be considered wrong even if one of the answers is correct.

3. If you change your mind, you must erase your mark. Attempting to cross out an incorrect answer like this ▓ will not work. You must erase any incorrect answer completely. An incomplete erasure might be read as a second answer.

4. All of your answering should be in the form of blackened spaces. The machine cannot read English. Do not write any notes in the margins.

5. MOST IMPORTANT: Answer each question in the right place. Question 1 must be answered in space 1; question 52 in space 52. If you should skip an answer space and mark a series of answers in the wrong places, you must erase all those answers and do the questions over, marking your answers in the proper places. You cannot afford to use the limited time in this way. Therefore, as you answer *each* question, look at its number and check that you are marking your answer in the space with the same number.

6. You may be wondering whether or not it is wise to guess when you are not sure of an answer, or whether it is better to skip a question when you are not certain of the answer. On the Address Checking Test there is no reason to skip questions or to guess. Simply answer every question, in order, as quickly and accurately as you can. In the Memory for Addresses Test, you must choose for yourself whether to skip questions or to guess. A correct answer gives you one point; a skipped space gives you nothing at all, but costs you nothing except the chance of getting the answer right; a wrong answer costs you 1/4 point. If you are really stumped, you may skip a question, BUT you must then remember to skip its answer space as well. The risk of losing your place if you skip questions is so great that we advise you to guess even if you are not sure of the answer. Our suggestion is that you answer every question in order, even if you have to guess. It is better to lose a few 1/4 points for wrong guesses than to lose valuable seconds figuring where you started marking answers in the wrong place, erasing, and remarking answers.

The complaint most frequently heard about the Clerk-Carrier Exam is, "There are too many questions and too little time." Very few people are able to finish. Simply do your best and do not worry about the questions that you were not able to get to.

HOW IS THE EXAM SCORED?

When the exam is over, the examiner will collect test booklets and answer sheets. The answer sheets will be sent to the test center in California where a machine will scan your answers and mark them right or wrong. Then your raw score will be calculated. On the Address Checking Test, your raw score is the number you got right minus the number you got wrong. On the Memory for Addresses Test, your raw score is the number you got right minus 1/4 the number you got wrong.

Your raw score is not your final score. The Postal Service takes the raw scores, combines them according to a formula of its own, and converts them to a scaled score, on a scale of 1 to 100. The entire process of conversion from raw to scaled score is confidential information. The score you receive is not your number right, is not your raw score, and is not a percent. The score you receive is a *scaled score*. Before reporting any scaled scores, the Postal Service adds any veterans' service points or any other advantages to which the applicant might be entitled. Veterans' service points are added only to passing scaled scores of 70 or more. A failing score cannot be brought to passing level by veterans' points. The score earned plus veterans' service points results in the final scaled score that finds its place onto the eligibility list.

A total scaled score of 70 is a passing score. The names of all persons with scaled scores of 70 or more are placed on the list sent to the local post office. Those names are placed on the list in order, with the highest scored at the top of the list. Hiring then takes place from the top of the list as vacancies occur.

The scoring process may take six or ten weeks or even longer. Be patient. If you pass the exam, you will receive notice of your scaled score and will be offered the opportunity to take the Number Series Test to qualify for placement on the Letter Sorting Machine Operator list. Applicants who fail the exam are not told their score. They are simply notified that they will not be considered for positions as clerks or carriers. People who fail the Clerk-Carrier Exam are not eligible to take the Number Series Test for Letter Sorting Machine Operator.

PART I
Diagnostic Exam

BEFORE YOU TAKE THE DIAGNOSTIC EXAM

The purpose of the Diagnostic Exam is to start you in your studies for the Clerk-Carrier Exam and to establish a base upon which you can build. The diagnostic exam will give you an idea of where you are now and of how far you need to go. By starting out with a full-length exam, you see from the begining how many questions you must answer and how quickly you must work to score high on this exam.

DIRECTIONS FOR TAKING THE DIAGNOSTIC EXAM

- Choose a work space that is quiet and well-lit.
- Clear the desk or tabletop of all clutter.
- Bring a stopwatch or kitchen timer and two or three number two pencils with good erasers to your work area.
- While the pencils should have plenty of exposed lead, you will find that you fill in answer circles more quickly if the pencils are not razor sharp. The little circles on the answer sheet must be completely filled in, and the fewer strokes needed to fill them, the faster you work.
  At the actual exam, where pencils are provided, do some scribbling to dull the point while you are waiting for the exam to begin.
- Tear out the answer sheets for the Diagnostic Exam and place them on the desk or table beside your book, to the right if you are right-handed, to the left if you are left-handed.
- Set the timer, read the directions for the Address Checking Test, and begin to work immediately.
- Stop as soon as time is up.
- Go directly from Address Checking to Memory for Addresses, and follow the directions for timing and taking this test.

DIRECTIONS FOR SCORING YOUR EXAM

- When you have completed both parts of the Diagnostic Exam, check your answers against the correct answers on page 40.
- Follow the directions for analyzing your Address Checking errors.
- Calculate your raw score for each part of the exam as instructed on the Score Sheet on page 29.
- Check to see where your scores fall on the Self-Evaluation Chart.
- Plot your scores on the Progress Graph.

After you have completed the Diagnostic Exam and analyzed your results, you will have a good picture of where you stand. Then you start learning how to add valuable points to your score by increasing your speed and accuracy and by memorizing more effectively. The ten Model Exams will give you plenty of practice in applying these new-found skills.

ANSWER SHEET FOR DIAGNOSTIC EXAM

ADDRESS CHECKING

1 Ⓐ Ⓓ	20 Ⓐ Ⓓ	39 Ⓐ Ⓓ	58 Ⓐ Ⓓ	77 Ⓐ Ⓓ
2 Ⓐ Ⓓ	21 Ⓐ Ⓓ	40 Ⓐ Ⓓ	59 Ⓐ Ⓓ	78 Ⓐ Ⓓ
3 Ⓐ Ⓓ	22 Ⓐ Ⓓ	41 Ⓐ Ⓓ	60 Ⓐ Ⓓ	79 Ⓐ Ⓓ
4 Ⓐ Ⓓ	23 Ⓐ Ⓓ	42 Ⓐ Ⓓ	61 Ⓐ Ⓓ	80 Ⓐ Ⓓ
5 Ⓐ Ⓓ	24 Ⓐ Ⓓ	43 Ⓐ Ⓓ	62 Ⓐ Ⓓ	81 Ⓐ Ⓓ
6 Ⓐ Ⓓ	25 Ⓐ Ⓓ	44 Ⓐ Ⓓ	63 Ⓐ Ⓓ	82 Ⓐ Ⓓ
7 Ⓐ Ⓓ	26 Ⓐ Ⓓ	45 Ⓐ Ⓓ	64 Ⓐ Ⓓ	83 Ⓐ Ⓓ
8 Ⓐ Ⓓ	27 Ⓐ Ⓓ	46 Ⓐ Ⓓ	65 Ⓐ Ⓓ	84 Ⓐ Ⓓ
9 Ⓐ Ⓓ	28 Ⓐ Ⓓ	47 Ⓐ Ⓓ	66 Ⓐ Ⓓ	85 Ⓐ Ⓓ
10 Ⓐ Ⓓ	29 Ⓐ Ⓓ	48 Ⓐ Ⓓ	67 Ⓐ Ⓓ	86 Ⓐ Ⓓ
11 Ⓐ Ⓓ	30 Ⓐ Ⓓ	49 Ⓐ Ⓓ	68 Ⓐ Ⓓ	87 Ⓐ Ⓓ
12 Ⓐ Ⓓ	31 Ⓐ Ⓓ	50 Ⓐ Ⓓ	69 Ⓐ Ⓓ	88 Ⓐ Ⓓ
13 Ⓐ Ⓓ	32 Ⓐ Ⓓ	51 Ⓐ Ⓓ	70 Ⓐ Ⓓ	89 Ⓐ Ⓓ
14 Ⓐ Ⓓ	33 Ⓐ Ⓓ	52 Ⓐ Ⓓ	71 Ⓐ Ⓓ	90 Ⓐ Ⓓ
15 Ⓐ Ⓓ	34 Ⓐ Ⓓ	53 Ⓐ Ⓓ	72 Ⓐ Ⓓ	91 Ⓐ Ⓓ
16 Ⓐ Ⓓ	35 Ⓐ Ⓓ	54 Ⓐ Ⓓ	73 Ⓐ Ⓓ	92 Ⓐ Ⓓ
17 Ⓐ Ⓓ	36 Ⓐ Ⓓ	55 Ⓐ Ⓓ	74 Ⓐ Ⓓ	93 Ⓐ Ⓓ
18 Ⓐ Ⓓ	37 Ⓐ Ⓓ	56 Ⓐ Ⓓ	75 Ⓐ Ⓓ	94 Ⓐ Ⓓ
19 Ⓐ Ⓓ	38 Ⓐ Ⓓ	57 Ⓐ Ⓓ	76 Ⓐ Ⓓ	95 Ⓐ Ⓓ

MEMORY FOR ADDRESSES

PRACTICE I

1 Ⓐ Ⓑ Ⓒ Ⓓ Ⓔ   23 Ⓐ Ⓑ Ⓒ Ⓓ Ⓔ   45 Ⓐ Ⓑ Ⓒ Ⓓ Ⓔ   67 Ⓐ Ⓑ Ⓒ Ⓓ Ⓔ

2 Ⓐ Ⓑ Ⓒ Ⓓ Ⓔ   24 Ⓐ Ⓑ Ⓒ Ⓓ Ⓔ   46 Ⓐ Ⓑ Ⓒ Ⓓ Ⓔ   68 Ⓐ Ⓑ Ⓒ Ⓓ Ⓔ

3 Ⓐ Ⓑ Ⓒ Ⓓ Ⓔ   25 Ⓐ Ⓑ Ⓒ Ⓓ Ⓔ   47 Ⓐ Ⓑ Ⓒ Ⓓ Ⓔ   69 Ⓐ Ⓑ Ⓒ Ⓓ Ⓔ

4 Ⓐ Ⓑ Ⓒ Ⓓ Ⓔ   26 Ⓐ Ⓑ Ⓒ Ⓓ Ⓔ   48 Ⓐ Ⓑ Ⓒ Ⓓ Ⓔ   70 Ⓐ Ⓑ Ⓒ Ⓓ Ⓔ

5 Ⓐ Ⓑ Ⓒ Ⓓ Ⓔ   27 Ⓐ Ⓑ Ⓒ Ⓓ Ⓔ   49 Ⓐ Ⓑ Ⓒ Ⓓ Ⓔ   71 Ⓐ Ⓑ Ⓒ Ⓓ Ⓔ

6 Ⓐ Ⓑ Ⓒ Ⓓ Ⓔ   28 Ⓐ Ⓑ Ⓒ Ⓓ Ⓔ   50 Ⓐ Ⓑ Ⓒ Ⓓ Ⓔ   72 Ⓐ Ⓑ Ⓒ Ⓓ Ⓔ

7 Ⓐ Ⓑ Ⓒ Ⓓ Ⓔ   29 Ⓐ Ⓑ Ⓒ Ⓓ Ⓔ   51 Ⓐ Ⓑ Ⓒ Ⓓ Ⓔ   73 Ⓐ Ⓑ Ⓒ Ⓓ Ⓔ

8 Ⓐ Ⓑ Ⓒ Ⓓ Ⓔ   30 Ⓐ Ⓑ Ⓒ Ⓓ Ⓔ   52 Ⓐ Ⓑ Ⓒ Ⓓ Ⓔ   74 Ⓐ Ⓑ Ⓒ Ⓓ Ⓔ

9 Ⓐ Ⓑ Ⓒ Ⓓ Ⓔ   31 Ⓐ Ⓑ Ⓒ Ⓓ Ⓔ   53 Ⓐ Ⓑ Ⓒ Ⓓ Ⓔ   75 Ⓐ Ⓑ Ⓒ Ⓓ Ⓔ

10 Ⓐ Ⓑ Ⓒ Ⓓ Ⓔ   32 Ⓐ Ⓑ Ⓒ Ⓓ Ⓔ   54 Ⓐ Ⓑ Ⓒ Ⓓ Ⓔ   76 Ⓐ Ⓑ Ⓒ Ⓓ Ⓔ

11 Ⓐ Ⓑ Ⓒ Ⓓ Ⓔ   33 Ⓐ Ⓑ Ⓒ Ⓓ Ⓔ   55 Ⓐ Ⓑ Ⓒ Ⓓ Ⓔ   77 Ⓐ Ⓑ Ⓒ Ⓓ Ⓔ

12 Ⓐ Ⓑ Ⓒ Ⓓ Ⓔ   34 Ⓐ Ⓑ Ⓒ Ⓓ Ⓔ   56 Ⓐ Ⓑ Ⓒ Ⓓ Ⓔ   78 Ⓐ Ⓑ Ⓒ Ⓓ Ⓔ

13 Ⓐ Ⓑ Ⓒ Ⓓ Ⓔ   35 Ⓐ Ⓑ Ⓒ Ⓓ Ⓔ   57 Ⓐ Ⓑ Ⓒ Ⓓ Ⓔ   79 Ⓐ Ⓑ Ⓒ Ⓓ Ⓔ

14 Ⓐ Ⓑ Ⓒ Ⓓ Ⓔ   36 Ⓐ Ⓑ Ⓒ Ⓓ Ⓔ   58 Ⓐ Ⓑ Ⓒ Ⓓ Ⓔ   80 Ⓐ Ⓑ Ⓒ Ⓓ Ⓔ

15 Ⓐ Ⓑ Ⓒ Ⓓ Ⓔ   37 Ⓐ Ⓑ Ⓒ Ⓓ Ⓔ   59 Ⓐ Ⓑ Ⓒ Ⓓ Ⓔ   81 Ⓐ Ⓑ Ⓒ Ⓓ Ⓔ

16 Ⓐ Ⓑ Ⓒ Ⓓ Ⓔ   38 Ⓐ Ⓑ Ⓒ Ⓓ Ⓔ   60 Ⓐ Ⓑ Ⓒ Ⓓ Ⓔ   82 Ⓐ Ⓑ Ⓒ Ⓓ Ⓔ

17 Ⓐ Ⓑ Ⓒ Ⓓ Ⓔ   39 Ⓐ Ⓑ Ⓒ Ⓓ Ⓔ   61 Ⓐ Ⓑ Ⓒ Ⓓ Ⓔ   83 Ⓐ Ⓑ Ⓒ Ⓓ Ⓔ

18 Ⓐ Ⓑ Ⓒ Ⓓ Ⓔ   40 Ⓐ Ⓑ Ⓒ Ⓓ Ⓔ   62 Ⓐ Ⓑ Ⓒ Ⓓ Ⓔ   84 Ⓐ Ⓑ Ⓒ Ⓓ Ⓔ

19 Ⓐ Ⓑ Ⓒ Ⓓ Ⓔ   41 Ⓐ Ⓑ Ⓒ Ⓓ Ⓔ   63 Ⓐ Ⓑ Ⓒ Ⓓ Ⓔ   85 Ⓐ Ⓑ Ⓒ Ⓓ Ⓔ

20 Ⓐ Ⓑ Ⓒ Ⓓ Ⓔ   42 Ⓐ Ⓑ Ⓒ Ⓓ Ⓔ   64 Ⓐ Ⓑ Ⓒ Ⓓ Ⓔ   86 Ⓐ Ⓑ Ⓒ Ⓓ Ⓔ

21 Ⓐ Ⓑ Ⓒ Ⓓ Ⓔ   43 Ⓐ Ⓑ Ⓒ Ⓓ Ⓔ   65 Ⓐ Ⓑ Ⓒ Ⓓ Ⓔ   87 Ⓐ Ⓑ Ⓒ Ⓓ Ⓔ

22 Ⓐ Ⓑ Ⓒ Ⓓ Ⓔ   44 Ⓐ Ⓑ Ⓒ Ⓓ Ⓔ   66 Ⓐ Ⓑ Ⓒ Ⓓ Ⓔ   88 Ⓐ Ⓑ Ⓒ Ⓓ Ⓔ

PRACTICE II

1 Ⓐ Ⓑ Ⓒ Ⓓ Ⓔ	23 Ⓐ Ⓑ Ⓒ Ⓓ Ⓔ	45 Ⓐ Ⓑ Ⓒ Ⓓ Ⓔ	67 Ⓐ Ⓑ Ⓒ Ⓓ Ⓔ
2 Ⓐ Ⓑ Ⓒ Ⓓ Ⓔ	24 Ⓐ Ⓑ Ⓒ Ⓓ Ⓔ	46 Ⓐ Ⓑ Ⓒ Ⓓ Ⓔ	68 Ⓐ Ⓑ Ⓒ Ⓓ Ⓔ
3 Ⓐ Ⓑ Ⓒ Ⓓ Ⓔ	25 Ⓐ Ⓑ Ⓒ Ⓓ Ⓔ	47 Ⓐ Ⓑ Ⓒ Ⓓ Ⓔ	69 Ⓐ Ⓑ Ⓒ Ⓓ Ⓔ
4 Ⓐ Ⓑ Ⓒ Ⓓ Ⓔ	26 Ⓐ Ⓑ Ⓒ Ⓓ Ⓔ	48 Ⓐ Ⓑ Ⓒ Ⓓ Ⓔ	70 Ⓐ Ⓑ Ⓒ Ⓓ Ⓔ
5 Ⓐ Ⓑ Ⓒ Ⓓ Ⓔ	27 Ⓐ Ⓑ Ⓒ Ⓓ Ⓔ	49 Ⓐ Ⓑ Ⓒ Ⓓ Ⓔ	71 Ⓐ Ⓑ Ⓒ Ⓓ Ⓔ
6 Ⓐ Ⓑ Ⓒ Ⓓ Ⓔ	28 Ⓐ Ⓑ Ⓒ Ⓓ Ⓔ	50 Ⓐ Ⓑ Ⓒ Ⓓ Ⓔ	72 Ⓐ Ⓑ Ⓒ Ⓓ Ⓔ
7 Ⓐ Ⓑ Ⓒ Ⓓ Ⓔ	29 Ⓐ Ⓑ Ⓒ Ⓓ Ⓔ	51 Ⓐ Ⓑ Ⓒ Ⓓ Ⓔ	73 Ⓐ Ⓑ Ⓒ Ⓓ Ⓔ
8 Ⓐ Ⓑ Ⓒ Ⓓ Ⓔ	30 Ⓐ Ⓑ Ⓒ Ⓓ Ⓔ	52 Ⓐ Ⓑ Ⓒ Ⓓ Ⓔ	74 Ⓐ Ⓑ Ⓒ Ⓓ Ⓔ
9 Ⓐ Ⓑ Ⓒ Ⓓ Ⓔ	31 Ⓐ Ⓑ Ⓒ Ⓓ Ⓔ	53 Ⓐ Ⓑ Ⓒ Ⓓ Ⓔ	75 Ⓐ Ⓑ Ⓒ Ⓓ Ⓔ
10 Ⓐ Ⓑ Ⓒ Ⓓ Ⓔ	32 Ⓐ Ⓑ Ⓒ Ⓓ Ⓔ	54 Ⓐ Ⓑ Ⓒ Ⓓ Ⓔ	76 Ⓐ Ⓑ Ⓒ Ⓓ Ⓔ
11 Ⓐ Ⓑ Ⓒ Ⓓ Ⓔ	33 Ⓐ Ⓑ Ⓒ Ⓓ Ⓔ	55 Ⓐ Ⓑ Ⓒ Ⓓ Ⓔ	77 Ⓐ Ⓑ Ⓒ Ⓓ Ⓔ
12 Ⓐ Ⓑ Ⓒ Ⓓ Ⓔ	34 Ⓐ Ⓑ Ⓒ Ⓓ Ⓔ	56 Ⓐ Ⓑ Ⓒ Ⓓ Ⓔ	78 Ⓐ Ⓑ Ⓒ Ⓓ Ⓔ
13 Ⓐ Ⓑ Ⓒ Ⓓ Ⓔ	35 Ⓐ Ⓑ Ⓒ Ⓓ Ⓔ	57 Ⓐ Ⓑ Ⓒ Ⓓ Ⓔ	79 Ⓐ Ⓑ Ⓒ Ⓓ Ⓔ
14 Ⓐ Ⓑ Ⓒ Ⓓ Ⓔ	36 Ⓐ Ⓑ Ⓒ Ⓓ Ⓔ	58 Ⓐ Ⓑ Ⓒ Ⓓ Ⓔ	80 Ⓐ Ⓑ Ⓒ Ⓓ Ⓔ
15 Ⓐ Ⓑ Ⓒ Ⓓ Ⓔ	37 Ⓐ Ⓑ Ⓒ Ⓓ Ⓔ	59 Ⓐ Ⓑ Ⓒ Ⓓ Ⓔ	81 Ⓐ Ⓑ Ⓒ Ⓓ Ⓔ
16 Ⓐ Ⓑ Ⓒ Ⓓ Ⓔ	38 Ⓐ Ⓑ Ⓒ Ⓓ Ⓔ	60 Ⓐ Ⓑ Ⓒ Ⓓ Ⓔ	82 Ⓐ Ⓑ Ⓒ Ⓓ Ⓔ
17 Ⓐ Ⓑ Ⓒ Ⓓ Ⓔ	39 Ⓐ Ⓑ Ⓒ Ⓓ Ⓔ	61 Ⓐ Ⓑ Ⓒ Ⓓ Ⓔ	83 Ⓐ Ⓑ Ⓒ Ⓓ Ⓔ
18 Ⓐ Ⓑ Ⓒ Ⓓ Ⓔ	40 Ⓐ Ⓑ Ⓒ Ⓓ Ⓔ	62 Ⓐ Ⓑ Ⓒ Ⓓ Ⓔ	84 Ⓐ Ⓑ Ⓒ Ⓓ Ⓔ
19 Ⓐ Ⓑ Ⓒ Ⓓ Ⓔ	41 Ⓐ Ⓑ Ⓒ Ⓓ Ⓔ	63 Ⓐ Ⓑ Ⓒ Ⓓ Ⓔ	85 Ⓐ Ⓑ Ⓒ Ⓓ Ⓔ
20 Ⓐ Ⓑ Ⓒ Ⓓ Ⓔ	42 Ⓐ Ⓑ Ⓒ Ⓓ Ⓔ	64 Ⓐ Ⓑ Ⓒ Ⓓ Ⓔ	86 Ⓐ Ⓑ Ⓒ Ⓓ Ⓔ
21 Ⓐ Ⓑ Ⓒ Ⓓ Ⓔ	43 Ⓐ Ⓑ Ⓒ Ⓓ Ⓔ	65 Ⓐ Ⓑ Ⓒ Ⓓ Ⓔ	87 Ⓐ Ⓑ Ⓒ Ⓓ Ⓔ
22 Ⓐ Ⓑ Ⓒ Ⓓ Ⓔ	44 Ⓐ Ⓑ Ⓒ Ⓓ Ⓔ	66 Ⓐ Ⓑ Ⓒ Ⓓ Ⓔ	88 Ⓐ Ⓑ Ⓒ Ⓓ Ⓔ

PRACTICE III

1 Ⓐ Ⓑ Ⓒ Ⓓ Ⓔ   23 Ⓐ Ⓑ Ⓒ Ⓓ Ⓔ   45 Ⓐ Ⓑ Ⓒ Ⓓ Ⓔ   67 Ⓐ Ⓑ Ⓒ Ⓓ Ⓔ

2 Ⓐ Ⓑ Ⓒ Ⓓ Ⓔ   24 Ⓐ Ⓑ Ⓒ Ⓓ Ⓔ   46 Ⓐ Ⓑ Ⓒ Ⓓ Ⓔ   68 Ⓐ Ⓑ Ⓒ Ⓓ Ⓔ

3 Ⓐ Ⓑ Ⓒ Ⓓ Ⓔ   25 Ⓐ Ⓑ Ⓒ Ⓓ Ⓔ   47 Ⓐ Ⓑ Ⓒ Ⓓ Ⓔ   69 Ⓐ Ⓑ Ⓒ Ⓓ Ⓔ

4 Ⓐ Ⓑ Ⓒ Ⓓ Ⓔ   26 Ⓐ Ⓑ Ⓒ Ⓓ Ⓔ   48 Ⓐ Ⓑ Ⓒ Ⓓ Ⓔ   70 Ⓐ Ⓑ Ⓒ Ⓓ Ⓔ

5 Ⓐ Ⓑ Ⓒ Ⓓ Ⓔ   27 Ⓐ Ⓑ Ⓒ Ⓓ Ⓔ   49 Ⓐ Ⓑ Ⓒ Ⓓ Ⓔ   71 Ⓐ Ⓑ Ⓒ Ⓓ Ⓔ

6 Ⓐ Ⓑ Ⓒ Ⓓ Ⓔ   28 Ⓐ Ⓑ Ⓒ Ⓓ Ⓔ   50 Ⓐ Ⓑ Ⓒ Ⓓ Ⓔ   72 Ⓐ Ⓑ Ⓒ Ⓓ Ⓔ

7 Ⓐ Ⓑ Ⓒ Ⓓ Ⓔ   29 Ⓐ Ⓑ Ⓒ Ⓓ Ⓔ   51 Ⓐ Ⓑ Ⓒ Ⓓ Ⓔ   73 Ⓐ Ⓑ Ⓒ Ⓓ Ⓔ

8 Ⓐ Ⓑ Ⓒ Ⓓ Ⓔ   30 Ⓐ Ⓑ Ⓒ Ⓓ Ⓔ   52 Ⓐ Ⓑ Ⓒ Ⓓ Ⓔ   74 Ⓐ Ⓑ Ⓒ Ⓓ Ⓔ

9 Ⓐ Ⓑ Ⓒ Ⓓ Ⓔ   31 Ⓐ Ⓑ Ⓒ Ⓓ Ⓔ   53 Ⓐ Ⓑ Ⓒ Ⓓ Ⓔ   75 Ⓐ Ⓑ Ⓒ Ⓓ Ⓔ

10 Ⓐ Ⓑ Ⓒ Ⓓ Ⓔ   32 Ⓐ Ⓑ Ⓒ Ⓓ Ⓔ   54 Ⓐ Ⓑ Ⓒ Ⓓ Ⓔ   76 Ⓐ Ⓑ Ⓒ Ⓓ Ⓔ

11 Ⓐ Ⓑ Ⓒ Ⓓ Ⓔ   33 Ⓐ Ⓑ Ⓒ Ⓓ Ⓔ   55 Ⓐ Ⓑ Ⓒ Ⓓ Ⓔ   77 Ⓐ Ⓑ Ⓒ Ⓓ Ⓔ

12 Ⓐ Ⓑ Ⓒ Ⓓ Ⓔ   34 Ⓐ Ⓑ Ⓒ Ⓓ Ⓔ   56 Ⓐ Ⓑ Ⓒ Ⓓ Ⓔ   78 Ⓐ Ⓑ Ⓒ Ⓓ Ⓔ

13 Ⓐ Ⓑ Ⓒ Ⓓ Ⓔ   35 Ⓐ Ⓑ Ⓒ Ⓓ Ⓔ   57 Ⓐ Ⓑ Ⓒ Ⓓ Ⓔ   79 Ⓐ Ⓑ Ⓒ Ⓓ Ⓔ

14 Ⓐ Ⓑ Ⓒ Ⓓ Ⓔ   36 Ⓐ Ⓑ Ⓒ Ⓓ Ⓔ   58 Ⓐ Ⓑ Ⓒ Ⓓ Ⓔ   80 Ⓐ Ⓑ Ⓒ Ⓓ Ⓔ

15 Ⓐ Ⓑ Ⓒ Ⓓ Ⓔ   37 Ⓐ Ⓑ Ⓒ Ⓓ Ⓔ   59 Ⓐ Ⓑ Ⓒ Ⓓ Ⓔ   81 Ⓐ Ⓑ Ⓒ Ⓓ Ⓔ

16 Ⓐ Ⓑ Ⓒ Ⓓ Ⓔ   38 Ⓐ Ⓑ Ⓒ Ⓓ Ⓔ   60 Ⓐ Ⓑ Ⓒ Ⓓ Ⓔ   82 Ⓐ Ⓑ Ⓒ Ⓓ Ⓕ

17 Ⓐ Ⓑ Ⓒ Ⓓ Ⓔ   39 Ⓐ Ⓑ Ⓒ Ⓓ Ⓔ   61 Ⓐ Ⓑ Ⓒ Ⓓ Ⓔ   83 Ⓐ Ⓑ Ⓒ Ⓓ Ⓔ

18 Ⓐ Ⓑ Ⓒ Ⓓ Ⓔ   40 Ⓐ Ⓑ Ⓒ Ⓓ Ⓔ   62 Ⓐ Ⓑ Ⓒ Ⓓ Ⓔ   84 Ⓐ Ⓑ Ⓒ Ⓓ Ⓔ

19 Ⓐ Ⓑ Ⓒ Ⓓ Ⓔ   41 Ⓐ Ⓑ Ⓒ Ⓓ Ⓔ   63 Ⓐ Ⓑ Ⓒ Ⓓ Ⓔ   85 Ⓐ Ⓑ Ⓒ Ⓓ Ⓔ

20 Ⓐ Ⓑ Ⓒ Ⓓ Ⓔ   42 Ⓐ Ⓑ Ⓒ Ⓓ Ⓔ   64 Ⓐ Ⓑ Ⓒ Ⓓ Ⓔ   86 Ⓐ Ⓑ Ⓒ Ⓓ Ⓔ

21 Ⓐ Ⓑ Ⓒ Ⓓ Ⓔ   43 Ⓐ Ⓑ Ⓒ Ⓓ Ⓔ   65 Ⓐ Ⓑ Ⓒ Ⓓ Ⓔ   87 Ⓐ Ⓑ Ⓒ Ⓓ Ⓔ

22 Ⓐ Ⓑ Ⓒ Ⓓ Ⓔ   44 Ⓐ Ⓑ Ⓒ Ⓓ Ⓔ   66 Ⓐ Ⓑ Ⓒ Ⓓ Ⓔ   88 Ⓐ Ⓑ Ⓒ Ⓓ Ⓔ

MEMORY FOR ADDRESSES TEST

1 Ⓐ Ⓑ Ⓒ Ⓓ Ⓔ
2 Ⓐ Ⓑ Ⓒ Ⓓ Ⓔ
3 Ⓐ Ⓑ Ⓒ Ⓓ Ⓔ
4 Ⓐ Ⓑ Ⓒ Ⓓ Ⓔ
5 Ⓐ Ⓑ Ⓒ Ⓓ Ⓔ
6 Ⓐ Ⓑ Ⓒ Ⓓ Ⓔ
7 Ⓐ Ⓑ Ⓒ Ⓓ Ⓔ
8 Ⓐ Ⓑ Ⓒ Ⓓ Ⓔ
9 Ⓐ Ⓑ Ⓒ Ⓓ Ⓔ
10 Ⓐ Ⓑ Ⓒ Ⓓ Ⓔ
11 Ⓐ Ⓑ Ⓒ Ⓓ Ⓔ
12 Ⓐ Ⓑ Ⓒ Ⓓ Ⓔ
13 Ⓐ Ⓑ Ⓒ Ⓓ Ⓔ
14 Ⓐ Ⓑ Ⓒ Ⓓ Ⓔ
15 Ⓐ Ⓑ Ⓒ Ⓓ Ⓔ
16 Ⓐ Ⓑ Ⓒ Ⓓ Ⓔ
17 Ⓐ Ⓑ Ⓒ Ⓓ Ⓔ
18 Ⓐ Ⓑ Ⓒ Ⓓ Ⓔ
19 Ⓐ Ⓑ Ⓒ Ⓓ Ⓔ
20 Ⓐ Ⓑ Ⓒ Ⓓ Ⓔ
21 Ⓐ Ⓑ Ⓒ Ⓓ Ⓔ
22 Ⓐ Ⓑ Ⓒ Ⓓ Ⓔ

23 Ⓐ Ⓑ Ⓒ Ⓓ Ⓔ
24 Ⓐ Ⓑ Ⓒ Ⓓ Ⓔ
25 Ⓐ Ⓑ Ⓒ Ⓓ Ⓔ
26 Ⓐ Ⓑ Ⓒ Ⓓ Ⓔ
27 Ⓐ Ⓑ Ⓒ Ⓓ Ⓔ
28 Ⓐ Ⓑ Ⓒ Ⓓ Ⓔ
29 Ⓐ Ⓑ Ⓒ Ⓓ Ⓔ
30 Ⓐ Ⓑ Ⓒ Ⓓ Ⓔ
31 Ⓐ Ⓑ Ⓒ Ⓓ Ⓔ
32 Ⓐ Ⓑ Ⓒ Ⓓ Ⓔ
33 Ⓐ Ⓑ Ⓒ Ⓓ Ⓔ
34 Ⓐ Ⓑ Ⓒ Ⓓ Ⓔ
35 Ⓐ Ⓑ Ⓒ Ⓓ Ⓔ
36 Ⓐ Ⓑ Ⓒ Ⓓ Ⓔ
37 Ⓐ Ⓑ Ⓒ Ⓓ Ⓔ
38 Ⓐ Ⓑ Ⓒ Ⓓ Ⓔ
39 Ⓐ Ⓑ Ⓒ Ⓓ Ⓔ
40 Ⓐ Ⓑ Ⓒ Ⓓ Ⓔ
41 Ⓐ Ⓑ Ⓒ Ⓓ Ⓔ
42 Ⓐ Ⓑ Ⓒ Ⓓ Ⓔ
43 Ⓐ Ⓑ Ⓒ Ⓓ Ⓔ
44 Ⓐ Ⓑ Ⓒ Ⓓ Ⓔ

45 Ⓐ Ⓑ Ⓒ Ⓓ Ⓔ
46 Ⓐ Ⓑ Ⓒ Ⓓ Ⓔ
47 Ⓐ Ⓑ Ⓒ Ⓓ Ⓔ
48 Ⓐ Ⓑ Ⓒ Ⓓ Ⓔ
49 Ⓐ Ⓑ Ⓒ Ⓓ Ⓔ
50 Ⓐ Ⓑ Ⓒ Ⓓ Ⓔ
51 Ⓐ Ⓑ Ⓒ Ⓓ Ⓔ
52 Ⓐ Ⓑ Ⓒ Ⓓ Ⓔ
53 Ⓐ Ⓑ Ⓒ Ⓓ Ⓔ
54 Ⓐ Ⓑ Ⓒ Ⓓ Ⓔ
55 Ⓐ Ⓑ Ⓒ Ⓓ Ⓔ
56 Ⓐ Ⓑ Ⓒ Ⓓ Ⓔ
57 Ⓐ Ⓑ Ⓒ Ⓓ Ⓔ
58 Ⓐ Ⓑ Ⓒ Ⓓ Ⓔ
59 Ⓐ Ⓑ Ⓒ Ⓓ Ⓔ
60 Ⓐ Ⓑ Ⓒ Ⓓ Ⓔ
61 Ⓐ Ⓑ Ⓒ Ⓓ Ⓔ
62 Ⓐ Ⓑ Ⓒ Ⓓ Ⓔ
63 Ⓐ Ⓑ Ⓒ Ⓓ Ⓕ
64 Ⓐ Ⓑ Ⓒ Ⓓ Ⓔ
65 Ⓐ Ⓑ Ⓒ Ⓓ Ⓔ
66 Ⓐ Ⓑ Ⓒ Ⓓ Ⓔ

67 Ⓐ Ⓑ Ⓒ Ⓓ Ⓔ
68 Ⓐ Ⓑ Ⓒ Ⓓ Ⓔ
69 Ⓐ Ⓑ Ⓒ Ⓓ Ⓔ
70 Ⓐ Ⓑ Ⓒ Ⓓ Ⓔ
71 Ⓐ Ⓑ Ⓒ Ⓓ Ⓔ
72 Ⓐ Ⓑ Ⓒ Ⓓ Ⓔ
73 Ⓐ Ⓑ Ⓒ Ⓓ Ⓔ
74 Ⓐ Ⓑ Ⓒ Ⓓ Ⓔ
75 Ⓐ Ⓑ Ⓒ Ⓓ Ⓔ
76 Ⓐ Ⓑ Ⓒ Ⓓ Ⓔ
77 Ⓐ Ⓑ Ⓒ Ⓓ Ⓔ
78 Ⓐ Ⓑ Ⓒ Ⓓ Ⓔ
79 Ⓐ Ⓑ Ⓒ Ⓓ Ⓔ
80 Ⓐ Ⓑ Ⓒ Ⓓ Ⓔ
81 Ⓐ Ⓑ Ⓒ Ⓓ Ⓔ
82 Ⓐ Ⓑ Ⓒ Ⓓ Ⓔ
83 Ⓐ Ⓑ Ⓒ Ⓓ Ⓔ
84 Ⓐ Ⓑ Ⓒ Ⓓ Ⓔ
85 Ⓐ Ⓑ Ⓒ Ⓓ Ⓔ
86 Ⓐ Ⓑ Ⓒ Ⓓ Ⓔ
87 Ⓐ Ⓑ Ⓒ Ⓓ Ⓔ
88 Ⓐ Ⓑ Ⓒ Ⓓ Ⓔ

SCORE SHEET FOR DIAGNOSTIC EXAM

ADDRESS CHECKING TEST

Number Right minus Number Wrong equals   Score

_____ – _____ = _____

MEMORY FOR ADDRESSES TEST

Number Right minus (Number Wrong ÷ 4) equals   Score

_____ – _____ = _____

SELF-EVALUATION CHART

The Self-Evaluation Chart will help you to rate yourself on the Diagnostic Exam and on all other Model Exams that follow. Calculate your score for each test as shown above. Then check to see where your score falls on the scale from Poor to Excellent. Lightly shade in the boxes in which your scores fall.

Test	Excellent	Good	Average	Fair	Poor
Address Checking	80–95	65–79	50–64	35–49	1–34
Memory for Addresses	75–88	60–74	45–59	30–44	1–29

DIAGNOSTIC EXAM

ADDRESS CHECKING TEST

TIME: 6 Minutes. 95 Questions.

DIRECTIONS: For each question, compare the address in the left column with the address in the right column. If the two addresses are ALIKE IN EVERY WAY, blacken space Ⓐ on your answer sheet. If the two addresses are DIFFERENT IN ANY WAY, blacken space Ⓓ on your answer sheet. Correct answers for this test are on page 40.

1.	.197 Wonderview Dr NW	197 Wonderview Dr NW
2.	.243 S Capistrano Ave	234 S Capistrano Ave
3.	.4300 Las Pillas Rd	4300 Las Pillas Rd
4.	.5551 N Ramara Ave	5551 N Ramara St
5.	.Walden Col 80480	Waldon Col 80480
6.	.2200 E Dunnington St	2200 E Dowington St
7.	.2700 Helena Way	2700 Helena Way
8.	.3968 S Zeno Ave	3968 S Zemo Ave
9.	.14011 Costilla Ave NE	14011 Costilla Ave SE
10.	.1899 N Dearborn Dr	1899 N Dearborn Dr
11.	.8911 Scranton Way	8911 Scranton Way
12.	.365 Liverpool St	356 Liverpool St
13.	.1397 Lewiston Pl	1297 Lewiston Pl
14.	.4588 Crystal Way	4588 Crystal Rd
15.	.Muscle Shoals AL 35660	Muscle Shoals AL 35660
16.	.988 Larkin Johnson Ave SE	988 Larkin Johnson Ave SE
17.	.5501 Greenville Blvd NE	5501 Greenview Blvd NE
18.	.7133 N Baranmor Pky	7133 N Baranmor Pky
19.	.10500 Montana Rd	10500 Montana Rd
20.	.4769 E Kalispell Dr	4769 E Kalispell Cir
21.	.Daytona Beach Fla 32016	Daytona Beach FL 32016
22.	.2227 W 94th Ave	2272 W 94th Ave
23.	.6399 E Ponce De Leon St	6399 E Ponce De Leon Ct
24.	.20800 N Rainbow Pl	20800 N Rainbow Pl
25.	.Sasser GA 31785	Sasser GA 31785
26.	.Washington D C 20018	Washington D C 20013
27.	.6500 Milwaukee NE	6500 Milwaukee SE
28.	.1300 Strasburg Dr	1300 Strasburg Dr
29.	.Burnettsville IN 47926	Bornettsville IN 47926

30...1594 S Frontage St	1594 S Frontage Ave
31...37099 Oliphant Ln	37909 Oliphant Ln
32...2248 Avonsdale Cir NW	2248 Avonsdale Cir NE
33...1733 Norlander Dr SE	1733 Norlander Dr SW
34...15469 W Oxalida Dr	15469 W Oxalido Dr
35...4192 E Commonwealth Ave	4192 E Commonwealth Ave
36...Kingsfield Maine 04947	Kingsfield Maine 04947
37...246 East Ramsdell Rd	246 East Ramsdale Rd
38...8456 Vina Del Maro Blvd	8456 Vina Del Maro Blvd
39...6688 N 26th Street	6888 N 26th Street
40...1477 Woodrow Wilson Blvd	1477 Woodrow Wilson Blvd
41...3724 S 18th Ave	3724 S 18th Ave
42...11454 S Lake Maggiore Blvd	11454 S Lake Maggiore Blvd
43...4832 N Bougainnvilla Ave	4832 N Bougainnvillia Ave
44...3713 Coffee Pot Riviera	3773 Coffee Pot Riviera
45...2800 S Freemont Ter	2800 S Freemond Ter
46...3654 S Urbane Dr	3654 S Urbane Cir
47...1408 Oklahoma Ave NE	1408 Oklahoma Ave NE
48...6201 Meadowland Ln	6201 Meadowlawn Ln
49...5799 S Augusta Ln	15799 S Augusta Ln
50...5115 Winchester Rd	5115 Westchester Rd
51...4611 N Kendall Pl	4611 N Kendall Pl
52...17045 Dormicone Cir	17045 Dormieone Cir
53...3349 Palma Del Mar Blvd	3346 Palma Del Mar Blvd
54...13211 E 182nd Ave	12311 E 182nd Ave
55...Evansville WY 82636	Evansville WI 82636
56...6198 N Albritton Rd	6198 N Albretton Rd
57...11230 Twinflower Cir	11230 Twintower Cir
58...6191 Lockett Station Rd	6191 Lockett Station Rd
59...1587 Vanderbilt Dr N	1587 Vanderbilt Dr S
60...Ontarioville IL 60103	Ontarioville IL 60103
61...4204 Bridgeton Ave	4204 Bridgeton Ave
62...31215 N Emerald Dr	31215 N Emerald Cir
63...4601 N Peniman Ave	4601 N Peniman Ave
64...3782 SE Verrazanna Bay	3782 SE Verrazana Bay
65...2766 N Thunderbird Ct	2766 N Thunderbird Ct
66...2166 N Elmorado Ct	2166 N Eldorado Ct
67...10538 Innsbruck Ln	1058 Innsbruck Ln
68...888 Lonesome Rd	8888 Lonesome Rd
69...4023 N Brainbridge Ave	4023 N Brainbridge Ave
70...3000 E Roberta Rd	30000 E Roberta Rd
71...Quenemo KS 66528	Quenemo KS 66528
72...13845 Donahoo St	13345 Donahoo St
73...10466 Gertrude NE	10466 Gertrude NE
74...2733 N 105th Ave	2733 S 105th Ave
75...3100 N Wyandotte Cir	3100 N Wyandotte Ave
76...11796 Summittcrest Dr	11769 Summittcrest Dr
77...Viburnum Miss 65566	Viburnom Miss 65566
78...9334 Kindleberger Rd	9334 Kindleberger Road
79...4801 Armourdale Pky	8401 Armourdale Pky
80...9392 Northrup Ave	9392 Northrop Ave
81...11736 Rottinghaus Rd	11736 Rottinghaus Rd
82...3878 Flammang Dr	3878 Flammang Dr

83. . .	2101 Johnstontown Way	2101 Johnsontown Way
84. . .	1177 Ghentwoodrow St	1177 Ghentwoodrow Ct
85. . .	888 Onadaga Ct	888 Onadaga Ct
86. . .	3205 N Rastetter Ave	3205 N Rastetter Ave
87. . .	1144 Yellowsands Dr NE	1144 Yellowsands Dr NW
88. . .	3197 Clerkenwell Ct	3197 Clerkenwell Ct
89. . .	3021 Pemaquid Way	3210 Pemaquid Way
90. . .	1398 Angelina Rd	1398 Angelino Rd
91. . .	4331 NW Zoeller Ave	4881 NW Zoeller Ave
92. . .	1805 Jeassamine Ln	1805 Jassamine Ln
93. . .	14411 Bellemeade Ave	14411 Bellemeade Ave
94. . .	Noquochoke MA 02790	Noguochoke MA 02790
95. . .	11601 Hagamann Cir	11601 Hagamann Ct

END OF ADDRESS CHECKING TEST

If you finish this test before time is up, use the remaining time to check over your work. Do not turn to the next page until you are told to do so.

PRACTICE FOR
MEMORY FOR ADDRESSES TEST

DIRECTIONS: The five boxes below are labelled A, B, C, D, and E. In each box there are three sets of number spans with names, and two names which are not associated with numbers. In the next THREE MINUTES, you must try to memorize the box location of each name and number span. The position of a name or number span within its box is not important. You need only remember the letter of the box in which the item is to be found. You will use these names and numbers to answer three sets of practice questions which are NOT scored and one actual test that is scored. Correct answers are on pages 40 and 41.

A	B	C	D	E
1800-2699 Teakwood	2800-3299 Teakwood	1400-1799 Teakwood	3300-3699 Teakwood	2700-2799 Teakwood
Windy	Oman	Melinda	Burnett	Stern
8600-8799 Prince	8800-9499 Prince	9500-9599 Prince	8100-8599 Prince	9600-9799 Prince
Langley	Rogers	Bonnie	Flower	Fairland
6300-6499 Bakers	5800-6299 Bakers	6500-6599 Bakers	5100-5799 Bakers	4800-4999 Bakers

PRACTICE I

DIRECTIONS: Use the next THREE MINUTES to mark on your answer sheet the letter of the box in which each item that follows is to be found. Try to mark each item without looking back at the boxes. If, however, you get stuck, you may refer to the boxes during this practice exercise. If you find that you must look back, try to memorize as you do so. This test is for practice only. It will not be scored.

1. 4800-4999 Bakers
2. Oman
3. Burnett
4. 3300-3699 Teakwood
5. Windy
6. 1800-2699 Teakwood
7. 9600-9799 Prince
8. Langley
9. Bonnie
10. Burnett
11. 6300-6499 Bakers
12. Rogers
13. 2800-3299 Teakwood
14. 8800-9499 Prince
15. 6500-6599 Bakers
16. 3300-3699 Teakwood
17. Fairland
18. 5100-5799 Bakers
19. Melinda
20. Stern
21. 8100-8599 Prince
22. Fairland

23. 5800-6299 Bakers
24. 9600-9799 Prince
25. 2700-2799 Teakwood
26. 8100-8599 Prince
27. Windy
28. 1400-1799 Teakwood
29. Oman
30. 9600-9799 Prince
31. 1800-2699 Teakwood
32. Langley
33. 2800-3299 Teakwood
34. Windy
35. 6500-6599 Bakers
36. Stern
37. Flower
38. Melinda
39. 4800-4999 Bakers
40. 1800-2699 Teakwood
41. 9600-9799 Prince
42. Windy
43. 2800-3299 Teakwood
44. Bonnie
45. Burnett
46. 6500-6599 Bakers
47. Stern
48. 1800-2699 Teakwood
49. Rogers
50. Flower
51. 8100-8599 Prince
52. 2700-2799 Teakwood
53. Melinda
54. 8600-8799 Prince
55. 4800-4999 Bakers
56. 8800-9499 Prince
57. Bonnie
58. 5100-5799 Bakers
59. 1800-2699 Teakwood
60. 5800-6299 Bakers
61. Stern
62. 9500-9599 Prince
63. 3300-3699 Teakwood
64. 5100-5799 Bakers
65. Langley
66. 1400-1799 Teakwood
67. 8100-8599 Prince
68. 4800-4999 Bakers
69. 8800-9499 Prince
70. 6300-6499 Bakers
71. Flower
72. Rogers
73. 4800-4999 Bakers
74. 6500-6599 Bakers
75. 1800-2699 Teakwood
76. Burnett
77. 9500-9599 Prince
78. 1400-1799 Teakwood
79. 4800-4999 Bakers
80. Melinda
81. Oman
82. 6500-6599 Bakers
83. Fairland
84. 2700-2799 Teakwood
85. 6300-6499 Bakers
86. Fairland
87. 2700-2799 Teakwood
88. 5800-6299 Bakers

PRACTICE II

DIRECTIONS: The next 88 questions constitute another practice exercise. Again, you should mark your answers on your answer sheet. Again, the time limit is THREE MINUTES. This time, however, you must NOT look at the boxes while answering the questions. You must rely on your memory in marking the box location of each item. This practice test will not be scored.

1. 4800-4999 Bakers
2. Oman
3. Burnett
4. 3300-3699 Teakwood
5. Windy
6. 1800-2699 Teakwood
7. 9600-9799 Prince
8. Langley
9. Bonnie
10. Burnett
11. 6300-6499 Bakers
12. Rogers
13. 2800-3299 Teakwood
14. 8800-9499 Prince
15. 6500-6599 Bakers
16. 3300-3699 Teakwood
17. Fairland
18. 5100-5799 Bakers
19. Melinda
20. Stern
21. 8100-8599 Prince
22. Fairland
23. 5800-6299 Bakers
24. 9600-9799 Prince
25. 2700-2799 Teakwood
26. 8100-8599 Prince
27. Windy
28. 1400-1799 Teakwood
29. Oman
30. 9600-9799 Prince
31. 1800-2699 Teakwood
32. Langley
33. 2800-3299 Teakwood
34. Windy
35. 6500-6599 Bakers
36. Stern
37. Flower
38. Melinda
39. 4800-4999 Bakers
40. 1800-2699 Teakwood
41. 9600-9799 Prince
42. Windy
43. 2800-3299 Teakwood
44. Bonnie

45. Burnett
46. 6500-6599 Bakers
47. Stern
48. 1800-2699 Teakwood
49. Rogers
50. Flower
51. 8100-8599 Prince
52. 2700-2799 Teakwood
53. Melinda
54. 8600-8799 Prince
55. 4800-4999 Bakers
56. 8800-9499 Prince
57. Bonnie
58. 5100-5799 Bakers
59. 1800-2699 Teakwood
60. 5800-6299 Bakers
61. Stern
62. 9500-9599 Prince
63. 3300-3699 Teakwood
64. 5100-5799 Bakers
65. Langley
66. 1400-1799 Teakwood
67. 8100-8599 Prince
68. 4800-4999 Baker
69. 8800-9499 Prince
70. 6300-6499 Bakers
71. Flower
72. Rogers
73. 4800-4999 Bakers
74. 6500-6599 Bakers
75. 1800-2699 Teakwood
76. Burnett
77. 9500-9599 Prince
78. 1400-1799 Teakwood
79. 4800-4999 Bakers
80. Melinda
81. Oman
82. 6500-6599 Bakers
83. Fairland
84. 2700-2799 Teakwood
85. 6300-6499 Bakers
86. Fairland
87. 2700-2799 Teakwood
88. 5800-6299 Bakers

PRACTICE III

DIRECTIONS: The names and addresses are repeated for you in the boxes below. Each name and each number span is in the same box in which you found it in the original set. You are now allowed FIVE MINUTES to study the locations again. Do your best to memorize the letter of the box in which each item is to be found. This is your last chance to see the boxes.

A	B	C	D	E
1800-2699 Teakwood Windy 8600-8799 Prince Langley 6300-6499 Bakers	2800-3299 Teakwood Oman 8800-9499 Prince Rogers 5800-6299 Bakers	1400-1799 Teakwood Melinda 9500-9599 Prince Bonnie 6500-6599 Bakers	3300-3699 Teakwood Burnett 8100-8599 Prince Flower 5100-5799 Bakers	2700-2799 Teakwood Stern 9600-9799 Prince Fairland 4800-4999 Bakers

DIRECTIONS: This is your last practice test. Mark the location of each of the 88 items on your answer sheet. You are allowed FIVE MINUTES to answer these questions. Do NOT look back at the boxes. This practice test will not be scored.

1. 3300-3699 Teakwood
2. 9600-9799 Prince
3. 4800-4999 Bakers
4. Windy
5. 1800-2699 Teakwood
6. Burnett
7. 2800-3299 Teakwood
8. 6300-6499 Bakers
9. Oman
10. 3300-3699 Teakwood
11. 8800-9499 Prince
12. 2800-3299 Teakwood
13. Rogers
14. 6500-6599 Bakers
15. Langley
16. 5100-5799 Bakers
17. Bonnie
18. 9600-9799 Prince
19. Burnett
20. 4800-4999 Bakers
21. Fairland
22. 8100-8599 Prince
23. Stern
24. 1800-2699 Teakwood
25. Melinda
26. 5800-6299 Bakers
27. Oman
28. 1400-1799 Teakwood
29. Windy
30. 9600-9799 Prince
31. 2700-2799 Teakwood
32. Flower
33. 8100-8599 Prince
34. Langley
35. 9600-9799 Prince
36. Melinda
37. Windy
38. Bonnie
39. 9600-9799 Prince
40. Fairland
41. 2800-3299 Teakwood
42. Stern
43. 6500-6599 Bakers
44. Windy
45. 5800-6299 Bakers
46. 2700-2799 Teakwood
47. Fairland
48. 6300-6499 Bakers
49. 2700-2799 Teakwood
50. Fairland
51. 6500-6599 Bakers
52. Oman

53. Melinda
54. 4800-4999 Bakers
55. 1400-1799 Teakwood
56. 9500-9599 Prince
57. Burnett
58. 1800-2699 Teakwood
59. 6500-6599 Bakers
60. Rogers
61. 4800-4999 Bakers
62. Flower
63. 6300-6499 Bakers
64. 8800-9499 Prince
65. 4800-4999 Bakers
66. 8100-8599 Prince
67. 1400-1799 Teakwood
68. Langley
69. 5100-5799 Bakers
70. 3300-3699 Teakwood

71. 9500-9599 Prince
72. Stern
73. 5800-6299 Bakers
74. 1800-2699 Teakwood
75. 5100-5799 Bakers
76. Bonnie
77. 8800-9499 Prince
78. 4800-4999 Bakers
79. 8600-8799 Prince
80. Melinda
81. 8800-9499 Prince
82. Flower
83. 6500-6599 Bakers
84. Burnett
85. 1800-2699 Teakwood
86. Stern
87. 8100-8599 Prince
88. Rogers

MEMORY FOR ADDRESSES TEST

TIME: 5 Minutes. 88 Questions.

DIRECTIONS: Mark your answers on the answer sheet in the section headed "MEMORY FOR ADDRESSES TEST." This test will be scored. You are NOT permitted to look at the boxes. Work from memory, as quickly and as accurately as you can. Correct answers are on page 41.

1. 9500-9599 Prince
2. 4800-4999 Bakers
3. Oman
4. 8100-8599 Prince
5. Windy
6. Fairland
7. 2800-3299 Teakwood
8. 5800-6299 Bakers
9. 8800-9499 Prince
10. Langley
11. 1800-2699 Teakwood
12. 2700-2799 Teakwood
13. Rogers
14. Oman
15. 6500-6599 Bakers
16. 9600-9799 Prince
17. 3300-3699 Teakwood
18. Melinda
19. 8100-8599 Prince
20. Stern
21. 6300-6499 Bakers
22. 8800-9499 Prince
23. 3300-3699 Teakwood
24. Burnett
25. Bonnie
26. Rogers
27. 9500-9599 Prince
28. 9600-9799 Prince
29. 6300-6499 Bakers
30. 1800-2699 Teakwood
31. Langley
32. 1400-1799 Teakwood
33. 2700-2799 Teakwood
34. Stern
35. 8800-9499 Prince
36. 3300-3699 Teakwood
37. Fairland
38. Flower
39. 5100-5799 Bakers

40. 8100-8599 Prince
41. 6500-6599 Bakers
42. Windy
43. 2800-3299 Teakwood
44. Melinda
45. 9600-9799 Prince
46. Bonnie
47. 1800-2699 Teakwood
48. 8600-8799 Prince
49. 5800-6299 Bakers
50. Burnett
51. Stern
52. 6300-6499 Bakers
53. 3300-3699 Teakwood
54. 8100-8599 Prince
55. Flower
56. 5100-5799 Bakers
57. 4800-4999 Bakers
58. 6300-6499 Bakers
59. Fairland
60. 2700-2799 Teakwood
61. 8600-8799 Prince
62. 8800-9499 Prince
63. Oman
64. Windy
65. Langley
66. 2800-3299 Teakwood
67. 9500-9599 Prince
68. 4800-4999 Bakers
69. 1400-1799 Teakwood
70. Windy
71. 5800-6299 Bakers
72. 1800-2699 Teakwood
73. Rogers
74. 6300-6499 Bakers
75. 5100-5799 Bakers
76. Fairland
77. 8600-8799 Prince
78. 8800-9499 Prince

79. Bonnie
80. Burnett
81. 2800-3299 Teakwood
82. 2700-2799 Teakwood
83. 9600-9799 Prince

84. Oman
85. 4800-4999 Bakers
86. 9500-9599 Prince
87. Rogers
88. Stern

END OF EXAM

CORRECT ANSWERS FOR DIAGNOSTIC EXAM

ADDRESS CHECKING TEST

1. A	13. D	25. A	37. D	49. D	61. A	73. A	85. A
2. D	14. D	26. D	38. A	50. D	62. D	74. D	86. A
3. A	15. A	27. D	39. D	51. A	63. A	75. D	87. D
4. D	16. A	28. A	40. A	52. A	64. D	76. D	88. A
5. D	17. D	29. D	41. A	53. D	65. A	77. D	89. D
6. D	18. A	30. D	42. A	54. D	66. D	78. D	90. D
7. A	19. A	31. D	43. D	55. D	67. D	79. D	91. D
8. D	20. D	32. D	44. D	56. D	68. D	80. D	92. D
9. D	21. D	33. D	45. D	57. D	69. A	81. A	93. A
10. A	22. D	34. D	46. D	58. A	70. D	82. A	94. D
11. A	23. D	35. A	47. A	59. D	71. A	83. D	95. D
12. D	24. A	36. A	48. D	60. A	72. D	84. D	

MEMORY FOR ADDRESSES—PRACTICE I

1. E	12. B	23. B	34. A	45. D	56. B	67. D	78. C
2. B	13. B	24. E	35. C	46. C	57. C	68. E	79. E
3. D	14. B	25. E	36. E	47. E	58. D	69. B	80. C
4. D	15. C	26. D	37. D	48. A	59. A	70. A	81. B
5. A	16. D	27. A	38. C	49. B	60. B	71. D	82. C
6. A	17. E	28. C	39. E	50. A	61. E	72. B	83. E
7. E	18. D	29. B	40. A	51. D	62. C	73. E	84. E
8. A	19. C	30. E	41. E	52. E	63. D	74. C	85. A
9. C	20. E	31. A	42. A	53. C	64. D	75. A	86. E
10. D	21. D	32. A	43. B	54. A	65. A	76. D	87. E
11. A	22. E	33. B	44. C	55. E	66. C	77. C	88. B

MEMORY FOR ADDRESSES—PRACTICE II

1. E	12. B	23. B	34. A	45. D	56. B	67. D	78. C
2. B	13. B	24. E	35. C	46. C	57. C	68. E	79. E
3. D	14. B	25. E	36. E	47. E	58. D	69. B	80. C
4. D	15. C	26. D	37. D	48. A	59. A	70. A	81. B
5. A	16. D	27. A	38. C	49. B	60. B	71. D	82. C
6. A	17. E	28. C	39. E	50. D	61. E	72. B	83. E
7. E	18. D	29. B	40. A	51. D	62. C	73. E	84. E
8. A	19. C	30. E	41. E	52. E	63. D	74. C	85. A
9. C	20. E	31. A	42. A	53. C	64. D	75. A	86. E
10. D	21. D	32. A	43. B	54. A	65. A	76. D	87. E
11. A	22. E	33. B	44. C	55. E	66. C	77. C	88. B

MEMORY FOR ADDRESSES—PRACTICE III

1. D	12. B	23. E	34. A	45. B	56. C	67. C	78. E
2. E	13. B	24. A	35. E	46. E	57. D	68. A	79. A
3. E	14. C	25. C	36. C	47. E	58. A	69. D	80. C
4. A	15. A	26. B	37. A	48. A	59. C	70. D	81. B
5. A	16. D	27. B	38. C	49. E	60. B	71. C	82. D
6. D	17. C	28. C	39. E	50. E	61. E	72. E	83. C
7. B	18. E	29. A	40. E	51. C	62. D	73. B	84. D
8. A	19. D	30. E	41. B	52. B	63. A	74. A	85. A
9. B	20. E	31. E	42. E	53. C	64. B	75. D	86. E
10. D	21. E	32. D	43. C	54. E	65. E	76. C	87. D
11. B	22. D	33. D	44. A	55. C	66. D	77. B	88. B

MEMORY FOR ADDRESSES TEST

1. C	12. E	23. D	34. E	45. E	56. D	67. C	78. B
2. E	13. B	24. D	35. B	46. C	57. E	68. E	79. C
3. B	14. B	25. C	36. D	47. A	58. A	69. C	80. D
4. D	15. C	26. B	37. E	48. A	59. E	70. A	81. B
5. A	16. E	27. C	38. D	49. B	60. E	71. B	82. E
6. E	17. D	28. E	39. D	50. D	61. A	72. A	83. E
7. B	18. C	29. A	40. D	51. E	62. B	73. B	84. B
8. B	19. D	30. A	41. C	52. A	63. B	74. A	85. E
9. B	20. E	31. A	42. A	53. D	64. A	75. D	86. C
10. A	21. A	32. C	43. B	54. D	65. A	76. E	87. B
11. A	22. B	33. E	44. C	55. D	66. B	77. A	88. E

ANALYZING YOUR ERRORS

The Address Checking Test of the Diagnostic Exam contains 35 addresses that are exactly alike and 60 addresses that are different. The chart below shows what kind of difference occurs in each of the addresses that contains a difference. Check your answers against this chart to see which kind of difference you missed most often. Note also the questions in which you thought you saw a difference but in which there really was none. Becoming aware of your errors will help you to eliminate those errors on future model exams and on the actual exam.

Type of Difference	Question Numbers	Number of Questions You Missed
Difference in NUMBERS	2, 12, 13, 22, 26, 31, 39, 44, 49, 53, 54, 67, 68, 70, 72, 76, 79, 89, 91	
Difference in ABBREVIATIONS	4, 9, 14, 20, 21, 23, 27, 30, 32, 33, 46, 55, 59, 62, 74, 75, 78, 84, 87, 95	
Difference in NAMES	5, 6, 8, 17, 29, 34, 37, 43, 45, 48, 50, 56, 57, 64, 66, 77, 80, 83, 90, 92, 94	
No Difference	1, 3, 7, 10, 11, 15, 16, 18, 19, 24, 25, 28, 35, 36, 38, 40, 41, 42, 47, 51, 52, 58, 60, 61, 63, 65, 69, 71, 73, 81, 82, 85, 86, 88, 93	

PROGRESS GRAPH

A Progress Graph like this one accompanies each Model Exam. After you score each exam, blacken the bar for each test to the score closest to the score you earned. The SAMPLE PROGRESS GRAPH below illustrates how to fill in the graph for scores of 70 on Address Checking and 50 on Memory for Addresses. Use the graph entitled YOUR PROGRESS GRAPH to record your scores for the Diagnostic Exam. Later on you may wish to transfer these scores to the Progress Graph for the next Model Exam so that you can see at a glance how much you are improving.

SAMPLE PROGRESS CHART

Blacken to the closest score to chart your progress.

Score		
95		
90		
85		
80		
75		
70		
65		
60		
55		
50		
45		
40		
35		
30		
25		
20		
15		
10		
5		
0		

Test	AC	M
Model Exam	Diag.	

AC = Address Checking
M = Memory for Addresses

YOUR PROGRESS CHART

Blacken to the closest score to chart your progress.

Score		
95		
90		
85		
80		
75		
70		
65		
60		
55		
50		
45		
40		
35		
30		
25		
20		
15		
10		
5		
0		

Test	AC	M
Model Exam	Diag.	

AC − Address Checking
M = Memory for Addresses

PART II
Test Strategies

HOW TO ANSWER ADDRESS CHECKING QUESTIONS

The Address Checking Test is not difficult, but it requires great speed and it carries a heavy penalty for inaccuracy. You must learn to spot differences very quickly and to make firm, fast decisions about addresses that are exactly alike. This chapter will help you to develop a system for comparing addresses. Once you have a system, practice with that system will help you to build up speed.

The directions make it very clear that if there is *any difference at all* between the two addresses they are to be marked as different. This means that once you spot a difference, mark the answer as Ⓓ and go immediately to the next question. There is no point in looking at the remainder of an address once you have found a difference. You will be amazed at how much time you can save by not reading the whole of every address.

READ EXACTLY WHAT YOU SEE

The best way to read addresses being compared is to read exactly what you see and to sound out words by syllables. For example:

If you see "St," read "es tee" not "street."
If you see "NH," read "en aitch" not "New Hampshire."
If you see "1035," read "one oh three five" not "one thousand thirty-five."
Read "sassafrass" as "sas-sa-frass."

Psychologists have discovered that the human mind always tries to complete a figure. If you read "Pky" as "Parkway," you will probably read "Pkwy" as "Parkway," and will never notice the difference. Your mind will complete the word without allowing you to focus on the letters. If, however, you read the abbreviation as an abbreviation, you will notice that the two abbreviations are different. If you read "Kansas City MO" as "Kansas City Missouri," you are unlikely to catch the difference with "Kansas City MD." But if you read "Kansas City em oh," you will readily pick up on "Kansas City em dee."

USE YOUR HANDS

Since speed is so important in answering Address Checking questions and since it is so easy to lose your place, you must use both hands during your work on this part. In the hand with which you write, hold your pencil poised at the number on your answer sheet. Run the index finger of your other hand under the addresses being compared. The finger will help you to focus on one line at a time, will help keep your eyes from jumping up or down a line. By holding your place on both question and answer sheet, you are less likely to skip a question or an answer space.

One effective way to tackle address checking questions quickly and accurately is to look for differences in only one area at a time. Every address consists of both numbers and words. If you narrow your focus to compare only the numbers or only the words, you are more likely to notice differences and less apt to see what you expect to see rather than what is actually printed on the page.

LOOK FOR DIFFERENCES IN NUMBERS

Look first at the numbers. Read the number in the left column, then skip immediately to the number in the right column. Do the two numbers contain the same number of digits?

A difference of this type should be easy to see. In the questions that follow, blacken Ⓐ if the two numbers are exactly alike and Ⓓ if the numbers are different in any way.

IS THE NUMBER OF DIGITS THE SAME?

1. 2003	2003	1. Ⓐ Ⓓ
2. 75864	75864	2. Ⓐ Ⓓ
3. 7300	730	3. Ⓐ Ⓓ
4. 50106	5016	4. Ⓐ Ⓓ
5. 2184	2184	5. Ⓐ Ⓓ

Answers: 1.A   2.A   3.D   4.D   5.A

Did you spot the differences? Train your eye to count digits rapidly.

IS THE ORDER OF DIGITS THE SAME?

1. 7516	7561	1. Ⓐ Ⓓ
2. 80302	80302	2. Ⓐ Ⓓ
3. 19832	18932	3. Ⓐ Ⓓ
4. 6186	6186	4. Ⓐ Ⓓ
5. 54601	54610	5. Ⓐ Ⓓ

Answers: 1.D   2.A   3.D   4.A   5.D

Did you get these all correct? If not, look again right now. See where you made your mistakes.

IS THERE A SUBSTITUTION OF ONE DIGIT FOR ANOTHER?

1. 16830	16830	1. Ⓐ Ⓓ
2. 94936	94636	2. Ⓐ Ⓓ
3. 3287	3285	3. Ⓐ Ⓓ
4. 54216	54216	4. Ⓐ Ⓓ
5. 32341	33341	5. Ⓐ Ⓓ

Answers: 1.A   2.D   3.D   4.A   5.D

Did you catch all the differences? Were you able to mark Ⓐ with confidence when there was no difference?

PRACTICE FINDING DIFFERENCES IN NUMBERS

In the following set of practice questions, all differences are in the numbers. Work quickly, focusing only on the numbers. You may find any of the three varieties of differences just described.

#	Left	Right	Answer
1	3685 Brite Ave	3865 Brite Ave	Ⓐ Ⓓ
2	Ware MA 08215	Ware MA 08215	Ⓐ Ⓓ
3	4001 Webster Rd	401 Webster Rd	Ⓐ Ⓓ
4	9789 Bell Rd	9786 Bell Rd	Ⓐ Ⓓ
5	Scarsdale NY 10583	Scarsdale NY 10583	Ⓐ Ⓓ
6	1482 Grand Blvd	1482 Grand Blvd	Ⓐ Ⓓ
7	Milwaukee WI 53202	Milwaukee WI 52302	Ⓐ Ⓓ
8	3542 W 48th St	3542 W 84th St	Ⓐ Ⓓ
9	9461 Hansen St	9461 Hansen St	Ⓐ Ⓓ
10	32322 Florence Pkwy	3232 Florence Pkwy	Ⓐ Ⓓ
11	Portland OR 97208	Portland OR 99208	Ⓐ Ⓓ
12	3999 Thompson Dr	3999 Thompson Dr	Ⓐ Ⓓ
13	1672 Sutton Pl	1972 Sutton Pl	Ⓐ Ⓓ
14	Omaha NE 68127	Omaha NE 68127	Ⓐ Ⓓ
15	1473 S 96th St	1743 S 96th St	Ⓐ Ⓓ
16	3425 Geary St	3425 Geary St	Ⓐ Ⓓ
17	Dallas TX 75234	Dallas TX 75234	Ⓐ Ⓓ
18	4094 Horchow Rd	4904 Horchow Rd	Ⓐ Ⓓ
19	San Francisco CA 94108	San Francisco CA 94108	Ⓐ Ⓓ
20	1410 Broadway	141 Broadway	Ⓐ Ⓓ
21	424 Fifth Ave	4240 Fifth Ave	Ⓐ Ⓓ
22	Westport CT 06880	Westport CT 06880	Ⓐ Ⓓ
23	1932 Wilton Rd	1923 Wilton Rd	Ⓐ Ⓓ
24	2052 Victoria Sta	2502 Victoria Sta	Ⓐ Ⓓ
25	1982 Carlton Pl	1982 Carlton Pl	Ⓐ Ⓓ

Answers:

1.D	6.A	11.D	16.A	21.D
2.A	7.D	12.A	17.A	22.A
3.D	8.D	13.D	18.D	23.D
4.D	9.A	14.A	19.A	24.D
5.A	10.D	15.D	20.D	25.A

Were you able to focus on the numbers? Were you able to spot the differences quickly? Could you make a rapid decision when there was no difference? If you got any of these questions wrong, look now to see why.

If you find a difference between the two numbers, mark Ⓓ and go on to the next question. Do not bother to look at the words in any pair of addresses in which you find a difference between the numbers.

If, while concentrating on numbers, you happen to catch a difference in spelling or abbreviations, by all means mark Ⓓ and go on to the next question. In other words, if you spot *any* difference between the addresses, even while you are looking for a specific type of difference, mark Ⓓ at once. A system may be useful, but do not stick to it slavishly when an answer is obvious.

LOOK FOR DIFFERENCES IN ABBREVIATIONS

When you are satisfied that the numbers are alike, and if no other difference has "struck you between the eyes," turn your attention to the abbreviations. Keep alert for differences such as:

Rd	Dr
Wy	Way
NH	NM

In comparing numbers, you began by looking at the numbers in the left column, then moved your eyes to focus on the right column. If you found a difference, you marked Ⓓ on your answer sheet, moved pencil and hand down one line and began again with the numbers of the next question. If you found no difference between the numbers, your eyes should have stopped at the right column. Look now at the abbreviations in the right column, then move your eyes to the left column to see if there are any differences. A difference is a difference, left to right or right to left, so do not waste time going back to the left column when you are focusing on the right. Try the next group of practice questions holding your place with pencil and finger and comparing the first question from left to right, the next question from right to left, and so on down the list. Remember to sound out the abbreviations exactly as you see them.

1 . . . 3238 NW 3rd St	3238 NE 3rd St	1.	ⒶⒹ
2 . . . 7865 Harkness Blvd	7865 Harkness Blvd	2.	ⒶⒹ
3 . . . Seattle WA 98102	Seattle WY 98102	3.	ⒶⒹ
4 . . . 342 Madison Ave	342 Madison St	4.	ⒶⒹ
5 . . . 723 Broadway E	723 Broadway E	5.	ⒶⒹ
6 . . . 4731 W 88th Dr	4731 W 88th Rd	6.	ⒶⒹ
7 . . . Boiceville NY 12412	Boiceville NY 12412	7.	ⒶⒹ
8 . . . 9021 Rodeo Dr	9021 Rodeo Drive	8.	ⒶⒹ
9 . . . 2093 Post St	2093 Post Rd	9.	ⒶⒹ
10 . . . New Orleans LA 70153	New Orleans LA 70153	10.	ⒶⒹ
11 . . . 5332 SW Bombay St	5332 SW Bombay St	11.	ⒶⒹ
12 . . . 416 Wellington Pkwy	416 Wellington Hwy	12.	ⒶⒹ
13 . . . 2096 Garden Ln	2096 Garden Wy	13.	ⒶⒹ
14 . . . 3220 W Grant Ave	3220 W Grant Ave	14.	ⒶⒹ
15 . . . Charlotte VT 05445	Charlotte VA 05445	15.	ⒶⒹ
16 . . . 4415 Oriental Blvd	4415 Oriental Blvd	16.	ⒶⒹ
17 . . . 6876 Raffles Rd	6876 Raffles Road	17.	ⒶⒹ
18 . . . 891 S Hotel Hwy	891 E Hotel Hwy	18.	ⒶⒹ
19 . . . 9500 London Br	9500 London Br	19.	ⒶⒹ
20 . . . 24A Motcomb St	24A Motcomb St	20.	ⒶⒹ
21 . . . 801 S Erleigh Ln	801 S Erleigh La	21.	ⒶⒹ
22 . . . 839 Casco St	839 Casco St	22.	ⒶⒹ
23 . . . Freeport ME 04033	Freeport NE 04033	23.	ⒶⒹ
24 . . . 3535 Island Ave	3535 Island Av	24.	ⒶⒹ
25 . . . 2186 Missouri Ave NE	2186 Missouri Ave NW	25.	ⒶⒹ

Answers:

1. D	6. D	11. A	16. A	21. D
2. A	7. A	12. D	17. D	22. A
3. D	8. D	13. D	18. D	23. D
4. D	9. D	14. A	19. A	24. D
5. A	10. A	15. D	20. A	25. D

LOOK FOR DIFFERENCES IN STREET OR CITY NAMES

If, after you have compared the numbers and the abbreviations, you have still not spotted any differences, you must look at the main words of the address. First of all, are the words in the two addresses really the same words?

1. Brookfield	Brookville	1. Ⓐ Ⓓ
2. Wayland	Wayland	2. Ⓐ Ⓓ
3. Ferncliff	Farmcliff	3. Ⓐ Ⓓ
4. Spring	Springs	4. Ⓐ Ⓓ
5. New City	New City	5. Ⓐ Ⓓ

Answers: 1.D 2.A 3.D 4.D 5.A

Sound out the words by syllables or spell them out. Is the spelling exactly the same? Are the same letters doubled? Are two letters reversed?

1. Beech	Beach	1. Ⓐ Ⓓ
2. Torrington	Torington	2. Ⓐ Ⓓ
3. Brayton	Brayton	3. Ⓐ Ⓓ
4. Collegiate	Collegaite	4. Ⓐ Ⓓ
5. Weston	Wetson	5. Ⓐ Ⓓ

Answers: 1.D 2.D 3.A 4.D 5.D

PRACTICE FINDING DIFFERENCES IN NAMES

Now try some practice questions in which differences may be found between the main words. Remember you can save precious time by reading one question from the left column to the right column and the next question from the right column to the left.

1 . . . 5254 Shaeffer St	5254 Schaeffer St	1. Ⓐ Ⓓ
2 . . . 8003 Sheraton Wy	8003 Sheraton Wy	2. Ⓐ Ⓓ
3 . . . 1937 Cordelia Terr	1937 Cordelia Terr	3. Ⓐ Ⓓ
4 . . . 392 Kauai Hwy	392 Kauaui Hwy	4. Ⓐ Ⓓ
5 . . . 7500 Preferred Rd	7500 Preffered Rd	5. Ⓐ Ⓓ
6 . . . Natick MA 01760	Natick MA 01760	6. Ⓐ Ⓓ
7 . . . 727 Stockbridge Rd	727 Stockbridge Rd	7. Ⓐ Ⓓ
8 . . . 294 Friend St	294 Freind St	8. Ⓐ Ⓓ
9 . . . 4550 Munching St	4550 Munchkin St	9. Ⓐ Ⓓ
10 . . . Gt Barrington MA 01230	Gt Barnington MA 01230	10. Ⓐ Ⓓ
11 . . . 7070 Baltic Wy	7070 Baltic Wy	11. Ⓐ Ⓓ
12 . . . 889 Safari St	889 Seafari St	12. Ⓐ Ⓓ
13 . . . Irvington NY 10533	Irvington NY 10533	13. Ⓐ Ⓓ
14 . . . 475 Ghirardelli Sq	475 Ghirardelli Sq	14. Ⓐ Ⓓ
15 . . . Sea Island GA 31561	Sea Inland GA 31561	15. Ⓐ Ⓓ
16 . . . 8486 Massachusetts Tpke	8486 Massachusetts Tpke	16. Ⓐ Ⓓ
17 . . . 6874 Cloister St	6874 Cloister St	17. Ⓐ Ⓓ
18 . . . 292 Westminster MI	292 Westminister MI	18. Ⓐ Ⓓ
19 . . . Providence RI 02903	Providence RI 02903	19. Ⓐ Ⓓ
20 . . . Arundel ME 04046	Anurdel ME 04046	20. Ⓐ Ⓓ
21 . . . 1000 Cadiz St	1000 Cadiz St	21. Ⓐ Ⓓ
22 . . . 821 Calphalon Wy	821 Caphalon Wy	22. Ⓐ Ⓓ
23 . . . Oakland CA 94604	Oakland CA 94604	23. Ⓐ Ⓓ
24 . . . 371 Himalaya St	371 Himalaya St	24. Ⓐ Ⓓ
25 . . . 1053 Columbus Cir	1053 Columbia Cir	25. Ⓐ Ⓓ

Answers:	1.D	6.A	11.A	16.A	21.A
	2.A	7.A	12.D	17.A	22.D
	3.A	8.D	13.A	18.D	23.A
	4.D	9.D	14.A	19.A	24.A
	5.D	10.D	15.D	20.D	25.D

Check your answers. Then look at the questions to see where you made your mistakes. If your mistakes fall into any sort of pattern, guard against those errors in the future. If your mistakes seem to be random, then practice and care should help you to improve.

Comparing first the numbers, then the little words and abbreviations, and finally the main words must be done in a flash. If you have gone through this process and have spotted no errors, mark Ⓐ on your answer sheet and go on to the next question. In order to complete the Address Checking Test, you can allow only *four seconds* for each question. That means you cannot afford to re-read a single address. Make your decision based on your first check and go right on.

Keeping these suggestions in mind, try the practice questions that follow. In these questions, you may find differences between numbers, abbreviations or main words, or you may find no difference at all. Work quickly, but do not time yourself on these practice questions.

ADDRESS CHECKING PRACTICE TEST

1 . . . 8690 W 134th St	8960 W 134th St	1.	ⒶⒹ
2 . . . 1912 Berkshire Wy	1912 Berkshire Wy	2.	ⒶⒹ
3 . . . 5331 W Professor St	5331 W Proffesor St	3.	ⒶⒹ
4 . . . Philadelphia PA 19124	Philadelphia PN 19124	4.	ⒶⒹ
5 . . . 7450 Saguenay St	7450 Saguenay St	5.	ⒶⒹ
6 . . . 8650 Christy St	8650 Christey St	6.	ⒶⒹ
7 . . . Lumberville PA 18933	Lumberville PA 19833	7.	ⒶⒹ
8 . . . 114 Alabama Ave NW	114 Alabama Av NW	8.	ⒶⒹ
9 . . . 1756 Waterford St	1756 Waterville St	9.	ⒶⒹ
10 . . . 2214 Wister Wy	2214 Wister Wy	10.	ⒶⒹ
11 . . . 2974 Repplier Rd	2974 Repplier Dr	11.	ⒶⒹ
12 . . . Essex CT 06426	Essex CT 06426	12.	ⒶⒹ
13 . . . 7676 N Bourbon St	7616 N Bourbon St	13.	ⒶⒹ
14 . . . 2762 Rosengarten Wy	2762 Rosengarden Wy	14.	ⒶⒹ
15 . . . 239 Windell Ave	239 Windell Ave	15.	ⒶⒹ
16 . . . 4667 Edgeworth Rd	4677 Edgeworth Rd	16.	ⒶⒹ
17 . . . 2661 Kennel St SE	2661 Kennel St SW	17.	ⒶⒹ
18 . . . Alamo TX 78516	Alamo TX 78516	18.	ⒶⒹ
19 . . . 3709 Columbine St	3709 Columbine St	19.	ⒶⒹ
20 . . . 9699 W 14th St	9699 W 14th Rd	20.	ⒶⒹ
21 . . . 2207 Markland Ave	2207 Markham Ave	21.	ⒶⒹ
22 . . . Los Angeles Ca 90013	Los Angeles CA 90018	22.	ⒶⒹ
23 . . . 4608 N Warnock St	4806 N Warnock St	23.	ⒶⒹ
24 . . . 7718 S Summer St	7718 S Sumner St	24.	ⒶⒹ

25 . . . New York, NY 10016	New York, NY 10016	25. Ⓐ Ⓓ
26 . . . 4514 Ft Hamilton Pk	4514 Ft Hamilton Pk	26. Ⓐ Ⓓ
27 . . . 5701 Kosciusko St	5701 Koscusko St	27. Ⓐ Ⓓ
28 . . . 5422 Evergreen St	4522 Evergreen St	28. Ⓐ Ⓓ
29 . . . Gainsville FL 32611	Gainsville FL 32611	29. Ⓐ Ⓓ
30 . . . 5018 Church St	5018 Church Ave	30. Ⓐ Ⓓ
31 . . . 1079 N Blake St	1097 N Blake St	31. Ⓐ Ⓓ
32 . . . 8072 W 20th Rd	8072 W 20th Dr	32. Ⓐ Ⓓ
33 . . . Onoro ME 04473	Orono ME 04473	33. Ⓐ Ⓓ
34 . . . 2175 Kimbell Rd	2175 Kimball Rd	34. Ⓐ Ⓓ
35 . . . 1243 Mermaid St	1243 Mermaid St	35. Ⓐ Ⓓ
36 . . . 4904 SW 134th St	4904 SW 134th St	36. Ⓐ Ⓓ
37 . . . 1094 Hancock St	1049 Hancock St	37. Ⓐ Ⓓ
38 . . . Des Moines IA 50311	Des Moines IA 50311	38. Ⓐ Ⓓ
39 . . . 4832 S Rinaldi Rd	4832 S Rinaldo Rd	39. Ⓐ Ⓓ
40 . . . 2015 Dorchester Rd	2015 Dorchester Rd	40. Ⓐ Ⓓ
41 . . . 5216 Woodbine St	5216 Woodburn St	41. Ⓐ Ⓓ
42 . . . Boulder CO 80302	Boulder CA 80302	42. Ⓐ Ⓓ
43 . . . 4739 N Marion St	479 N Marion St	43. Ⓐ Ⓓ
44 . . . 3720 Nautilus Wy	3720 Nautilus Way	44. Ⓐ Ⓓ
45 . . . 3636 Gramercy Pk	3636 Gramercy Pk	45. Ⓐ Ⓓ
46 . . . 757 Johnson Ave	757 Johnston Ave	46. Ⓐ Ⓓ
47 . . . 3045 Brighton 12th St	3054 Brighton 12th St	47. Ⓐ Ⓓ
48 . . . 237 Ovington Avc	237 Ovington Ave	48. Ⓐ Ⓓ
49 . . . Kalamazoo MI 49007	Kalamazoo MI 49007	49. Ⓐ Ⓓ
50 . . . Missoula MT 59812	Missoula MS 59812	50. Ⓐ Ⓓ
51 . . . Stillwater OK 74704	Stillwater OK 47404	51. Ⓐ Ⓓ
52 . . . 4746 Empire Blvd	4746 Empire Bldg	52. Ⓐ Ⓓ
53 . . . 6321 St Johns Pl	6321 St Johns Pl	53. Ⓐ Ⓓ
54 . . . 2242 Vanderbilt Ave	2242 Vanderbilt Ave	54. Ⓐ Ⓓ
55 . . . 542 Ditmas Blvd	542 Ditmars Blvd	55. Ⓐ Ⓓ
56 . . . 4603 W Argyle Rd	4603 W Argyle Rd	56. Ⓐ Ⓓ
57 . . . 653 Knickerbocker Ave NE	653 Knickerbocker Ave NE	57. Ⓐ Ⓓ
58 . . . 3651 Midwood Terr	3651 Midwood Terr	58. Ⓐ Ⓓ
59 . . . Chapel Hill NC 27514	Chaple Hill NC 27514	59. Ⓐ Ⓓ
60 . . . 3217 Vernon Pl NW	3217 Vernon Dr NW	60. Ⓐ Ⓓ
61 . . . 1094 Rednor Pkwy	1049 Rednor Pkwy	61. Ⓐ Ⓓ
62 . . . 986 S Doughty Blvd	986 S Douty Blvd	62. Ⓐ Ⓓ
63 . . . Lincoln NE 68508	Lincoln NE 65808	63. Ⓐ Ⓓ
64 . . . 1517 LaSalle Ave	1517 LaSalle Ave	64. Ⓐ Ⓓ
65 . . . 3857 S Morris St	3857 S Morriss St	65. Ⓐ Ⓓ
66 . . . 6104 Saunders Expy	614 Saunders Expy	66. Ⓐ Ⓓ
67 . . . 2541 Appleton St	2541 Appleton Rd	67. Ⓐ Ⓓ
68 . . . Washington DC 20052	Washington DC 20052	68. Ⓐ Ⓓ
69 . . . 6439 Kessler Blvd S	6439 Kessler Blvd S	69. Ⓐ Ⓓ
70 . . . 4786 Catalina Dr	4786 Catalana Dr	70. Ⓐ Ⓓ
71 . . . 132 E Hampton Pkwy	1322 E Hampton Pkwy	71. Ⓐ Ⓓ
72 . . . 1066 Goethe Sq S	1066 Geothe Sq S	72. Ⓐ Ⓓ
73 . . . 1118 Jerriman Wy	1218 Jerriman Wy	73. Ⓐ Ⓓ
74 . . . 5798 Gd Central Pkwy	5798 Gd Central Pkwy	74. Ⓐ Ⓓ
75 . . . Delaware OH 43015	Delaware OK 43015	75. Ⓐ Ⓓ
76 . . . Corvallis OR 97331	Corvallis OR 97331	76. Ⓐ Ⓓ

77 . . . 4231 Keating Ave N	4231 Keating Av N	77. Ⓐ Ⓓ
78 . . . 5689 Central Pk Pl	5869 Central Pk Pl	78. Ⓐ Ⓓ
79 . . . 1108 Lyndhurst Dr	1108 Lyndhurst Dr	79. Ⓐ Ⓓ
80 . . . 842 Chambers Ct	842 Chamber Ct	80. Ⓐ Ⓓ
81 . . . Athens OH 45701	Athens GA 45701	81. Ⓐ Ⓓ
82 . . . Tulsa OK 74171	Tulsa OK 71471	82. Ⓐ Ⓓ
83 . . . 6892 Beech Grove Ave	6892 Beech Grove Ave	83. Ⓐ Ⓓ
84 . . . 2939 E Division St	2939 W Division St	84. Ⓐ Ⓓ
85 . . . 1554 Pitkin Ave	1554 Pitkin Ave	85. Ⓐ Ⓓ
86 . . . 905 St Edwards Plz	950 St Edwards Plz	86. Ⓐ Ⓓ
87 . . . 1906 W 152nd St	1906 W 152nd St	87. Ⓐ Ⓓ
88 . . . 3466 Glenmore Ave	3466 Glenville Ave	88. Ⓐ Ⓓ
89 . . . Middlebury VT 05753	Middlebery VT 05753	89. Ⓐ Ⓓ
90 . . . Evanston IL 60201	Evanston IN 60201	90. Ⓐ Ⓓ
91 . . . 9401 W McDonald Ave	9401 W MacDonald Ave	91. Ⓐ Ⓓ
92 . . . 5527 Albermarle Rd	5527 Albermarle Rd	92. Ⓐ Ⓓ
93 . . . 9055 Carter Dr	9055 Carter Rd	93. Ⓐ Ⓓ
94 . . . Greenvale NY 11548	Greenvale NY 11458	94. Ⓐ Ⓓ
95 . . . 1149 Cherry Gr S	1149 Cherry Gr S	95. Ⓐ Ⓓ

ANSWERS TO PRACTICE TEST

1.D	13.D	25.A	37.D	49.A	61.D	73.D	85.A
2.A	14.D	26.A	38.A	50.D	62.D	74.A	86.D
3.D	15.A	27.D	39.D	51.D	63.D	75.D	87.A
4.D	16.D	28.D	40.A	52.D	64.A	76.A	88.D
5.A	17.D	29.A	41.D	53.A	65.D	77.D	89.D
6.D	18.A	30.D	42.D	54.A	66.D	78.D	90.D
7.D	19.A	31.D	43.D	55.D	67.D	79.A	91.D
8.D	20.D	32.D	44.D	56.A	68.A	80.D	92.A
9.D	21.D	33.D	45.A	57.A	69.A	81.D	93.D
10.A	22.D	34.D	46.D	58.A	70.D	82.D	94.D
11.D	23.D	35.A	47.D	59.D	71.D	83.A	95.A
12.A	24.D	36.A	48.A	60.D	72.D	84.D	

Use the chart below to analyze your errors on the Practice Test.

ANALYSIS OF DIFFERENCES

Type of Difference	Question Numbers	Number of Questions You Missed
Difference in NUMBERS	1, 7, 13, 16, 22, 23, 28, 31, 37, 43, 47, 51, 61, 63, 66, 71, 73, 78, 82, 86, 94	
Difference in ABBREVIATIONS	4, 8, 11, 17, 20, 30, 32, 42, 44, 50, 52, 60, 67, 75, 77, 81, 84, 90, 93	
Difference in NAMES	3, 6, 9, 14, 21, 24, 27, 33, 34, 39, 41, 46, 55, 59, 62, 65, 70, 72, 80, 88, 89, 91	
No Difference	2, 5, 10, 12, 15, 18, 19, 25, 26, 29, 35, 36, 38, 40, 45, 48, 49, 53, 54, 56, 57, 58, 64, 68, 69, 74, 76, 79, 83 85, 87, 92, 95	

The Model Exams that follow will offer you plenty of practice with Address Checking questions. Flip back to this chapter between Model Exams as you work through the book. Reread the chapter the day before your exam for a quick refresher.

REMEMBER: Look first for differences between numbers.

Next, look at the abbreviations and little words.

Read what is written, as it is written.

Finally, sound out or spell out the main words.

When you find any difference, mark Ⓓ and go immediately to the next question.

If you find no difference, do not linger. Mark Ⓐ and move right on to the next question.

Do NOT read the whole address as a unit.

HOW TO ANSWER MEMORY
FOR ADDRESSES QUESTIONS

Memorizing is a special skill, simple for some few people, a chore for most. If you are one of the lucky ones with a good visual memory—that is, if you can look at a page and remember not only what was on the page but how the page looked—you will find this test very easy. You need only picture where on the page each item is located. If, however, you do not have this gift, then the Memory for Addresses Test may appear to be frighteningly difficult. This chapter contains suggestions to help you memorize more efficiently and tips to help you cope with this particular memorizing test.

The first thing you must do in this test is to memorize the location of 25 addresses which are presented in five different boxes labelled A, B, C, D, and E. Here is a typical set of addresses. Look at it carefully and commit it to memory, following the step-by-step analysis that follows.

A	B	C	D	E
3200–3499 Apple Book 7400–7699 Tripp Silver 5900–6499 Budd	1000–2199 Apple Taxter 7900–8499 Tripp Bloom 6800–7199 Budd	3500–3599 Apple Superior 7700–7799 Tripp Malter 4500–5199 Budd	2200–2899 Apple Brayton 6800–7399 Tripp Moore 5500–6799 Budd	2900–3199 Apple Miller 7800–7899 Tripp Clayton 5200–5499 Budd

Step One: The fewer items you have to memorize, the easier your job will be. Therefore, the first step is to eliminate any unnecessary items. Concentrate on the number spans. In this case, every one is different. This means there is no need to remember the street names associated with the number spans, so you can immediately narrow down the information to be memorized to this:

A	B	C	D	E
3200–3499 Book 7400–7699 Silver 5900–6499	1000–2199 Taxter 7900–8499 Bloom 6800–7199	3500–3599 Superior 7700–7799 Malter 4500–5199	2200–2899 Brayton 6800–7399 Moore 5500–6799	2900–3199 Miller 7800–7899 Clayton 5200–5499

Step Two: Close examination of each number span reveals that the first number of each span always ends in *00* and the second number always ends in *99*. With this knowledge, you can ignore half of each number, reducing your memorization to the following:

A	B	C	D	E
32–34 Book 74–76 Silver 59–64	10–21 Taxter 79–84 Bloom 68–71	35–35 Superior 77–77 Malter 45–51	22–28 Brayton 68–73 Moore 55–67	29–31 Miller 78–78 Clayton 52–54

Step Three: Now look only at the first number in each span. Only two spans begin with the same number (68–71 in box B and 68–73 in box D). This means that you can eliminate the second number from all but these two spans. Thus, you have narrowed down the information to be memorized from 30 four-digit numbers and 25 names to 17 two-digit numbers and 10 names. You can answer every question on the test by remembering only this information:

A	B	C	D	E
32 Book 74 Silver 59	10 Taxter 79 Bloom 68–71	35 Superior 77 Malter 45	22 Brayton 68–73 Moore 55	29 Miller 78 Clayton 52

Of course, each exam offers a different set of names and numbers. You must mentally go through all these steps with each exam, blocking out all unnecessary material and memorizing only what you need to know. On the actual exam, you cannot use scratch paper and cannot learn the names and numbers by writing them down.

You must be certain to memorize enough to differentiate the addresses from box to box. If by any chance you find an exact duplication of number spans, you must memorize the names that go with those number spans.

To simplify your task still further, consider that if you memorize which addresses belong in each of four boxes, those addresses that you have not memorized automatically belong in the fifth box. And so, you really need memorize the locations of only twenty items. Suddenly, the Memory for Addresses Test does not seem so hard after all.

DECIDING WHAT TO MEMORIZE

You must practice the narrowing down process so that you can decide very quickly what it is that you must memorize in order to answer the questions on the Memory for Addresses Test. The exercise that follows presents two sorting schemes. Examine the boxes in each row. Then fill in the empty boxes with the information you must memorize for each scheme.

1.

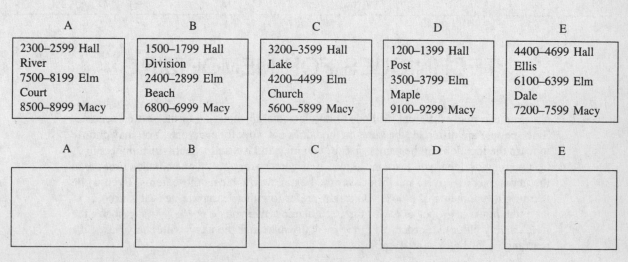

A	B	C	D	E
2300–2599 Hall River 7500–8199 Elm Court 8500–8999 Macy	1500–1799 Hall Division 2400–2899 Elm Beach 6800–6999 Macy	3200–3599 Hall Lake 4200–4499 Elm Church 5600–5899 Macy	1200–1399 Hall Post 3500–3799 Elm Maple 9100–9299 Macy	4400–4699 Hall Ellis 6100–6399 Elm Dale 7200–7599 Macy

A	B	C	D	E

2.

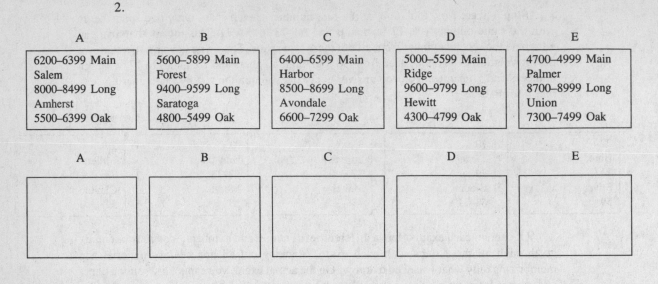

A	B	C	D	E
6200–6399 Main Salem 8000–8499 Long Amherst 5500–6399 Oak	5600–5899 Main Forest 9400–9599 Long Saratoga 4800–5499 Oak	6400–6599 Main Harbor 8500–8699 Long Avondale 6600–7299 Oak	5000–5599 Main Ridge 9600–9799 Long Hewitt 4300–4799 Oak	4700–4999 Main Palmer 8700–8999 Long Union 7300–7499 Oak

A	B	C	D	E

Answers:

1.

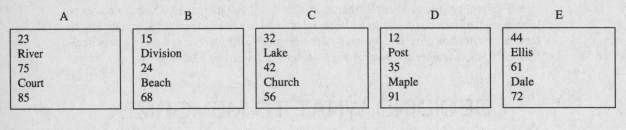

A	B	C	D	E
23 River 75 Court 85	15 Division 24 Beach 68	32 Lake 42 Church 56	12 Post 35 Maple 91	44 Ellis 61 Dale 72

2.

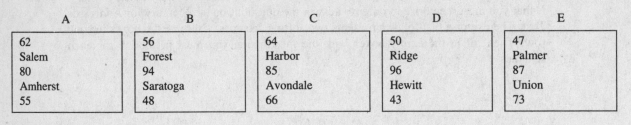

A	B	C	D	E
62 Salem 80 Amherst 55	56 Forest 94 Saratoga 48	64 Harbor 85 Avondale 66	50 Ridge 96 Hewitt 43	47 Palmer 87 Union 73

TECHNIQUES FOR MEMORIZING

You can use many different methods to do the actual memorizing of the sorting scheme. Since people are different, the same method does not work for everyone. You may choose to learn the locations of the names first, or you may find it easier to learn the numbers first. Or you may find that you learn most quickly if you concentrate on one box at a time, read the items over and over, and then cover the box and try to repeat those items. Even while learning the contents of a box, you might prefer to either learn one item at a time or to learn the items in groups of two or three. Remember that you do not have to memorize the items in any particular order. You may mentally rearrange the items within any box if the rearrangement helps you learn.

Here is one memory strategy that works for many people:

- First, narrow down the information in each box to the bare essentials.
- Next, group together all the necessary numbers and names in each box.
- Then, combine the names in such a way that they form a word or an image that helps you fix each box in your mind.

Let's try this strategy on the sorting scheme that follows:

A	B	C	D	E
5500–5899 Town Marshall 2200–2499 Park Endicott 1700–1999 Grand	6300–6500 Town Needham 1800–2199 Park Haymarket 1100–1299 Grand	5900–6299 Town Prescott 2600–2899 Park Draper 4200–4499 Grand	4800–5299 Town Whitehall 1500–1699 Park Houseman 6200–6399 Grand	3700–3999 Town Rider 1300–1499 Park Carthage 3100–3399 Grand

Step One: Narrow down the information to the barest essentials.

A	B	C	D	E
55 Marshall 22 Endicott 17	63 Needham 18 Haymarket 11	59 Prescott 26 Draper 42	48 Whitehall 15 Houseman 62	37 Rider 13 Carthage 31

Step Two: Group together the numbers and the names in each box.

A	B	C	D	E
55 22 17 Marshall Endicott	63 18 11 Needham Haymarket	59 26 42 Prescott Draper	48 15 62 Whitehall Houseman	37 13 31 Rider Carthage

Step Three: Combine the names to form a word or an image that will help you fix each box in your mind.

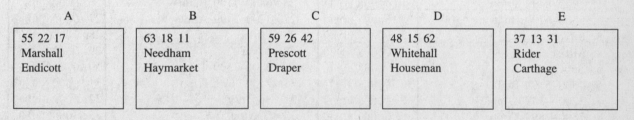

A	B	C	D	E
55 22 17 A *Marshal* at the *End* of a parade	63 18 11 A *Needle* in a *Haystack*	59 26 42 A man *Pressing Drapes*	48 15 62 A *White House*	37 13 31 A child *Riding* in a *Cart*

NOTE: The image you choose may be different from the one given. The object is to choose an image that helps you to remember what is in each box. The best image is the one that works for you.

Try a different memory strategy on each of the first few model exams in this book. Once you decide which strategy is best for you, develop your skill and speed in using it on the remaining model exams.

While working on questions in this chapter, forget about time limits. The time pressure in the actual exam is very real, but use the model exams to develop your speed. In this chapter concentrate on skills. Look again now at the addresses for Practice Exercise 1. Try to memorize as little information as possible, but memorize it thoroughly. When you feel that you are ready, answer the following questions. While you are answering the questions in Set 1, you may refer to the address boxes whenever you need to. Do not look back at the address boxes when you answer the questions in Set 2. Correct answers to these questions are on page 62.

PRACTICE EXERCISE 1

A	B	C	D	E
3200–3499 Apple Book 7400–7699 Tripp Silver 5900–6499 Budd	1000–2199 Apple Taxter 7900–8499 Tripp Bloom 6800–7199 Budd	3500–3599 Apple Superior 7700–7799 Tripp Malter 4500–5199 Budd	2200–2899 Apple Brayton 6800–7399 Tripp Moore 5500–6799 Budd	2900–3199 Apple Miller 7800–7899 Tripp Clayton 5200–5499 Budd

SET 1

1. 7900–8499 Tripp
2. 5500–6799 Budd
3. Silver
4. Miller
5. Superior
6. 4500–5199 Budd
7. 3200—3499 Apple
8. 7800–7899 Tripp
9. 5900–6499 Budd
10. Book
11. Brayton
12. 2900–3199 Apple
13. 1000–2199 Apple
14. Taxter
15. 5200–5499 Budd
16. Clayton
17. 7400–7699 Tripp
18. 6800–7199 Budd
19. 3500–3599 Apple
20. Moore
21. 2200–2899 Apple
22. Bloom
23. Malter
24. 5900–6499 Budd
25. 7700–7799 Tripp

26. 6800–7199 Budd
27. 3200–3499 Apple
28. Miller
29. Silver
30. 6800–7399 Tripp
31. 7400-7699 Tripp
32. Superior
33. Clayton
34. 1000–2199 Apple
35. 5500–6799 Budd
36. 5200–5499 Budd
37. Book
38. Brayton
39. 2900–3199 Apple
40. 7900–8499 Tripp
41. 4500–5199 Budd
42. Taxter
43. 7800–7899 Tripp
44. 3500–3599 Apple
45. 7400–7699 Tripp
46. 5200–5499 Budd
47. Silver
48. Brayton
49. 3200–3499 Apple
50. 7900–8499 Tripp

1. Ⓐ Ⓑ Ⓒ Ⓓ Ⓔ
2. Ⓐ Ⓑ Ⓒ Ⓓ Ⓔ
3. Ⓐ Ⓑ Ⓒ Ⓓ Ⓔ
4. Ⓐ Ⓑ Ⓒ Ⓓ Ⓔ
5. Ⓐ Ⓑ Ⓒ Ⓓ Ⓔ
6. Ⓐ Ⓑ Ⓒ Ⓓ Ⓔ
7. Ⓐ Ⓑ Ⓒ Ⓓ Ⓔ
8. Ⓐ Ⓑ Ⓒ Ⓓ Ⓔ
9. Ⓐ Ⓑ Ⓒ Ⓓ Ⓔ
10. Ⓐ Ⓑ Ⓒ Ⓓ Ⓔ
11. Ⓐ Ⓑ Ⓒ Ⓓ Ⓔ
12. Ⓐ Ⓑ Ⓒ Ⓓ Ⓔ
13. Ⓐ Ⓑ Ⓒ Ⓓ Ⓔ
14. Ⓐ Ⓑ Ⓒ Ⓓ Ⓔ
15. Ⓐ Ⓑ Ⓒ Ⓓ Ⓔ
16. Ⓐ Ⓑ Ⓒ Ⓓ Ⓔ
17. Ⓐ Ⓑ Ⓒ Ⓓ Ⓔ
18. Ⓐ Ⓑ Ⓒ Ⓓ Ⓔ
19. Ⓐ Ⓑ Ⓒ Ⓓ Ⓔ
20. Ⓐ Ⓑ Ⓒ Ⓓ Ⓔ
21. Ⓐ Ⓑ Ⓒ Ⓓ Ⓔ
22. Ⓐ Ⓑ Ⓒ Ⓓ Ⓔ
23. Ⓐ Ⓑ Ⓒ Ⓓ Ⓔ
24. Ⓐ Ⓑ Ⓒ Ⓓ Ⓔ
25. Ⓐ Ⓑ Ⓒ Ⓓ Ⓔ

26. Ⓐ Ⓑ Ⓒ Ⓓ Ⓔ
27. Ⓐ Ⓑ Ⓒ Ⓓ Ⓔ
28. Ⓐ Ⓑ Ⓒ Ⓓ Ⓔ
29. Ⓐ Ⓑ Ⓒ Ⓓ Ⓔ
30. Ⓐ Ⓑ Ⓒ Ⓓ Ⓔ
31. Ⓐ Ⓑ Ⓒ Ⓓ Ⓔ
32. Ⓐ Ⓑ Ⓒ Ⓓ Ⓔ
33. Ⓐ Ⓑ Ⓒ Ⓓ Ⓔ
34. Ⓐ Ⓑ Ⓒ Ⓓ Ⓔ
35. Ⓐ Ⓑ Ⓒ Ⓓ Ⓔ
36. Ⓐ Ⓑ Ⓒ Ⓓ Ⓔ
37. Ⓐ Ⓑ Ⓒ Ⓓ Ⓔ
38. Ⓐ Ⓑ Ⓒ Ⓓ Ⓔ
39. Ⓐ Ⓑ Ⓒ Ⓓ Ⓔ
40. Ⓐ Ⓑ Ⓒ Ⓓ Ⓔ
41. Ⓐ Ⓑ Ⓒ Ⓓ Ⓔ
42. Ⓐ Ⓑ Ⓒ Ⓓ Ⓔ
43. Ⓐ Ⓑ Ⓒ Ⓓ Ⓔ
44. Ⓐ Ⓑ Ⓒ Ⓓ Ⓔ
45. Ⓐ Ⓑ Ⓒ Ⓓ Ⓔ
46. Ⓐ Ⓑ Ⓒ Ⓓ Ⓔ
47. Ⓐ Ⓑ Ⓒ Ⓓ Ⓔ
48. Ⓐ Ⓑ Ⓒ Ⓓ Ⓔ
49. Ⓐ Ⓑ Ⓒ Ⓓ Ⓔ
50. Ⓐ Ⓑ Ⓒ Ⓓ Ⓔ

51. 4500–5199 Budd
52. Moore
53. Miller
54. 5200–5499 Budd
55. 6800–7399 Tripp
56. 3500–3599 Apple
57. Taxter
58. Silver
59. 5900–6499 Budd
60. Bloom
61. 7700–7799 Tripp
62. Brayton
63. 2900–3199 Apple
64. Book
65. 7800–7899 Tripp
66. Clayton
67. 6800–7199 Budd
68. 2200–2899 Apple
69. Superior

51. Ⓐ Ⓑ Ⓒ Ⓓ Ⓔ
52. Ⓐ Ⓑ Ⓒ Ⓓ Ⓔ
53. Ⓐ Ⓑ Ⓒ Ⓓ Ⓔ
54. Ⓐ Ⓑ Ⓒ Ⓓ Ⓔ
55. Ⓐ Ⓑ Ⓒ Ⓓ Ⓔ
56. Ⓐ Ⓑ Ⓒ Ⓓ Ⓔ
57. Ⓐ Ⓑ Ⓒ Ⓓ Ⓔ
58. Ⓐ Ⓑ Ⓒ Ⓓ Ⓔ
59. Ⓐ Ⓑ Ⓒ Ⓓ Ⓔ
60. Ⓐ Ⓑ Ⓒ Ⓓ Ⓔ
61. Ⓐ Ⓑ Ⓒ Ⓓ Ⓔ
62. Ⓐ Ⓑ Ⓒ Ⓓ Ⓔ
63. Ⓐ Ⓑ Ⓒ Ⓓ Ⓔ
64. Ⓐ Ⓑ Ⓒ Ⓓ Ⓔ
65. Ⓐ Ⓑ Ⓒ Ⓓ Ⓔ
66. Ⓐ Ⓑ Ⓒ Ⓓ Ⓔ
67. Ⓐ Ⓑ Ⓒ Ⓓ Ⓔ
68. Ⓐ Ⓑ Ⓒ Ⓓ Ⓔ
69. Ⓐ Ⓑ Ⓒ Ⓓ Ⓔ

70. Malter
71. 1000–2199 Apple
72. 7400–7699 Tripp
73. 5500–6799 Budd
74. 7900–8499 Tripp
75. 5200–5499 Budd
76. 3200–3499 Apple
77. 7700–7799 Tripp
78. Silver
79. 2200–2899 Apple
80. Clayton
81. Bloom
82. Brayton
83. 6800–7199 Budd
84. 1000–2199 Apple
85. 6800–7399 Tripp
86. 7800–7899 Tripp
87. Superior
88. Taxter

70. Ⓐ Ⓑ Ⓒ Ⓓ Ⓔ
71. Ⓐ Ⓑ Ⓒ Ⓓ Ⓔ
72. Ⓐ Ⓑ Ⓒ Ⓓ Ⓔ
73. Ⓐ Ⓑ Ⓒ Ⓓ Ⓔ
74. Ⓐ Ⓑ Ⓒ Ⓓ Ⓔ
75. Ⓐ Ⓑ Ⓒ Ⓓ Ⓔ
76. Ⓐ Ⓑ Ⓒ Ⓓ Ⓔ
77. Ⓐ Ⓑ Ⓒ Ⓓ Ⓔ
78. Ⓐ Ⓑ Ⓒ Ⓓ Ⓔ
79. Ⓐ Ⓑ Ⓒ Ⓓ Ⓔ
80. Ⓐ Ⓑ Ⓒ Ⓓ Ⓔ
81. Ⓐ Ⓑ Ⓒ Ⓓ Ⓔ
82. Ⓐ Ⓑ Ⓒ Ⓓ Ⓔ
83. Ⓐ Ⓑ Ⓒ Ⓓ Ⓔ
84. Ⓐ Ⓑ Ⓒ Ⓓ Ⓔ
85. Ⓐ Ⓑ Ⓒ Ⓓ Ⓔ
86. Ⓐ Ⓑ Ⓒ Ⓓ Ⓔ
87. Ⓐ Ⓑ Ⓒ Ⓓ Ⓔ
88. Ⓐ Ⓑ Ⓒ Ⓓ Ⓔ

SET 2

Mark as your answer the letter of the box in which each address appears. Do *not* look back at the address boxes while answering these questions.

1. 7900–8499 Tripp
2. Bloom
3. Book
4. 3500–3599 Apple
5. 5900–6499 Budd
6. 7400–7699 Tripp
7. Miller
8. Malter
9. 1000–2199 Apple
10. 5500–6799 Budd
11. 2900–3199 Apple
12. 5200–5499 Budd
13. Taxter
14. Clayton
15. Silver
16. 3200–3499 Apple
17. 7900–8499 Tripp
18. 5500–6799 Budd
19. Brayton
20. Bloom
21. 7400–7699 Tripp
22. 3500–3599 Apple
23. 5200–5499 Budd
24. Malter

1. Ⓐ Ⓑ Ⓒ Ⓓ Ⓔ
2. Ⓐ Ⓑ Ⓒ Ⓓ Ⓔ
3. Ⓐ Ⓑ Ⓒ Ⓓ Ⓔ
4. Ⓐ Ⓑ Ⓒ Ⓓ Ⓔ
5. Ⓐ Ⓑ Ⓒ Ⓓ Ⓔ
6. Ⓐ Ⓑ Ⓒ Ⓓ Ⓔ
7. Ⓐ Ⓑ Ⓒ Ⓓ Ⓔ
8. Ⓐ Ⓑ Ⓒ Ⓓ Ⓔ
9. Ⓐ Ⓑ Ⓒ Ⓓ Ⓔ
10. Ⓐ Ⓑ Ⓒ Ⓓ Ⓔ
11. Ⓐ Ⓑ Ⓒ Ⓓ Ⓔ
12. Ⓐ Ⓑ Ⓒ Ⓓ Ⓔ
13. Ⓐ Ⓑ Ⓒ Ⓓ Ⓔ
14. Ⓐ Ⓑ Ⓒ Ⓓ Ⓔ
15. Ⓐ Ⓑ Ⓒ Ⓓ Ⓔ
16. Ⓐ Ⓑ Ⓒ Ⓓ Ⓔ
17. Ⓐ Ⓑ Ⓒ Ⓓ Ⓔ
18. Ⓐ Ⓑ Ⓒ Ⓓ Ⓔ
19. Ⓐ Ⓑ Ⓒ Ⓓ Ⓔ
20. Ⓐ Ⓑ Ⓒ Ⓓ Ⓔ
21. Ⓐ Ⓑ Ⓒ Ⓓ Ⓔ
22. Ⓐ Ⓑ Ⓒ Ⓓ Ⓔ
23. Ⓐ Ⓑ Ⓒ Ⓓ Ⓔ
24. Ⓐ Ⓑ Ⓒ Ⓓ Ⓔ

25. Clayton
26. 3200–3499 Apple
27. 6800–7399 Tripp
28. 4500–5199 Budd
29. Book
30. Superior
31. 5900–6499 Budd
32. 1000–2199 Apple
33. 7900–8499 Tripp
34. Miller
35. Silver
36. 2900–3199 Apple
37. 5500–6799 Budd
38. 7700–7799 Tripp
39. Bloom
40. Brayton
41. 7800–7899 Tripp
42. 6800–7199 Budd
43. 2200–2899 Apple
44. Taxter
45. Moore
46. 5500–6799 Budd
47. 7900–8499 Tripp
48. 1000–2199 Apple

25. Ⓐ Ⓑ Ⓒ Ⓓ Ⓔ
26. Ⓐ Ⓑ Ⓒ Ⓓ Ⓔ
27. Ⓐ Ⓑ Ⓒ Ⓓ Ⓔ
28. Ⓐ Ⓑ Ⓒ Ⓓ Ⓔ
29. Ⓐ Ⓑ Ⓒ Ⓓ Ⓔ
30. Ⓐ Ⓑ Ⓒ Ⓓ Ⓔ
31. Ⓐ Ⓑ Ⓒ Ⓓ Ⓔ
32. Ⓐ Ⓑ Ⓒ Ⓓ Ⓔ
33. Ⓐ Ⓑ Ⓒ Ⓓ Ⓔ
34. Ⓐ Ⓑ Ⓒ Ⓓ Ⓔ
35. Ⓐ Ⓑ Ⓒ Ⓓ Ⓔ
36. Ⓐ Ⓑ Ⓒ Ⓓ Ⓔ
37. Ⓐ Ⓑ Ⓒ Ⓓ Ⓔ
38. Ⓐ Ⓑ Ⓒ Ⓓ Ⓔ
39. Ⓐ Ⓑ Ⓒ Ⓓ Ⓔ
40. Ⓐ Ⓑ Ⓒ Ⓓ Ⓔ
41. Ⓐ Ⓑ Ⓒ Ⓓ Ⓔ
42. Ⓐ Ⓑ Ⓒ Ⓓ Ⓔ
43. Ⓐ Ⓑ Ⓒ Ⓓ Ⓔ
44. Ⓐ Ⓑ Ⓒ Ⓓ Ⓔ
45. Ⓐ Ⓑ Ⓒ Ⓓ Ⓔ
46. Ⓐ Ⓑ Ⓒ Ⓓ Ⓔ
47. Ⓐ Ⓑ Ⓒ Ⓓ Ⓔ
48. Ⓐ Ⓑ Ⓒ Ⓓ Ⓔ

49. Malter	49. Ⓐ Ⓑ Ⓒ Ⓓ Ⓔ	69. 5500–6799 Budd	69. Ⓐ Ⓑ Ⓒ Ⓓ Ⓔ
50. 5900–6499 Budd	50. Ⓐ Ⓑ Ⓒ Ⓓ Ⓔ	70. 4500–5199 Budd	70. Ⓐ Ⓑ Ⓒ Ⓓ Ⓔ
51. 6800–7199 Budd	51. Ⓐ Ⓑ Ⓒ Ⓓ Ⓔ	71. Taxter	71. Ⓐ Ⓑ Ⓒ Ⓓ Ⓔ
52. 7800–7899 Tripp	52. Ⓐ Ⓑ Ⓒ Ⓓ Ⓔ	72. Moore	72. Ⓐ Ⓑ Ⓒ Ⓓ Ⓔ
53. Silver	53. Ⓐ Ⓑ Ⓒ Ⓓ Ⓔ	73. 1000–2199 Apple	73. Ⓐ Ⓑ Ⓒ Ⓓ Ⓔ
54. Superior	54. Ⓐ Ⓑ Ⓒ Ⓓ Ⓔ	74. 6800–7399 Tripp	74. Ⓐ Ⓑ Ⓒ Ⓓ Ⓔ
55. Malter	55. Ⓐ Ⓑ Ⓒ Ⓓ Ⓔ	75. 5900–6499 Budd	75. Ⓐ Ⓑ Ⓒ Ⓓ Ⓔ
56. 3200–3499 Apple	56. Ⓐ Ⓑ Ⓒ Ⓓ Ⓔ	76. 4500–5199 Budd	76. Ⓐ Ⓑ Ⓒ Ⓓ Ⓔ
57. 2900–3199 Apple	57. Ⓐ Ⓑ Ⓒ Ⓓ Ⓔ	77. 3200–3499 Apple	77. Ⓐ Ⓑ Ⓒ Ⓓ Ⓔ
58. 3500–3599 Apple	59. Ⓐ Ⓑ Ⓒ Ⓓ Ⓔ	78. 5200–5499 Budd	78. Ⓐ Ⓑ Ⓒ Ⓓ Ⓔ
59. 7900–8499 Tripp	59. Ⓐ Ⓑ Ⓒ Ⓓ Ⓔ	79. 6800–7199 Budd	79. Ⓐ Ⓑ Ⓒ Ⓓ Ⓔ
60. 5500–6799 Budd	60. Ⓐ Ⓑ Ⓒ Ⓓ Ⓔ	80. 2900–3199 Apple	80. Ⓐ Ⓑ Ⓒ Ⓓ Ⓔ
61. 6800–7199 Budd	61. Ⓐ Ⓑ Ⓒ Ⓓ Ⓔ	81. 5900–6499 Budd	81. Ⓐ Ⓑ Ⓒ Ⓓ Ⓔ
62. Bloom	62. Ⓐ Ⓑ Ⓒ Ⓓ Ⓔ	82. 7700–7799 Tripp	82. Ⓐ Ⓑ Ⓒ Ⓓ Ⓔ
63. Brayton	63. Ⓐ Ⓑ Ⓒ Ⓓ Ⓔ	83. Taxter	83. Ⓐ Ⓑ Ⓒ Ⓓ Ⓔ
64. 2200–2899 Apple	64. Ⓐ Ⓑ Ⓒ Ⓓ Ⓔ	84. Moore	84. Ⓐ Ⓑ Ⓒ Ⓓ Ⓔ
65. 7400–7699 Tripp	65. Ⓐ Ⓑ Ⓒ Ⓓ Ⓔ	85. Clayton	85. Ⓐ Ⓑ Ⓒ Ⓓ Ⓔ
66. 6800–7399 Tripp	66. Ⓐ Ⓑ Ⓒ Ⓓ Ⓔ	86. 3200–3499 Apple	86. Ⓐ Ⓑ Ⓒ Ⓓ Ⓔ
67. Clayton	67. Ⓐ Ⓑ Ⓒ Ⓓ Ⓔ	87. 6800–7399 Tripp	87. Ⓐ Ⓑ Ⓒ Ⓓ Ⓔ
68. 7700–7799 Tripp	68. Ⓐ Ⓑ Ⓒ Ⓓ Ⓔ	88. 7800–7899 Tripp	88. Ⓐ Ⓑ Ⓒ Ⓓ Ⓔ

ANSWERS TO PRACTICE EXERCISE 1

SET 1

1. B	12. E	23. C	34. B	45. A	56. C	67. B	78. A
2. D	13. B	24. A	35. D	46. E	57. B	68. D	79. D
3. A	14. B	25. C	36. E	47. A	58. A	69. C	80. E
4. E	15. E	26. B	37. A	48. D	59. A	70. C	81. B
5. C	16. E	27. A	38. D	49. A	60. B	71. B	82. D
6. C	17. A	28. E	39. E	50. B	61. C	72. A	83. B
7. A	18. B	29. A	40. B	51. C	62. D	73. D	84. B
8. E	19. C	30. D	41. C	52. D	63. E	74. B	85. D
9. A	20. D	31. A	42. B	53. E	64. A	75. E	86. E
10. A	21. D	32. C	43. E	54. E	65. E	76. A	87. C
11. D	22. B	33. E	44. C	55. D	66. E	77. C	88. B

SET 2

1. B	12. E	23. E	34. E	45. D	56. A	67. E	78. E
2. B	13. B	24. C	35. A	46. D	57. E	68 C	79. B
3. A	14. E	25. E	36. E	47. B	58. C	69. D	80. E
4. C	15. A	26. A	37. D	48. B	59. B	70. C	81. A
5. A	16. A	27. D	38. C	49. C	60. D	71. B	82. C
6. A	17. B	28. C	39. B	50. A	61. B	72. D	83. B
7. E	18. D	29. A	40. D	51. B	62. B	73. B	84. D
8. C	19. D	30. C	41. E	52. E	63. D	74. D	85. E
9. B	20. B	31. A	42. B	53. A	64. D	75. A	86. A
10. D	21. A	32. B	43. D	54. C	65. A	76. C	87. D
11. E	22. C	33. B	44. B	55. C	66. D	77. A	88. E

Here is another set of boxes for you to try out the techniques you have just learned. Begin by narrowing the memorizing task to the fewest and simplest possible items. Then try to memorize the box in which each item is located. Finally, see how well you can do with identifying the box location of each practice question. Mark your answer by blackening the space that contains the letter of the box in which each address is found. If necessary, you may look at the boxes for the first set of practice questios. Answer the second set of practice questions without looking at the boxes. Once again, take as much time as you need to memorize before you begin answering questions. Work to perfect your technique. Correct answers for these questions are on page 67.

PRACTICE EXERCISE 2

A	B	C	D	E
8300–8599 Lane Penny 1400–2199 Hill Townsend 7200–8199 Crest	4000–4399 Lane Cooper 2200–2599 Hill Reimer 8800–9599 Crest	1000–1399 Lane Murray 9600–9899 Hill Densen 3400–3999 Crest	5400–6099 Lane Brook 6500–6599 Hill Glendale 9100–9299 Crest	4500–6099 Lane Fernwood 3100–3399 Hill Avon 2600–2899 Crest

SET 1

You may refer to the address boxes while answering these questions.

1. 9600–9899 Hill
2. Reimer
3. 2600–2899 Crest
4. 8300–8599 Lane
5. 8800–9599 Crest
6. Densen
7. Avon
8. 6500–6599 Hill
9. 5400–6099 Lane
10. 1400–2199 Hill
11. Glendale
12. Cooper
13. 7200–8199 Crest
14. 4500–6099 Lane
15. 4000–4399 Lane
16. Murray
17. Penny
18. 9100–9299 Crest
19. 2200–2599 Hill
20. 3100–3399 Hill
21. Brook

1. Ⓐ Ⓑ Ⓒ Ⓓ Ⓔ
2. Ⓐ Ⓑ Ⓒ Ⓓ Ⓔ
3. Ⓐ Ⓑ Ⓒ Ⓓ Ⓔ
4. Ⓐ Ⓑ Ⓒ Ⓓ Ⓔ
5. Ⓐ Ⓑ Ⓒ Ⓓ Ⓔ
6. Ⓐ Ⓑ Ⓒ Ⓓ Ⓔ
7. Ⓐ Ⓑ Ⓒ Ⓓ Ⓔ
8. Ⓐ Ⓑ Ⓒ Ⓓ Ⓔ
9. Ⓐ Ⓑ Ⓒ Ⓓ Ⓔ
10. Ⓐ Ⓑ Ⓒ Ⓓ Ⓔ
11. Ⓐ Ⓑ Ⓒ Ⓓ Ⓔ
12. Ⓐ Ⓑ Ⓒ Ⓓ Ⓔ
13. Ⓐ Ⓑ Ⓒ Ⓓ Ⓔ
14. Ⓐ Ⓑ Ⓒ Ⓓ Ⓔ
15. Ⓐ Ⓑ Ⓒ Ⓓ Ⓔ
16. Ⓐ Ⓑ Ⓒ Ⓓ Ⓔ
17. Ⓐ Ⓑ Ⓒ Ⓓ Ⓔ
18. Ⓐ Ⓑ Ⓒ Ⓓ Ⓔ
19. Ⓐ Ⓑ Ⓒ Ⓓ Ⓔ
20. Ⓐ Ⓑ Ⓒ Ⓓ Ⓔ
21. Ⓐ Ⓑ Ⓒ Ⓓ Ⓔ

22. Townsend	22. Ⓐ Ⓑ Ⓒ Ⓓ Ⓔ
23. 1000–1399 Lane	23. Ⓐ Ⓑ Ⓒ Ⓓ Ⓔ
24. 3400–3999 Crest	24. Ⓐ Ⓑ Ⓒ Ⓓ Ⓔ
25. Fernwood	25. Ⓐ Ⓑ Ⓒ Ⓓ Ⓔ
26. 8800–9599 Crest	26. Ⓐ Ⓑ Ⓒ Ⓓ Ⓔ
27. 1400–2199 Hill	27. Ⓐ Ⓑ Ⓒ Ⓓ Ⓔ
28. Glendale	28. Ⓐ Ⓑ Ⓒ Ⓓ Ⓔ
29. 4500–6099 Lane	29. Ⓐ Ⓑ Ⓒ Ⓓ Ⓔ
30. 3400–3999 Crest	30. Ⓐ Ⓑ Ⓒ Ⓓ Ⓔ
31. Avon	31. Ⓐ Ⓑ Ⓒ Ⓓ Ⓔ
32. Densen	32. Ⓐ Ⓑ Ⓒ Ⓓ Ⓔ
33. 2200–2599 Hill	33. Ⓐ Ⓑ Ⓒ Ⓓ Ⓔ
34. 8300–8599 Lane	34. Ⓐ Ⓑ Ⓒ Ⓓ Ⓔ
35. 7200–8199 Crest	35. Ⓐ Ⓑ Ⓒ Ⓓ Ⓔ
36. 4000–4399 Lane	36. Ⓐ Ⓑ Ⓒ Ⓓ Ⓔ
37. Reimer	37. Ⓐ Ⓑ Ⓒ Ⓓ Ⓔ
38. Cooper	38. Ⓐ Ⓑ Ⓒ Ⓓ Ⓔ
39. 6500–6599 Hill	39. Ⓐ Ⓑ Ⓒ Ⓓ Ⓔ
40. 2600–2899 Crest	40. Ⓐ Ⓑ Ⓒ Ⓓ Ⓔ
41. 1000–1399 Lane	41. Ⓐ Ⓑ Ⓒ Ⓓ Ⓔ
42. Townsend	42. Ⓐ Ⓑ Ⓒ Ⓓ Ⓔ
43. Brook	43. Ⓐ Ⓑ Ⓒ Ⓓ Ⓔ
44. 9100–9299 Crest	44. Ⓐ Ⓑ Ⓒ Ⓓ Ⓔ
45. 3100–3399 Hill	45. Ⓐ Ⓑ Ⓒ Ⓓ Ⓔ
46. 4500–6099 Lane	46. Ⓐ Ⓑ Ⓒ Ⓓ Ⓔ
47. Penny	47. Ⓐ Ⓑ Ⓒ Ⓓ Ⓔ
48. Murray	48. Ⓐ Ⓑ Ⓒ Ⓓ Ⓔ
49. 9600–9899 Hill	49. Ⓐ Ⓑ Ⓒ Ⓓ Ⓔ
50. Fernwood	50. Ⓐ Ⓑ Ⓒ Ⓓ Ⓔ
51. 1400–2199 Hill	51. Ⓐ Ⓑ Ⓒ Ⓓ Ⓔ
52. 8800–9599 Crest	52. Ⓐ Ⓑ Ⓒ Ⓓ Ⓔ
53. 4500–6099 Lane	53. Ⓐ Ⓑ Ⓒ Ⓓ Ⓔ
54. Brook	54. Ⓐ Ⓑ Ⓒ Ⓓ Ⓔ
55. 8300–8599 Lane	55. Ⓐ Ⓑ Ⓒ Ⓓ Ⓔ
56. 2600–2899 Crest	56. Ⓐ Ⓑ Ⓒ Ⓓ Ⓔ
57. Fernwood	57. Ⓐ Ⓑ Ⓒ Ⓓ Ⓔ
58. Densen	58. Ⓐ Ⓑ Ⓒ Ⓓ Ⓔ
59. 9600–9899 Hill	59. Ⓐ Ⓑ Ⓒ Ⓓ Ⓔ
60. 8800–9599 Crest	60. Ⓐ Ⓑ Ⓒ Ⓓ Ⓔ
61. 7200–8199 Crest	61. Ⓐ Ⓑ Ⓒ Ⓓ Ⓔ
62. 1400–2199 Hill	62. Ⓐ Ⓑ Ⓒ Ⓓ Ⓔ
63. Cooper	63. Ⓐ Ⓑ Ⓒ Ⓓ Ⓔ
64. Glendale	64. Ⓐ Ⓑ Ⓒ Ⓓ Ⓔ
65. Avon	65. Ⓐ Ⓑ Ⓒ Ⓓ Ⓔ
66. 3100–3399 Hill	66. Ⓐ Ⓑ Ⓒ Ⓓ Ⓔ
67. 4500–6099 Lane	67. Ⓐ Ⓑ Ⓒ Ⓓ Ⓔ
68. 5400–6099 Lane	68. Ⓐ Ⓑ Ⓒ Ⓓ Ⓔ
69. 2200–2599 Hill	69. Ⓐ Ⓑ Ⓒ Ⓓ Ⓔ
70. 3400–3999 Crest	70. Ⓐ Ⓑ Ⓒ Ⓓ Ⓔ
71. Townsend	71. Ⓐ Ⓑ Ⓒ Ⓓ Ⓔ
72. Penny	72. Ⓐ Ⓑ Ⓒ Ⓓ Ⓔ
73. Murray	73. Ⓐ Ⓑ Ⓒ Ⓓ Ⓔ

74. 9100–9299 Crest
75. 6500–6599 Hill
76. 1000–1399 Lane
77. 4000–4399 Lane
78. Reimer
79. Brook
80. 3100–3399 Hill
81. 8300–8599 Lane
82. 5400–6099 Lane
83. Fernwood
84. 9600–9899 Hill
85. 8800–9599 Crest
86. 2600–2899 Crest
87. Brook
88. Avon

74. Ⓐ Ⓑ Ⓒ Ⓓ Ⓔ
75. Ⓐ Ⓑ Ⓒ Ⓓ Ⓔ
76. Ⓐ Ⓑ Ⓒ Ⓓ Ⓔ
77. Ⓐ Ⓑ Ⓒ Ⓓ Ⓔ
78. Ⓐ Ⓑ Ⓒ Ⓓ Ⓔ
79. Ⓐ Ⓑ Ⓒ Ⓓ Ⓔ
80. Ⓐ Ⓑ Ⓒ Ⓓ Ⓔ
81. Ⓐ Ⓑ Ⓒ Ⓓ Ⓔ
82. Ⓐ Ⓑ Ⓒ Ⓓ Ⓔ
83. Ⓐ Ⓑ Ⓒ Ⓓ Ⓔ
84. Ⓐ Ⓑ Ⓒ Ⓓ Ⓔ
85. Ⓐ Ⓑ Ⓒ Ⓓ Ⓔ
86. Ⓐ Ⓑ Ⓒ Ⓓ Ⓔ
87. Ⓐ Ⓑ Ⓒ Ⓓ Ⓔ
88. Ⓐ Ⓑ Ⓒ Ⓓ Ⓔ

SET 2

Do *not* look back at the address boxes while answering these questions.

1. 1400–2199 Hill
2. 9600–9899 Hill
3. 3400–3999 Crest
4. 4500–6099 Lane
5. Reimer
6. Fernwood
7. 6500–6599 Hill
8. 5400–6099 Lane
9. 2600–2899 Crest
10. 9100–9299 Crest
11. Avon
12. Densen
13. Penny
14. 4000–4399 Lane
15. 7200–8199 Crest
16. 2200–2599 Hill
17. Townsend
18. Murray
19. 8300–8599 Lane
20. 1000–1399 Lane
21. Cooper
22. 3100–3399 Hill
23. 8800–9599 Crest
24. Glendale
25. Brook
26. 6500–6599 Hill
27. 2600–2899 Crest
28. 4000–4399 Lane
29. 3400–3999 Crest

1. Ⓐ Ⓑ Ⓒ Ⓓ Ⓔ
2. Ⓐ Ⓑ Ⓒ Ⓓ Ⓔ
3. Ⓐ Ⓑ Ⓒ Ⓓ Ⓔ
4. Ⓐ Ⓑ Ⓒ Ⓓ Ⓔ
5. Ⓐ Ⓑ Ⓒ Ⓓ Ⓔ
6. Ⓐ Ⓑ Ⓒ Ⓓ Ⓔ
7. Ⓐ Ⓑ Ⓒ Ⓓ Ⓔ
8. Ⓐ Ⓑ Ⓒ Ⓓ Ⓔ
9. Ⓐ Ⓑ Ⓒ Ⓓ Ⓔ
10. Ⓐ Ⓑ Ⓒ Ⓓ Ⓔ
11. Ⓐ Ⓑ Ⓒ Ⓓ Ⓔ
12. Ⓐ Ⓑ Ⓒ Ⓓ Ⓔ
13. Ⓐ Ⓑ Ⓒ Ⓓ Ⓔ
14. Ⓐ Ⓑ Ⓒ Ⓓ Ⓔ
15. Ⓐ Ⓑ Ⓒ Ⓓ Ⓔ
16. Ⓐ Ⓑ Ⓒ Ⓓ Ⓔ
17. Ⓐ Ⓑ Ⓒ Ⓓ Ⓔ
18. Ⓐ Ⓑ Ⓒ Ⓓ Ⓔ
19. Ⓐ Ⓑ Ⓒ Ⓓ Ⓔ
20. Ⓐ Ⓑ Ⓒ Ⓓ Ⓔ
21. Ⓐ Ⓑ Ⓒ Ⓓ Ⓔ
22. Ⓐ Ⓑ Ⓒ Ⓓ Ⓔ
23. Ⓐ Ⓑ Ⓒ Ⓓ Ⓔ
24. Ⓐ Ⓑ Ⓒ Ⓓ Ⓔ
25. Ⓐ Ⓑ Ⓒ Ⓓ Ⓔ
26. Ⓐ Ⓑ Ⓒ Ⓓ Ⓔ
27. Ⓐ Ⓑ Ⓒ Ⓓ Ⓔ
28. Ⓐ Ⓑ Ⓒ Ⓓ Ⓔ
29. Ⓐ Ⓑ Ⓒ Ⓓ Ⓔ

30. Cooper	30. Ⓐ Ⓑ Ⓒ Ⓓ Ⓔ
31. Glendale	31. Ⓐ Ⓑ Ⓒ Ⓓ Ⓔ
32. 4500–6099 Lane	32. Ⓐ Ⓑ Ⓒ Ⓓ Ⓔ
33. 1400–2199 Hill	33. Ⓐ Ⓑ Ⓒ Ⓓ Ⓔ
34. 1000–1399 Lane	34. Ⓐ Ⓑ Ⓒ Ⓓ Ⓔ
35. Avon	35. Ⓐ Ⓑ Ⓒ Ⓓ Ⓔ
36. Reimer	36. Ⓐ Ⓑ Ⓒ Ⓓ Ⓔ
37. 8300–8599 Lane	37. Ⓐ Ⓑ Ⓒ Ⓓ Ⓔ
38. 9600–9899 Hill	38. Ⓐ Ⓑ Ⓒ Ⓓ Ⓔ
39. 9100–9299 Crest	39. Ⓐ Ⓑ Ⓒ Ⓓ Ⓔ
40. 5400–6099 Lane	40. Ⓐ Ⓑ Ⓒ Ⓓ Ⓔ
41. 3100–3399 Hill	41. Ⓐ Ⓑ Ⓒ Ⓓ Ⓔ
42. Fernwood	42. Ⓐ Ⓑ Ⓒ Ⓓ Ⓔ
43. Brook	43. Ⓐ Ⓑ Ⓒ Ⓓ Ⓔ
44. Penny	44. Ⓐ Ⓑ Ⓒ Ⓓ Ⓔ
45. Densen	45. Ⓐ Ⓑ Ⓒ Ⓓ Ⓔ
46. 2200–2599 Hill	46. Ⓐ Ⓑ Ⓒ Ⓓ Ⓔ
47. 7200–8199 Crest	47. Ⓐ Ⓑ Ⓒ Ⓓ Ⓔ
48. 8800–9599 Crest	48. Ⓐ Ⓑ Ⓒ Ⓓ Ⓔ
49. Murray	49. Ⓐ Ⓑ Ⓒ Ⓓ Ⓔ
50. Townsend	50. Ⓐ Ⓑ Ⓒ Ⓓ Ⓔ
51. 4500–6099 Lane	51. Ⓐ Ⓑ Ⓒ Ⓓ Ⓔ
52. 6500–6599 Hill	52. Ⓐ Ⓑ Ⓒ Ⓓ Ⓔ
53. 4000–4399 Lane	53. Ⓐ Ⓑ Ⓒ Ⓓ Ⓔ
54. 7200–8199 Crest	54. Ⓐ Ⓑ Ⓒ Ⓓ Ⓔ
55. 8300–8599 Lane	55. Ⓐ Ⓑ Ⓒ Ⓓ Ⓔ
56. 3400–3999 Crest	56. Ⓐ Ⓑ Ⓒ Ⓓ Ⓔ
57. Densen	57. Ⓐ Ⓑ Ⓒ Ⓓ Ⓔ
58. Glendale	58. Ⓐ Ⓑ Ⓒ Ⓓ Ⓔ
59. Fernwood	59. Ⓐ Ⓑ Ⓒ Ⓓ Ⓔ
60. 2200–2599 Hill	60. Ⓐ Ⓑ Ⓒ Ⓓ Ⓔ
61. 9600–9899 Hill	61. Ⓐ Ⓑ Ⓒ Ⓓ Ⓔ
62. 2600–2899 Crest	62. Ⓐ Ⓑ Ⓒ Ⓓ Ⓔ
63. 8300–8599 Lane	63. Ⓐ Ⓑ Ⓒ Ⓓ Ⓔ
64. 7200–8199 Crest	64. Ⓐ Ⓑ Ⓒ Ⓓ Ⓔ
65. 4500–6099 Lane	65. Ⓐ Ⓑ Ⓒ Ⓓ Ⓔ
66. Avon	66. Ⓐ Ⓑ Ⓒ Ⓓ Ⓔ
67. Penny	67. Ⓐ Ⓑ Ⓒ Ⓓ Ⓔ
68. 3100–3399 Hill	68. Ⓐ Ⓑ Ⓒ Ⓓ Ⓔ
69. 5400–6099 Lane	69. Ⓐ Ⓑ Ⓒ Ⓓ Ⓔ
70. 8800–9599 Crest	70. Ⓐ Ⓑ Ⓒ Ⓓ Ⓔ
71. Murray	71. Ⓐ Ⓑ Ⓒ Ⓓ Ⓔ
72. 1400–2199 Hill	72. Ⓐ Ⓑ Ⓒ Ⓓ Ⓔ
73. 1000–1399 Lane	73. Ⓐ Ⓑ Ⓒ Ⓓ Ⓔ
74. 9100–9299 Crest	74. Ⓐ Ⓑ Ⓒ Ⓓ Ⓔ
75. 3400–3999 Crest	75. Ⓐ Ⓑ Ⓒ Ⓓ Ⓔ
76. Townsend	76. Ⓐ Ⓑ Ⓒ Ⓓ Ⓔ
77. Cooper	77. Ⓐ Ⓑ Ⓒ Ⓓ Ⓔ
78. 6500–6599 Hill	78. Ⓐ Ⓑ Ⓒ Ⓓ Ⓔ
79. 4000–4399 Lane	79. Ⓐ Ⓑ Ⓒ Ⓓ Ⓔ
80. Reimer	80. Ⓐ Ⓑ Ⓒ Ⓓ Ⓔ
81. Brook	81. Ⓐ Ⓑ Ⓒ Ⓓ Ⓔ

82. 3100–3399 Hill
83. 8800–9599 Crest
84. 5400–6099 Lane
85. 6500–6599 Hill
86. 9100–9299 Crest
87. 8300–8599 Lane
88. Fernwood

82. Ⓐ Ⓑ Ⓒ Ⓓ Ⓔ
83. Ⓐ Ⓑ Ⓒ Ⓓ Ⓔ
84. Ⓐ Ⓑ Ⓒ Ⓓ Ⓔ
85. Ⓐ Ⓑ Ⓒ Ⓓ Ⓔ
86. Ⓐ Ⓑ Ⓒ Ⓓ Ⓔ
87. Ⓐ Ⓑ Ⓒ Ⓓ Ⓔ
88. Ⓐ Ⓑ Ⓒ Ⓓ Ⓔ

ANSWERS TO PRACTICE EXERCISE 2

SET 1

1. C	12. B	23. C	34. A	45. E	56. E	67. E	78. B
2. B	13. A	24. C	35. A	46. E	57. E	68. D	79. D
3. E	14. E	25. E	36. B	47. A	58. C	69. B	80. E
4. A	15. B	26. B	37. B	48. C	59. C	70. C	81. A
5. B	16. C	27. A	38. B	49. C	60. B	71. A	82. D
6. C	17. A	28. D	39. D	50. E	61. A	72. A	83. E
7. E	18. D	29. E	40. E	51. A	62. A	73. C	84. C
8. D	19. B	30. C	41. C	52. B	63. B	74. D	85. B
9. D	20. E	31. E	42. A	53. E	64. D	75. D	86. E
10. A	21. D	32. C	43. D	54. D	65. E	76. C	87. D
11. D	22. A	33. B	44. D	55. A	66. E	77. B	88. E

SET 2

1. A	12. C	23. B	34. C	45. C	56. C	67. A	78. D
2. C	13. A	24. D	35. E	46. B	57. C	68. E	79. B
3. C	14. B	25. D	36. B	47. A	58. D	69. D	80. B
4. E	15. A	26. D	37. A	48. B	59. E	70. B	81. D
5. B	16. B	27. E	38. C	49. C	60. B	71. C	82. E
6. E	17. A	28. B	39. D	50. A	61. C	72. A	83. B
7. D	18. C	29. C	40. D	51. E	62. E	73. C	84. D
8. D	19. A	30. B	41. E	52. D	63. A	74. D	85. D
9. E	20. C	31. D	42. E	53. B	64. A	75. C	86. D
10. D	21. B	32. E	43. D	54. A	65. E	76. A	87. A
11. E	22. E	33. A	44. A	55. A	66. E	77. B	88. E

As you go through the model exams in this book, remember all the tricks and techniques you have learned, and apply them. Also, work to develop your own memory scheme. Try to leave enough time between model exams so that your memory of a previous set of boxes does not interfere with the task at hand. Come back to this chapter to brush up whenever necessary. Reread the chapter the day before your exam, but do NOT do a model exam that day. You want your mind to be like a clean slate in order to learn the sorting scheme on your actual Clerk-Carrier Exam.

IMPORTANT NOTE: Clerk-Carrier Exams in past years have provided at least two practice tests to familiarize you with the Memory for Addresses Test. These practice tests are presented only to help candidates learn how to answer Memory for Addresses questions and are not scored. If you have done all the exercises in this book, you will already be familiar with how to answer Memory for Addresses questions, and you can use some of the practice test time for memorizing the boxes instead of answering the practice questions. In this way, you can gain five to ten minutes of additional memorizing time, which can add valuable points to your score.

PART III
Ten Sample Exams

ANSWER SHEET FOR
FIRST MODEL EXAM

ADDRESS CHECKING

1 Ⓐ Ⓓ	20 Ⓐ Ⓓ	39 Ⓐ Ⓓ	58 Ⓐ Ⓓ	77 Ⓐ Ⓓ
2 Ⓐ Ⓓ	21 Ⓐ Ⓓ	40 Ⓐ Ⓓ	59 Ⓐ Ⓓ	78 Ⓐ Ⓓ
3 Ⓐ Ⓓ	22 Ⓐ Ⓓ	41 Ⓐ Ⓓ	60 Ⓐ Ⓓ	79 Ⓐ Ⓓ
4 Ⓐ Ⓓ	23 Ⓐ Ⓓ	42 Ⓐ Ⓓ	61 Ⓐ Ⓓ	80 Ⓐ Ⓓ
5 Ⓐ Ⓓ	24 Ⓐ Ⓓ	43 Ⓐ Ⓓ	62 Ⓐ Ⓓ	81 Ⓐ Ⓓ
6 Ⓐ Ⓓ	25 Ⓐ Ⓓ	44 Ⓐ Ⓓ	63 Ⓐ Ⓓ	82 Ⓐ Ⓓ
7 Ⓐ Ⓓ	26 Ⓐ Ⓓ	45 Ⓐ Ⓓ	64 Ⓐ Ⓓ	83 Ⓐ Ⓓ
8 Ⓐ Ⓓ	27 Ⓐ Ⓓ	46 Ⓐ Ⓓ	65 Ⓐ Ⓓ	84 Ⓐ Ⓓ
9 Ⓐ Ⓓ	28 Ⓐ Ⓓ	47 Ⓐ Ⓓ	66 Ⓐ Ⓓ	85 Ⓐ Ⓓ
10 Ⓐ Ⓓ	29 Ⓐ Ⓓ	48 Ⓐ Ⓓ	67 Ⓐ Ⓓ	86 Ⓐ Ⓓ
11 Ⓐ Ⓓ	30 Ⓐ Ⓓ	49 Ⓐ Ⓓ	68 Ⓐ Ⓓ	87 Ⓐ Ⓓ
12 Ⓐ Ⓓ	31 Ⓐ Ⓓ	50 Ⓐ Ⓓ	69 Ⓐ Ⓓ	88 Ⓐ Ⓓ
13 Ⓐ Ⓓ	32 Ⓐ Ⓓ	51 Ⓐ Ⓓ	70 Ⓐ Ⓓ	89 Ⓐ Ⓓ
14 Ⓐ Ⓓ	33 Ⓐ Ⓓ	52 Ⓐ Ⓓ	71 Ⓐ Ⓓ	90 Ⓐ Ⓓ
15 Ⓐ Ⓓ	34 Ⓐ Ⓓ	53 Ⓐ Ⓓ	72 Ⓐ Ⓓ	91 Ⓐ Ⓓ
16 Ⓐ Ⓓ	35 Ⓐ Ⓓ	54 Ⓐ Ⓓ	73 Ⓐ Ⓓ	92 Ⓐ Ⓓ
17 Ⓐ Ⓓ	36 Ⓐ Ⓓ	55 Ⓐ Ⓓ	74 Ⓐ Ⓓ	93 Ⓐ Ⓓ
18 Ⓐ Ⓓ	37 Ⓐ Ⓓ	56 Ⓐ Ⓓ	75 Ⓐ Ⓓ	94 Ⓐ Ⓓ
19 Ⓐ Ⓓ	38 Ⓐ Ⓓ	57 Ⓐ Ⓓ	76 Ⓐ Ⓓ	95 Ⓐ Ⓓ

TEAR HERE

MEMORY FOR ADDRESSES

PRACTICE I

1 Ⓐ Ⓑ Ⓒ Ⓓ Ⓔ	23 Ⓐ Ⓑ Ⓒ Ⓓ Ⓔ	45 Ⓐ Ⓑ Ⓒ Ⓓ Ⓔ	67 Ⓐ Ⓑ Ⓒ Ⓓ Ⓔ
2 Ⓐ Ⓑ Ⓒ Ⓓ Ⓔ	24 Ⓐ Ⓑ Ⓒ Ⓓ Ⓔ	46 Ⓐ Ⓑ Ⓒ Ⓓ Ⓔ	68 Ⓐ Ⓑ Ⓒ Ⓓ Ⓔ
3 Ⓐ Ⓑ Ⓒ Ⓓ Ⓔ	25 Ⓐ Ⓑ Ⓒ Ⓓ Ⓔ	47 Ⓐ Ⓑ Ⓒ Ⓓ Ⓔ	69 Ⓐ Ⓑ Ⓒ Ⓓ Ⓔ
4 Ⓐ Ⓑ Ⓒ Ⓓ Ⓔ	26 Ⓐ Ⓑ Ⓒ Ⓓ Ⓔ	48 Ⓐ Ⓑ Ⓒ Ⓓ Ⓔ	70 Ⓐ Ⓑ Ⓒ Ⓓ Ⓔ
5 Ⓐ Ⓑ Ⓒ Ⓓ Ⓔ	27 Ⓐ Ⓑ Ⓒ Ⓓ Ⓔ	49 Ⓐ Ⓑ Ⓒ Ⓓ Ⓔ	71 Ⓐ Ⓑ Ⓒ Ⓓ Ⓔ
6 Ⓐ Ⓑ Ⓒ Ⓓ Ⓔ	28 Ⓐ Ⓑ Ⓒ Ⓓ Ⓔ	50 Ⓐ Ⓑ Ⓒ Ⓓ Ⓔ	72 Ⓐ Ⓑ Ⓒ Ⓓ Ⓔ
7 Ⓐ Ⓑ Ⓒ Ⓓ Ⓔ	29 Ⓐ Ⓑ Ⓒ Ⓓ Ⓔ	51 Ⓐ Ⓑ Ⓒ Ⓓ Ⓔ	73 Ⓐ Ⓑ Ⓒ Ⓓ Ⓔ
8 Ⓐ Ⓑ Ⓒ Ⓓ Ⓔ	30 Ⓐ Ⓑ Ⓒ Ⓓ Ⓔ	52 Ⓐ Ⓑ Ⓒ Ⓓ Ⓔ	74 Ⓐ Ⓑ Ⓒ Ⓓ Ⓔ
9 Ⓐ Ⓑ Ⓒ Ⓓ Ⓔ	31 Ⓐ Ⓑ Ⓒ Ⓓ Ⓔ	53 Ⓐ Ⓑ Ⓒ Ⓓ Ⓔ	75 Ⓐ Ⓑ Ⓒ Ⓓ Ⓔ
10 Ⓐ Ⓑ Ⓒ Ⓓ Ⓔ	32 Ⓐ Ⓑ Ⓒ Ⓓ Ⓔ	54 Ⓐ Ⓑ Ⓒ Ⓓ Ⓔ	76 Ⓐ Ⓑ Ⓒ Ⓓ Ⓔ
11 Ⓐ Ⓑ Ⓒ Ⓓ Ⓔ	33 Ⓐ Ⓑ Ⓒ Ⓓ Ⓔ	55 Ⓐ Ⓑ Ⓒ Ⓓ Ⓔ	77 Ⓐ Ⓑ Ⓒ Ⓓ Ⓔ
12 Ⓐ Ⓑ Ⓒ Ⓓ Ⓔ	34 Ⓐ Ⓑ Ⓒ Ⓓ Ⓔ	56 Ⓐ Ⓑ Ⓒ Ⓓ Ⓔ	78 Ⓐ Ⓑ Ⓒ Ⓓ Ⓔ
13 Ⓐ Ⓑ Ⓒ Ⓓ Ⓔ	35 Ⓐ Ⓑ Ⓒ Ⓓ Ⓔ	57 Ⓐ Ⓑ Ⓒ Ⓓ Ⓔ	79 Ⓐ Ⓑ Ⓒ Ⓓ Ⓔ
14 Ⓐ Ⓑ Ⓒ Ⓓ Ⓔ	36 Ⓐ Ⓑ Ⓒ Ⓓ Ⓔ	58 Ⓐ Ⓑ Ⓒ Ⓓ Ⓔ	80 Ⓐ Ⓑ Ⓒ Ⓓ Ⓔ
15 Ⓐ Ⓑ Ⓒ Ⓓ Ⓔ	37 Ⓐ Ⓑ Ⓒ Ⓓ Ⓔ	59 Ⓐ Ⓑ Ⓒ Ⓓ Ⓔ	81 Ⓐ Ⓑ Ⓒ Ⓓ Ⓔ
16 Ⓐ Ⓑ Ⓒ Ⓓ Ⓔ	38 Ⓐ Ⓑ Ⓒ Ⓓ Ⓔ	60 Ⓐ Ⓑ Ⓒ Ⓓ Ⓔ	82 Ⓐ Ⓑ Ⓒ Ⓓ Ⓔ
17 Ⓐ Ⓑ Ⓒ Ⓓ Ⓔ	39 Ⓐ Ⓑ Ⓒ Ⓓ Ⓔ	61 Ⓐ Ⓑ Ⓒ Ⓓ Ⓔ	83 Ⓐ Ⓑ Ⓒ Ⓓ Ⓔ
18 Ⓐ Ⓑ Ⓒ Ⓓ Ⓔ	40 Ⓐ Ⓑ Ⓒ Ⓓ Ⓔ	62 Ⓐ Ⓑ Ⓒ Ⓓ Ⓔ	84 Ⓐ Ⓑ Ⓒ Ⓓ Ⓔ
19 Ⓐ Ⓑ Ⓒ Ⓓ Ⓔ	41 Ⓐ Ⓑ Ⓒ Ⓓ Ⓔ	63 Ⓐ Ⓑ Ⓒ Ⓓ Ⓔ	85 Ⓐ Ⓑ Ⓒ Ⓓ Ⓔ
20 Ⓐ Ⓑ Ⓒ Ⓓ Ⓔ	42 Ⓐ Ⓑ Ⓒ Ⓓ Ⓔ	64 Ⓐ Ⓑ Ⓒ Ⓓ Ⓔ	86 Ⓐ Ⓑ Ⓒ Ⓓ Ⓔ
21 Ⓐ Ⓑ Ⓒ Ⓓ Ⓔ	43 Ⓐ Ⓑ Ⓒ Ⓓ Ⓔ	65 Ⓐ Ⓑ Ⓒ Ⓓ Ⓔ	87 Ⓐ Ⓑ Ⓒ Ⓓ Ⓔ
22 Ⓐ Ⓑ Ⓒ Ⓓ Ⓔ	44 Ⓐ Ⓑ Ⓒ Ⓓ Ⓔ	66 Ⓐ Ⓑ Ⓒ Ⓓ Ⓔ	88 Ⓐ Ⓑ Ⓒ Ⓓ Ⓔ

PRACTICE II

1 Ⓐ Ⓑ Ⓒ Ⓓ Ⓔ   23 Ⓐ Ⓑ Ⓒ Ⓓ Ⓔ   45 Ⓐ Ⓑ Ⓒ Ⓓ Ⓔ   67 Ⓐ Ⓑ Ⓒ Ⓓ Ⓔ

2 Ⓐ Ⓑ Ⓒ Ⓓ Ⓔ   24 Ⓐ Ⓑ Ⓒ Ⓓ Ⓔ   46 Ⓐ Ⓑ Ⓒ Ⓓ Ⓔ   68 Ⓐ Ⓑ Ⓒ Ⓓ Ⓔ

3 Ⓐ Ⓑ Ⓒ Ⓓ Ⓔ   25 Ⓐ Ⓑ Ⓒ Ⓓ Ⓔ   47 Ⓐ Ⓑ Ⓒ Ⓓ Ⓔ   69 Ⓐ Ⓑ Ⓒ Ⓓ Ⓔ

4 Ⓐ Ⓑ Ⓒ Ⓓ Ⓔ   26 Ⓐ Ⓑ Ⓒ Ⓓ Ⓔ   48 Ⓐ Ⓑ Ⓒ Ⓓ Ⓔ   70 Ⓐ Ⓑ Ⓒ Ⓓ Ⓔ

5 Ⓐ Ⓑ Ⓒ Ⓓ Ⓔ   27 Ⓐ Ⓑ Ⓒ Ⓓ Ⓔ   49 Ⓐ Ⓑ Ⓒ Ⓓ Ⓔ   71 Ⓐ Ⓑ Ⓒ Ⓓ Ⓔ

6 Ⓐ Ⓑ Ⓒ Ⓓ Ⓔ   28 Ⓐ Ⓑ Ⓒ Ⓓ Ⓔ   50 Ⓐ Ⓑ Ⓒ Ⓓ Ⓔ   72 Ⓐ Ⓑ Ⓒ Ⓓ Ⓔ

7 Ⓐ Ⓑ Ⓒ Ⓓ Ⓔ   29 Ⓐ Ⓑ Ⓒ Ⓓ Ⓔ   51 Ⓐ Ⓑ Ⓒ Ⓓ Ⓔ   73 Ⓐ Ⓑ Ⓒ Ⓓ Ⓔ

8 Ⓐ Ⓑ Ⓒ Ⓓ Ⓔ   30 Ⓐ Ⓑ Ⓒ Ⓓ Ⓔ   52 Ⓐ Ⓑ Ⓒ Ⓓ Ⓔ   74 Ⓐ Ⓑ Ⓒ Ⓓ Ⓔ

9 Ⓐ Ⓑ Ⓒ Ⓓ Ⓔ   31 Ⓐ Ⓑ Ⓒ Ⓓ Ⓔ   53 Ⓐ Ⓑ Ⓒ Ⓓ Ⓔ   75 Ⓐ Ⓑ Ⓒ Ⓓ Ⓔ

10 Ⓐ Ⓑ Ⓒ Ⓓ Ⓔ   32 Ⓐ Ⓑ Ⓒ Ⓓ Ⓔ   54 Ⓐ Ⓑ Ⓒ Ⓓ Ⓔ   76 Ⓐ Ⓑ Ⓒ Ⓓ Ⓔ

11 Ⓐ Ⓑ Ⓒ Ⓓ Ⓔ   33 Ⓐ Ⓑ Ⓒ Ⓓ Ⓔ   55 Ⓐ Ⓑ Ⓒ Ⓓ Ⓔ   77 Ⓐ Ⓑ Ⓒ Ⓓ Ⓔ

12 Ⓐ Ⓑ Ⓒ Ⓓ Ⓔ   34 Ⓐ Ⓑ Ⓒ Ⓓ Ⓔ   56 Ⓐ Ⓑ Ⓒ Ⓓ Ⓔ   78 Ⓐ Ⓑ Ⓒ Ⓓ Ⓔ

13 Ⓐ Ⓑ Ⓒ Ⓓ Ⓔ   35 Ⓐ Ⓑ Ⓒ Ⓓ Ⓔ   57 Ⓐ Ⓑ Ⓒ Ⓓ Ⓔ   79 Ⓐ Ⓑ Ⓒ Ⓓ Ⓔ

14 Ⓐ Ⓑ Ⓒ Ⓓ Ⓔ   36 Ⓐ Ⓑ Ⓒ Ⓓ Ⓔ   58 Ⓐ Ⓑ Ⓒ Ⓓ Ⓔ   80 Ⓐ Ⓑ Ⓒ Ⓓ Ⓔ

15 Ⓐ Ⓑ Ⓒ Ⓓ Ⓔ   37 Ⓐ Ⓑ Ⓒ Ⓓ Ⓔ   59 Ⓐ Ⓑ Ⓒ Ⓓ Ⓔ   81 Ⓐ Ⓑ Ⓒ Ⓓ Ⓔ

16 Ⓐ Ⓑ Ⓒ Ⓓ Ⓔ   38 Ⓐ Ⓑ Ⓒ Ⓓ Ⓔ   60 Ⓐ Ⓑ Ⓒ Ⓓ Ⓔ   82 Ⓐ Ⓑ Ⓒ Ⓓ Ⓔ

17 Ⓐ Ⓑ Ⓒ Ⓓ Ⓔ   39 Ⓐ Ⓑ Ⓒ Ⓓ Ⓔ   61 Ⓐ Ⓑ Ⓒ Ⓓ Ⓔ   83 Ⓐ Ⓑ Ⓒ Ⓓ Ⓔ

18 Ⓐ Ⓑ Ⓒ Ⓓ Ⓔ   40 Ⓐ Ⓑ Ⓒ Ⓓ Ⓔ   62 Ⓐ Ⓑ Ⓒ Ⓓ Ⓔ   84 Ⓐ Ⓑ Ⓒ Ⓓ Ⓔ

19 Ⓐ Ⓑ Ⓒ Ⓓ Ⓔ   41 Ⓐ Ⓑ Ⓒ Ⓓ Ⓔ   63 Ⓐ Ⓑ Ⓒ Ⓓ Ⓔ   85 Ⓐ Ⓑ Ⓒ Ⓓ Ⓔ

20 Ⓐ Ⓑ Ⓒ Ⓓ Ⓔ   42 Ⓐ Ⓑ Ⓒ Ⓓ Ⓔ   64 Ⓐ Ⓑ Ⓒ Ⓓ Ⓔ   86 Ⓐ Ⓑ Ⓒ Ⓓ Ⓔ

21 Ⓐ Ⓑ Ⓒ Ⓓ Ⓔ   43 Ⓐ Ⓑ Ⓒ Ⓓ Ⓔ   65 Ⓐ Ⓑ Ⓒ Ⓓ Ⓔ   87 Ⓐ Ⓑ Ⓒ Ⓓ Ⓔ

22 Ⓐ Ⓑ Ⓒ Ⓓ Ⓔ   44 Ⓐ Ⓑ Ⓒ Ⓓ Ⓔ   66 Ⓐ Ⓑ Ⓒ Ⓓ Ⓔ   88 Ⓐ Ⓑ Ⓒ Ⓓ Ⓔ

PRACTICE III

1 Ⓐ Ⓑ Ⓒ Ⓓ Ⓔ   23 Ⓐ Ⓑ Ⓒ Ⓓ Ⓔ   45 Ⓐ Ⓑ Ⓒ Ⓓ Ⓔ   67 Ⓐ Ⓑ Ⓒ Ⓓ Ⓔ

2 Ⓐ Ⓑ Ⓒ Ⓓ Ⓔ   24 Ⓐ Ⓑ Ⓒ Ⓓ Ⓔ   46 Ⓐ Ⓑ Ⓒ Ⓓ Ⓔ   68 Ⓐ Ⓑ Ⓒ Ⓓ Ⓔ

3 Ⓐ Ⓑ Ⓒ Ⓓ Ⓔ   25 Ⓐ Ⓑ Ⓒ Ⓓ Ⓔ   47 Ⓐ Ⓑ Ⓒ Ⓓ Ⓔ   69 Ⓐ Ⓑ Ⓒ Ⓓ Ⓔ

4 Ⓐ Ⓑ Ⓒ Ⓓ Ⓔ   26 Ⓐ Ⓑ Ⓒ Ⓓ Ⓔ   48 Ⓐ Ⓑ Ⓒ Ⓓ Ⓔ   70 Ⓐ Ⓑ Ⓒ Ⓓ Ⓔ

5 Ⓐ Ⓑ Ⓒ Ⓓ Ⓔ   27 Ⓐ Ⓑ Ⓒ Ⓓ Ⓔ   49 Ⓐ Ⓑ Ⓒ Ⓓ Ⓔ   71 Ⓐ Ⓑ Ⓒ Ⓓ Ⓔ

6 Ⓐ Ⓑ Ⓒ Ⓓ Ⓔ   28 Ⓐ Ⓑ Ⓒ Ⓓ Ⓔ   50 Ⓐ Ⓑ Ⓒ Ⓓ Ⓔ   72 Ⓐ Ⓑ Ⓒ Ⓓ Ⓔ

7 Ⓐ Ⓑ Ⓒ Ⓓ Ⓔ   29 Ⓐ Ⓑ Ⓒ Ⓓ Ⓔ   51 Ⓐ Ⓑ Ⓒ Ⓓ Ⓔ   73 Ⓐ Ⓑ Ⓒ Ⓓ Ⓔ

8 Ⓐ Ⓑ Ⓒ Ⓓ Ⓔ   30 Ⓐ Ⓑ Ⓒ Ⓓ Ⓔ   52 Ⓐ Ⓑ Ⓒ Ⓓ Ⓔ   74 Ⓐ Ⓑ Ⓒ Ⓓ Ⓔ

9 Ⓐ Ⓑ Ⓒ Ⓓ Ⓔ   31 Ⓐ Ⓑ Ⓒ Ⓓ Ⓔ   53 Ⓐ Ⓑ Ⓒ Ⓓ Ⓔ   75 Ⓐ Ⓑ Ⓒ Ⓓ Ⓔ

10 Ⓐ Ⓑ Ⓒ Ⓓ Ⓔ   32 Ⓐ Ⓑ Ⓒ Ⓓ Ⓔ   54 Ⓐ Ⓑ Ⓒ Ⓓ Ⓔ   76 Ⓐ Ⓑ Ⓒ Ⓓ Ⓔ

11 Ⓐ Ⓑ Ⓒ Ⓓ Ⓔ   33 Ⓐ Ⓑ Ⓒ Ⓓ Ⓔ   55 Ⓐ Ⓑ Ⓒ Ⓓ Ⓔ   77 Ⓐ Ⓑ Ⓒ Ⓓ Ⓔ

12 Ⓐ Ⓑ Ⓒ Ⓓ Ⓔ   34 Ⓐ Ⓑ Ⓒ Ⓓ Ⓔ   56 Ⓐ Ⓑ Ⓒ Ⓓ Ⓔ   78 Ⓐ Ⓑ Ⓒ Ⓓ Ⓔ

13 Ⓐ Ⓑ Ⓒ Ⓓ Ⓔ   35 Ⓐ Ⓑ Ⓒ Ⓓ Ⓔ   57 Ⓐ Ⓑ Ⓒ Ⓓ Ⓔ   79 Ⓐ Ⓑ Ⓒ Ⓓ Ⓔ

14 Ⓐ Ⓑ Ⓒ Ⓓ Ⓔ   36 Ⓐ Ⓑ Ⓒ Ⓓ Ⓔ   58 Ⓐ Ⓑ Ⓒ Ⓓ Ⓔ   80 Ⓐ Ⓑ Ⓒ Ⓓ Ⓔ

15 Ⓐ Ⓑ Ⓒ Ⓓ Ⓔ   37 Ⓐ Ⓑ Ⓒ Ⓓ Ⓔ   59 Ⓐ Ⓑ Ⓒ Ⓓ Ⓔ   81 Ⓐ Ⓑ Ⓒ Ⓓ Ⓔ

16 Ⓐ Ⓑ Ⓒ Ⓓ Ⓔ   38 Ⓐ Ⓑ Ⓒ Ⓓ Ⓔ   60 Ⓐ Ⓑ Ⓒ Ⓓ Ⓔ   82 Ⓐ Ⓑ Ⓒ Ⓓ Ⓔ

17 Ⓐ Ⓑ Ⓒ Ⓓ Ⓔ   39 Ⓐ Ⓑ Ⓒ Ⓓ Ⓔ   61 Ⓐ Ⓑ Ⓒ Ⓓ Ⓔ   83 Ⓐ Ⓑ Ⓒ Ⓓ Ⓔ

18 Ⓐ Ⓑ Ⓒ Ⓓ Ⓔ   40 Ⓐ Ⓑ Ⓒ Ⓓ Ⓔ   62 Ⓐ Ⓑ Ⓒ Ⓓ Ⓔ   84 Ⓐ Ⓑ Ⓒ Ⓓ Ⓔ

19 Ⓐ Ⓑ Ⓒ Ⓓ Ⓔ   41 Ⓐ Ⓑ Ⓒ Ⓓ Ⓔ   63 Ⓐ Ⓑ Ⓒ Ⓓ Ⓔ   85 Ⓐ Ⓑ Ⓒ Ⓓ Ⓔ

20 Ⓐ Ⓑ Ⓒ Ⓓ Ⓔ   42 Ⓐ Ⓑ Ⓒ Ⓓ Ⓔ   64 Ⓐ Ⓑ Ⓒ Ⓓ Ⓔ   86 Ⓐ Ⓑ Ⓒ Ⓓ Ⓔ

21 Ⓐ Ⓑ Ⓒ Ⓓ Ⓔ   43 Ⓐ Ⓑ Ⓒ Ⓓ Ⓔ   65 Ⓐ Ⓑ Ⓒ Ⓓ Ⓔ   87 Ⓐ Ⓑ Ⓒ Ⓓ Ⓔ

22 Ⓐ Ⓑ Ⓒ Ⓓ Ⓔ   44 Ⓐ Ⓑ Ⓒ Ⓓ Ⓔ   66 Ⓐ Ⓑ Ⓒ Ⓓ Ⓔ   88 Ⓐ Ⓑ Ⓒ Ⓓ Ⓔ

PRACTICE III

MEMORY FOR ADDRESSES TEST

1 Ⓐ Ⓑ Ⓒ Ⓓ Ⓔ
2 Ⓐ Ⓑ Ⓒ Ⓓ Ⓔ
3 Ⓐ Ⓑ Ⓒ Ⓓ Ⓔ
4 Ⓐ Ⓑ Ⓒ Ⓓ Ⓔ
5 Ⓐ Ⓑ Ⓒ Ⓓ Ⓔ
6 Ⓐ Ⓑ Ⓒ Ⓓ Ⓔ
7 Ⓐ Ⓑ Ⓒ Ⓓ Ⓔ
8 Ⓐ Ⓑ Ⓒ Ⓓ Ⓔ
9 Ⓐ Ⓑ Ⓒ Ⓓ Ⓔ
10 Ⓐ Ⓑ Ⓒ Ⓓ Ⓔ
11 Ⓐ Ⓑ Ⓒ Ⓓ Ⓔ
12 Ⓐ Ⓑ Ⓒ Ⓓ Ⓔ
13 Ⓐ Ⓑ Ⓒ Ⓓ Ⓔ
14 Ⓐ Ⓑ Ⓒ Ⓓ Ⓔ
15 Ⓐ Ⓑ Ⓒ Ⓓ Ⓔ
16 Ⓐ Ⓑ Ⓒ Ⓓ Ⓔ
17 Ⓐ Ⓑ Ⓒ Ⓓ Ⓔ
18 Ⓐ Ⓑ Ⓒ Ⓓ Ⓔ
19 Ⓐ Ⓑ Ⓒ Ⓓ Ⓔ
20 Ⓐ Ⓑ Ⓒ Ⓓ Ⓔ
21 Ⓐ Ⓑ Ⓒ Ⓓ Ⓔ
22 Ⓐ Ⓑ Ⓒ Ⓓ Ⓔ

23 Ⓐ Ⓑ Ⓒ Ⓓ Ⓔ
24 Ⓐ Ⓑ Ⓒ Ⓓ Ⓔ
25 Ⓐ Ⓑ Ⓒ Ⓓ Ⓔ
26 Ⓐ Ⓑ Ⓒ Ⓓ Ⓔ
27 Ⓐ Ⓑ Ⓒ Ⓓ Ⓔ
28 Ⓐ Ⓑ Ⓒ Ⓓ Ⓔ
29 Ⓐ Ⓑ Ⓒ Ⓓ Ⓔ
30 Ⓐ Ⓑ Ⓒ Ⓓ Ⓔ
31 Ⓐ Ⓑ Ⓒ Ⓓ Ⓔ
32 Ⓐ Ⓑ Ⓒ Ⓓ Ⓔ
33 Ⓐ Ⓑ Ⓒ Ⓓ Ⓔ
34 Ⓐ Ⓑ Ⓒ Ⓓ Ⓔ
35 Ⓐ Ⓑ Ⓒ Ⓓ Ⓔ
36 Ⓐ Ⓑ Ⓒ Ⓓ Ⓔ
37 Ⓐ Ⓑ Ⓒ Ⓓ Ⓔ
38 Ⓐ Ⓑ Ⓒ Ⓓ Ⓔ
39 Ⓐ Ⓑ Ⓒ Ⓓ Ⓔ
40 Ⓐ Ⓑ Ⓒ Ⓓ Ⓔ
41 Ⓐ Ⓑ Ⓒ Ⓓ Ⓔ
42 Ⓐ Ⓑ Ⓒ Ⓓ Ⓔ
43 Ⓐ Ⓑ Ⓒ Ⓓ Ⓔ
44 Ⓐ Ⓑ Ⓒ Ⓓ Ⓔ

45 Ⓐ Ⓑ Ⓒ Ⓓ Ⓔ
46 Ⓐ Ⓑ Ⓒ Ⓓ Ⓔ
47 Ⓐ Ⓑ Ⓒ Ⓓ Ⓔ
48 Ⓐ Ⓑ Ⓒ Ⓓ Ⓔ
49 Ⓐ Ⓑ Ⓒ Ⓓ Ⓔ
50 Ⓐ Ⓑ Ⓒ Ⓓ Ⓔ
51 Ⓐ Ⓑ Ⓒ Ⓓ Ⓔ
52 Ⓐ Ⓑ Ⓒ Ⓓ Ⓔ
53 Ⓐ Ⓑ Ⓒ Ⓓ Ⓔ
54 Ⓐ Ⓑ Ⓒ Ⓓ Ⓔ
55 Ⓐ Ⓑ Ⓒ Ⓓ Ⓔ
56 Ⓐ Ⓑ Ⓒ Ⓓ Ⓔ
57 Ⓐ Ⓑ Ⓒ Ⓓ Ⓔ
58 Ⓐ Ⓑ Ⓒ Ⓓ Ⓔ
59 Ⓐ Ⓑ Ⓒ Ⓓ Ⓔ
60 Ⓐ Ⓑ Ⓒ Ⓓ Ⓔ
61 Ⓐ Ⓑ Ⓒ Ⓓ Ⓔ
62 Ⓐ Ⓑ Ⓒ Ⓓ Ⓔ
63 Ⓐ Ⓑ Ⓒ Ⓓ Ⓔ
64 Ⓐ Ⓑ Ⓒ Ⓓ Ⓔ
65 Ⓐ Ⓑ Ⓒ Ⓓ Ⓔ
66 Ⓐ Ⓑ Ⓒ Ⓓ Ⓔ

67 Ⓐ Ⓑ Ⓒ Ⓓ Ⓔ
68 Ⓐ Ⓑ Ⓒ Ⓓ Ⓔ
69 Ⓐ Ⓑ Ⓒ Ⓓ Ⓔ
70 Ⓐ Ⓑ Ⓒ Ⓓ Ⓔ
71 Ⓐ Ⓑ Ⓒ Ⓓ Ⓔ
72 Ⓐ Ⓑ Ⓒ Ⓓ Ⓔ
73 Ⓐ Ⓑ Ⓒ Ⓓ Ⓔ
74 Ⓐ Ⓑ Ⓒ Ⓓ Ⓔ
75 Ⓐ Ⓑ Ⓒ Ⓓ Ⓔ
76 Ⓐ Ⓑ Ⓒ Ⓓ Ⓔ
77 Ⓐ Ⓑ Ⓒ Ⓓ Ⓔ
78 Ⓐ Ⓑ Ⓒ Ⓓ Ⓔ
79 Ⓐ Ⓑ Ⓒ Ⓓ Ⓔ
80 Ⓐ Ⓑ Ⓒ Ⓓ Ⓔ
81 Ⓐ Ⓑ Ⓒ Ⓓ Ⓔ
82 Ⓐ Ⓑ Ⓒ Ⓓ Ⓔ
83 Ⓐ Ⓑ Ⓒ Ⓓ Ⓔ
84 Ⓐ Ⓑ Ⓒ Ⓓ Ⓔ
85 Ⓐ Ⓑ Ⓒ Ⓓ Ⓔ
86 Ⓐ Ⓑ Ⓒ Ⓓ Ⓔ
87 Ⓐ Ⓑ Ⓒ Ⓓ Ⓔ
88 Ⓐ Ⓑ Ⓒ Ⓓ Ⓔ

SCORE SHEET FOR
FIRST MODEL EXAM

ADDRESS CHECKING TEST

Number Right minus Number Wrong equals   Score

_____ – _____ = _____

MEMORY FOR ADDRESSES TEST

Number Right minus (Number Wrong ÷ 4) equals   Score

_____ – _____ = _____

PROGRESS GRAPH

Blacken the bars for Model Exam 1 to the scores you earned.

Score		
95		
90		
85		
80		
75		
70		
65		
60		
55		
50		
45		
40		
35		
30		
25		
20		
15		
10		
5		
0		
Test	AC | M	AC | M
Model Exam	Diag.	1

AC = Address Checking   M = Memory for Addresses

FIRST MODEL EXAM

ADDRESS CHECKING TEST

TIME: 6 Minutes. 95 Questions.

DIRECTIONS: For each question, compare the address in the left column with the address in the right column. If the addresses are ALIKE IN EVERY WAY, blacken space Ⓐ on your answer sheet. If the two addresses are DIFFERENT IN ANY WAY, blacken space Ⓓ on your answer sheet. Correct answers for this test are on page 87.

1. . .7399 NW Candleworth Dr	7399 NW Candleworth Dr
2. . .New Castle AL 35119	New Castle AL 35119
3. . .2098 NE Catalpa Ln	2098 NW Catalpa Ln
4. . .17001 NE Rappaix Court	17001 NE Rappaix Court
5. . .10091 NE Larryvale Rd	10091 NE Larryville Rd
6. . .2896 NE Wallaston Way	2896 NE Walleston Way
7. . .Timonium MD 21093	Timanium MD 21093
8. . .7749 NW Barracuda Cove Ct	7749 NW Barracuda Cove Ct
9. . .6099 NW Atterbury Rd	6099 NW Atterbury Dr
10. . .2198 NE Springs St	2198 NW Springs St
11. . .6089 SE Flintshire Rd	6089 SW Flintshire Rd
12. . .13111 SE Throgmorton Ct	13111 SE Throgmorton Ct
13. . Estacada OR 97023	Estacada OK 97023
14. . .5301 NE Monocacy Cir	5301 NE Monocacy Ct
15. . .6066 NW Schissler Ave	6606 NW Schissler Ave
16. . .1915 NE Chapletowne Cir	1915 NE Chapeltowne Cir
17. . .4505 NE Reisterstown Plaza	4505 NE Reisterstown Plaza
18. . .3399 NW Ivydene Ter	3399 NW Ivydene Trl
19. . .8605 Commanche Ave	8605 Commanche Ave
20. . .Winnemucca NV 89445	Winnemocca NV 89445
21. . .467 SE Chatterleigh Cir	467 SE Chatterleigh Cir
22. . .3300 SE Golupski Rd	3300 SE Golpski Rd
23. . .4884 NW Farmvale Ave	4884 NW Farmdale Ave
24. . .Kalamazoo MI 49009	Kalamazoo MI 49009
25. . .11676 SE Harryweiss Rd	11676 SE Harrywise Rd
26. . .4395 Auchentoroly Ter	4395 Auchentoroly Ter
27. . .11321 NE Pageland Rd	11321 NE Pageland Rd
28. . .2488 Jeannett Ave	2488 Jeannett Ave
29. . .1900 Gilford Ter	1900 Gulford Ter

30...5177 NE Bridgehampton Dr	5177 NE Bridgehampton Dr
31...7333 Martingale Ave	7333 Martingale Ave
32...11577 Delagrange Way	11571 Delagrange Way
33...13852 NE 68th Ave	13852 NE 86th Ave
34...11736 NE Uffington Rd	17736 NE Uffington Rd
35...21199 NW Huntington Ave	21199 NW Huntingdon Ave
36...Merriweather NY 11548	Merriweather NY 11548
37...11001 NE Cedarcrest Rd	11001 NE Cedarchest Rd
38...3569 NE Tazewell Rd	3569 NE Tazewell Rd
39...5297 Popperdam Creek	5297 Pepperdam Creek
40...2288 Dundawan Rd	2288 Dundawan Rd
41...17299 Rhuddlan Rd	17299 Rhuddlan Rd
42...37719 Underwood Ct	37719 Underwood Cir
43...22700 S Strathdale Rd	22700 S Strathdale Rd
44...Homeworth OH 44634	Homeworth OH 46434
45...3727 NW Ayleshire Rd	3727 NE Ayleshire Rd
46...4585 E Englemeade Ave	4585 E Englemeade Ave
47...37741 NE Jacqueline Ln	34771 NE Jacqueline Ln
48...3800 N Grinnalds Ave	3800 N Grinnalds St
49...10990 NE Kennicott Rd	10990 NE Kenningcott Rd
50...Vanderpool TX 78885	Vanderpool TX 78885
51...11799 NE Brattel Rd	11799 NE Brattle Rd
52...2196 Leadenhall Court	2196 Leadenhall Court
53...Albuquerque NM 87109	Albuquerque NM 81709
54...3789 Featherstone Ln	8789 Featherstone Ln
55...18076 Martinque Rd	18076 Martinque Ct
56...60111 Debonair Ct	6011 Debonair Ct
57...4131 NE Tussock Rd	4131 NE Tussock Road
58...299 Susquehanna Ave E	299 Susquehanna Ave W
59...53116 NE T Avenue	53116 NE T Avenue
60...16917 Saint Elmo Ave	16917 Saint Almo Ave
61...10401 Olde Georgetown Rd SE	10401 Old Georgetown Rd SE
62...7550 Wisconsin Ave	7550 Wisconsin St
63...8054 Aberdeen Rd	8054 Aberdeen Rd
64...Wheelersburg KY 41473	Wheelersburg KY 41473
65...3138 Edgemere Ave	3138 Edgemore Ave
66...11595 Heathcliff Dr	11595 Heathcliff Dr
67...13531 N Keutel Rd	13531 N Kratel Rd
68...7585 Breezewick Cir	78575 Breezewick Cir
69...15530 NE Jimrowe Cir	15530 NE Jimrowe Ct
70...2001 Quantico Way	2001 Guantico Way
71...8899 Randolph Springs Pl	8899 Rudolph Springs Pl
72...4010 Oakleigh Beach Rd	4010 Oakleigh Beach Rd
73...3977 Mc Teague Ave	3977 Mc Teague Ave
74...13827 N Lavington Pl	13827 N Lavingston Pl
75...17390 Youngstown Ave NE	17390 Youngstown Ave SE
76...15999 Brookview Ave	15999 Brookview Ave
77...12733 NE 88th Ave	1273 NE 88th Ave
78...P.O. Box 34001	P.O. Box 34007
79...Selinsgrove PA 17870	Selingrove PA 17870
80...3425 Chelmareford Trl	3245 Chelmareford Trl
81...6080 Knickerbocker Cir	6080 Knickerbocker Dr
82...1700 Alconbury Rd	1700 Alconbury Rd

83...2620 Winnettka St   2620 Winnettka St
84...2367 Essextowne Cir   2367 Essextowne Cir
85...3588 Investment Pl   3588 Investment Pl
86...11888 Margarette Ave   11888 Margaretta Ave
87...4756 Ridervale Rd   4756 Riderview Rd
88...16491 Zeppelin Ave   16491 Zepperlin Ave
89...10195 Highway 210 N   10195 Highway 201 N
90...11811 Vailthorn Ln   11181 Vailthorn Ln
91...7299 E 41st Street   7299 W 41st Street
92...P.O. Box 30399   P.O. Box 30399
93...4710 Bethesda Ave N   4710 Bethesda Blvd N
94...Waynesboro MS 39367   Waynesboro MN 39367
95...99 NW M Street   99 NW M Street

END OF ADDRESS CHECKING TEST

If you finish this test before time is up, use the remaining time to check over your work. Do not turn the page until you are told to do so.

PRACTICE FOR
MEMORY FOR ADDRESSES TEST

DIRECTIONS: The five boxes below are labelled A, B, C, D, and E. In each box are three sets of number spans with names and two names which are not associated with numbers. In the next THREE MINUTES, you must try to memorize the box location of each name and number span. The position of a name or number span within its box is not important. You need only remember the letter of the box in which the item is to be found. You will use these names and numbers to answer three sets of practice questions which are NOT scored and one actual test that is scored. Correct answers are on pages 87 and 88.

A	B	C	D	E
2200-2899 Mills	4100-4299 Mills	4400-4599 Mills	3500-3899 Mills	2900-3499 Mills
Carmen	Center	Noya	Turner	Dalewood
4900-4999 Cass	4000-4299 Cass	3400-3999 Cass	4600-4799 Cass	4400-4499 Cass
Nevada	Florence	Daisey	Palm	Mooney
2400-2999 Leon	3200-3799 Leon	1900-2299 Leon	3100-3199 Leon	1600-1899 Leon

PRACTICE I

DIRECTIONS: Use the next THREE MINUTES to mark on your answer sheet the letter of the box in which each item that follows is to be found. Try to mark each item without looking back at the boxes. If, however, you get stuck, you may refer to the boxes during this practice exercise. If you find that you must look at the boxes, try to memorize as you do so. This test is for practice only. It will not be scored.

1. 1900-2299 Leon
2. 4400-4499 Cass
3. Center
4. Palm
5. 3500-3899 Mills
6. 4400-4499 Cass
7. Palm
8. Carmen
9. 4400-4499 Cass
10. Daisey
11. Dalewood
12. Nevada
13. 2900-3499 Mills
14. 1900-2299 Leon
15. 3500-3899 Mills
16. 2400-2999 Leon
17. 4400-4499 Cass
18. 4100-4299 Mills
19. Florence
20. 3500-3899 Mills

21. 4900-4999 Cass
22. 1600-1899 Leon
23. Dalewood
24. Center
25. 4600-4799 Cass
26. 1600-1899 Leon
27. 2200-2899 Mills
28. 4900-4999 Cass
29. 4100-4299 Mills
30. 1600-1899 Leon
31. Dalewood
32. Turner
33. Center
34. Daisey
35. 4000-4299 Cass
36. 3500-3899 Mills
37. Carmen
38. 2900-3499 Mills
39. 1900-2299 Leon
40. 4900-4999 Cass
41. Mooney
42. 4100-4299 Mills
43. Palm
44. Nevada
45. 3400-3999 Cass
46. Carmen
47. Noya
48. 1600-1899 Leon
49. 3400-3999 Cass
50. Dalewood
51. Carmen
52. 4400-4599 Mills
53. 3200-3799 Leon
54. 2200-2899 Mills

55. 3100-3199 Leon
56. Nevada
57. 2400-2999 Leon
58. 3400-3999 Cass
59. Mooney
60. Florence
61. 4100-4299 Mills
62. 3100-3199 Leon
63. 4600-4799 Cass
64. 2900-3499 Mills
65. Center
66. 2400-2999 Leon
67. Mooney
68. 4900-4999 Cass
69. 4400-4599 Mills
70. Noya
71. Palm
72. 2400-2999 Leon
73. 4400-4499 Cass
74. 4100-4299 Mills
75. 3200-3799 Leon
76. 3500-3899 Mills
77. 4000-4299 Cass
78. Dalewood
79. 4400-4599 Mills
80. Daisey
81. 4000-4299 Cass
82. Mooney
83. 2400-2999 Leon
84. 2900-3499 Mills
85. Noya
86. 4900-4999 Cass
87. Carmen
88. 2900-3499 Mills

PRACTICE II

DIRECTIONS: This is another practice test. Again, the time limit is THREE MINUTES. This time you must NOT look back at the boxes while answering the questions. This practice test will NOT be scored.

1. 3400-3999 Cass
2. 1600-1899 Leon
3. Nevada
4. Daisey
5. 2200-2899 Mills
6. 4400-4599 Mills
7. 4600-4799 Cass
8. Mooney
9. 4400-4499 Cass
10. Turner
11. Florence
12. 2400-2999 Leon
13. 4900-4999 Cass
14. 3200-3799 Leon
15. Carmen
16. 3500-3899 Mills
17. 4000-4299 Cass
18. Center
19. 1900-2299 Leon
20. 3100-3199 Leon
21. Palm
22. Dalewood
23. 2900-3499 Mills
24. 4100-4299 Mills
25. Turner
26. Palm
27. 4000-4299 Cass
28. 3500-3899 Mills
29. 1600-1899 Leon
30. Florence
31. Daisey
32. Nevada
33. 1900-2299 Leon
34. 4600-4799 Cass
35. 4100-4299 Mills
36. 3200-3799 Leon
37. 4000-4299 Cass
38. Mooney
39. Noya
40. Center
41. 2400-2999 Leon
42. 3400-3999 Cass
43. 2900-3499 Mills
44. 4400-4499 Cass
45. 3500-3899 Mills
46. Carmen
47. Center
48. Turner
49. 4900-4999 Cass
50. 2200-2899 Mills
51. Mooney
52. 4100-4299 Mills
53. 4600-4799 Cass
54. Noya
55. Florence
56. 3500-3899 Mills
57. 1900-2299 Leon
58. 3100-3199 Leon
59. 2400-2999 Leon
60. 4000-4299 Cass
61. 2900-3499 Mills
62. 3200-3799 Leon
63. Daisey
64. Turner
65. Dalewood
66. Palm
67. 4900-4999 Cass
68. 4100-4299 Mills
69. 3400-3999 Cass
70. 3500-3899 Mills
71. 4600-4799 Cass
72. 1900-2299 Leon
73. 4000-4299 Cass
74. 2200-2899 Mills
75. Nevada
76. Palm
77. Dalewood
78. 2400-2999 Leon
79. 4000-4299 Cass
80. 4400-4599 Mills
81. Noya
82. Carmen
83. 3100-3199 Leon
84. 3200-3799 Leon
85. 4100-4299 Mills
86. 2900-3499 Mills
87. Daisey
88. 4900-4999 Cass

PRACTICE III

DIRECTIONS: The names and addresses are repeated for you in the boxes below. Each name and each number span is in the same box in which you found it in the original set. You will now be allowed FIVE MINUTES to study the locations again. Do your best to memorize the letter of the box in which each item is to be found. This is your last chance to see the boxes.

A	B	C	D	E
2200-2899 Mills	4100-4299 Mills	4400-4599 Mills	3500-3899 Mills	2900-3499 Mills
Carmen	Center	Noya	Turner	Dalewood
4900-4999 Cass	4000-4299 Cass	3400-3999 Cass	4600-4799 Cass	4400-4499 Cass
Nevada	Florence	Daisey	Palm	Mooney
2400-2999 Leon	3200-3799 Leon	1900-2299 Leon	3100-3199 Leon	1600-1899 Leon

DIRECTIONS: This is your last practice test. Mark the location of each of the 88 items on your answer sheet. You will have FIVE MINUTES to answer these questions. Do NOT look back at the boxes. This practice test will not be scored.

1. 4400-4499 Cass
2. 1900-2299 Leon
3. 2200-2899 Mills
4. Center
5. Palm
6. 2400-2999 Leon
7. 4000-4299 Cass
8. 4400-4599 Mills
9. Turner
10. Mooney
11. 4900-4999 Cass
12. 4100-4299 Mills
13. 3200-3799 Leon
14. Florence
15. 3100-3199 Leon
16. Noya
17. Carmen
18. 4400-4499 Cass
19. 3500-3899 Mills
20. 2200-2899 Mills
21. 4100-4299 Mills
22. Daisey
23. Dalewood
24. Nevada
25. 3200-3799 Leon
26. 4900-4999 Cass
27. 2400-2999 Leon
28. 4400-4499 Cass
29. 4400-4599 Mills
30. Center
31. 4100-4299 Mills
32. 4600-4799 Cass
33. Carmen
34. 3200-3799 Leon
35. Mooney
36. 4900-4999 Cass
37. 1900-2299 Leon
38. 2900-3499 Mills
39. 1600-1899 Leon
40. 4400-4499 Cass
41. Noya
42. Daisey
43. 2200-2899 Mills
44. 3500-3899 Mills
45. Nevada
46. 3400-3999 Cass

47. 4000-4299 Cass
48. Center
49. Florence
50. Palm
51. 4400-4599 Mills
52. 3100-3199 Leon
53. 2400-2999 Leon
54. 4000-4299 Cass
55. 4400-4599 Mills
56. Dalewood
57. Turner
58. 3400-3999 Cass
59. 1600-1899 Leon
60. 4600-4799 Cass
61. 4100-4299 Mills
62. 2200-2899 Mills
63. Florence
64. Noya
65. 3100-3199 Leon
66. 4900-4999 Cass
67. 1600-1899 Leon
68. 2900-3499 Mills
69. Palm
70. Dalewood
71. Nevada
72. 4400-4499 Cass
73. 1900-2299 Leon
74. 4400-4599 Mills
75. Center
76. 4600-4799 Cass
77. 3200-3799 Leon
78. 4000-4299 Cass
79. 3500-3899 Mills
80. Daisey
81. Florence
82. Mooney
83. 3100-3199 Leon
84. Palm
85. 3400-3999 Cass
86. 4400-4599 Mills
87. 4100-4299 Mills
88. Carmen

MEMORY FOR ADDRESSES TEST

TIME: 5 Minutes. 88 Questions.

DIRECTIONS: Mark your answers on the answer sheet in the section headed "MEMORY FOR ADDRESSES TEST." This test will be scored. You are NOT permitted to look at the boxes. Work from memory, as quickly and as accurately as you can. Correct answers are on page 88.

1. 4900-4999 Cass
2. 1600-1899 Leon
3. Daisey
4. 4400-4599 Mills
5. Palm
6. Dalewood
7. 2900-3499 Mills
8. 3200-3799 Leon
9. 4000-4299 Cass
10. Nevada
11. 4400-4499 Cass
12. 3100-3199 Leon
13. 3500-3899 Mills
14. Carmen
15. Noya
16. 2200-2899 Mills
17. 1900-2299 Leon
18. Mooney
19. 4100-4299 Mills
20. 3400-3999 Cass
21. 4600-4799 Cass
22. Turner
23. Center
24. 2400-2999 Leon
25. Florence
26. 4100-4299 Mills
27. 4400-4499 Cass
28. 1900-2299 Leon
29. Palm
30. 1600-1899 Leon
31. 3500-3899 Mills
32. 4600-4799 Cass
33. Turner
34. 4400-4599 Mills
35. 2900-3499 Mills
36. Carmen
37. Center
38. 4900-4999 Cass

39. 3200-3799 Leon
40. 3100-3199 Leon
41. Nevada
42. Daisey
43. Dalewood
44. 2200-2899 Mills
45. 4400-4499 Cass
46. Noya
47. Turner
48. 4000-4299 Cass
49. 2900-3499 Mills
50. 3100-3199 Leon
51. Nevada
52. 4000-4299 Cass
53. 4400-4599 Mills
54. 2400-2999 Leon
55. Daisey
56. 2900-3499 Mills
57. 1900-2299 Leon
58. Center
59. Mooney
60. 4400-4499 Cass
61. 2200-2899 Mills
62. Noya
63. 4600-4799 Cass
64. 3200-3799 Leon
65. 3500-3899 Mills
66. 4100-4299 Mills
67. Dalewood
68. Florence
69. 4600-4799 Cass
70. 3500-3899 Mills
71. 2400-2999 Leon
72. Daisey
73. 3400-3999 Cass
74. 3100-3199 Leon
75. 4400-4499 Cass
76. 4100-4299 Mills

77. Center
78. Nevada
79. 2900-3499 Mills
80. 1900-2299 Leon
81. 4900-4999 Cass
82. Carmen

83. Mooney
84. 2900-3499 Mills
85. 4000-4299 Cass
86. 1600-1899 Leon
87. 3200-3799 Leon
88. Palm

END OF EXAM

ADDRESS CHECKING ERROR ANALYSIS CHART

Type of Difference	Question Numbers	Number of Questions You Missed
Difference in NUMBERS	15, 32, 33, 34, 44, 47, 53, 54, 56, 68, 77, 78, 80, 89, 90	
Difference in ABBREVIATIONS	3, 9, 10, 11, 13, 14, 18, 42, 45, 48, 55, 57, 58, 62, 69, 75, 81, 91, 93, 94	
Difference in NAMES	5, 6, 7, 16, 20, 22, 23, 25, 29, 35, 37, 39, 49, 51, 60, 61, 65, 67, 70, 71, 74, 79, 86, 87, 88	
No Difference	1, 2, 4, 8, 12, 17, 19, 21, 24, 26, 27, 28, 30, 31, 36, 38, 40, 41, 43, 46, 50, 52, 59, 63, 64, 66, 72, 73, 76, 82, 83, 84, 85, 92, 95	

SELF-EVALUATION CHART

Test	Excellent	Good	Average	Fair	Poor
Address Checking	80-95	65-79	50-64	35-49	1-34
Memory for Addresses	75-88	60-74	45-59	30-44	1-29

CORRECT ANSWERS FOR FIRST MODEL EXAM

ADDRESS CHECKING TEST

1. A	13. D	25. D	37. D	49. D	61. D	73. A	85. A
2. A	14. D	26. A	38. A	50. A	62. D	74. D	86. D
3. D	15. D	27. A	39. D	51. D	63. A	75. D	87. D
4. A	16. D	28. A	40. A	52. A	64. A	76. A	88. D
5. D	17. A	29. D	41. A	53. D	65. D	77. D	89. D
6. D	18. D	30. A	42. D	54. D	66. A	78. D	90. D
7. D	19. A	31. A	43. A	55. D	67. D	79. D	91. D
8. A	20. D	32. D	44. D	56. D	68. D	80. D	92. A
9. D	21. A	33. D	45. D	57. D	69. D	81. D	93. D
10. D	22. D	34. D	46. A	58. D	70. D	82. A	94. D
11. D	23. D	35. D	47. D	59. A	71. D	83. A	95. A
12. A	24. A	36. A	48. D	60. D	72. A	84. A	

MEMORY FOR ADDRESSES—PRACTICE I

1. C	12. A	23. E	34. C	45. C	56. A	67. E	78. E
2. E	13. E	24. B	35. B	46. A	57. A	68. A	79. C
3. B	14. C	25. D	36. D	47. C	58. C	69. C	80. C
4. D	15. D	26. E	37. A	48. E	59. E	70. C	81. B
5. D	16. A	27. A	38. E	49. C	60. B	71. D	82. E
6. E	17. E	28. A	39. C	50. E	61. B	72. A	83. A
7. D	18. B	29. B	40. A	51. A	62. D	73. E	84. E
8. A	19. B	30. E	41. E	52. C	63. D	74. B	85. C
9. E	20. D	31. E	42. B	53. B	64. E	75. B	86. A
10. C	21. A	32. D	43. D	54. A	65. B	76. D	87. A
11. E	22. E	33. B	44. A	55. D	66. A	77. B	88. E

MEMORY FOR ADDRESSES—PRACTICE II

1. C	12. A	23. E	34. D	45. D	56. D	67. A	78. A
2. E	13. A	24. B	35. B	46. A	57. C	68. B	79. B
3. A	14. B	25. D	36. B	47. B	58. D	69. C	80. C
4. C	15. A	26. D	37. B	48. D	59. A	70. D	81. C
5. A	16. D	27. B	38. E	49. A	60. B	71. D	82. A
6. C	17. B	28. D	39. C	50. A	61. E	72. C	83. D
7. D	18. B	29. E	40. B	51. E	62. B	73. B	84. B
8. E	19. C	30. B	41. A	52. B	63. C	74. A	85. B
9. E	20. D	31. C	42. C	53. D	64. D	75. A	86. E
10. D	21. D	32. A	43. E	54. C	65. E	76. D	87. C
11. B	22. E	33. C	44. E	55. B	66. D	77. E	88. A

MEMORY FOR ADDRESSES—PRACTICE III

1. E	12. B	23. E	34. B	45. A	56. E	67. E	78. B
2. C	13. B	24. A	35. E	46. C	57. D	68. E	79. D
3. A	14. B	25. B	36. A	47. B	58. C	69. D	80. C
4. B	15. D	26. A	37. C	48. B	59. E	70. E	81. B
5. D	16. C	27. A	38. E	49. B	60. D	71. A	82. E
6. A	17. A	28. E	39. E	50. D	61. B	72. E	83. D
7. B	18. E	29. C	40. E	51. C	62. A	73. C	84. D
8. C	19. D	30. B	41. C	52. D	63. B	74. C	85. C
9. D	20. A	31. B	42. C	53. A	64. C	75. B	86. C
10. E	21. B	32. D	43. A	54. B	65. D	76. D	87. B
11. A	22. C	33. A	44. D	55. C	66. A	77. B	88. A

MEMORY FOR ADDRESSES TEST

1. A	12. D	23. B	34. C	45. E	56. E	67. E	78. A
2. E	13. D	24. A	35. E	46. C	57. C	68. B	79. E
3. C	14. A	25. B	36. A	47. D	58. B	69. D	80. C
4. C	15. C	26. B	37. B	48. B	59. E	70. D	81. A
5. D	16. A	27. E	38. A	49. E	60. E	71. A	82. A
6. E	17. C	28. C	39. B	50. D	61. A	72. C	83. E
7. E	18. E	29. D	40. D	51. A	62. C	73. C	84. E
8. B	19. B	30. E	41. A	52. B	63. D	74. D	85. B
9. B	20. C	31. D	42. C	53. C	64. B	75. E	86. E
10. A	21. D	32. D	43. E	54. A	65. D	76. B	87. B
11. E	22. D	33. D	44. A	55. C	66. B	77. B	88. D

ANSWER SHEET FOR SECOND MODEL EXAM

ADDRESS CHECKING

1 Ⓐ Ⓓ	20 Ⓐ Ⓓ	39 Ⓐ Ⓓ	58 Ⓐ Ⓓ	77 Ⓐ Ⓓ
2 Ⓐ Ⓓ	21 Ⓐ Ⓓ	40 Ⓐ Ⓓ	59 Ⓐ Ⓓ	78 Ⓐ Ⓓ
3 Ⓐ Ⓓ	22 Ⓐ Ⓓ	41 Ⓐ Ⓓ	60 Ⓐ Ⓓ	79 Ⓐ Ⓓ
4 Ⓐ Ⓓ	23 Ⓐ Ⓓ	42 Ⓐ Ⓓ	61 Ⓐ Ⓓ	80 Ⓐ Ⓓ
5 Ⓐ Ⓓ	24 Ⓐ Ⓓ	43 Ⓐ Ⓓ	62 Ⓐ Ⓓ	81 Ⓐ Ⓓ
6 Ⓐ Ⓓ	25 Ⓐ Ⓓ	44 Ⓐ Ⓓ	63 Ⓐ Ⓓ	82 Ⓐ Ⓓ
7 Ⓐ Ⓓ	26 Ⓐ Ⓓ	45 Ⓐ Ⓓ	64 Ⓐ Ⓓ	83 Ⓐ Ⓓ
8 Ⓐ Ⓓ	27 Ⓐ Ⓓ	46 Ⓐ Ⓓ	65 Ⓐ Ⓓ	84 Ⓐ Ⓓ
9 Ⓐ Ⓓ	28 Ⓐ Ⓓ	47 Ⓐ Ⓓ	66 Ⓐ Ⓓ	85 Ⓐ Ⓓ
10 Ⓐ Ⓓ	29 Ⓐ Ⓓ	48 Ⓐ Ⓒ	67 Ⓐ Ⓓ	86 Ⓐ Ⓓ
11 Ⓐ Ⓓ	30 Ⓐ Ⓓ	49 Ⓐ Ⓓ	68 Ⓐ Ⓓ	87 Ⓐ Ⓓ
12 Ⓐ Ⓓ	31 Ⓐ Ⓓ	50 Ⓐ Ⓓ	69 Ⓐ Ⓓ	88 Ⓐ Ⓓ
13 Ⓐ Ⓓ	32 Ⓐ Ⓓ	51 Ⓐ Ⓓ	70 Ⓐ Ⓓ	89 Ⓐ Ⓓ
14 Ⓐ Ⓓ	33 Ⓐ Ⓓ	52 Ⓐ Ⓓ	71 Ⓐ Ⓓ	90 Ⓐ Ⓓ
15 Ⓐ Ⓓ	34 Ⓐ Ⓓ	53 Ⓐ Ⓓ	72 Ⓐ Ⓓ	91 Ⓐ Ⓓ
16 Ⓐ Ⓓ	35 Ⓐ Ⓓ	54 Ⓐ Ⓓ	73 Ⓐ Ⓓ	92 Ⓐ Ⓓ
17 Ⓐ Ⓓ	36 Ⓐ Ⓓ	55 Ⓐ Ⓓ	74 Ⓐ Ⓓ	93 Ⓐ Ⓓ
18 Ⓐ Ⓓ	37 Ⓐ Ⓓ	56 Ⓐ Ⓓ	75 Ⓐ Ⓓ	94 Ⓐ Ⓓ
19 Ⓐ Ⓓ	38 Ⓐ Ⓓ	57 Ⓐ Ⓓ	76 Ⓐ Ⓓ	95 Ⓐ Ⓓ

TEAR HERE

MEMORY FOR ADDRESSES

PRACTICE I

1 Ⓐ Ⓑ Ⓒ Ⓓ Ⓔ	23 Ⓐ Ⓑ Ⓒ Ⓓ Ⓔ	45 Ⓐ Ⓑ Ⓒ Ⓓ Ⓔ	67 Ⓐ Ⓑ Ⓒ Ⓓ Ⓔ
2 Ⓐ Ⓑ Ⓒ Ⓓ Ⓔ	24 Ⓐ Ⓑ Ⓒ Ⓓ Ⓔ	46 Ⓐ Ⓑ Ⓒ Ⓓ Ⓔ	68 Ⓐ Ⓑ Ⓒ Ⓓ Ⓔ
3 Ⓐ Ⓑ Ⓒ Ⓓ Ⓔ	25 Ⓐ Ⓑ Ⓒ Ⓓ Ⓔ	47 Ⓐ Ⓑ Ⓒ Ⓓ Ⓔ	69 Ⓐ Ⓑ Ⓒ Ⓓ Ⓔ
4 Ⓐ Ⓑ Ⓒ Ⓓ Ⓔ	26 Ⓐ Ⓑ Ⓒ Ⓓ Ⓔ	48 Ⓐ Ⓑ Ⓒ Ⓓ Ⓔ	70 Ⓐ Ⓑ Ⓒ Ⓓ Ⓔ
5 Ⓐ Ⓑ Ⓒ Ⓓ Ⓔ	27 Ⓐ Ⓑ Ⓒ Ⓓ Ⓔ	49 Ⓐ Ⓑ Ⓒ Ⓓ Ⓔ	71 Ⓐ Ⓑ Ⓒ Ⓓ Ⓔ
6 Ⓐ Ⓑ Ⓒ Ⓓ Ⓔ	28 Ⓐ Ⓑ Ⓒ Ⓓ Ⓔ	50 Ⓐ Ⓑ Ⓒ Ⓓ Ⓔ	72 Ⓐ Ⓑ Ⓒ Ⓓ Ⓔ
7 Ⓐ Ⓑ Ⓒ Ⓓ Ⓔ	29 Ⓐ Ⓑ Ⓒ Ⓓ Ⓔ	51 Ⓐ Ⓑ Ⓒ Ⓓ Ⓔ	73 Ⓐ Ⓑ Ⓒ Ⓓ Ⓔ
8 Ⓐ Ⓑ Ⓒ Ⓓ Ⓔ	30 Ⓐ Ⓑ Ⓒ Ⓓ Ⓔ	52 Ⓐ Ⓑ Ⓒ Ⓓ Ⓔ	74 Ⓐ Ⓑ Ⓒ Ⓓ Ⓔ
9 Ⓐ Ⓑ Ⓒ Ⓓ Ⓔ	31 Ⓐ Ⓑ Ⓒ Ⓓ Ⓔ	53 Ⓐ Ⓑ Ⓒ Ⓓ Ⓔ	75 Ⓐ Ⓑ Ⓒ Ⓓ Ⓔ
10 Ⓐ Ⓑ Ⓒ Ⓓ Ⓔ	32 Ⓐ Ⓑ Ⓒ Ⓓ Ⓔ	54 Ⓐ Ⓑ Ⓒ Ⓓ Ⓔ	76 Ⓐ Ⓑ Ⓒ Ⓓ Ⓔ
11 Ⓐ Ⓑ Ⓒ Ⓓ Ⓔ	33 Ⓐ Ⓑ Ⓒ Ⓓ Ⓔ	55 Ⓐ Ⓑ Ⓒ Ⓓ Ⓔ	77 Ⓐ Ⓑ Ⓒ Ⓓ Ⓔ
12 Ⓐ Ⓑ Ⓒ Ⓓ Ⓔ	34 Ⓐ Ⓑ Ⓒ Ⓓ Ⓔ	56 Ⓐ Ⓑ Ⓒ Ⓓ Ⓔ	78 Ⓐ Ⓑ Ⓒ Ⓓ Ⓔ
13 Ⓐ Ⓑ Ⓒ Ⓓ Ⓔ	35 Ⓐ Ⓑ Ⓒ Ⓓ Ⓔ	57 Ⓐ Ⓑ Ⓒ Ⓓ Ⓔ	79 Ⓐ Ⓑ Ⓒ Ⓓ Ⓔ
14 Ⓐ Ⓑ Ⓒ Ⓓ Ⓔ	36 Ⓐ Ⓑ Ⓒ Ⓓ Ⓔ	58 Ⓐ Ⓑ Ⓒ Ⓓ Ⓔ	80 Ⓐ Ⓑ Ⓒ Ⓓ Ⓔ
15 Ⓐ Ⓑ Ⓒ Ⓓ Ⓔ	37 Ⓐ Ⓑ Ⓒ Ⓓ Ⓔ	59 Ⓐ Ⓑ Ⓒ Ⓓ Ⓔ	81 Ⓐ Ⓑ Ⓒ Ⓓ Ⓔ
16 Ⓐ Ⓑ Ⓒ Ⓓ Ⓔ	38 Ⓐ Ⓑ Ⓒ Ⓓ Ⓔ	60 Ⓐ Ⓑ Ⓒ Ⓓ Ⓔ	82 Ⓐ Ⓑ Ⓒ Ⓓ Ⓔ
17 Ⓐ Ⓑ Ⓒ Ⓓ Ⓔ	39 Ⓐ Ⓑ Ⓒ Ⓓ Ⓔ	61 Ⓐ Ⓑ Ⓒ Ⓓ Ⓔ	83 Ⓐ Ⓑ Ⓒ Ⓓ Ⓔ
18 Ⓐ Ⓑ Ⓒ Ⓓ Ⓔ	40 Ⓐ Ⓑ Ⓒ Ⓓ Ⓔ	62 Ⓐ Ⓑ Ⓒ Ⓓ Ⓔ	84 Ⓐ Ⓑ Ⓒ Ⓓ Ⓔ
19 Ⓐ Ⓑ Ⓒ Ⓓ Ⓔ	41 Ⓐ Ⓑ Ⓒ Ⓓ Ⓔ	63 Ⓐ Ⓑ Ⓒ Ⓓ Ⓔ	85 Ⓐ Ⓑ Ⓒ Ⓓ Ⓔ
20 Ⓐ Ⓑ Ⓒ Ⓓ Ⓔ	42 Ⓐ Ⓑ Ⓒ Ⓓ Ⓔ	64 Ⓐ Ⓑ Ⓒ Ⓓ Ⓔ	86 Ⓐ Ⓑ Ⓒ Ⓓ Ⓔ
21 Ⓐ Ⓑ Ⓒ Ⓓ Ⓔ	43 Ⓐ Ⓑ Ⓒ Ⓓ Ⓔ	65 Ⓐ Ⓑ Ⓒ Ⓓ Ⓔ	87 Ⓐ Ⓑ Ⓒ Ⓓ Ⓔ
22 Ⓐ Ⓑ Ⓒ Ⓓ Ⓔ	44 Ⓐ Ⓑ Ⓒ Ⓓ Ⓔ	66 Ⓐ Ⓑ Ⓒ Ⓓ Ⓔ	88 Ⓐ Ⓑ Ⓒ Ⓓ Ⓔ

PRACTICE II

1 Ⓐ Ⓑ Ⓒ Ⓓ Ⓔ	23 Ⓐ Ⓑ Ⓒ Ⓓ Ⓔ	45 Ⓐ Ⓑ Ⓒ Ⓓ Ⓔ	67 Ⓐ Ⓑ Ⓒ Ⓓ Ⓔ
2 Ⓐ Ⓑ Ⓒ Ⓓ Ⓔ	24 Ⓐ Ⓑ Ⓒ Ⓓ Ⓔ	46 Ⓐ Ⓑ Ⓒ Ⓓ Ⓔ	68 Ⓐ Ⓑ Ⓒ Ⓓ Ⓔ
3 Ⓐ Ⓑ Ⓒ Ⓓ Ⓔ	25 Ⓐ Ⓑ Ⓒ Ⓓ Ⓔ	47 Ⓐ Ⓑ Ⓒ Ⓓ Ⓔ	69 Ⓐ Ⓑ Ⓒ Ⓓ Ⓔ
4 Ⓐ Ⓑ Ⓒ Ⓓ Ⓔ	26 Ⓐ Ⓑ Ⓒ Ⓓ Ⓔ	48 Ⓐ Ⓑ Ⓒ Ⓓ Ⓔ	70 Ⓐ Ⓑ Ⓒ Ⓓ Ⓔ
5 Ⓐ Ⓑ Ⓒ Ⓓ Ⓔ	27 Ⓐ Ⓑ Ⓒ Ⓓ Ⓔ	49 Ⓐ Ⓑ Ⓒ Ⓓ Ⓔ	71 Ⓐ Ⓑ Ⓒ Ⓓ Ⓔ
6 Ⓐ Ⓑ Ⓒ Ⓓ Ⓔ	28 Ⓐ Ⓑ Ⓒ Ⓓ Ⓔ	50 Ⓐ Ⓑ Ⓒ Ⓓ Ⓔ	72 Ⓐ Ⓑ Ⓒ Ⓓ Ⓔ
7 Ⓐ Ⓑ Ⓒ Ⓓ Ⓔ	29 Ⓐ Ⓑ Ⓒ Ⓓ Ⓔ	51 Ⓐ Ⓑ Ⓒ Ⓓ Ⓔ	73 Ⓐ Ⓑ Ⓒ Ⓓ Ⓔ
8 Ⓐ Ⓑ Ⓒ Ⓓ Ⓔ	30 Ⓐ Ⓑ Ⓒ Ⓓ Ⓔ	52 Ⓐ Ⓑ Ⓒ Ⓓ Ⓔ	74 Ⓐ Ⓑ Ⓒ Ⓓ Ⓔ
9 Ⓐ Ⓑ Ⓒ Ⓓ Ⓔ	31 Ⓐ Ⓑ Ⓒ Ⓓ Ⓔ	53 Ⓐ Ⓑ Ⓒ Ⓓ Ⓔ	75 Ⓐ Ⓑ Ⓒ Ⓓ Ⓔ
10 Ⓐ Ⓑ Ⓒ Ⓓ Ⓔ	32 Ⓐ Ⓑ Ⓒ Ⓓ Ⓔ	54 Ⓐ Ⓑ Ⓒ Ⓓ Ⓔ	76 Ⓐ Ⓑ Ⓒ Ⓓ Ⓔ
11 Ⓐ Ⓑ Ⓒ Ⓓ Ⓔ	33 Ⓐ Ⓑ Ⓒ Ⓓ Ⓔ	55 Ⓐ Ⓑ Ⓒ Ⓓ Ⓔ	77 Ⓐ Ⓑ Ⓒ Ⓓ Ⓔ
12 Ⓐ Ⓑ Ⓒ Ⓓ Ⓔ	34 Ⓐ Ⓑ Ⓒ Ⓓ Ⓔ	56 Ⓐ Ⓑ Ⓒ Ⓓ Ⓔ	78 Ⓐ Ⓑ Ⓒ Ⓓ Ⓔ
13 Ⓐ Ⓑ Ⓒ Ⓓ Ⓔ	35 Ⓐ Ⓑ Ⓒ Ⓓ Ⓔ	57 Ⓐ Ⓑ Ⓒ Ⓓ Ⓔ	79 Ⓐ Ⓑ Ⓒ Ⓓ Ⓔ
14 Ⓐ Ⓑ Ⓒ Ⓓ Ⓔ	36 Ⓐ Ⓑ Ⓒ Ⓓ Ⓔ	58 Ⓐ Ⓑ Ⓒ Ⓓ Ⓔ	80 Ⓐ Ⓑ Ⓒ Ⓓ Ⓔ
15 Ⓐ Ⓑ Ⓒ Ⓓ Ⓔ	37 Ⓐ Ⓑ Ⓒ Ⓓ Ⓔ	59 Ⓐ Ⓑ Ⓒ Ⓓ Ⓔ	81 Ⓐ Ⓑ Ⓒ Ⓓ Ⓔ
16 Ⓐ Ⓑ Ⓒ Ⓓ Ⓔ	38 Ⓐ Ⓑ Ⓒ Ⓓ Ⓔ	60 Ⓐ Ⓑ Ⓒ Ⓓ Ⓔ	82 Ⓐ Ⓑ Ⓒ Ⓓ Ⓔ
17 Ⓐ Ⓑ Ⓒ Ⓓ Ⓔ	39 Ⓐ Ⓑ Ⓒ Ⓓ Ⓔ	61 Ⓐ Ⓑ Ⓒ Ⓓ Ⓔ	83 Ⓐ Ⓑ Ⓒ Ⓓ Ⓔ
18 Ⓐ Ⓑ Ⓒ Ⓓ Ⓔ	40 Ⓐ Ⓑ Ⓒ Ⓓ Ⓔ	62 Ⓐ Ⓑ Ⓒ Ⓓ Ⓔ	84 Ⓐ Ⓑ Ⓒ Ⓓ Ⓔ
19 Ⓐ Ⓑ Ⓒ Ⓓ Ⓔ	41 Ⓐ Ⓑ Ⓒ Ⓓ Ⓔ	63 Ⓐ Ⓑ Ⓒ Ⓓ Ⓕ	85 Ⓐ Ⓑ Ⓒ Ⓓ Ⓔ
20 Ⓐ Ⓑ Ⓒ Ⓓ Ⓔ	42 Ⓐ Ⓑ Ⓒ Ⓓ Ⓔ	64 Ⓐ Ⓑ Ⓒ Ⓓ Ⓔ	86 Ⓐ Ⓑ Ⓒ Ⓓ Ⓔ
21 Ⓐ Ⓑ Ⓒ Ⓓ Ⓔ	43 Ⓐ Ⓑ Ⓒ Ⓓ Ⓔ	65 Ⓐ Ⓑ Ⓒ Ⓓ Ⓔ	87 Ⓐ Ⓑ Ⓒ Ⓓ Ⓔ
22 Ⓐ Ⓑ Ⓒ Ⓓ Ⓔ	44 Ⓐ Ⓑ Ⓒ Ⓓ Ⓔ	66 Ⓐ Ⓑ Ⓒ Ⓓ Ⓔ	88 Ⓐ Ⓑ Ⓒ Ⓓ Ⓔ

PRACTICE III

1 Ⓐ Ⓑ Ⓒ Ⓓ Ⓔ	23 Ⓐ Ⓑ Ⓒ Ⓓ Ⓔ	45 Ⓐ Ⓑ Ⓒ Ⓓ Ⓔ	67 Ⓐ Ⓑ Ⓒ Ⓓ Ⓔ
2 Ⓐ Ⓑ Ⓒ Ⓓ Ⓔ	24 Ⓐ Ⓑ Ⓒ Ⓓ Ⓔ	46 Ⓐ Ⓑ Ⓒ Ⓓ Ⓔ	68 Ⓐ Ⓑ Ⓒ Ⓓ Ⓔ
3 Ⓐ Ⓑ Ⓒ Ⓓ Ⓔ	25 Ⓐ Ⓑ Ⓒ Ⓓ Ⓔ	47 Ⓐ Ⓑ Ⓒ Ⓓ Ⓔ	69 Ⓐ Ⓑ Ⓒ Ⓓ Ⓔ
4 Ⓐ Ⓑ Ⓒ Ⓓ Ⓔ	26 Ⓐ Ⓑ Ⓒ Ⓓ Ⓔ	48 Ⓐ Ⓑ Ⓒ Ⓓ Ⓔ	70 Ⓐ Ⓑ Ⓒ Ⓓ Ⓔ
5 Ⓐ Ⓑ Ⓒ Ⓓ Ⓔ	27 Ⓐ Ⓑ Ⓒ Ⓓ Ⓔ	49 Ⓐ Ⓑ Ⓒ Ⓓ Ⓔ	71 Ⓐ Ⓑ Ⓒ Ⓓ Ⓔ
6 Ⓐ Ⓑ Ⓒ Ⓓ Ⓔ	28 Ⓐ Ⓑ Ⓒ Ⓓ Ⓔ	50 Ⓐ Ⓑ Ⓒ Ⓓ Ⓔ	72 Ⓐ Ⓑ Ⓒ Ⓓ Ⓔ
7 Ⓐ Ⓑ Ⓒ Ⓓ Ⓔ	29 Ⓐ Ⓑ Ⓒ Ⓓ Ⓔ	51 Ⓐ Ⓑ Ⓒ Ⓓ Ⓔ	73 Ⓐ Ⓑ Ⓒ Ⓓ Ⓔ
8 Ⓐ Ⓑ Ⓒ Ⓓ Ⓔ	30 Ⓐ Ⓑ Ⓒ Ⓓ Ⓔ	52 Ⓐ Ⓑ Ⓒ Ⓓ Ⓔ	74 Ⓐ Ⓑ Ⓒ Ⓓ Ⓔ
9 Ⓐ Ⓑ Ⓒ Ⓓ Ⓔ	31 Ⓐ Ⓑ Ⓒ Ⓓ Ⓔ	53 Ⓐ Ⓑ Ⓒ Ⓓ Ⓔ	75 Ⓐ Ⓑ Ⓒ Ⓓ Ⓔ
10 Ⓐ Ⓑ Ⓒ Ⓓ Ⓔ	32 Ⓐ Ⓑ Ⓒ Ⓓ Ⓔ	54 Ⓐ Ⓑ Ⓒ Ⓓ Ⓔ	76 Ⓐ Ⓑ Ⓒ Ⓓ Ⓔ
11 Ⓐ Ⓑ Ⓒ Ⓓ Ⓔ	33 Ⓐ Ⓑ Ⓒ Ⓓ Ⓔ	55 Ⓐ Ⓑ Ⓒ Ⓓ Ⓔ	77 Ⓐ Ⓑ Ⓒ Ⓓ Ⓔ
12 Ⓐ Ⓑ Ⓒ Ⓓ Ⓔ	34 Ⓐ Ⓑ Ⓒ Ⓓ Ⓔ	56 Ⓐ Ⓑ Ⓒ Ⓓ Ⓔ	78 Ⓐ Ⓑ Ⓒ Ⓓ Ⓔ
13 Ⓐ Ⓑ Ⓒ Ⓓ Ⓔ	35 Ⓐ Ⓑ Ⓒ Ⓓ Ⓔ	57 Ⓐ Ⓑ Ⓒ Ⓓ Ⓔ	79 Ⓐ Ⓑ Ⓒ Ⓓ Ⓔ
14 Ⓐ Ⓑ Ⓒ Ⓓ Ⓔ	36 Ⓐ Ⓑ Ⓒ Ⓓ Ⓔ	58 Ⓐ Ⓑ Ⓒ Ⓓ Ⓔ	80 Ⓐ Ⓑ Ⓒ Ⓓ Ⓔ
15 Ⓐ Ⓑ Ⓒ Ⓓ Ⓔ	37 Ⓐ Ⓑ Ⓒ Ⓓ Ⓔ	59 Ⓐ Ⓑ Ⓒ Ⓓ Ⓔ	81 Ⓐ Ⓑ Ⓒ Ⓓ Ⓔ
16 Ⓐ Ⓑ Ⓒ Ⓓ Ⓔ	38 Ⓐ Ⓑ Ⓒ Ⓓ Ⓔ	60 Ⓐ Ⓑ Ⓒ Ⓓ Ⓔ	82 Ⓐ Ⓑ Ⓒ Ⓓ Ⓔ
17 Ⓐ Ⓑ Ⓒ Ⓓ Ⓔ	39 Ⓐ Ⓑ Ⓒ Ⓓ Ⓔ	61 Ⓐ Ⓑ Ⓒ Ⓓ Ⓔ	83 Ⓐ Ⓑ Ⓒ Ⓓ Ⓔ
18 Ⓐ Ⓑ Ⓒ Ⓓ Ⓔ	40 Ⓐ Ⓑ Ⓒ Ⓓ Ⓔ	62 Ⓐ Ⓑ Ⓒ Ⓓ Ⓔ	84 Ⓐ Ⓑ Ⓒ Ⓓ Ⓔ
19 Ⓐ Ⓑ Ⓒ Ⓓ Ⓔ	41 Ⓐ Ⓑ Ⓒ Ⓓ Ⓔ	63 Ⓐ Ⓑ Ⓒ Ⓓ Ⓔ	85 Ⓐ Ⓑ Ⓒ Ⓓ Ⓔ
20 Ⓐ Ⓑ Ⓒ Ⓓ Ⓔ	42 Ⓐ Ⓑ Ⓒ Ⓓ Ⓔ	64 Ⓐ Ⓑ Ⓒ Ⓓ Ⓔ	86 Ⓐ Ⓑ Ⓒ Ⓓ Ⓔ
21 Ⓐ Ⓑ Ⓒ Ⓓ Ⓔ	43 Ⓐ Ⓑ Ⓒ Ⓓ Ⓔ	65 Ⓐ Ⓑ Ⓒ Ⓓ Ⓔ	87 Ⓐ Ⓑ Ⓒ Ⓓ Ⓔ
22 Ⓐ Ⓑ Ⓒ Ⓓ Ⓔ	44 Ⓐ Ⓑ Ⓒ Ⓓ Ⓔ	66 Ⓐ Ⓑ Ⓒ Ⓓ Ⓔ	88 Ⓐ Ⓑ Ⓒ Ⓓ Ⓔ

MEMORY FOR ADDRESSES TEST

1 Ⓐ Ⓑ Ⓒ Ⓓ Ⓔ	23 Ⓐ Ⓑ Ⓒ Ⓓ Ⓔ	45 Ⓐ Ⓑ Ⓒ Ⓓ Ⓔ	67 Ⓐ Ⓑ Ⓒ Ⓓ Ⓔ
2 Ⓐ Ⓑ Ⓒ Ⓓ Ⓔ	24 Ⓐ Ⓑ Ⓒ Ⓓ Ⓔ	46 Ⓐ Ⓑ Ⓒ Ⓓ Ⓔ	68 Ⓐ Ⓑ Ⓒ Ⓓ Ⓔ
3 Ⓐ Ⓑ Ⓒ Ⓓ Ⓔ	25 Ⓐ Ⓑ Ⓒ Ⓓ Ⓔ	47 Ⓐ Ⓑ Ⓒ Ⓓ Ⓔ	69 Ⓐ Ⓑ Ⓒ Ⓓ Ⓔ
4 Ⓐ Ⓑ Ⓒ Ⓓ Ⓔ	26 Ⓐ Ⓑ Ⓒ Ⓓ Ⓔ	48 Ⓐ Ⓑ Ⓒ Ⓓ Ⓔ	70 Ⓐ Ⓑ Ⓒ Ⓓ Ⓔ
5 Ⓐ Ⓑ Ⓒ Ⓓ Ⓔ	27 Ⓐ Ⓑ Ⓒ Ⓓ Ⓔ	49 Ⓐ Ⓑ Ⓒ Ⓓ Ⓔ	71 Ⓐ Ⓑ Ⓒ Ⓓ Ⓔ
6 Ⓐ Ⓑ Ⓒ Ⓓ Ⓔ	28 Ⓐ Ⓑ Ⓒ Ⓓ Ⓔ	50 Ⓐ Ⓑ Ⓒ Ⓓ Ⓔ	72 Ⓐ Ⓑ Ⓒ Ⓓ Ⓔ
7 Ⓐ Ⓑ Ⓒ Ⓓ Ⓔ	29 Ⓐ Ⓑ Ⓒ Ⓓ Ⓔ	51 Ⓐ Ⓑ Ⓒ Ⓓ Ⓔ	73 Ⓐ Ⓑ Ⓒ Ⓓ Ⓔ
8 Ⓐ Ⓑ Ⓒ Ⓓ Ⓔ	30 Ⓐ Ⓑ Ⓒ Ⓓ Ⓔ	52 Ⓐ Ⓑ Ⓒ Ⓓ Ⓔ	74 Ⓐ Ⓑ Ⓒ Ⓓ Ⓔ
9 Ⓐ Ⓑ Ⓒ Ⓓ Ⓔ	31 Ⓐ Ⓑ Ⓒ Ⓓ Ⓔ	53 Ⓐ Ⓑ Ⓒ Ⓓ Ⓔ	75 Ⓐ Ⓑ Ⓒ Ⓓ Ⓔ
10 Ⓐ Ⓑ Ⓒ Ⓓ Ⓔ	32 Ⓐ Ⓑ Ⓒ Ⓓ Ⓔ	54 Ⓐ Ⓑ Ⓒ Ⓓ Ⓔ	76 Ⓐ Ⓑ Ⓒ Ⓓ Ⓔ
11 Ⓐ Ⓑ Ⓒ Ⓓ Ⓔ	33 Ⓐ Ⓑ Ⓒ Ⓓ Ⓔ	55 Ⓐ Ⓑ Ⓒ Ⓓ Ⓔ	77 Ⓐ Ⓑ Ⓒ Ⓓ Ⓔ
12 Ⓐ Ⓑ Ⓒ Ⓓ Ⓔ	34 Ⓐ Ⓑ Ⓒ Ⓓ Ⓔ	56 Ⓐ Ⓑ Ⓒ Ⓓ Ⓔ	78 Ⓐ Ⓑ Ⓒ Ⓓ Ⓔ
13 Ⓐ Ⓑ Ⓒ Ⓓ Ⓔ	35 Ⓐ Ⓑ Ⓒ Ⓓ Ⓔ	57 Ⓐ Ⓑ Ⓒ Ⓓ Ⓔ	79 Ⓐ Ⓑ Ⓒ Ⓓ Ⓔ
14 Ⓐ Ⓑ Ⓒ Ⓓ Ⓔ	36 Ⓐ Ⓑ Ⓒ Ⓓ Ⓔ	58 Ⓐ Ⓑ Ⓒ Ⓓ Ⓔ	80 Ⓐ Ⓑ Ⓒ Ⓓ Ⓔ
15 Ⓐ Ⓑ Ⓒ Ⓓ Ⓔ	37 Ⓐ Ⓑ Ⓒ Ⓓ Ⓔ	59 Ⓐ Ⓑ Ⓒ Ⓓ Ⓔ	81 Ⓐ Ⓑ Ⓒ Ⓓ Ⓔ
16 Ⓐ Ⓑ Ⓒ Ⓓ Ⓔ	38 Ⓐ Ⓑ Ⓒ Ⓓ Ⓔ	60 Ⓐ Ⓑ Ⓒ Ⓓ Ⓔ	82 Ⓐ Ⓑ Ⓒ Ⓓ Ⓔ
17 Ⓐ Ⓑ Ⓒ Ⓓ Ⓔ	39 Ⓐ Ⓑ Ⓒ Ⓓ Ⓔ	61 Ⓐ Ⓑ Ⓒ Ⓓ Ⓔ	83 Ⓐ Ⓑ Ⓒ Ⓓ Ⓔ
18 Ⓐ Ⓑ Ⓒ Ⓓ Ⓔ	40 Ⓐ Ⓑ Ⓒ Ⓓ Ⓔ	62 Ⓐ Ⓑ Ⓒ Ⓓ Ⓔ	84 Ⓐ Ⓑ Ⓒ Ⓓ Ⓔ
19 Ⓐ Ⓑ Ⓒ Ⓓ Ⓔ	41 Ⓐ Ⓑ Ⓒ Ⓓ Ⓔ	63 Ⓐ Ⓑ Ⓒ Ⓓ Ⓔ	85 Ⓐ Ⓑ Ⓒ Ⓓ Ⓔ
20 Ⓐ Ⓑ Ⓒ Ⓓ Ⓔ	42 Ⓐ Ⓑ Ⓒ Ⓓ Ⓔ	64 Ⓐ Ⓑ Ⓒ Ⓓ Ⓔ	86 Ⓐ Ⓑ Ⓒ Ⓓ Ⓔ
21 Ⓐ Ⓑ Ⓒ Ⓓ Ⓔ	43 Ⓐ Ⓑ Ⓒ Ⓓ Ⓔ	65 Ⓐ Ⓑ Ⓒ Ⓓ Ⓔ	87 Ⓐ Ⓑ Ⓒ Ⓓ Ⓔ
22 Ⓐ Ⓑ Ⓒ Ⓓ Ⓔ	44 Ⓐ Ⓑ Ⓒ Ⓓ Ⓔ	66 Ⓐ Ⓑ Ⓒ Ⓓ Ⓔ	88 Ⓐ Ⓑ Ⓒ Ⓓ Ⓔ

SCORE SHEET FOR SECOND MODEL EXAM

ADDRESS CHECKING TEST

Number Right minus Number Wrong equals   Score

_____ – _____ = _____

MEMORY FOR ADDRESSES TEST

Number Right minus (Number Wrong ÷ 4) equals   Score

_____ – _____ = _____

PROGRESS GRAPH

Blacken the bars for Model Exam 2 to the scores you earned.

Score			
95			
90			
85			
80			
75			
70			
65			
60			
55			
50			
45			
40			
35			
30			
25			
20			
15			
10			
5			
0			

Test	AC| M	AC| M	AC| M
Model Exam	Diag.	1	2

AC = Address Checking   M = Memory for Addresses

SECOND MODEL EXAM

ADDRESS CHECKING TEST

TIME: 6 Minutes. 95 Questions.

DIRECTIONS: For each question, compare the address in the left column with the address in the right column. If the two addresses are ALIKE IN EVERY WAY, blacken space Ⓐ on your answer sheet. If the two addresses are DIFFERENT IN ANY WAY, blacken space Ⓓ on your answer sheet. Correct answers for this test are on page 105.

1...12310 Clairmond Pl	12310 Clarimond Pl
2...24038 Johnson Rd	24038 Johnston Rd
3...578 Abraham Kazan Blvd	5788 Abraham Kazan Blvd
4...11390 W Wynnewood Rd	11390 E Wynnewood Rd
5...11000 W 221st St	11000 W 221st St
6...Canadiqua NY 14424	Canadiqua NY 14424
7...13450 Montgomery Park	13450 Montegomery Park
8...16235 Zimbrich Dr	16235 Zimbrench Dr
9...43961 Remmington Ave	43691 Remmington Ave
10...11236 Shorewood Ln	11236 Sherwood Ln
11...16002 Dalewood Gardens	1602 Dalewood Gardens
12...11335 Yarkerdale Dr	11335 Yorkerdale Dr
13...12305 NE Teutonia Ave	12305 NW Teutonia Ave
14...1508 Duanesburg Rd	1508 Duanesburg Rd
15...Wachapregue VA 23480	Wachapergue VA 23480
16...34001 E Atkinson Cir	34001 E Atkinson Ct
17...43872 E Tottenham Rd	43872 E Tottenham Rd
18...13531 Yancey Ave NE	13531 Yancey Ave NW
19...14615 Lost Mountain Trl	14615 Last Mountain Trl
20...11633 N Abingdon Pl	11633 N Abingdon Pl
21...14609 Lakeview Ter	14609 Lakeview Park
22...10001 N Magee Ave	10001 N McGee Ave
23...14617 Quattara Blvd	14716 Quattara Blvd
24...98 North Timberland Rd	98 North Timberland Rd
25...14615 Coca Cola Park	14615 Coca Cola Pky
26...13444 Glenthorne Way	13444 Glenthorne Way
27...16567 Pinnacle Rd	16567 Pinnacel Rd
28...12726 N Montaine Park	12726 S Montaine Park
29...5071 E Trelawne Dr	5071 E Treelawne Dr

30. . .5304 SE Winterroth St	5304 SE Winterroth St
31. . .Emancipation PR 00802	Emancipation PR 00802
32. . .11925 Resolute Cir	11925 Resolute Dr
33. . .31011 Lynchford Park A	31011 Lynchford Park B
34. . .12306 Woolacott Rd	12306 Woolacott St
35. . .31991 Abbottsford Rd	31991 Abbottsford Rd
36. . .14201 W Galbraith Ave	14201 W Galbraith Ave
37. . .11367 Olentangy Ln	11367 Olengtongy Ln
38. . .11235 N Zumstein Ave	11235 N Zomstein Ave
39. . .21003 NE Cronwell Blvd	21003 NE Cromwell Blvd
40. . .11450 S Westonridge Dr	14150 S Westonridge Dr
41. . .22122 Jonquilmeadow Rd	22122 Jonquilmeadow Rd
42. . .4434 N Glenorchard Pl	4434 N Glenorchard Ln
43. . .12087 Neyartnell Pky	12087 Neyartell Pky
44. . .31756 Falconbridge Dr	31756 Falconbridge Dr
45. . .Stambaugh MI 49964	Stanbaugh MI 49964
46. . .16735 Halidonhill Ln	16735 Hanlidonhill Ln
47. . .13299 La Boiteaux Ave	1329 La Boiteaux Ave
48. . .10154 Ottercreek Rd	10154 Ottercreek Rd
49. . .4867 NE Kellerman Ct	4867 NE Kellerman Ct
50. . .16089 Carnation Cir	16089 Carnation Dr
51. . .12196 SE Kensington Pl	12196 SE Kensington Pl
52. . .7800 SE Grantham Way	7800 SE Grantham Way
53. . .10697 Indianbluff Dr	10997 Indianbluff Dr
54. . .2200 Amberacres Rd	2200 Amberacers Rd
55. . .3901 Paulmeadows Dr	3901 Paulmeadows Dr
56. . .4201 Tanagerwoods Ln	4201 Tanagerwoods Ln
57. . .1399 Clarendon Ave NE	1399 Clarendon Ave SE
58. . .6377 Kuenerle Ct NE	6377 Kuenerle Cir NE
59. . .12397 Reicosky Ln NW	12397 Reikosky Ln NW
60. . .4600 Henrietta Ave SE	4600 Henrietta Ave SE
61. . .5263 Tuscarawas W	5263 Tuscarawas W
62. . .3567 Villa Padova Dr NW	3567 Villa Padova Dr NW
63. . .1190 Edinberry Dr SE	1190 Edinbury Dr SE
64. . .1107 NE Julie Ann Cir	1107 NE Julie Anna Cir
65. . .11300 South Central Ave	11300 South Center Ave
66. . .11205 Trenaman Cir	11205 Trenamar Cir
67. . .2288 Altament Ave	2288 Altament St
68. . .4056 Sprucewood Ln NW	4056 Sprucewood Ln SW
69. . .Cynthiana OH 45624	Cynthiana OH 45642
70. . .1257 Zesiger Ave	1257 Zesinger Ave
71. . .2697 Demington Ave NW	2697 Demington Ave NW
72. . .3401 East Nimidila Rd	3401 East Nimidila Rd
73. . .801 Airymeadows Ln	801 Airymeadows Ln
74. . .1795 NE 24th Avenue	1795 NW 24th Avenue
75. . .PO Box 41001	PO Box 41081
76. . .11299 Wolverine Ct SE	11929 Wolverine Ct SE
77. . .1800 Youngdale Ave NW	1800 Youngdale St NW
78. . .25011 Fulmore Pl NW	25011 Filmore Pl NW
79. . .5700 Inverness Pky NW	5700 Inverness Pky NW
80. . .699 Mount Marie Ave SE	699 Mount Maria Ave SE
81. . .1166 Schwalm Ave SE	1166 Schwalm Ave SE
82. . .7744 Otterbein Trl	7744 Otterbein Trl

83...Fort Steilacoon WA 98494	Fort Stielacoon WA 98494
84...1155 Parkridge Cir NW	1155 Partridge Cir NW
85...3477 Eastbury Ave NE	3477 Eastbury St NE
86...25501 Gambrinus Ct SE	2501 Gambrinus Ct SE
87...11089 Nicklaus St NW	11909 Nicklaus St NW
88...5500 Knollridge Dr NW	5500 Knollridge Cir NW
89...2203 Forestdale Pl SE	2203 Forestdale Pl NE
90...11449 Vaniman Trl	11449 Vaniman Trl
91...9903 Hometown Rd S	9903 Hometown Rd S
92...13468 Ritchie Ave	13486 Ritchie Ave
93...Tununak AK 99681	Tununak AR 99681
94...400 Nimishillen Church Rd	400 Nimishollen Church Rd
95...3577 Brunnerdale Ct NW	3577 Brunnerdale St NW

END OF ADDRESS CHECKING TEST

If you finish this test before time is up, use the remaining time to check over your work. Do not turn the page until you are told to do so.

PRACTICE FOR
MEMORY FOR ADDRESSES TEST

DIRECTIONS: The five boxes below are labelled A, B, C, D, and E. In each box are three sets of number spans with names and two names which are not associated with numbers. In the next THREE MINUTES, you must try to memorize the box location of each name and number span. The rosition of a name or number span within its box is not important. You need only remember the letter of the box in which the item is to be found. You will use these names and numbers to answer three sets of practice questions which are NOT scored and one actual test which is scored. Correct answers are on pages 105 and 106.

A	B	C	D	E
1500-1699 Indio	3300-3999 Indio	9600-9699 Indio	7200-8999 Indio	6400-6999 Indio
Main	Hawthorne	Dogwood	Fulton	Melody
2300-2999 Bombay	5200-5999 Bombay	6200-6999 Bombay	2100-2299 Bombay	3600-3999 Bombay
Holly	Linwood	Murray	Quartz	Flint
9200-9499 Lecroy	5600-5999 Lecroy	2800-2999 Lecroy	9500-9999 Lecroy	3200-3999 Lecroy

PRACTICE I

DIRECTIONS: Use the next THREE MINUTES to mark on your answer sheet the letter of the box in which each item that follows is to be found. Try to mark each item without looking back at the boxes. If however, you get stuck, you may refer to the boxes during this practice exercise. If you find that you must look at the boxes, try to memorize as you do so. This test is for practice only. It will not be scored.

1. 3200-3999 Lecroy
2. 3300-3999 Indio
3. Melody
4. Flint
5. 2800-2999 Lecroy
6. 2100-2299 Bombay
7. 6400-6999 Indio
8. Hawthorne
9. Holly
10. 1500-1699 Indio
11. Linwood
12. 2100-2299 Bombay
13. 9600-9699 Indio
14. 6400-6999 Indio
15. 2100-2299 Bombay
16. Linwood
17. Flint
18. 5600-5999 Lecroy
19. 3600-3999 Bombay
20. 7200-8999 Indio
21. Dogwood
22. Main

23. 6400-6999 Indio
24. Quartz
25. 5600-5999 Lecroy
26. 3200-3999 Lecroy
27. Murray
28. 1500-1699 Indio
29. 6400-6999 Indio
30. 2100-2299 Bombay
31. Holly
32. 9500-9999 Lecroy
33. 5200-5999 Bombay
34. Flint
35. 3300-3999 Indio
36. 9200-9499 Lecroy
37. 2100-2299 Bombay
38. Flint
39. Dogwood
40. 6400-6999 Indio
41. Holly
42. Hawthorne
43. 7200-8999 Indio
44. Main
45. 2800-2999 Lecroy
46. Murray
47. 3300-3999 Indio
48. 3200-3999 Lecroy
49. Quartz
50. 5600-5999 Lecroy
51. 2300-2999 Bombay
52. 2800-2999 Lecroy
53. Fulton
54. 7200-8999 Indio
55. 3600-3999 Bombay
56. Melody
57. Hawthorne
58. Flint
59. 3300-3999 Indio
60. Main
61. 5600-5999 Lecroy
62. 7200-8999 Indio
63. 2300-2999 Bombay
64. 9500-9999 Lecroy
65. 9600-9699 Indio
66. Linwood
67. 3200-3999 Lecro
68. Holly
69. 3600-3999 Bombay
70. 1500-1699 Indio
71. Murray
72. 9500-9999 Lecroy
73. Holly
74. 7200-8999 Indio
75. Quartz
76. Dogwood
77. 2300-2999 Bombay
78. 9500-9999 Lecroy
79. 5200-5999 Bombay
80. Fulton
81. 3600-3999 Bombay
82. Melody
83. 9200-9499 Lecroy
84. 1500-1699 Indio
85. 6200-6999 Bombay
86. Linwood
87. Flint
88. 9600-9699 Indio

PRACTICE II

DIRECTIONS: The next 88 questions constitute another practice exercise. Again, you should mark your answers on your answer sheet. Again, the time limit is THREE MINUTES. This time, however, you must NOT look at the boxes while answering the questions. You must rely on your memory in marking the box location of each item. This practice test will not be scored.

1. 6200-6999 Bombay
2. 9200-9499 Lecroy
3. 3600-3999 Bombay
4. 3300-3999 Indio
5. Murray
6. Holly
7. 1500-1699 Indio
8. 3200-3999 Lecroy
9. 5600-5999 Lecroy
10. Main
11. Melody
12. 2100-2299 Bombay
13. 9600-9699 Indio
14. 6400-6999 Indio
15. Dogwood
16. 9500-9999 Lecroy
17. 7200-8999 Indio
18. Hawthorne
19. 2300-2999 Bombay
20. Linwood
21. 5200-5999 Bombay
22. Fulton
23. Flint
24. 2800-2999 Lecroy
25. Quartz
26. 3300-3999 Indio
27. 2100-2299 Bombay
28. 9200-9499 Lecroy
29. Holly
30. Main
31. 7200-8999 Indio
32. 6200-6999 Bombay
33. 2800-2999 Lecroy
34. 2300-2999 Bombay
35. Fulton
36. Dogwood
37. Melody
38. 6400-6999 Indio
39. 5200-5999 Bombay
40. 9200-9499 Lecroy
41. Linwood
42. Flint
43. 1500-1699 Indio
44. 9500-9999 Lecroy
45. 3300-3999 Indio
46. Hawthorne
47. 3600-3999 Bombay
48. 9600-9699 Indio
49. Murray
50. 5200-5999 Bombay
51. 9500-9999 Lecroy
52. 1500-1699 Indio
53. Melody
54. 7200-8999 Indio
55. Quartz
56. 2800-2999 Lecroy
57. 6400-6999 Indio
1500-1699 Indio
58.
59. Linwood
60. Hawthorne
61. 6200-6999 Bombay
62. 2300-2999 Bombay
63. 3200-3999 Lecroy
64. 2100-2299 Bombay
65. 9200-9499 Lecroy
66. Main
67. Fulton
68. Flint
69. 3300-3999 Indio
70. 5200-5999 Bombay
71. Murray
72. 9600-9699 Indio
73. 5600-5999 Lecroy
74. 3200-3999 Lecroy
75. 1500-1699 Indio
76. 2300-2999 Bombay
77. 3600-3999 Bombay
78. 6400-6999 Indio
79. Quartz
80. Main
81. Linwood
82. 7200-8999 Indio
83. 9200-9499 Lecroy
84. 2100-2299 Bombay
85. 9500-9999 Lecroy
86. 6200-6999 Bombay
87. Flint
88. Hawthorne

PRACTICE III

DIRECTIONS: The names and addresses are repeated for you in the boxes below. Each name and each number span is in the same box in which you found it in the original set. You will now be allowed FIVE MINUTES to study the locations again. Do your best to memorize the letter of the box in which each item is located. This is your last chance to see the boxes.

A	B	C	D	E
1500-1699 Indio Main 2300-2999 Bombay Holly 9200-9499 Lecroy	3300-3999 Indio Hawthorne 5200-5999 Bombay Linwood 5600-5999 Lecroy	9600-9699 Indio Dogwood 6200-6999 Bombay Murray 2800-2999 Lecroy	7200-8999 Indio Fulton 2100-2299 Bombay Quartz 9500-9999 Lecroy	6400-6999 Indio Melody 3600-3999 Bombay Flint 3200-3999 Lecroy

DIRECTIONS: This is your last practice test. Mark the location of each of the 88 items on your answer sheet. You will have FIVE MINUTES to answer these questions. Do NOT look back at the boxes. This practice test will not be scored.

1. 7200-8999 Indio
2. Hawthorne
3. 2300-2999 Bombay
4. 5600-5999 Lecroy
5. Murray
6. 2100-2299 Bombay
7. 6400-6999 Indio
8. 3200-3999 Lecroy
9. Holly
10. Flint
11. 9500-9999 Lecroy
12. 1500-1699 Indio
13. 9600-9699 Indio
14. 3600-3999 Bombay
15. Quartz
16. 3300-3999 Indio
17. Linwood
18. 5200-5999 Bombay
19. 9200-9499 Lecroy
20. 5600-5999 Lecroy
21. Dogwood
22. Fulton
23. 2800-2999 Lecroy
24. 2300-2999 Bombay
25. 7200-8999 Indio
26. Melody
27. Main
28. 2100-2299 Bombay
29. 9500-9999 Lecroy
30. Quartz
31. 9600-9699 Indio
32. 3200-3999 Lecroy
33. 3300-3999 Indio
34. 6200-6999 Bombay
35. 9500-9999 Lecroy
36. Linwood
37. Melody
38. 9200-9499 Lecroy
39. 5200-5999 Bombay
40. 1500-1699 Indio
41. Fulton
42. Hawthorne
43. 2300-2999 Bombay
44. 6400-6999 Indio
45. 5600-5999 Lecroy
46. Main
47. Flint
48. 9600-9699 Indio
49. 9200-9499 Lecroy
50. 2100-2299 Bombay
51. Quartz
52. Dogwood

53. 2800-2999 Lecroy
54. 7200-8999 Indio
55. 5600-5999 Lecroy
56. 3600-3999 Bombay
57. Holly
58. Murray
59. 9600-9699 Indio
60. 5200-5999 Bombay
61. 3200-3999 Lecroy
62. 9600-9699 Indio
63. Linwood
64. 2100-2299 Bombay
65. 1500-1699 Indio
66. 6200-6999 Bombay
67. Fulton
68. Holly
69. 9200-9499 Lecroy
70. 5200-5999 Bombay

71. 7200-8999 Indio
72. 3600-3999 Bombay
73. Melody
74. Flint
75. 6400-6999 Indio
76. 6200-6999 Bombay
77. 9600-9699 Indio
78. Hawthorne
79. Main
80. 9500-9999 Lecroy
81. 5600-5999 Lecroy
82. Murray
83. 2300-2999 Bombay
84. Quartz
85. Dogwood
86. 3300-3999 Indio
87. 3600-3999 Bombay
88. 5600-5999 Lecroy

MEMORY FOR ADDRESSES TEST

TIME: 5 Minutes. 88 Questions.

DIRECTIONS: Mark your answers on the answer sheet in the section headed "MEMORY FOR ADDRESSES TEST." This test will be scored. You are NOT permitted to look at the boxes. Work from memory, as quickly and as accurately as you can. Correct answers are on page106.

1. 2100-2299 Bombay
2. 7200-8999 Indio
3. 2800-2999 Lecroy
4. 1500-1699 Indio
5. 3200-3999 Lecroy
6. Fulton
7. Linwood
8. 5200-5999 Bombay
9. 3600-3999 Bombay
10. Melody
11. Holly
12. 6400-6999 Indio
13. 9200-9499 Lecroy
14. 9600-9699 Indio
15. 2300-2999 Bombay
16. Fulton
17. Flint
18. Main
19. 6200-6999 Bombay
20. 9600-9699 Indio
21. 9500-9999 Lecroy
22. 5600-5999 Lecroy
23. Hawthorne
24. Murray
25. Dogwood
26. 6200-6999 Bombay
27. 6400-6999 Indio
28. 2800-2999 Lecroy
29. Quartz
30. Flint
31. 1500-1699 Indio
32. 2100-2299 Bombay
33. 7200-8999 Indio
34. 5600-5999 Lecroy
35. 9600-9699 Indio
36. Main
37. Holly
38. 2300-2999 Bombay
39. 9500-9999 Lecroy
40. Melody
41. 5200-5999 Bombay
42. 3300-3999 Indio
43. 3200-3999 Lecroy
44. 9200-9499 Lecroy
45. Dogwood
46. 3300-3999 Indio
47. 6200-6999 Bombay
48. 9500-9999 Lecroy
49. Flint
50. Main
51. 3200-3999 Lecroy
52. 2100-2299 Bombay
53. 9600-9699 Indio
54. 5200-5999 Bombay
55. 9200-9499 Lecroy
56. Hawthorne
57. Quartz
58. 1500-1699 Indio
59. 2300-2999 Bombay
60. Fulton
61. Melody
62. 5600-5999 Lecroy
63. 6400-6999 Indio
64. 7200-8999 Indio
65. Holly
66. Linwood
67. Murray
68. 9500-9999 Lecroy
69. 5200-5999 Bombay
70. Fulton
71. Hawthorne
72. 6200-6999 Bombay
73. 9600-9699 Indio
74. 6400-6999 Indio
75. Quartz
76. 2300-2999 Bombay
77. 9200-9499 Lecroy
78. Linwood

79. 2100-2299 Bombay
80. Flint
81. 3300-3999 Indio
82. 3600-3999 Bombay
83. 3200-3999 Lecroy

84. 7200-8999 Indio
85. Melody
86. Main
87. 5600-5999 Lecroy
88. Holly

END OF EXAM

By now you should be able to analyze your own pattern of errors. Make up a tally sheet by cross-checking your incorrect answers against the correct answers and against the questions themselves. Mark your tally sheet like this

ADDRESS CHECKING ERROR ANALYSIS CHART

Type of Error	Tally	Total Number
Number of addresses which were alike and you incorrectly marked "different"		
Number of addresses which were different and you incorrectly marked "alike"		
Number of addresses in which you missed a difference in NUMBERS		
Number of addresses in which you missed a difference in ABBREVIATIONS		
Number of addresses in which you missed a difference in NAMES		

SELF-EVALUATION CHART

Test	Excellent	Good	Average	Fair	Poor
Address Checking	80-95	65-79	50-64	35-49	1-34
Memory for Addresses	75-88	60-74	45-59	30-44	1-29

CORRECT ANSWERS FOR SECOND MODEL EXAM

ADDRESS CHECKING TEST

1. D	13. D	25. D	37. D	49. A	61. A	73. A	85. D
2. D	14. A	26. A	38. D	50. D	62. A	74. D	86. D
3. D	15. D	27. D	39. D	51. A	63. D	75. D	87. D
4. D	16. D	28. D	40. D	52. A	64. D	76. D	88. D
5. A	17. A	29. D	41. D	53. D	65. D	77. D	89. D
6. A	18. D	30. A	42. D	54. D	66. D	78. D	90. A
7. D	19. D	31. A	43. D	55. A	67. D	79. A	91. A
8. D	20. A	32. D	44. A	56. A	68. D	80. D	92. D
9. D	21. D	33. D	45. D	57. D	69. D	81. A	93. D
10. D	22. D	34. D	46. D	58. D	70. D	82. A	94. D
11. D	23. D	35. D	47. D	59. D	71. A	83. D	95. D
12. D	24. A	36. A	48. A	60. A	72. A	84. D	

MEMORY FOR ADDRESSES—PRACTICE I

1. E	12. D	23. E	34. E	45. C	56. E	67. E	78. D
2. B	13. C	24. D	35. B	46. C	57. B	68. A	79. B
3. E	14. E	25. B	36. A	47. B	58. E	69. E	80. D
4. E	15. D	26. E	37. D	48. E	59. B	70. A	81. E
5. C	16. B	27. C	38. E	49. D	60. A	71. C	82. E
6. D	17. E	28. A	39. C	50. B	61. B	72. D	83. A
7. E	18. B	29. E	40. E	51. A	62. D	73. A	84. A
8. B	19. E	30. D	41. A	52. C	63. A	74. D	85. C
9. A	20. D	31. A	42. B	53. D	64. D	75. D	86. B
10. A	21. C	32. D	43. D	54. D	65. C	76. C	87. E
11. B	22. A	33. B	44. A	55. E	66. B	77. A	88. C

MEMORY FOR ADDRESSES—PRACTICE II

1. C	12. D	23. E	34. A	45. B	56. C	67. D	78. E
2. A	13. C	24. C	35. D	46. B	57. E	68. E	79. D
3. E	14. E	25. D	36. C	47. E	58. A	69. B	80. A
4. B	15. C	26. B	37. E	48. C	59. B	70. B	81. B
5. C	16. D	27. D	38. E	49. C	60. B	71. C	82. B
6. A	17. D	28. A	39. B	50. B	61. C	72. C	83. A
7. A	18. B	29. A	40. A	51. D	62. A	73. B	84. D
8. E	19. A	30. A	41. B	52. A	63. E	74. E	85. D
9. B	20. B	31. D	42. E	53. E	64. D	75. A	86. C
10. A	21. B	32. C	43. A	54. D	65. A	76. A	87. E
11. E	22. D	33. C	44. D	55. D	66. A	77. E	88. B

MEMORY FOR ADDRESSES—PRACTICE III

1. D	12. A	23. C	34. C	45. B	56. E	67. D	78. B
2. B	13. C	24. A	35. D	46. A	57. A	68. A	79. A
3. A	14. E	25. D	36. B	47. E	58. C	69. A	80. D
4. B	15. D	26. E	37. E	48. C	59. C	70. B	81. B
5. C	16. B	27. A	38. A	49. A	60. B	71. D	82. C
6. D	17. B	28. D	39. B	50. D	61. E	72. E	83. A
7. E	18. B	29. D	40. A	51. D	62. C	73. E	84. D
8. E	19. A	30. D	41. D	52. C	63. B	74. E	85. C
9. A	20. B	31. C	42. B	53. C	64. D	75. E	86. B
10. E	21. C	32. E	43. A	54. D	65. A	76. C	87. E
11. D	22. D	33. B	44. E	55. B	66. C	77. C	88. B

MEMORY FOR ADDRESSES TEST

1. D	12. E	23. B	34. B	45. C	56. B	67. C	78. B
2. D	13. A	24. C	35. C	46. B	57. D	68. D	79. D
3. C	14. C	25. C	36. A	47. C	58. A	69. B	80. E
4. A	15. A	26. C	37. A	48. D	59. A	70. D	81. B
5. E	16. D	27. E	38. A	49. E	60. D	71. B	82. E
6. D	17. E	28. C	39. D	50. A	61. E	72. C	83. E
7. B	18. A	29. D	40. E	51. E	62. B	73. C	84. D
8. B	19. C	30. E	41. B	52. D	63. E	74. E	85. E
9. E	20. C	31. A	42. B	53. C	64. D	75. D	86. A
10. E	21. D	32. D	43. E	54. B	65. A	76. A	87. B
11. A	22. B	33. D	44. A	55. A	66. B	77. A	88. A

PRACTICE II

1. Ⓐ Ⓑ Ⓒ Ⓓ Ⓔ
2. Ⓐ Ⓑ Ⓒ Ⓓ Ⓔ
3. Ⓐ Ⓑ Ⓒ Ⓓ Ⓔ
4. Ⓐ Ⓑ Ⓒ Ⓓ Ⓔ
5. Ⓐ Ⓑ Ⓒ Ⓓ Ⓔ
6. Ⓐ Ⓑ Ⓒ Ⓓ Ⓔ
7. Ⓐ Ⓑ Ⓒ Ⓓ Ⓔ
8. Ⓐ Ⓑ Ⓒ Ⓓ Ⓔ
9. Ⓐ Ⓑ Ⓒ Ⓓ Ⓔ
10. Ⓐ Ⓑ Ⓒ Ⓓ Ⓔ
11. Ⓐ Ⓑ Ⓒ Ⓓ Ⓔ
12. Ⓐ Ⓑ Ⓒ Ⓓ Ⓔ
13. Ⓐ Ⓑ Ⓒ Ⓓ Ⓔ
14. Ⓐ Ⓑ Ⓒ Ⓓ Ⓔ
15. Ⓐ Ⓑ Ⓒ Ⓓ Ⓔ
16. Ⓐ Ⓑ Ⓒ Ⓓ Ⓔ
17. Ⓐ Ⓑ Ⓒ Ⓓ Ⓔ
18. Ⓐ Ⓑ Ⓒ Ⓓ Ⓔ
19. Ⓐ Ⓑ Ⓒ Ⓓ Ⓔ
20. Ⓐ Ⓑ Ⓒ Ⓓ Ⓔ
21. Ⓐ Ⓑ Ⓒ Ⓓ Ⓔ
22. Ⓐ Ⓑ Ⓒ Ⓓ Ⓔ

23. Ⓐ Ⓑ Ⓒ Ⓓ Ⓔ
24. Ⓐ Ⓑ Ⓒ Ⓓ Ⓔ
25. Ⓐ Ⓑ Ⓒ Ⓓ Ⓔ
26. Ⓐ Ⓑ Ⓒ Ⓓ Ⓔ
27. Ⓐ Ⓑ Ⓒ Ⓓ Ⓔ
28. Ⓐ Ⓑ Ⓒ Ⓓ Ⓔ
29. Ⓐ Ⓑ Ⓒ Ⓓ Ⓔ
30. Ⓐ Ⓑ Ⓒ Ⓓ Ⓔ
31. Ⓐ Ⓑ Ⓒ Ⓓ Ⓔ
32. Ⓐ Ⓑ Ⓒ Ⓓ Ⓔ
33. Ⓐ Ⓑ Ⓒ Ⓓ Ⓔ
34. Ⓐ Ⓑ Ⓒ Ⓓ Ⓔ
35. Ⓐ Ⓑ Ⓒ Ⓓ Ⓔ
36. Ⓐ Ⓑ Ⓒ Ⓓ Ⓔ
37. Ⓐ Ⓑ Ⓒ Ⓓ Ⓔ
38. Ⓐ Ⓑ Ⓒ Ⓓ Ⓔ
39. Ⓐ Ⓑ Ⓒ Ⓓ Ⓔ
40. Ⓐ Ⓑ Ⓒ Ⓓ Ⓔ
41. Ⓐ Ⓑ Ⓒ Ⓓ Ⓔ
42. Ⓐ Ⓑ Ⓒ Ⓓ Ⓔ
43. Ⓐ Ⓑ Ⓒ Ⓓ Ⓔ
44. Ⓐ Ⓑ Ⓒ Ⓓ Ⓔ

45. Ⓐ Ⓑ Ⓒ Ⓓ Ⓔ
46. Ⓐ Ⓑ Ⓒ Ⓓ Ⓔ
47. Ⓐ Ⓑ Ⓒ Ⓓ Ⓔ
48. Ⓐ Ⓑ Ⓒ Ⓓ Ⓔ
49. Ⓐ Ⓑ Ⓒ Ⓓ Ⓔ
50. Ⓐ Ⓑ Ⓒ Ⓓ Ⓔ
51. Ⓐ Ⓑ Ⓒ Ⓓ Ⓔ
52. Ⓐ Ⓑ Ⓒ Ⓓ Ⓔ
53. Ⓐ Ⓑ Ⓒ Ⓓ Ⓔ
54. Ⓐ Ⓑ Ⓒ Ⓓ Ⓔ
55. Ⓐ Ⓑ Ⓒ Ⓓ Ⓔ
56. Ⓐ Ⓑ Ⓒ Ⓓ Ⓔ
57. Ⓐ Ⓑ Ⓒ Ⓓ Ⓔ
58. Ⓐ Ⓑ Ⓒ Ⓓ Ⓔ
59. Ⓐ Ⓑ Ⓒ Ⓓ Ⓔ
60. Ⓐ Ⓑ Ⓒ Ⓓ Ⓔ
61. Ⓐ Ⓑ Ⓒ Ⓓ Ⓔ
62. Ⓐ Ⓑ Ⓒ Ⓓ Ⓔ
63. Ⓐ Ⓑ Ⓒ Ⓓ Ⓕ
64. Ⓐ Ⓑ Ⓒ Ⓓ Ⓔ
65. Ⓐ Ⓑ Ⓒ Ⓓ Ⓔ
66. Ⓐ Ⓑ Ⓒ Ⓓ Ⓔ

67. Ⓐ Ⓑ Ⓒ Ⓓ Ⓔ
68. Ⓐ Ⓑ Ⓒ Ⓓ Ⓔ
69. Ⓐ Ⓑ Ⓒ Ⓓ Ⓔ
70. Ⓐ Ⓑ Ⓒ Ⓓ Ⓔ
71. Ⓐ Ⓑ Ⓒ Ⓓ Ⓔ
72. Ⓐ Ⓑ Ⓒ Ⓓ Ⓔ
73. Ⓐ Ⓑ Ⓒ Ⓓ Ⓔ
74. Ⓐ Ⓑ Ⓒ Ⓓ Ⓔ
75. Ⓐ Ⓑ Ⓒ Ⓓ Ⓔ
76. Ⓐ Ⓑ Ⓒ Ⓓ Ⓔ
77. Ⓐ Ⓑ Ⓒ Ⓓ Ⓔ
78. Ⓐ Ⓑ Ⓒ Ⓓ Ⓔ
79. Ⓐ Ⓑ Ⓒ Ⓓ Ⓔ
80. Ⓐ Ⓑ Ⓒ Ⓓ Ⓔ
81. Ⓐ Ⓑ Ⓒ Ⓓ Ⓔ
82. Ⓐ Ⓑ Ⓒ Ⓓ Ⓔ
83. Ⓐ Ⓑ Ⓒ Ⓓ Ⓔ
84. Ⓐ Ⓑ Ⓒ Ⓓ Ⓔ
85. Ⓐ Ⓑ Ⓒ Ⓓ Ⓔ
86. Ⓐ Ⓑ Ⓒ Ⓓ Ⓔ
87. Ⓐ Ⓑ Ⓒ Ⓓ Ⓔ
88. Ⓐ Ⓑ Ⓒ Ⓓ Ⓔ

PRACTICE III

1 Ⓐ Ⓑ Ⓒ Ⓓ Ⓔ
2 Ⓐ Ⓑ Ⓒ Ⓓ Ⓔ
3 Ⓐ Ⓑ Ⓒ Ⓓ Ⓔ
4 Ⓐ Ⓑ Ⓒ Ⓓ Ⓔ
5 Ⓐ Ⓑ Ⓒ Ⓓ Ⓔ
6 Ⓐ Ⓑ Ⓒ Ⓓ Ⓔ
7 Ⓐ Ⓑ Ⓒ Ⓓ Ⓔ
8 Ⓐ Ⓑ Ⓒ Ⓓ Ⓔ
9 Ⓐ Ⓑ Ⓒ Ⓓ Ⓔ
10 Ⓐ Ⓑ Ⓒ Ⓓ Ⓔ
11 Ⓐ Ⓑ Ⓒ Ⓓ Ⓔ
12 Ⓐ Ⓑ Ⓒ Ⓓ Ⓔ
13 Ⓐ Ⓑ Ⓒ Ⓓ Ⓔ
14 Ⓐ Ⓑ Ⓒ Ⓓ Ⓔ
15 Ⓐ Ⓑ Ⓒ Ⓓ Ⓔ
16 Ⓐ Ⓑ Ⓒ Ⓓ Ⓔ
17 Ⓐ Ⓑ Ⓒ Ⓓ Ⓔ
18 Ⓐ Ⓑ Ⓒ Ⓓ Ⓔ
19 Ⓐ Ⓑ Ⓒ Ⓓ Ⓔ
20 Ⓐ Ⓑ Ⓒ Ⓓ Ⓔ
21 Ⓐ Ⓑ Ⓒ Ⓓ Ⓔ
22 Ⓐ Ⓑ Ⓒ Ⓓ Ⓔ

23 Ⓐ Ⓑ Ⓒ Ⓓ Ⓔ
24 Ⓐ Ⓑ Ⓒ Ⓓ Ⓔ
25 Ⓐ Ⓑ Ⓒ Ⓓ Ⓔ
26 Ⓐ Ⓑ Ⓒ Ⓓ Ⓔ
27 Ⓐ Ⓑ Ⓒ Ⓓ Ⓔ
28 Ⓐ Ⓑ Ⓒ Ⓓ Ⓔ
29 Ⓐ Ⓑ Ⓒ Ⓓ Ⓔ
30 Ⓐ Ⓑ Ⓒ Ⓓ Ⓔ
31 Ⓐ Ⓑ Ⓒ Ⓓ Ⓔ
32 Ⓐ Ⓑ Ⓒ Ⓓ Ⓔ
33 Ⓐ Ⓑ Ⓒ Ⓓ Ⓔ
34 Ⓐ Ⓑ Ⓒ Ⓓ Ⓔ
35 Ⓐ Ⓑ Ⓒ Ⓓ Ⓔ
36 Ⓐ Ⓑ Ⓒ Ⓓ Ⓔ
37 Ⓐ Ⓑ Ⓒ Ⓓ Ⓔ
38 Ⓐ Ⓑ Ⓒ Ⓓ Ⓔ
39 Ⓐ Ⓑ Ⓒ Ⓓ Ⓔ
40 Ⓐ Ⓑ Ⓒ Ⓓ Ⓔ
41 Ⓐ Ⓑ Ⓒ Ⓓ Ⓔ
42 Ⓐ Ⓑ Ⓒ Ⓓ Ⓔ
43 Ⓐ Ⓑ Ⓒ Ⓓ Ⓔ
44 Ⓐ Ⓑ Ⓒ Ⓓ Ⓔ

45 Ⓐ Ⓑ Ⓒ Ⓓ Ⓔ
46 Ⓐ Ⓑ Ⓒ Ⓓ Ⓔ
47 Ⓐ Ⓑ Ⓒ Ⓓ Ⓔ
48 Ⓐ Ⓑ Ⓒ Ⓓ Ⓔ
49 Ⓐ Ⓑ Ⓒ Ⓓ Ⓔ
50 Ⓐ Ⓑ Ⓒ Ⓓ Ⓔ
51 Ⓐ Ⓑ Ⓒ Ⓓ Ⓔ
52 Ⓐ Ⓑ Ⓒ Ⓓ Ⓔ
53 Ⓐ Ⓑ Ⓒ Ⓓ Ⓔ
54 Ⓐ Ⓑ Ⓒ Ⓓ Ⓔ
55 Ⓐ Ⓑ Ⓒ Ⓓ Ⓔ
56 Ⓐ Ⓑ Ⓒ Ⓓ Ⓔ
57 Ⓐ Ⓑ Ⓒ Ⓓ Ⓔ
58 Ⓐ Ⓑ Ⓒ Ⓓ Ⓔ
59 Ⓐ Ⓑ Ⓒ Ⓓ Ⓔ
60 Ⓐ Ⓑ Ⓒ Ⓓ Ⓔ
61 Ⓐ Ⓑ Ⓒ Ⓓ Ⓔ
62 Ⓐ Ⓑ Ⓒ Ⓓ Ⓔ
63 Ⓐ Ⓑ Ⓒ Ⓓ Ⓕ
64 Ⓐ Ⓑ Ⓒ Ⓓ Ⓔ
65 Ⓐ Ⓑ Ⓒ Ⓓ Ⓔ
66 Ⓐ Ⓑ Ⓒ Ⓓ Ⓔ

67 Ⓐ Ⓑ Ⓒ Ⓓ Ⓔ
68 Ⓐ Ⓑ Ⓒ Ⓓ Ⓔ
69 Ⓐ Ⓑ Ⓒ Ⓓ Ⓔ
70 Ⓐ Ⓑ Ⓒ Ⓓ Ⓔ
71 Ⓐ Ⓑ Ⓒ Ⓓ Ⓔ
72 Ⓐ Ⓑ Ⓒ Ⓓ Ⓔ
73 Ⓐ Ⓑ Ⓒ Ⓓ Ⓔ
74 Ⓐ Ⓑ Ⓒ Ⓓ Ⓔ
75 Ⓐ Ⓑ Ⓒ Ⓓ Ⓔ
76 Ⓐ Ⓑ Ⓒ Ⓓ Ⓔ
77 Ⓐ Ⓑ Ⓒ Ⓓ Ⓔ
78 Ⓐ Ⓑ Ⓒ Ⓓ Ⓔ
79 Ⓐ Ⓑ Ⓒ Ⓓ Ⓔ
80 Ⓐ Ⓑ Ⓒ Ⓓ Ⓔ
81 Ⓐ Ⓑ Ⓒ Ⓓ Ⓔ
82 Ⓐ Ⓑ Ⓒ Ⓓ Ⓔ
83 Ⓐ Ⓑ Ⓒ Ⓓ Ⓔ
84 Ⓐ Ⓑ Ⓒ Ⓓ Ⓔ
85 Ⓐ Ⓑ Ⓒ Ⓓ Ⓔ
86 Ⓐ Ⓑ Ⓒ Ⓓ Ⓔ
87 Ⓐ Ⓑ Ⓒ Ⓓ Ⓔ
88 Ⓐ Ⓑ Ⓒ Ⓓ Ⓔ

MEMORY FOR ADDRESSES TEST

1 Ⓐ Ⓑ Ⓒ Ⓓ Ⓔ	23 Ⓐ Ⓑ Ⓒ Ⓓ Ⓔ	45 Ⓐ Ⓑ Ⓒ Ⓓ Ⓔ	67 Ⓐ Ⓑ Ⓒ Ⓓ Ⓔ
2 Ⓐ Ⓑ Ⓒ Ⓓ Ⓔ	24 Ⓐ Ⓑ Ⓒ Ⓓ Ⓔ	46 Ⓐ Ⓑ Ⓒ Ⓓ Ⓔ	68 Ⓐ Ⓑ Ⓒ Ⓓ Ⓔ
3 Ⓐ Ⓑ Ⓒ Ⓓ Ⓔ	25 Ⓐ Ⓑ Ⓒ Ⓓ Ⓔ	47 Ⓐ Ⓑ Ⓒ Ⓓ Ⓔ	69 Ⓐ Ⓑ Ⓒ Ⓓ Ⓔ
4 Ⓐ Ⓑ Ⓒ Ⓓ Ⓔ	26 Ⓐ Ⓑ Ⓒ Ⓓ Ⓔ	48 Ⓐ Ⓑ Ⓒ Ⓓ Ⓔ	70 Ⓐ Ⓑ Ⓒ Ⓓ Ⓔ
5 Ⓐ Ⓑ Ⓒ Ⓓ Ⓔ	27 Ⓐ Ⓑ Ⓒ Ⓓ Ⓔ	49 Ⓐ Ⓑ Ⓒ Ⓓ Ⓔ	71 Ⓐ Ⓑ Ⓒ Ⓓ Ⓔ
6 Ⓐ Ⓑ Ⓒ Ⓓ Ⓔ	28 Ⓐ Ⓑ Ⓒ Ⓓ Ⓔ	50 Ⓐ Ⓑ Ⓒ Ⓓ Ⓔ	72 Ⓐ Ⓑ Ⓒ Ⓓ Ⓔ
7 Ⓐ Ⓑ Ⓒ Ⓓ Ⓔ	29 Ⓐ Ⓑ Ⓒ Ⓓ Ⓔ	51 Ⓐ Ⓑ Ⓒ Ⓓ Ⓔ	73 Ⓐ Ⓑ Ⓒ Ⓓ Ⓔ
8 Ⓐ Ⓑ Ⓒ Ⓓ Ⓔ	30 Ⓐ Ⓑ Ⓒ Ⓓ Ⓔ	52 Ⓐ Ⓑ Ⓒ Ⓓ Ⓔ	74 Ⓐ Ⓑ Ⓒ Ⓓ Ⓔ
9 Ⓐ Ⓑ Ⓒ Ⓓ Ⓔ	31 Ⓐ Ⓑ Ⓒ Ⓓ Ⓔ	53 Ⓐ Ⓑ Ⓒ Ⓓ Ⓔ	75 Ⓐ Ⓑ Ⓒ Ⓓ Ⓔ
10 Ⓐ Ⓑ Ⓒ Ⓓ Ⓔ	32 Ⓐ Ⓑ Ⓒ Ⓓ Ⓔ	54 Ⓐ Ⓑ Ⓒ Ⓓ Ⓔ	76 Ⓐ Ⓑ Ⓒ Ⓓ Ⓔ
11 Ⓐ Ⓑ Ⓒ Ⓓ Ⓔ	33 Ⓐ Ⓑ Ⓒ Ⓓ Ⓔ	55 Ⓐ Ⓑ Ⓒ Ⓓ Ⓔ	77 Ⓐ Ⓑ Ⓒ Ⓓ Ⓔ
12 Ⓐ Ⓑ Ⓒ Ⓓ Ⓔ	34 Ⓐ Ⓑ Ⓒ Ⓓ Ⓔ	56 Ⓐ Ⓑ Ⓒ Ⓓ Ⓔ	78 Ⓐ Ⓑ Ⓒ Ⓓ Ⓔ
13 Ⓐ Ⓑ Ⓒ Ⓓ Ⓔ	35 Ⓐ Ⓑ Ⓒ Ⓓ Ⓔ	57 Ⓐ Ⓑ Ⓒ Ⓓ Ⓔ	79 Ⓐ Ⓑ Ⓒ Ⓓ Ⓔ
14 Ⓐ Ⓑ Ⓒ Ⓓ Ⓔ	36 Ⓐ Ⓑ Ⓒ Ⓓ Ⓔ	58 Ⓐ Ⓑ Ⓒ Ⓓ Ⓔ	80 Ⓐ Ⓑ Ⓒ Ⓓ Ⓔ
15 Ⓐ Ⓑ Ⓒ Ⓓ Ⓔ	37 Ⓐ Ⓑ Ⓒ Ⓓ Ⓔ	59 Ⓐ Ⓑ Ⓒ Ⓓ Ⓔ	81 Ⓐ Ⓑ Ⓒ Ⓓ Ⓔ
16 Ⓐ Ⓑ Ⓒ Ⓓ Ⓔ	38 Ⓐ Ⓑ Ⓒ Ⓓ Ⓔ	60 Ⓐ Ⓑ Ⓒ Ⓓ Ⓔ	82 Ⓐ Ⓑ Ⓒ Ⓓ Ⓔ
17 Ⓐ Ⓑ Ⓒ Ⓓ Ⓔ	39 Ⓐ Ⓑ Ⓒ Ⓓ Ⓔ	61 Ⓐ Ⓑ Ⓒ Ⓓ Ⓔ	83 Ⓐ Ⓑ Ⓒ Ⓓ Ⓔ
18 Ⓐ Ⓑ Ⓒ Ⓓ Ⓔ	40 Ⓐ Ⓑ Ⓒ Ⓓ Ⓔ	62 Ⓐ Ⓑ Ⓒ Ⓓ Ⓔ	84 Ⓐ Ⓑ Ⓒ Ⓓ Ⓔ
19 Ⓐ Ⓑ Ⓒ Ⓓ Ⓔ	41 Ⓐ Ⓑ Ⓒ Ⓓ Ⓔ	63 Ⓐ Ⓑ Ⓒ Ⓓ Ⓔ	85 Ⓐ Ⓑ Ⓒ Ⓓ Ⓔ
20 Ⓐ Ⓑ Ⓒ Ⓓ Ⓔ	42 Ⓐ Ⓑ Ⓒ Ⓓ Ⓔ	64 Ⓐ Ⓑ Ⓒ Ⓓ Ⓔ	86 Ⓐ Ⓑ Ⓒ Ⓓ Ⓔ
21 Ⓐ Ⓑ Ⓒ Ⓓ Ⓔ	43 Ⓐ Ⓑ Ⓒ Ⓓ Ⓔ	65 Ⓐ Ⓑ Ⓒ Ⓓ Ⓔ	87 Ⓐ Ⓑ Ⓒ Ⓓ Ⓔ
22 Ⓐ Ⓑ Ⓒ Ⓓ Ⓔ	44 Ⓐ Ⓑ Ⓒ Ⓓ Ⓔ	66 Ⓐ Ⓑ Ⓒ Ⓓ Ⓔ	88 Ⓐ Ⓑ Ⓒ Ⓓ Ⓔ

SCORE SHEET FOR THIRD MODEL EXAM

ADDRESS CHECKING TEST

Number Right minus Number Wrong equals   Score

_____ − _____ = _____

MEMORY FOR ADDRESSES TEST

Number Right minus (Number Wrong ÷ 4) equals   Score

_____ − _____ = _____

PROGRESS GRAPH

Blacken the bars for Model Exam 3 to the scores you earned.

Score				
95				
90				
85				
80				
75				
70				
65				
60				
55				
50				
45				
40				
35				
30				
25				
20				
15				
10				
5				
0				
Test	AC I M	AC I M	AC I M	AC I M
Model Exam	Diag.	1	2	3

AC = Address Checking   M = Memory for Addresses

THIRD MODEL EXAM

ADDRESS CHECKING TEST

TIME: 6 Minutes. 95 Questions.

*DIRECTIONS: For each question, compare the address in the left column with the address in the right column. If the two addresses are **ALIKE IN EVERY WAY**, blacken space Ⓐ on your answer sheet. If the two addresses are **DIFFERENT IN ANY WAY**, blacken space Ⓓ on your answer sheet. Correct answers for this test are on page 123.*

1.	1897 Smicksburg Rd	1897 Smithsburg Rd
2.	3609 E Paseo Aldeano	3909 E Paseo Aldeano
3.	11787 Ornamental Ln	1787 Ornamental Ln
4.	1096 Camino Grande E	1096 Camino Grande E
5.	2544 E Radcliff Ave	2544 E Redcliff Ave
6.	5796 E Narragansett Dr	5796 E Narragasett Dr
7.	12475 Ebbtide Way W	12475 Ebbtide Way W
8.	14396 N Via Armando	14396 S Via Armando
9.	2155 S Del Giorgio Rd	2155 S Del Giorgio Rd
10.	16550 Bainbridge Cir	16505 Bainbridge Cir
11.	1826 Milneburg Rd	1826 Milneburg St
12.	Eureka KS 67045	Eureka KY 67045
13.	4010 Glenaddie Ave	4010 Glenaddie Ave
14.	13501 Stratford Rd	13501 Standford Rd
15.	3296 W 64th St	3296 E 64th St
16.	2201 Tennessee Cir	2201 Tennessee Cir
17.	1502 Avenue M NE	1502 Avenue N NE
18.	1096 SE Longrone Dr	1096 SE Longrone Dr
19.	1267 Darthmouth Ct	1267 Darthmont Ct
20.	825 Ophanage Rd	825 Ophanage Rd
21.	1754 Golden Springs Rd	1754 Golden Springs Road
22.	1015 Tallwoods Ln	1015 Tallwoods Ln
23.	1097 Lambada Dr	1097 Lambadd Dr
24.	Vredenburgh AL 36481	Verdenburgh AL 36481
25.	1800 Monticello Ave	1800 Monticello Ave
26.	1723 Yellowbird Ln	1723 Yellowbird Ct
27.	700 Valca Materials Rd	700 Valca Materials Rd
28.	1569 Ladywood Ln N	1569 Ladywood Ln W
29.	3256 Interurban Dr	3256 Interurban Dr

30...1507 Haughton Cir	1507 Haughton Ct
31...8971 Robertson Ave	8971 Robinson Ave
32...3801 NE 49th Street	3801 NW 49th Street
33...4102 Chalkville Rd	4102 Chalkview Rd
34...1709 Ingersoll Cir	1709 Ingersoll Cir
35...6800 N Nantucket Ln	6800 N Nantucket Ln
36...12401 Tarrymore Dr	12401 Terrymore Dr
37...1097 Huntsville Ave	1097 Huntsville Ave
38...3566 Lornaridge Pl	3566 Lornaridge Pl
39...2039 Klondike Ave SW	2039 Klondie Ave SW
40...3267 Mayland Ln	3267 Maryland Ln
41...12956 Strawberry Ln	12596 Strawberry Ln
42...De Armanville AL 36257	De Armanville AL 36257
43...6015 Anniston Dr	6015 Anneston Dr
44...1525 E 90th St	1525 E 90th St
45...1299 Chappaque Rd	1266 Chappaque Rd
46...2156 Juliette Dr	2156 Juliaetta Dr
47...999 N Hollingsworth St	999 S Hollingsworth St
48...16901 Odum Crest Ln	19601 Odum Crest Ln
49...9787 Zellmark Dr	9787 Zealmark Dr
50...11103 NE Feasell Ave	11103 NE Feasell Ave
51...51121 N Mattison Rd	51121 S Mattison Rd
52...8326 Blackjack Ln	8326 Blackjack Blvd
53...18765 Lagarde Ave	18765 Lagrande Ave
54...11297 Gallatin Ln	11297 Gallatin Ln
55...Wormleysburg PA 17043	Wormleysburg PA 17043
56...22371 N Sprague Ave	22371 S Sprague Ave
57...15014 Warrior River Rd	15014 Warrior River Rd
58...45721 Hueytown Plaza	45721 Hueytowne Plaza
59...8973 Tedescki Dr	8793 Tedescki Dr
60...12995 Raimond Muscoda Pl	12995 Raimont Muscoda Pl
61...Phippsburg CO 80469	Phippsburg CA 80469
62...52003 W 49th Ave	52003 W 46th Ave
63...17201 Zenobia Cir	17210 Zenobia Cir
64...4800 Garrison Cir	4800 Garrison Dr
65...Los Angeles CA 90070	Los Angeles CA 90076
66...14798 W 62nd Ave	14198 W 62nd Ave
67...7191 E Eldridge Way	7191 E Eldridge Way
68...1279 S Quintard Dr	1279 S Guintard Dr
69...21899 Dellwood Ave	21899 Dillwood Ave
70...7191 Zenophone Cir	7191 Zenohone Cir
71...4301 Los Encinos Way	4301 Los Encinas Way
72...19700 Ostronic Dr NW	19700 Ostronic Dr NE
73...23291 Van Velsire Dr	23219 Van Velsire Dr
74...547 Paradise Valley Rd	547 Paradise Valley Ct
75...23167 Saltillo Ave	23167 Santillo Ave
76...43001 Mourning Dove Way	43001 Mourning Dove Way
77...21183 Declaration Ave	21183 Declaration Ave
78...10799 Via Sierra Ramal Ave	10799 Via Sierra Ramel Ave
79...16567 Hermosillia Ct	16597 Hermosillia Ct
80...Villamont VA 24178	Villamont VA 24178
81...18794 Villaboso Ave	18794 Villeboso Ave
82...24136 Ranthom Ave	24136 Ranthon Ave

83...13489 Golondrina Pl	13489 Golondrina St
84...6598 Adamsville Ave	6598 Adamsville Ave
85...12641 Indals Pl NE	12641 Indals Pl NW
86...19701 SE 2nd Avenue	19701 NE 2nd Avenue
87...22754 Cachalote Ln	22754 Cachalott Ln
88...12341 Kingfisher Rd	12341 Kingsfisher Rd
89...24168 Lorenzana Dr	24168 Lorenzano Dr
90...32480 Blackfriar Rd	32480 Blackfriar Rd
91...16355 Wheeler Dr	16355 Wheelen Dr
92...5100 Magna Carta Rd	5100 Magna Certa Rd
93...2341 N Federalist Pl	2341 N Federalist Pl
94...22200 Timpangos Rd	22200 Timpangos Rd
95...19704 Calderon Rd	19704 Calderon Rd

END OF ADDRESS CHECKING TEST

If you finish this test before time is up, use the remaining time to check over your work. Do not turn the page until you are told to do so.

PRACTICE FOR
MEMORY FOR ADDRESSES TEST

DIRECTIONS: The five boxes below are labelled A, B, C, D, and E. In each box are three sets of number spans with names and two names which are not associated with numbers. In the next THREE MINUTES, you must try to memorize the box location of each name and number span. The position of a name or number span within its box is not important. You need only remember the letter of the box in which the item is to be found. You will use these names and numbers to answer three sets of practice questions which are NOT scored and one actual test which is scored. Correct answers are on pages 123 and 124.

A	B	C	D	E
3100-3599 Ronald	4200-4599 Ronald	2400-2999 Ronald	3600-4199 Ronald	1900-2299 Ronald
Seville	Buckeye	Bowie	Phillis	Yuma
8500-8999 Tonka	8400-8499 Tonka	7600-7999 Tonka	8300-8399 Tonka	8100-8299 Tonka
Fiesta	Midway	Park	Falcon	Young
7700-7799 Walnut	2600-3999 Walnut	8000-8099 Walnut	7900-7990 Walnut	7800-7899 Walnut

PRACTICE I

DIRECTIONS: Use the next THREE MINUTES to mark on your answer sheet the letter of the box in which each item that follows is to be found. Try to mark each item without looking back at the boxes. If, however, you get stuck, you may refer to the boxes during this practice exercise. If you find that you must look at the boxes, try to memorize as you do so. This test is for practice only. It will not be scored.

1. 7800-7899 Walnut
2. Bowie
3. 1900-2299 Ronald
4. 8400-8499 Tonka
5. Phillis
6. 7700-7799 Walnut
7. 3100-3599 Ronald
8. 1900-2299 Ronald
9. 3100-3599 Ronald
10. 7600-7999 Tonka
11. Buckeye
12. 3600-4199 Ronald
13. 2600-3999 Walnut
14. Yuma
15. 2400-2999 Ronald
16. 8500-8999 Tonka
17. Young
18. Midway
19. 4200-4599 Ronald
20. 8100-8299 Tonka
21. 2400-2999 Ronald
22. 8500-8999 Tonka

23. 8000-8099 Walnut
24. 3600-4199 Ronald
25. 2600-3999 Walnut
26. 7800-7899 Walnut
27. Seville
28. Young
29. Park
30. 8300-8399 Tonka
31. Phillis
32. Bowie
33. 1900-2299 Ronald
34. Falcon
35. 4200-4599 Ronald
36. Midway
37. 3100-3599 Ronald
38. 8100-8299 Tonka
39. Buckeye
40. Yuma
41. Seville
42. 2600-3999 Walnut
43. 8300-8399 Tonka
44. 8000-8099 Walnut
45. 7800-7899 Walnut
46. Fiesta
47. 8300-8399 Tonka
48. 4200-4599 Ronald
49. 1900-2299 Ronald
50. 7600-7999 Tonka
51. Seville
52. 7800-7899 Walnut
53. Fiesta
54. Buckeye
55. 2600-3999 Walnut

56. 8100-8299 Tonka
57. 8500-8999 Tonka
58. 2400-2999 Ronald
59. 8300-8399 Tonka
60. 8500-8999 Tonka
61. 8000-8099 Walnut
62. Seville
63. 8400-8499 Tonka
64. 3600-4199 Ronald
65. 3100-3599 Ronald
66. 8000-8099 Walnut
67. 3600-4199 Ronald
68. 8400-8499 Tonka
69. 8000-8099 Walnut
70. 7700-7799 Walnut
71. 1900-2299 Ronald
72. 8400-8499 Tonka
73. Fiesta
74. 7800-7899 Walnut
75. 8000-8099 Walnut
76. 7900-7999 Walnut
77. 2600-3999 Walnut
78. 3100-3599 Ronald
79. 8100-8299 Tonka
80. 2400-2999 Ronald
81. Fiesta
82. 7700-7799 Walnut
83. 4200-4599 Ronald
84. Midway
85. Fiesta
86. 1900-2299 Ronald
87. Park
88. 2400-2999 Ronald

PRACTICE II

DIRECTIONS: The next 88 questions constitute another practice exercise. Again, you should mark your answers on your answer sheet. Again, the time limit is THREE MINUTES. This time, however, you must NOT look at the boxes while answering the questions. You must rely on your memory in marking the box location of each item. This practice test will not be scored.

1. 3600-4199 Ronald
2. 7600-7999 Tonka
3. Fiesta
4. Buckeye
5. 7800-7899 Walnut
6. 8400-8499 Tonka
7. 1900-2299 Ronald
8. 7700-7799 Walnut
9. Phillis
10. Young
11. Midway
12. 8000-8099 Walnut
13. 8500-8999 Tonka
14. 3100-3599 Ronald
15. 8300-8399 Tonka
16. Yuma
17. Bowie
18. Seville
19. 2600-3999 Walnut
20. 8100-8299 Tonka
21. 4200-4599 Ronald
22. 3600-4199 Ronald
23. 7900-7999 Walnut
24. Park
25. Falcon
26. 8500-8999 Tonka
27. 8000-8099 Walnut
28. 4200-4599 Ronald
29. 3600-4199 Ronald
30. Yuma
31. Buckeye
32. 8300-8399 Tonka
33. 7900-7999 Walnut
34. Young
35. Phillis
36. 2600-3999 Walnut
37. 3100-3599 Ronald
38. 8400-8499 Tonka
39. Midway
40. Falcon
41. 8100-8299 Tonka
42. 4200-4599 Ronald
43. 7600-7999 Tonka
44. Seville
45. Bowie
46. 7800-7899 Walnut
47. 7700-7799 Walnut
48. Park
49. 8400-8499 Tonka
50. 7900-7999 Walnut
51. 1900-2299 Ronald
52. 3100-3599 Ronald
53. Fiesta
54. 8000-8099 Walnut
55. 3600-4199 Ronald
56. Phillis
57. Seville
58. 8500-8999 Tonka
59. 8100-8299 Tonka
60. Buckeye
61. 2600-3999 Walnut
62. 4200-4599 Ronald
63. Midway
64. 2400-2999 Ronald
65. 7700-7799 Walnut
66. Yuma
67. 7800-7899 Walnut
68. 8300-8399 Tonka
69. Falcon
70. Young
71. Seville
72. 7600-7999 Tonka
73. 8000-8099 Walnut
74. 2400-2999 Ronald
75. 3100-3599 Ronald
76. 7700-7799 Walnut
77. 8500-8999 Tonka
78. Yuma
79. Fiesta
80. 4200-4599 Ronald
81. 8100-8299 Tonka
82. 7900-7999 Walnut
83. Phillis
84. Midway
85. Park
86. 8400-8499 Tonka
87. 2600-3999 Walnut
88. 4200-4599 Ronald

PRACTICE III

DIRECTIONS: The names and addresses are repeated for you in the boxes below. Each name and each number span is in the same box in which you found it in the original set. You will now be allowed FIVE MINUTES to study the locations again. Do your best to memorize the letter of the box in which each item is located. This is your last chance to see the boxes.

A	B	C	D	E
3100-3599 Ronald Seville 8500-8999 Tonka Fiesta 7700-7799 Walnut	4200-4599 Ronald Buckeye 8400-8499 Tonka Midway 2600-3999 Walnut	2400-2999 Ronald Bowie 7600-7999 Tonka Park 8000-8099 Walnut	3600-4199 Ronald Phillis 8300-8399 Tonka Falcon 7900-7990 Walnut	1900-2299 Ronald Yuma 8100-8299 Tonka Young 7800-7899 Walnut

DIRECTIONS: This is your last practice test. Mark the location of each of the 88 items on your answer sheet. You will have FIVE MINUTES to answer these questions. Do NOT look back at the boxes. This practice test will not be scored.

1. 8100-8299 Tonka
2. 7700-7799 Walnut
3. Bowie
4. Young
5. 4200-4599 Ronald
6. 7800-7899 Walnut
7. 8400-8499 Tonka
8. 2400-2999 Ronald
9. 1900-2299 Ronald
10. Seville
11. Park
12. Phillis
13. 8500-8999 Tonka
14. 8000-8099 Walnut
15. 2600-3999 Walnut
16. 3600-4199 Ronald
17. Fiesta
18. 7600-7999 Tonka
19. 7800-7899 Walnut
20. 3100-3599 Ronald
21. 7900-7999 Walnut
22. 8500-8999 Tonka
23. Bowie
24. Buckeye
25. Falcon
26. 2400-2999 Ronald
27. 7700-7799 Walnut
28. 8300-8399 Tonka
29. Yuma
30. Midway
31. 3100-3599 Ronald
32. Buckeye
33. 7600-7999 Tonka
34. Falcon
35. 7800-7899 Walnut
36. 1900-2299 Ronald
37. Phillis
38. Midway
39. 7700-7799 Walnut
40. 8500-8999 Tonka
41. 2600-3999 Walnut
42. Park
43. Bowie
44. 3600-4199 Ronald
45. 7900-7999 Walnut
46. 8100-8299 Tonka
47. Young
48. Yuma
49. 8000-8099 Walnut
50. 4200-4599 Ronald
51. 2400-2999 Ronald
52. 8300-8399 Tonka

53. 8400-8499 Tonka
54. Seville
55. Fiesta
56. 4200-4599 Ronald
57. 7800-7899 Walnut
58. 3100-3599 Ronald
59. 1900-2299 Ronald
60. Buckeye
61. Phillis
62. 8400-8499 Tonka
63. 7700-7799 Walnut
64. 3600-4199 Ronald
65. Midway
66. Park
67. 8100-8299 Tonka
68. 7800-7899 Walnut
69. 8500-8999 Tonka
70. 2400-2999 Ronald

71. 3100-3599 Ronald
72. Bowie
73. Young
74. 7900-7999 Walnut
75. 7600-7999 Tonka
76. 8000-8099 Walnut
77. 8300-8399 Tonka
78. Seville
79. Yuma
80. Buckeye
81. 1900-2299 Ronald
82. 4200-4599 Ronald
83. Falcon
84. Fiesta
85. 3600-4199 Ronald
86. 8100-8299 Tonka
87. 7700-7799 Walnut
88. 8000-8099 Walnut

MEMORY FOR ADDRESSES TEST

TIME: 5 Minutes. 88 Questions.

DIRECTIONS: Mark your answers on the answer sheet in the section headed "MEMORY FOR ADDRESSES TEST." This test will be scored. You are NOT permitted to look at the boxes. Work from memory, as quickly and as accurately as you can. Correct answers are on page 124.

1. Falcon
2. Bowie
3. 3600-4199 Ronald
4. 2600-3999 Walnut
5. 8500-8999 Tonka
6. 8100-8299 Tonka
7. 7900-7999 Walnut
8. 4200-4599 Ronald
9. Yuma
10. Midway
11. Park
12. 7700-7799 Walnut
13. 3100-3599 Ronald
14. 8100-8299 Tonka
15. Young
16. Phillis
17. 2400-2999 Ronald
18. 7800-7899 Walnut
19. 8000-8099 Walnut
20. Buckeye
21. Fiesta
22. 1900-2299 Ronald
23. 8300-8399 Tonka
24. Buckeye
25. Young
26. 4200-4599 Ronald
27. 7700-7799 Walnut
28. 3600-4199 Ronald
29. 7900-7999 Walnut
30. 8500-8999 Tonka
31. Seville
32. Yuma
33. 8100-8299 Tonka
34. 2600-3999 Walnut
35. 3100-3599 Ronald
36. 2400-2999 Ronald
37. Midway
38. 8400-8499 Tonka
39. 7800-7899 Walnut
40. 8000-8099 Walnut
41. 7600-7999 Tonka
42. 1900-2299 Ronald
43. Phillis
44. Bowie
45. 8500-8999 Tonka
46. Midway
47. 8000-8099 Walnut
48. Falcon
49. 1900-2299 Ronald
50. 7800-7899 Walnut
51. Phillis
52. 7600-7999 Tonka
53. 3100-3599 Ronald
54. 7900-7999 Walnut
55. 8400-8499 Tonka
56. Yuma
57. Seville
58. 8100-8299 Tonka
59. 7700-7799 Walnut
60. 2600-3999 Walnut
61. Fiesta
62. Park
63. 8300-8399 Tonka
64. 2400-2999 Ronald
65. 4200-4599 Ronald
66. Young
67. Bowie
68. 3600-4199 Ronald
69. Seville
70. 8100-8299 Tonka
71. 2600-3999 Walnut
72. 7600-7999 Tonka
73. 3100-3599 Ronald
74. 8000-8099 Walnut
75. Midway
76. Falcon
77. 8300-8399 Tonka
78. 4200-4599 Ronald

79. 7700-7799 Walnut
80. Yuma
81. Fiesta
82. 2400-2999 Ronald
83. Midway

84. 8400-8499 Tonka
85. 7900-7999 Walnut
86. 1900-2299 Ronald
87. 8500-8999 Tonka
88. Phillis

END OF EXAM

ADDRESS CHECKING ERROR ANALYSIS CHART

Type of Error	Tally	Total Number
Number of addresses which were alike and you incorrectly marked "different"		
Number of addresses which were different and you incorrectly marked "alike"		
Number of addresses in which you missed a difference in NUMBERS		
Number of addresses in which you missed a difference in ABBREVIATIONS		
Number of addresses in which you missed a difference in NAMES		

SELF-EVALUATION CHART

Test	Excellent	Good	Average	Fair	Poor
Address Checking	80-95	65-79	50-64	35-49	1-34
Memory for Addresses	75-88	60-74	45-59	30-44	1-29

CORRECT ANSWERS FOR THIRD MODEL EXAM

ADDRESS CHECKING TEST

1. D	13. A	25. A	37. A	49. D	61. D	73. D	85. D
2. D	14. D	26. D	38. A	50. A	62. D	74. D	86. D
3. D	15. D	27. A	39. D	51. D	63. D	75. D	87. D
4. A	16. A	28. D	40. D	52. D	64. D	76. A	88. D
5. D	17. D	29. A	41. D	53. D	65. D	77. A	89. D
6. D	18. A	30. D	42. A	54. A	66. D	78. D	90. A
7. A	19. D	31. D	43. D	55. A	67. A	79. D	91. D
8. D	20. A	32. D	44. A	56. D	68. D	80. A	92. D
9. A	21. D	33. D	45. D	57. A	69. D	81. D	93. A
10. D	22. A	34. A	46. D	58. D	70. D	82. D	94. A
11. D	23. D	35. A	47. D	59. D	71. D	83. D	95. A
12. D	24. D	36. D	48. D	60. D	72. D	84. A	

MEMORY FOR ADDRESSES—PRACTICE I

1. E	12. D	23. C	34. D	45. E	56. E	67. D	78. A
2. C	13. B	24. D	35. B	46. A	57. A	68. B	79. E
3. E	14. E	25. B	36. B	47. D	58. C	69. C	80. C
4. B	15. C	26. E	37. A	48. B	59. D	70. A	81. A
5. D	16. A	27. A	38. E	49. E	60. A	71. E	82. A
6. A	17. E	28. E	39. B	50. C	61. C	72. B	83. B
7. A	18. B	29. C	40. E	51. A	62. A	73. A	84. B
8. E	19. B	30. D	41. A	52. E	63. B	74. E	85. A
9. A	20. E	31. D	42. B	53. A	64. D	75. C	86. E
10. C	21. C	32. C	43. D	54. B	65. A	76. D	87. C
11. B	22. A	33. E	44. C	55. B	66. C	77. B	88. C

MEMORY FOR ADDRESSES—PRACTICE II

1. D	12. C	23. D	34. E	45. C	56. D	67. E	78. E
2. C	13. A	24. C	35. D	46. E	57. A	68. D	79. A
3. A	14. A	25. D	36. B	47. A	58. A	69. D	80. B
4. B	15. D	26. A	37. A	48. C	59. E	70. E	81. E
5. E	16. E	27. C	38. B	49. B	60. B	71. A	82. D
6. B	17. C	28. B	39. B	50. D	61. B	72. C	83. D
7. E	18. A	29. D	40. D	51. E	62. B	73. C	84. B
8. A	19. B	30. E	41. E	52. A	63. B	74. C	85. C
9. D	20. E	31. B	42. B	53. A	64. C	75. A	86. B
10. E	21. B	32. D	43. C	54. C	65. A	76. A	87. B
11. B	22. D	33. D	44. A	55. D	66. E	77. A	88. B

MEMORY FOR ADDRESSES—PRACTICE III

1. E	12. D	23. C	34. D	45. D	56. B	67. E	78. A
2. A	13. A	24. B	35. E	46. E	57. E	68. E	79. E
3. C	14. C	25. D	36. E	47. E	58. A	69. A	80. B
4. E	15. B	26. C	37. D	48. E	59. E	70. C	81. E
5. B	16. D	27. A	38. B	49. C	60. B	71. A	82. B
6. E	17. A	28. D	39. A	50. B	61. D	72. C	83. D
7. B	18. C	29. E	40. A	51. C	62. B	73. E	84. A
8. C	19. E	30. B	41. B	52. D	63. A	74. D	85. D
9. E	20. A	31. A	42. C	53. B	64. D	75. C	86. E
10. A	21. D	32. B	43. C	54. A	65. B	76. C	87. A
11. C	22. A	33. C	44. D	55. A	66. C	77. D	88. C

MEMORY FOR ADDRESSES TEST

1. D	12. A	23. D	34. B	45. A	56. E	67. C	78. B
2. C	13. A	24. B	35. A	46. B	57. A	68. D	79. A
3. D	14. E	25. E	36. C	47. C	58. E	69. A	80. E
4. B	15. E	26. B	37. B	48. D	59. A	70. E	81. A
5. A	16. D	27. A	38. B	49. E	60. B	71. B	82. C
6. E	17. C	28. D	39. E	50. E	61. A	72. C	83. B
7. D	18. E	29. D	40. C	51. D	62. C	73. A	84. B
8. B	19. C	30. A	41. C	52. C	63. D	74. C	85. D
9. E	20. B	31. A	42. E	53. A	64. C	75. B	86. E
10. B	21. A	32. E	43. D	54. D	65. B	76. D	87. A
11. C	22. E	33. E	44. C	55. B	66. E	77. D	88. D

CÓMO UTILIZAR ESTE LIBRO

Empiece ahora. Lo ideal es empezar a estudiar dos o tres meses antes del examen. El Examen para Cartero le exige memorizar un esquema de clasificación postal. Con el fin de ofrecerle a usted la oportunidad de crear su propio método de memorización y de practicar con esta clase de problemas, hemos creado once exámenes modelos, cada uno de ellos con un esquema diferente, para ser memorizados. Deje transcurrir cierto tiempo entre cada modelo de examen, de manera que la memorización que haya hecho usted de un esquema no interfiera con la memorización y las respuestas a preguntas basadas en otro esquema. Si ha empezado lo suficientemente pronto, deje transcurrir una semana entre cada modelo de examen.

Prepárese para hacer el modelo de examen preliminar. Escoja un lugar tranquilo y bien iluminado para trabajar. Limpie su mesa o su escritorio de cualquier cosa que le pueda distraer. Afile dos lápices #2 que tengan goma de borrar. Tenga un cronómetro o un reloj de cocina en su área de trabajo, o pídale a un amigo que le controle el tiempo. Separe la hoja de respuestas, ponga el reloj en marcha, lea las instrucciones y empiece la "Prueba de Comprobación de Direcciones". Trabaje rápida y precisamente. Cuando se acabe el tiempo, trace una línea negra debajo de la última pregunta contestada y debajo del espacio de la respuesta. Conteste las preguntas restantes simplemente para hacer una práctica extra. Las preguntas que usted responda una vez que el tiempo sea finalizado no cuentan en su puntuación, pero cada pregunta que usted contesta le ayuda a desarrollar su destreza.

Continúe de manera similar con la "Memoria para las Direcciones." Esta prueba consiste en tres grupos de preguntas de práctica para ayudarle a memorizar el esquema de clasificación. Debe contestar todas las preguntas. Pero en el momento de determinar su puntuación, sólamente debe contar el último grupo de preguntas encabezado con el título "Prueba de Memoria para las Direcciones". Cuando haya completado el examen preliminar, compruebe sus respuestas con las respuestas correctas que están al final del examen. Seguidamente calcule su puntuación en la hoja de resultados, basándose sólamente en aquellas preguntas contestadas antes del tiempo limite.

No se desanime si obtiene una puntuación baja. Recuerde que éste era un examen preliminar. Todavía no ha tenido usted ninguna clase de instrucciones, sugerencias, ni práctica exhaustiva. Para obtener más ayuda, pase a los siguientes capítulos.

Los dos capítulos de la sección en espanol le proporcionarán consejos concretos sobre técnicas para manejar las preguntas de este examen. Lea cuidadosamente estos capítulos y siga al pie de la letra todas las sugerencias antes de pasar a los modelos restantes de examen. Puede usted volver a consultar estos capítulos, si lo necesita, mientras hace los siguientes exámenes, para recordar algunas indicaciones que le ayudarán a mejorar su puntuación.

Dejando suficiente tiempo entre ellos, haga los exámenes restantes exactamente de la misma manera en que hizo el examen preliminar. Cronometre su tiempo de una manera precisa; no haga trampas; responda a todas las preguntas, pero no cuente aquéllas que fueron contestadas después de que se acabó el tiempo al calcular su puntuación. (En el examen verdadero usted se detendrá, naturalmente, cuando el tiempo haya finalizado.) Rellene las gráficas de comparación de manera que pueda comprobar su progreso.

Si no termina la Prueba de Comprobación de Direcciones, no se alarme. La precisión también cuenta y mucha gente que no termina obtiene también altas puntuaciones con su precisión. No deje que su actuación en la Comprobación de Direcciones afecte su actuación en la Memoria para las Direcciones.

La mejor actuación que usted pueda hacer es suficiente. Después del duro trabajo que ha realizado, usted está preparado para hacerlo lo mejor posible.

CÓMO CONTESTAR LAS PREGUNTAS DE COMPROBACIÓN DE DIRECCIONES

La Prueba de Comprobación de Direcciones no es difícil, pero requiere velocidad y la imprecisión está muy penalizada. Debe usted aprender a ver las diferencias rápidamente y tomar firmes decisiones sobre direcciones que son exactamente iguales. Este capítulo le ayudará a desarrollar un método para comparar direcciones. Una vez que adquiera el método, el practicarlo le ayudará a adquirir velocidad.

Las instrucciones dejan bien claro que si hay *la más mínima* diferencia entre las dos direcciones, deben señalarse como diferentes. Esto significa que en cuanto vea que hay una diferencia, marque de la Ⓓ y pase a la siguiente pregunta inmediatamente. No tiene sentido mirar el resto de la dirección una vez que haya notado una diferencia. Le sorprenderá comprobar cuánto tiempo puede ahorrar al no mirar la dirección completa.

La mejor manera de leer las direcciones que debe comparar es leer exactamente lo que usted ve y pronunciar las palabras por sílabas. Por ejemplo:

Si ve "St", lea "ese te" y no "street".
Si ve "NH", lea "ene hache" y no "New Hampshire".
Si ve "1035", lea "uno cero tres cinco" y no "mil treinta y cinco".
Lea "sassafrass" como "sas-sa-frass".

Los psicólogos han descubierto que la mente humana siempre trata de completar una figura. Si usted lee "Pky" como "Parkway," probablemente leerá "Pkwy" como "Parkway" y nunca notará la diferencia. Su mente completará la palabra sin permitirle concentrarse en las letras. Si, de todas maneras, lee la abreviación como abreviatura, se dará cuenta de que las dos abreviaturas son diferentes. Si lee "Kansas City MO" como "Kansas City Missouri", no tiene muchas probabilidades de ver la diferencia con "Kansas City MD". Pero si lee "Kansas City eme o", verá que es diferente de "Kansas City eme de".

Una manera efectiva de resolver las preguntas de comprobación de direcciones rápida y precisamente es buscar las diferencias en una sola área a la vez. Cada dirección consiste en unos números y unas palabras. Si compara usted sólo los números o sólo las palabras, tiene usted más probabilidades de ver las diferencias y menos oportunidades de ver lo que usted espera ver en vez de lo que está realmente impreso en la página.

Mire primero los números. Lea el número de la columna izquierda y vaya inmediatamente al número de la columna derecha. ¿Tienen los dos números el mismo número de dígitos? Una diferencia de este tipo debería ser evidente de inmediato. En las preguntas que siguen, ennegrezca el espacio Ⓐ si los dos números son exactamente iguales y el Ⓓ si hay alguna diferencia entre ellos.

1. 6321	6321	1. Ⓐ Ⓓ
2. 57012	57012	2. Ⓐ Ⓓ
3. 8411	841	3. Ⓐ Ⓓ
4. 6032	60302	4. Ⓐ Ⓓ
5. 9486	9486	5. Ⓐ Ⓓ

Respuestas: 1. A 2. A 3. D 4. D 5. A

¿Ha visto usted las diferencias? Acostumbre a sus ojos a contar los dígitos rápidamente.

¿Están los dígitos en el mismo orden, o hay alguna inversión?

1. 8912	8921		1. Ⓐ Ⓓ
2. 40629	40629		2. Ⓐ Ⓓ
3. 36826	38626		3. Ⓐ Ⓓ
4. 7185	7185		4. Ⓐ Ⓓ
5. 63523	63532		5. Ⓐ Ⓓ

Respuestas: 1. D 2. A 3. D 4. A 5. D

¿Las ha contestado todas correctamente? En caso contrario, vuelva a mirar los números ahora mismo y vea dónde se ha equivocado.

¿Son todos los dígitos iguales?

1. 54126	54126		1. Ⓐ Ⓓ
2. 81531	81731		2. Ⓐ Ⓓ
3. 6189	6186		3. Ⓐ Ⓓ
4. 90340	90340		4. Ⓐ Ⓓ
5. 42333	42233		5. Ⓐ Ⓓ

Respuestas: 1. A 2. D 3. D 4. A 5. D

¿Ha visto usted todas las diferencias? ¿Ha marcado usted la Ⓐ con toda seguridad cuando no había ninguna diferencia?

En el próximo grupo de preguntas de práctica, todas las diferencias èstán en los números. Trabaje rápidamente, concentrándose en los números. Puede encontrar cualquiera de las tres clases de diferencias que acabamos de describir.

1 . . . 2301 Central Ave	2310 Central Ave	1. Ⓐ Ⓓ
2 . . . Rawlins WY 82301	Rawlins Wy 82301	2. Ⓐ Ⓓ
3 . . . 4802 Sheboygan Ave	4082 Sheboygan Ave	3. Ⓐ Ⓓ
4 . . . 1150 Webster St	1151 Webster St	4. Ⓐ Ⓓ
5 . . . Madison WI 53707	Madison WI 53707	5. Ⓐ Ⓓ
6 . . . 7856 Pinckney St	7856 Pinckney St	6. Ⓐ Ⓓ
7 . . . Frankfort KY 40601	Frankfort KY 40610	7. Ⓐ Ⓓ
8 . . . 7091 E 68th St	7091 E 86th St	8. Ⓐ Ⓓ
9 . . . 3503 Rowe Blvd	3503 Rowe Blvd	9. Ⓐ Ⓓ
10 . . . 1020 Goldstein Wy	10200 Goldstein Wy	10. Ⓐ Ⓓ
11 . . . Angola LA 70712	Angola LA 70721	11. Ⓐ Ⓓ
12 . . . 8955 Whithall Dr	8955 Whithall Dr	12. Ⓐ Ⓓ
13 . . . 3572 Continental St	3592 Continental St	13. Ⓐ Ⓓ
14 . . . Windham ME 04062	Windham ME 04062	14. Ⓐ Ⓓ
15 . . . 1424 S Federal St	4124 S Federal St	15. Ⓐ Ⓓ
16 . . . 3785 N Liberty St	3785 N Liberty St	16. Ⓐ Ⓓ
17 . . . Topeka KS 66612	Topeka KS 66612	17. Ⓐ Ⓓ
18 . . . 3134 Interline Ave	3184 Interline Ave	18. Ⓐ Ⓓ
19 . . . Anamosa IA 52205	Anamosa IA 52205	19. Ⓐ Ⓓ
20 . . . 1172 Airline Hwy	11720 Airline Hwy	20. Ⓐ Ⓓ
21 . . . 3016 Cambridge St	3160 Cambridge St	21. Ⓐ Ⓓ

22 . . . Springfield IL 62706	Springfield IL 62706		22. Ⓐ Ⓓ
23 . . . 1385 Hancock St	1583 Hancock St		23. Ⓐ Ⓓ
24 . . . 3572 Louisville Rd	3573 Louisville Rd		24. Ⓐ Ⓓ
25 . . . 5825 Florida Blvd	5825 Florida Blvd		25. Ⓐ Ⓓ

Respuestas:

1. D	6. A	11. D	16. A	21. D
2. A	7. D	12. A	17. A	22. A
3. D	8. D	13. D	18. D	23. D
4. D	9. A	14. A	19. A	24. D
5. A	10. D	15. D	20. D	25. A

¿Se ha concentrado usted en los números? ¿Ha sido capaz de notar rápidamente las diferencias? ¿Ha podido tomar una decisión rápida cuando no había ninguna diferencia? Si ha contestado alguna de las preguntas incorrectamente, compruebe ahora por qué.

Si ve alguna diferencia entre los dos números, marque una Ⓓ y pase a la pregunta siguiente. No mire las palabras de un par de direcciones cuyos números son diferentes.

Si al concentrarse en los números ve usted alguna diferencia en las palabras o abreviaturas, no dude en marcar una Ⓓ y pasar a la pregunta siguiente. En otras palabras, si nota usted cualquier diferencia entre las direcciones, incluso cuando está buscando una clase concreta de diferencia, no dude en marcar una Ⓓ. Tener un método ayuda mucho, pero no se ciña a él estrictamente cuando la respuesta es obvia.

Cuando se ha asegurado de que los números son iguales y no ha notado usted ninguna otra diferencia por casualidad, pase a concentrarse en las abreviaturas. Tenga cuidado con diferencias como:

Rd	Dr
Wy	Way
NH	NM

Haga las siguientes preguntas de práctica, pronunciando las abreviaturas tal y como usted las ve.

1 . . . 523 E 12th St	523 E 12th Rd		1. Ⓐ Ⓓ
2 . . . 6776 NW Washington St	6776 NW Washington St		2. Ⓐ Ⓓ
3 . . . Framingham MA 01701	Framingham ME 01701		3. Ⓐ Ⓓ
4 . . . 2500 Broenig Hwy	2500 Broenig Tpke		4. Ⓐ Ⓓ
5 . . . 4703 Calvert St N	4703 Calvert St N		5. Ⓐ Ⓓ
6 . . . 4333 State House Ln	4333 State House Wy		6. Ⓐ Ⓓ
7 . . . Palestine TX 75801	Palestine TX 75801		7. Ⓐ Ⓓ
8 . . . 152 E 100 North	152 S 100 North		8. Ⓐ Ⓓ
9 . . . 2001 SW State St	2001 SW State Rd		9. Ⓐ Ⓓ
10 . . . Winchester VA 22601	Winchester VA 22601		10. Ⓐ Ⓓ
11 . . . 2039 Sycamore Ave	2039 Sycamore Ave		11. Ⓐ Ⓓ
12 . . . 2744 N Liveoak St	2744 N Liveoak Rd		12. Ⓐ Ⓓ
13 . . . P O Box 3083b	P O Box 3083d		13. Ⓐ Ⓓ
14 . . . 4110 Chain Bridge Rd	4110 Chain Bridge Rd		14. Ⓐ Ⓓ
15 . . . American Falls ID 83211	American Falls IA 83211		15. Ⓐ Ⓓ
16 . . . 6281 Public Square W	6281 Public Square W		16. Ⓐ Ⓓ
17 . . . 3324 N Rapp Road	3324 N Rapp Rd		17. Ⓐ Ⓓ
18 . . . 800A W Church St	800A E Church St		18. Ⓐ Ⓓ
19 . . . 6012 Mulberry Hill	6012 Mulberry Hill		19. Ⓐ Ⓓ
20 . . . 501 N Government Way	501 N Government Way		20. Ⓐ Ⓓ
21 . . . 1973 W Jourdan Ln	1973 W Jourdan La		21. Ⓐ Ⓓ

22 . . . 221 S Interocean Ave	221 S Interocean Ave	22. Ⓐ Ⓓ
23 . . . Summerville GA 30747	Summerville CA 30747	23. Ⓐ Ⓓ
24 . . . 108 S Madison Sq	108 S Madison Cir	24. Ⓐ Ⓓ
25 . . . 2177 Railroad Rd	2177 Railroad Rdge	25. Ⓐ Ⓓ

Respuestas:

1. D	6. D	11. A	16. A	21. D
2. A	7. A	12. D	17. D	22. A
3. D	8. D	13. D	18. D	23. D
4. D	9. D	14. A	19. A	24. D
5. A	10. A	15. D	20. A	25. D

Si ha cometido algún error, vuelva a mirar las direcciones otra vez. Ahora ya usted debe saber ver las diferencias más simples antes de buscar las diferencias ortográficas más difíciles de encontrar.

Si después de haber comparado números y abreviaturas, no ha encontrado aún ninguna diferencia, debe mirar las palabras principales de la dirección. Antes que todo, ¿son las palabras de las dos direcciones realmente las mismas palabras?

1. Alameda	Alamada	1. Ⓐ Ⓓ
2. Longworth	Longworth	2. Ⓐ Ⓓ
3. Raynold	Raynard	3. Ⓐ Ⓓ
4. Workman	Workmen	4. Ⓐ Ⓓ
5. Santa Monica	Santa Monica	5. Ⓐ Ⓓ

Respuestas: 1. D   2. A   3. D   4. D   5. A

Pronuncie las palabras en voz alta o sepárelas por sílabas. ¿Es la ortografía exactamente la misma? ¿Están repetidas las mismas letras? ¿Hay letras que estén en orden invertido?

1. Fairway	Fareway	1. Ⓐ Ⓓ
2. Roswell	Rosswell	2. Ⓐ Ⓓ
3. Cleburne	Cleburne	3. Ⓐ Ⓓ
4. Tuscarawas	Tuscawaras	4. Ⓐ Ⓓ
5. Kehukee Park	Kekuhee Park	5. Ⓐ Ⓓ

Respuestas: 1. D   2. D   3. A   4. D   5. D

Intente ahora contestar estas preguntas de práctica en las cuales las diferencias se hallan en las palabras principales.

1 . . . 1011 Burkemont Ave	1011 Burkmont Ave	1. Ⓐ Ⓓ
2 . . . 2830 Napoleon Rd	2830 Napoleon Rd	2. Ⓐ Ⓓ
3 . . . 4314 Mahoning Ave	4314 Mahoning Ave	3. Ⓐ Ⓓ
4 . . . 10470 Smucker Rd	10470 Schmucker Rd	4. Ⓐ Ⓓ
5 . . . 4214 Lakeville Dr	4214 Lakeland Dr	5. Ⓐ Ⓓ
6 . . . Carneys Point NJ 08069	Carneys Point NJ 08069	6. Ⓐ Ⓓ
7 . . . 3301 Hocking Pkwy	3301 Hocking Pkwy	7. Ⓐ Ⓓ
8 . . . 3516 University Blvd	3516 Universal Blvd	8. Ⓐ Ⓓ
9 . . . 1483 Spencer Hill Rd	1483 Spenser Hill Rd	9. Ⓐ Ⓓ
10 . . . Ogdenburg NY 13669	Ogdensburg NY 13669	10. Ⓐ Ⓓ

11 . . . 277R Portsmouth Ave	277R Portsmouth Ave	11. Ⓐ Ⓓ
12 . . . 10775 N St Helen Rd	10775 N St Helena Rd	12. Ⓐ Ⓓ
13 . . . 1555 Lourdes Trail	1555 Lourdes Trail	13. Ⓐ Ⓓ
14 . . . 428 Muskingum Dr	428 Muskingum Dr	14. Ⓐ Ⓓ
15 . . . Ansonville NC 28007	Arsonville NC 28007	15. Ⓐ Ⓓ
16 . . . 2606 Quinsigamond Cir	2606 Quinsigamond Cir	16. Ⓐ Ⓓ
17 . . . 670 W Boylston St	670 W Boylston St	17. Ⓐ Ⓓ
18 . . . 2783 Freedlander Dr	2783 Freelander Dr	18. Ⓐ Ⓓ
19 . . . North Platte NE 69101	North Platte NE 69101	19. Ⓐ Ⓓ
20 . . . Neosho MO 64850	Noesho MO 64850	20. Ⓐ Ⓓ
21 . . . 9555 Plainfield Rd	9555 Plainfield Rd	21. Ⓐ Ⓓ
22 . . . 2009 W Wilson St	2009 W Willson St	22. Ⓐ Ⓓ
23 . . . 1636 Prescott Hill	1636 Prescott Hill	23. Ⓐ Ⓓ
24 . . . 3996 Massasoit Blvd	3996 Massasoit Blvd	24. Ⓐ Ⓓ
25 . . . 1450 Vermilion St	1450 Vermillion St	25. Ⓐ Ⓓ

Respuestas:

1. D	6. A	11. A	16. A	21. A
2. A	7. A	12. D	17. A	22. D
3. A	8. D	13. A	18. D	23. A
4. D	9. D	14. A	19. A	24. A
5. D	10. D	15. D	20. D	25. D

Compruebe sus respuestas. Luego mire las preguntas para ver dónde se ha equivocado. Si sus errores son siempre del mismo tipo, concéntrese en evitarlos en el futuro. Si son errores casuales, la práctica y el prestar más atención le ayudarán a mejorar.

El comparar primero los números, luego las palabras cortas y las abreviaturas, y luego las palabras principales debe hacerse en muy poco tiempo. Si ha pasado usted ya este proceso y no ha cometido errores, no se detenga en la pregunta. No la vuelva a mirar para ver si se ha dejado algo. Confíe en sí mismo. Marque una Ⓐ y pase a la siguiente pregunta.

Teniendo en cuenta estas sugerencias, intente ahora hacer las siguientes preguntas de práctica. En estas preguntas las diferencias pueden estar en los números, en las prequeñas palabras o en las palabras principales, o puede no haber diferencias.

1 . . . 1386 NE 46th Rd	1368 NE 46th Rd	1. Ⓐ Ⓓ
2 . . . 5985 Kootenai St	5985 Kootenai St	2. Ⓐ Ⓓ
3 . . . 2422 Trocaire Dr	2422 Trocarie Dr	3. Ⓐ Ⓓ
4 . . . New Philadelphia PA 44663	New Philadelphia OH 44663	4. Ⓐ Ⓓ
5 . . . 2950 Jamacha Hwy E	2950 Jamacha Hwy E	5. Ⓐ Ⓓ
6 . . . 6740 Hendersonville St	6740 Hendersenville St	6. Ⓐ Ⓓ
7 . . . Mission Viego CA 92692	Mission Viego CA 92629	7. Ⓐ Ⓓ
8 . . . 1216 Houbolt Ave SE	1216 Houbolt Av SE	8. Ⓐ Ⓓ
9 . . . 3230 Appleyard Alley	3230 Appletree Alley	9. Ⓐ Ⓓ
10 . . . 3152 N Altama Hwy	3152 N Altama Hwy	10. Ⓐ Ⓓ
11 . . . 68544 S Citywide Rd	68544 S Citywide Dr	11. Ⓐ Ⓓ
12 . . . Kaneohe HI 96744	Kaneohe HI 96744	12. Ⓐ Ⓓ
13 . . . 4106 Nanaline Blvd	4706 Nanaline Blvd	13. Ⓐ Ⓓ
14 . . . 8063 Candelaria Hall	8063 Candaleria Hall	14. Ⓐ Ⓓ
15 . . . 6521 Middlebush Mile	6521 Middlebush Mile	15. Ⓐ Ⓓ
16 . . . 3233 W Wisconsin Ave	3323 W Wisconsin Ave	16. Ⓐ Ⓓ
17 . . . 24777 SE 248th St	24777 NE 248th St	17. Ⓐ Ⓓ
18 . . . 4632 Feelane Way	4632 Feelane Way	18. Ⓐ Ⓓ

19 . . . 1415 SE Truxton Ave	1415 SE Truxton Ave	19. Ⓐ Ⓓ
20 . . . 1121 West Rockefeller Rd	1121 West Rockefeller St	20. Ⓐ Ⓓ
21 . . . 6109 Wilshire Blvd	6109 Wiltshire Blvd	21. Ⓐ Ⓓ
22 . . . Albuquerque NM 87102	Albuquerque NM 87201	22. Ⓐ Ⓓ
23 . . . 2753 W Okmulgee Dr	2783 W Okmulgee Dr	23. Ⓐ Ⓓ
24 . . . 2085 N Fishers Ln	2085 N Fischers Ln	24. Ⓐ Ⓓ
25 . . . Window Rock AZ 86515	Window Rock AZ 86515	25. Ⓐ Ⓓ
26 . . . 2850 Youngfield St NE	2850 Youngfield St NE	26. Ⓐ Ⓓ
27 . . . 1791 Dauphin Pkwy	1791 Daphne Pkwy	27. Ⓐ Ⓓ
28 . . . 5433 W Placerita Canyon Rd	4533 W Placerita Canyon Rd	28. Ⓐ Ⓓ
29 . . . Lindsborg KS 67456	Lindsborg KS 67456	29. Ⓐ Ⓓ
30 . . . 1501 Morningside Blvd	1501 Morningside Pkwy	30. Ⓐ Ⓓ
31 . . . 1857 E Claflin Ave	1875 E Claflin Ave	31. Ⓐ Ⓓ
32 . . . 4625 NW Peterson Rd	4625 NW Peterson Dr	32. Ⓐ Ⓓ
33 . . . 6493 Valparaiso Blvd	6493 Valpariaiso Blvd	33. Ⓐ Ⓓ
34 . . . 2814 Huntington Pike	2814 Huntingdon Pike	34. Ⓐ Ⓓ
35 . . . 2201 Silver Lake Rd W	2201 Silver Lake Rd W	35. Ⓐ Ⓓ
36 . . . 9392 SE 182nd St	9392 SE 182nd St	36. Ⓐ Ⓓ
37 . . . 3524 Gwynedd Hwy	3452 Gwynedd Hwy	37. Ⓐ Ⓓ
38 . . . 2877 Warren Wilson Rd	2877 Warren Wilson Rd	38. Ⓐ Ⓓ
39 . . . 45177 Ludovic St	45177 Ludovici St	39. Ⓐ Ⓓ
40 . . . 1451 Steubenville Rd	1451 Steubenville Rd	40. Ⓐ Ⓓ
41 . . . 2826 Beatties Ford Rd	2826 Beattles Ford Rd	41. Ⓐ Ⓓ
42 . . . Emmitsburg MD 21727	Emmitsburg MO 21727	42. Ⓐ Ⓓ
43 . . . 6843 Summersworth St	684 Summersworth St	43. Ⓐ Ⓓ
44 . . . 2099 S Kingshighway St	2099 S Kings Highway St	44. Ⓐ Ⓓ
45 . . . 2601 Enterprise Blvd	2601 Enterprise Blvd	45. Ⓐ Ⓓ
46 . . . 3102 St Anselm Dr	3102 St Anselms Dr	46. Ⓐ Ⓓ
47 . . . 6842 SE Brighton 8th St	6482 SE Brighton 8th St	47. Ⓐ Ⓓ
48 . . . 5494 Syndicate St N	5494 Syndicate St N	48. Ⓐ Ⓓ
49 . . . Soldotna AK 99669	Soldotna AK 99669	49. Ⓐ Ⓓ
50 . . . Randolph Center VT 05061	Randolph Center VA 05061	50. Ⓐ Ⓓ
51 . . . Wenatchee WA 98801	Wenatchee WA 99801	51. Ⓐ Ⓓ
52 . . . 105 S Liberty Square Bldg	105 S Liberty Square Blvd	52. Ⓐ Ⓓ
53 . . . 22101 Georgetown Pike NE	22101 Georgetown Pike NE	53. Ⓐ Ⓓ
54 . . . 3003 Ala Moana Blvd	3003 Ala Moana Blvd	54. Ⓐ Ⓓ
55 . . . 6324 NW Needy Rd	6324 NW Reedy Rd	55. Ⓐ Ⓓ
56 . . . 9347 W Initiative Hwy	9347 W Initiative Hwy	56. Ⓐ Ⓓ
57 . . . 2451 NE Marquis Tower	2451 NE Marquis Tower	57. Ⓐ Ⓓ
58 . . . 41250 W Morrissey Blvd	41250 W Morrissey Blvd	58. Ⓐ Ⓓ
59 . . . 1201 Capitol Access Rd	1201 Capital Access Rd	59. Ⓐ Ⓓ
60 . . . 8825 Old Sunnycook Pl	8825 Old Sunnycook Dr	60. Ⓐ Ⓓ
61 . . . 4837 Penitentiary Mall	4873 Penitentiary Mall	61. Ⓐ Ⓓ
62 . . . 4498 Bullet Hill Rd	4498 Bullet Mill Rd	62. Ⓐ Ⓓ
63 . . . Carson City NV 89710	Carson City NV 89701	63. Ⓐ Ⓓ
64 . . . 810 W San Mateo Dr	810 W San Mateo Dr	64. Ⓐ Ⓓ
65 . . . 8751 Woolverton St	8751 Woolworthton St	65. Ⓐ Ⓓ
66 . . . 3658 Deaderick St E	3858 Deaderick St E	66. Ⓐ Ⓓ
67 . . . 1204 Kanawha Blvd E	1204 Kanawha Pkwy E	67. Ⓐ Ⓓ
68 . . . 1603 Mursfreesboro Rd	1603 Murfreesboro Rd	68. Ⓐ Ⓓ
69 . . . 1355 Norman Dale Arcade	1355 Norman Dale Arcade	69. Ⓐ Ⓓ
70 . . . 6044 W Briarcliffe Rd	6044 W Briarclift Rd	70. Ⓐ Ⓓ

71 . . . 187A Old Churchmans Rd	1817A Old Churchmans Rd	71. Ⓐ Ⓓ
72 . . . 1066 Goethe Sq SE	1066 Goethe Sq SW	72. Ⓐ Ⓓ
73 . . . Sheboygan WI 53081	Sheboygan WI 50381	73. Ⓐ Ⓓ
74 . . . 8056 W Comanche St	8056 W Comanche St	74. Ⓐ Ⓓ
75 . . . Cleveland Heights OH 44118	Cleveland Heights OK 44118	75. Ⓐ Ⓓ
76 . . . Accokeek MD 20607	Accokeek MD 20607	76. Ⓐ Ⓓ
77 . . . 3929 Greenmanville Ave E	3929 Greenmanville Av E	77. Ⓐ Ⓓ
78 . . . 4687 Scofieldtown Rd	4867 Scofieldtown Rd	78. Ⓐ Ⓓ
79 . . . 3418 Bryn Point Rd	3418 Bryn Point Rd	79. Ⓐ Ⓓ
80 . . . 4301 SW Torrance Blvd	4301 SW Torrence Blvd	80. Ⓐ Ⓓ
81 . . . Green River WY 82935	Green River KY 82935	81. Ⓐ Ⓓ
82 . . . Moncks Corner SC 29461	Moncks Corner SC 24961	82. Ⓐ Ⓓ
83 . . . 32901 McMorran Blvd	32901 McMorran Blvd	83. Ⓐ Ⓓ
84 . . . 1849 SW Bronough Ave	1849 NW Bronough Ave	84. Ⓐ Ⓓ
85 . . . 3525 Quaker Bridge Rd	3525 Quaker Bridge Rd	85. Ⓐ Ⓓ
86 . : . 5196 Last Chance Gulph Rd	5169 Last Chance Gulph Rd	86. Ⓐ Ⓓ
87 . . . 8971 146th Ave NE	8971 146th Ave NE	87. Ⓐ Ⓓ
88 . . . 1665 W Conservatory Dr	1665 W Conservation Dr	88. Ⓐ Ⓓ
89 . . . Indian Springs NV 89108	Indian Spring NV 89108	89. Ⓐ Ⓓ
90 . . . Bellingham WA 98225	Bellingham MA 98225	90. Ⓐ Ⓓ
91 . . . 11909 Gallisteo Blvd	11909 Gallileo Blvd	91. Ⓐ Ⓓ
92 . . . 6545 Mercantile Way N	6545 Mercantile Way N	92. Ⓐ Ⓓ
93 . . . 2501 E Sahara Rd	2501 E Sahara Dr	93. Ⓐ Ⓓ
94 . . . Fuquay-Varina NC 27526	Fuquay-Varina NC 27256	94. Ⓐ Ⓓ
95 . . . 1932 Wynnton Pkwy SE	1932 Wynnton Pkwy SE	95. Ⓐ Ⓓ

Respuestas:

1. D	13. D	25. A	37. D	49. A	61. D	73. D	85. A
2. A	14. D	26. A	38. A	50. D	62. D	74. A	86. D
3. D	15. A	27. D	39. D	51. D	63. D	75. D	87. A
4. D	16. D	28. D	40. A	52. D	64. A	76. A	88. D
5. A	17. D	29. A	41. D	53. A	65. D	77. D	89. D
6. D	18. A	30. D	42. D	54. A	66. D	78. D	90. D
7. D	19. A	31. D	43. D	55. D	67. D	79. A	91. D
8. D	20. D	32. D	44. D	56. A	68. A	80. D	92. A
9. D	21. D	33. D	45. A	57. A	69. A	81. D	93. D
10. A	22. D	34. D	46. D	58. A	70. D	82. D	94. D
11. D	23. D	35. A	47. D	59. D	71. D	83. A	95. A
12. A	24. D	36. A	48. A	60. D	72. D	84. D	

Emplee el cuadro siguiente para analizar sus faltas en el examen de práctica.

ANÁLISIS DE DISCREPANCIAS

Clase de Discrepancia	Numeros de los Problemas	Cantidad de Errores
Discrepancias entre las CIFRAS	1, 7, 13, 16, 22, 23, 28, 31, 37, 43, 47, 51, 61, 63, 66, 71, 73, 78, 82, 86, 94	
Discrepancias entre las ABREVIATURAS	4, 8, 11, 17, 20, 30, 32, 42, 50, 52, 60, 67, 72, 75, 77, 81, 84, 90, 93	
Discrepancias entre los NOMBRES	3, 6, 9, 14, 21, 24, 27, 33, 34, 39, 41, 44, 46, 55, 59, 62, 65, 70, 80, 88, 89, 91	
No hay Discrepancias	2, 5, 10, 12, 15, 18, 19, 25, 26, 29, 35, 36, 38, 40, 45, 48, 49, 53, 54, 56, 57, 58, 64, 68, 69, 74, 76, 79, 83, 85, 87, 92, 95	

Los Modelos de Examen que siguen le proporcionarán una amplia práctica para responder a preguntas de Comprobación de Direcciones. Vuelva a leer este capítulo entre exámenes a medida que avanza a lo largo del libro. Lea el capítulo el día antes de hacer un examen para refrescar sus ideas.

RECUERDE: Busque primero las diferencias entre números.
Después pase a las abreviaturas y pequeñas palabras.
Lea lo que está escrito, tal y como está escrito.
Finalmente, pronuncie en voz alta o deletree las palabras principales.
Si no ve alguna diferencia, no se detenga. Marque una A y pase inmediatamente a la siguiente pregunta.
NO lea toda la dirección como una unidad.

CÓMO CONTESTAR LAS PREGUNTAS DE MEMORIZACIÓN DE DIRECCIONES

La memorización es una aptitud especial, fácil para algunas personas pero difícil para la mayoría. Si es usted una de las afortunadas personas con buena memoria visual—es decir, si después de mirar una página puede recordar no sólo qué había en la página sino también cómo era la página—encontrará muy fácil esta prueba. Sólo necesita registrar visualmente en qué parte de la página está localizada cada cosa. Pero si usted no posee este don, la Prueba de Memoria para las Direcciones puede parecerle enormemente difícil. Este capítulo contiene algunas sugerencias que le ayudarán a memorizar más fácilmente y le indicarán algunos trucos para pasar esta prueba de memorización.

A	B	C	D	E
2100-2199 Costa Verde 9000-9299 Jugo Casa 7100-7199 Rana	2200-2699 Costa Grande 7400-7899 Jugo Ladera 6400-7099 Rana	3200-3399 Costa Rancho 7100-7399 Jugo Toro 6000-6399 Rana	1300-2099 Costa Sociedad 7900-8199 Jugo Alba 7200-7499 Rana	2700-3199 Costa Arce 8200-8999 Jugo Pluma 5800-5999 Rana

Cuantas menos cosas tenga que recordar, más fácil será su trabajo. Por lo tanto, el primer paso es eliminar cosas innecesarias. Concéntrese en las combinaciones de números. En este caso, todas son diferentes. Esto significa que no es necesario recordar los nombres de las calles asociadas con las combinaciones de números, por lo que puede usted reducir inmediatamente la información por recordar a la siguiente:

A	B	C	D	E
2100-2199 Verde 9000-9299 Casa 7100-7199	2200-2699 Grande 7400-7899 Ladera 6400-7099	3200-3399 Rancho 7100-7399 Toro 6000-6399	1300-2099 Sociedad 7900-8199 Alba 7200-7499	2700-3199 Arce 8200-8999 Pluma 5800-5999

Un examen más detenido de cada combinación de números revela que el primer número de cada combinación termina en 00 y el segundo en 99. Sabiendo esto, puede usted ignorar la mitad de cada número, reduciendo por tanto su ejercicio de memorización a lo siguiente:

A	B	C	D	E
21-21 Verde 90-92 Casa 71-71	22-26 Grande 74-78 Ladera 64-70	32-33 Rancho 71-73 Toro 60-63	13-20 Sociedad 79-81 Alba 72-74	27-31 Arce 82-89 Pluma 58-59

Mire ahora el primer número de cada combinación. Sólo dos combinaciones empiecen con el mismo número (71-71 en el recuadro A y 71-73 en el recuadro C). Esto significa que puede usted eliminar el segundo número de todas las combinaciones con la excepción de estas dos. Por tanto, ya ha reducido la información que tiene que memorizar de 30 números de 4 dígitos a 17 números de 2 dígitos y 10 nombres. Puede usted responder a todas las preguntas de la prueba recordando simplemente esta información:

A	B	C	D	E
21 Verde 90 Casa 71-71	22 Grande 74 Ladera 64	32 Rancho 71-73 Toro 60	13 Sociedad 79 Alba 72	27 Arce 82 Pluma 58

Por supuesto, en cada examen hay un número diferente de nombres y de números. En cada examen usted debe seguir mentalmente estos pasos, desechando el material innecesario y memorizando tan sólo aquello que usted debe saber. En el examen verdadero no dispondrá de papel adicional y por tanto no podrá aprenderse los nombres y números escribiéndolos.

Debe asegurarse de memorizar lo suficiente para diferenciar las direcciones de cada recuardro. Si por casualidad encuentra una repetición exacta de combinación de números, deberá memorizar los nombres que van con esas combinaciones de números.

Para simplificar aún más su tarea, tenga en cuenta que si memoriza todas las direcciones de cuatro recuadros, las direcciones que no haya memorizado están en el quinto recuadro. Por tanto, realmente sólo necesita memorizar la localización de veinte direcciones. Después de todo, por tanto, la Prueba de Memoria para las Direcciones no parece tan dura.

Hay varios métodos que usted puede utilizar para memorizar las direcciones del examen verdadero. Cada persona es diferente y el mismo método no es útil para todo el mundo. Usted puede decidir aprender primero la localización de ocho números, o puede encontrar que es más fácil aprender todos los números en primer lugar. O quizás aprenda más rápido si se concentra en un solo recuadro a la vez, leyendo su contenido una y otra vez, cubriendo luego el recuadro y tratando de repetir las direcciones. Incluso, al leer el contenido de un recuadro, puede aprender mejor una sola dirección, repitiéndose a sí mismo, una y otra vez, "21A, 21A, 21A", y así con todas las direcciones. O puede encontrar que es más eficaz aprender "21, 90, 71A". Utilice el método que más le convenga.

Pruebe estrategias diferentes en cada uno de los exámenes de este libro. Una vez que haya decidido cuál es la estrategia que más le conviene, amplíe su velocidad y su destreza siguiendo el mismo método en los restantes exámenes modelos.

Recuerde que la localización de cada dirección dentro del recuadro no tiene ninguna importancia. Usted no necesita recordar qué número de qué nombre va primero o último. Por lo tanto, no memorice el contenido de un recuadro por orden de posición. Puede usted redistribuir mentalmente el contenido del recuadro si cree que esto le ayuda a aprenderlo. Esta redistribución puede ser útil para aprender qué nombres se encuentran en cada recuadro. Sea creativo. Puede decirse a sí mismo, por ejemplo, "A la casa verde".

Vaya probando cuál es el método de aprendizaje que le va mejor. Debe usted practicar el reducir la información que debe aprenderse de manera que pueda decidir rápidamente qué es exactamente lo que debe memorizar. El proceso de reducir la información a memorizar debe hacerlo en el mínimo tiempo posible para no reducir el tiempo que usted tiene para memorizar las direcciones.

He aquí otro grupo de recuadros. Intente aplicar las técnicas que acaba de aprender al estudiarlos. Empiece reduciendo la tarea de memorización al mínimo número de direcciones posible. Seguidamente trate de memorizar el recuadro en que se encuentra cada dirección. Finalmente, compruebe cómo le va al identificar la localización en el recuadro de cada pregunta de práctica. Marque su respuesta ennegreciendo el espacio que contiene la letra del recuadro en que se encuentra cada dirección. Si lo necesita, usted puede mirar los recuadros para contestar el primer grupo de preguntas de práctica. Trate de contestar el segundo grupo de preguntas sin mirar los recuadros.

A	B	C	D	E
4500-4699 Pine Post 2300-2499 Main Linda 7000-7599 Ward	5600-5899 Pine Smith 1200-1799 Main Rivera 6400-6999 Ward	5100-5199 Pine London 1800-2299 Main Front 5300-5699 Ward	5200-5599 Pine China 3200-3699 Main Boca 5900-6399 Ward	4700-5099 Pine Coral 2500-3199 Main Mosca 5700-5899 Ward

1. 1800-2299 Main
2. Linda
3. 4700-5099 Pine
4. 5300-5699 Ward
5. Rivera
6. Coral
7. 3200-3699 Main
8. 1200-1799 Main
9. Front
10. 4500-4699 Pine
11. 5700-5899 Ward
12. Mosca
13. 5200-5599 Pine
14. 2300-2499 Main
15. 5900-6399 Ward
16. Smith
17. 5600-5899 Pine
18. 5100-5199 Pine
19. Boca
20. Post
21. 2500-3199 Main
22. London
23. China
24. 5300-5699 Ward
25. 6400-6999 Ward
26. 7000-7599 Ward
27. Coral
28. 4500-4699 Pine
29. 1200-1799 Main
30. 2500-3199 Main
31. Linda
32. Boca
33. 6400-6999 Ward
34. 2500-3199 Main
35. 5700-5899 Ward
36. 5600-5899 Pine

1. Ⓐ Ⓑ Ⓒ Ⓓ Ⓔ
2. Ⓐ Ⓑ Ⓒ Ⓓ Ⓔ
3. Ⓐ Ⓑ Ⓒ Ⓓ Ⓔ
4. Ⓐ Ⓑ Ⓒ Ⓓ Ⓔ
5. Ⓐ Ⓑ Ⓒ Ⓓ Ⓔ
6. Ⓐ Ⓑ Ⓒ Ⓓ Ⓔ
7. Ⓐ Ⓑ Ⓒ Ⓓ Ⓔ
8. Ⓐ Ⓑ Ⓒ Ⓓ Ⓔ
9. Ⓐ Ⓑ Ⓒ Ⓓ Ⓔ
10. Ⓐ Ⓑ Ⓒ Ⓓ Ⓔ
11. Ⓐ Ⓑ Ⓒ Ⓓ Ⓔ
12. Ⓐ Ⓑ Ⓒ Ⓓ Ⓔ
13. Ⓐ Ⓑ Ⓒ Ⓓ Ⓔ
14. Ⓐ Ⓑ Ⓒ Ⓓ Ⓔ
15. Ⓐ Ⓑ Ⓒ Ⓓ Ⓔ
16. Ⓐ Ⓑ Ⓒ Ⓓ Ⓔ
17. Ⓐ Ⓑ Ⓒ Ⓓ Ⓔ
18. Ⓐ Ⓑ Ⓒ Ⓓ Ⓔ
19. Ⓐ Ⓑ Ⓒ Ⓓ Ⓔ
20. Ⓐ Ⓑ Ⓒ Ⓓ Ⓔ
21. Ⓐ Ⓑ Ⓒ Ⓓ Ⓔ
22. Ⓐ Ⓑ Ⓒ Ⓓ Ⓔ
23. Ⓐ Ⓑ Ⓒ Ⓓ Ⓔ
24. Ⓐ Ⓑ Ⓒ Ⓓ Ⓔ
25. Ⓐ Ⓑ Ⓒ Ⓓ Ⓔ
26. Ⓐ Ⓑ Ⓒ Ⓓ Ⓔ
27. Ⓐ Ⓑ Ⓒ Ⓓ Ⓔ
28. Ⓐ Ⓑ Ⓒ Ⓓ Ⓔ
29. Ⓐ Ⓑ Ⓒ Ⓓ Ⓔ
30. Ⓐ Ⓑ Ⓒ Ⓓ Ⓔ
31. Ⓐ Ⓑ Ⓒ Ⓓ Ⓔ
32. Ⓐ Ⓑ Ⓒ Ⓓ Ⓔ
33. Ⓐ Ⓑ Ⓒ Ⓓ Ⓔ
34. Ⓐ Ⓑ Ⓒ Ⓓ Ⓔ
35. Ⓐ Ⓑ Ⓒ Ⓓ Ⓔ
36. Ⓐ Ⓑ Ⓒ Ⓓ Ⓔ

37. China	37. Ⓐ Ⓑ Ⓒ Ⓓ Ⓔ
38. Boca	38. Ⓐ Ⓑ Ⓒ Ⓓ Ⓔ
39. 5100-5199 Pine	39. Ⓐ Ⓑ Ⓒ Ⓓ Ⓔ
40. 3200-3699 Main	40. Ⓐ Ⓑ Ⓒ Ⓓ Ⓔ
41. 5700-5899 Ward	41. Ⓐ Ⓑ Ⓒ Ⓓ Ⓔ
42. 1200-1799 Main	42. Ⓐ Ⓑ Ⓒ Ⓓ Ⓔ
43. 7000-7599 Ward	43. Ⓐ Ⓑ Ⓒ Ⓓ Ⓔ
44. Post	44. Ⓐ Ⓑ Ⓒ Ⓓ Ⓔ
45. Smith	45. Ⓐ Ⓑ Ⓒ Ⓓ Ⓔ
46. 4500-4699 Pine	46. Ⓐ Ⓑ Ⓒ Ⓓ Ⓔ
47. 1200-1799 Main	47. Ⓐ Ⓑ Ⓒ Ⓓ Ⓔ
48. 5300-5699 Ward	48. Ⓐ Ⓑ Ⓒ Ⓓ Ⓔ
49. Mosca	49. Ⓐ Ⓑ Ⓒ Ⓓ Ⓔ
50. Rivera	50. Ⓐ Ⓑ Ⓒ Ⓓ Ⓔ
51. 2500-3199 Main	51. Ⓐ Ⓑ Ⓒ Ⓓ Ⓔ
52. 5200-5599 Pine	52. Ⓐ Ⓑ Ⓒ Ⓓ Ⓔ
53. 6400-6999 Ward	53. Ⓐ Ⓑ Ⓒ Ⓓ Ⓔ
54. Linda	54. Ⓐ Ⓑ Ⓒ Ⓓ Ⓔ
55. Coral	55. Ⓐ Ⓑ Ⓒ Ⓓ Ⓔ
56. Front	56. Ⓐ Ⓑ Ⓒ Ⓓ Ⓔ
57. 5600-5899 Pine	57. Ⓐ Ⓑ Ⓒ Ⓓ Ⓔ
58. 4700-5099 Pine	58. Ⓐ Ⓑ Ⓒ Ⓓ Ⓔ
59. 1800-2299 Main	59. Ⓐ Ⓑ Ⓒ Ⓓ Ⓔ
60. 2300-2499 Main	60. Ⓐ Ⓑ Ⓒ Ⓓ Ⓔ
61. 5900-6399 Ward	61. Ⓐ Ⓑ Ⓒ Ⓓ Ⓔ
62. London	62. Ⓐ Ⓑ Ⓒ Ⓓ Ⓔ
63. Smith	63. Ⓐ Ⓑ Ⓒ Ⓓ Ⓔ
64. 1200-1799 Main	64. Ⓐ Ⓑ Ⓒ Ⓓ Ⓔ
65. 4700-5099 Pine	65. Ⓐ Ⓑ Ⓒ Ⓓ Ⓔ
66. 6400-6999 Ward	66. Ⓐ Ⓑ Ⓒ Ⓓ Ⓔ
67. 5700-5899 Ward	67. Ⓐ Ⓑ Ⓒ Ⓓ Ⓔ
68. Rivera	68. Ⓐ Ⓑ Ⓒ Ⓓ Ⓔ
69. Linda	69. Ⓐ Ⓑ Ⓒ Ⓓ Ⓔ
70. 4500-4699 Pine	70. Ⓐ Ⓑ Ⓒ Ⓓ Ⓔ
71. 7000-7599 Ward	71. Ⓐ Ⓑ Ⓒ Ⓓ Ⓔ
72. 3200-3699 Main	72. Ⓐ Ⓑ Ⓒ Ⓓ Ⓔ
73. 4700-5099 Pine	73. Ⓐ Ⓑ Ⓒ Ⓓ Ⓔ
74. Coral	74. Ⓐ Ⓑ Ⓒ Ⓓ Ⓔ
75. Front	75. Ⓐ Ⓑ Ⓒ Ⓓ Ⓔ
76. 3200-3699 Main	76. Ⓐ Ⓑ Ⓒ Ⓓ Ⓔ
77. 2300-2499 Main	77. Ⓐ Ⓑ Ⓒ Ⓓ Ⓔ
78. 5100-5199 Pine	78. Ⓐ Ⓑ Ⓒ Ⓓ Ⓔ
79. 5600-5899 Pine	79. Ⓐ Ⓑ Ⓒ Ⓓ Ⓔ
80. Mosca	80. Ⓐ Ⓑ Ⓒ Ⓓ Ⓔ
81. Post	81. Ⓐ Ⓑ Ⓒ Ⓓ Ⓔ
82. China	82. Ⓐ Ⓑ Ⓒ Ⓓ Ⓔ
83. 1200-1799 Main	83. Ⓐ Ⓑ Ⓒ Ⓓ Ⓔ
84. Boca	84. Ⓐ Ⓑ Ⓒ Ⓓ Ⓔ
85. 2500-3199 Main	85. Ⓐ Ⓑ Ⓒ Ⓓ Ⓔ
86. 4700-5099 Pine	86. Ⓐ Ⓑ Ⓒ Ⓓ Ⓔ
87. 7000-7599 Ward	87. Ⓐ Ⓑ Ⓒ Ⓓ Ⓔ
88. 4500-4699 Pine	88. Ⓐ Ⓑ Ⓒ Ⓓ Ⓔ

Ahora trate de contestar las siguientes preguntas sin mirar los recuadros.

1.	1800-2299 Main	1. Ⓐ Ⓑ Ⓒ Ⓓ Ⓔ
2.	4700-5099 Pine	2. Ⓐ Ⓑ Ⓒ Ⓓ Ⓔ
3.	7000-7599 Ward	3. Ⓐ Ⓑ Ⓒ Ⓓ Ⓔ
4.	Smith	4. Ⓐ Ⓑ Ⓒ Ⓓ Ⓔ
5.	Boca	5. Ⓐ Ⓑ Ⓒ Ⓓ Ⓔ
6.	4500-4699 Pine	6. Ⓐ Ⓑ Ⓒ Ⓓ Ⓔ
7.	1200-1799 Main	7. Ⓐ Ⓑ Ⓒ Ⓓ Ⓔ
8.	5300-5699 Ward	8. Ⓐ Ⓑ Ⓒ Ⓓ Ⓔ
9.	Rivera	9. Ⓐ Ⓑ Ⓒ Ⓓ Ⓔ
10.	Coral	10. Ⓐ Ⓑ Ⓒ Ⓓ Ⓔ
11.	5700-5899 Ward	11. Ⓐ Ⓑ Ⓒ Ⓓ Ⓔ
12.	3200-3699 Main	12. Ⓐ Ⓑ Ⓒ Ⓓ Ⓔ
13.	5100-5199 Pine	13. Ⓐ Ⓑ Ⓒ Ⓓ Ⓔ
14.	London	14. Ⓐ Ⓑ Ⓒ Ⓓ Ⓔ
15.	Linda	15. Ⓐ Ⓑ Ⓒ Ⓓ Ⓔ
16.	Coral	16. Ⓐ Ⓑ Ⓒ Ⓓ Ⓔ
17.	2300-2499 Main	17. Ⓐ Ⓑ Ⓒ Ⓓ Ⓔ
18.	2500-3199 Main	18. Ⓐ Ⓑ Ⓒ Ⓓ Ⓔ
19.	5600-5899 Pine	19. Ⓐ Ⓑ Ⓒ Ⓓ Ⓔ
20.	5200-5599 Pine	20. Ⓐ Ⓑ Ⓒ Ⓓ Ⓔ
21.	Mosca	21. Ⓐ Ⓑ Ⓒ Ⓓ Ⓔ
22.	Front	22. Ⓐ Ⓑ Ⓒ Ⓓ Ⓔ
23.	Post	23. Ⓐ Ⓑ Ⓒ Ⓓ Ⓔ
24.	6400-6999 Ward	24. Ⓐ Ⓑ Ⓒ Ⓓ Ⓔ
25.	5900-6399 Ward	25. Ⓐ Ⓑ Ⓒ Ⓓ Ⓔ
26.	China	26. Ⓐ Ⓑ Ⓒ Ⓓ Ⓔ
27.	5200-5599 Pine	27. Ⓐ Ⓑ Ⓒ Ⓓ Ⓔ
28.	2500-3199 Main	28. Ⓐ Ⓑ Ⓒ Ⓓ Ⓔ
29.	5700-5899 Ward	29. Ⓐ Ⓑ Ⓒ Ⓓ Ⓔ
30.	2300-2499 Main	30. Ⓐ Ⓑ Ⓒ Ⓓ Ⓔ
31.	4500-4699 Pine	31. Ⓐ Ⓑ Ⓒ Ⓓ Ⓔ
32.	Smith	32. Ⓐ Ⓑ Ⓒ Ⓓ Ⓔ
33.	Rivera	33. Ⓐ Ⓑ Ⓒ Ⓓ Ⓔ
34.	5100-5199 Pine	34. Ⓐ Ⓑ Ⓒ Ⓓ Ⓔ
35.	5300-5699 Ward	35. Ⓐ Ⓑ Ⓒ Ⓓ Ⓔ
36.	1200-1799 Main	36. Ⓐ Ⓑ Ⓒ Ⓓ Ⓔ
37.	Rivera	37. Ⓐ Ⓑ Ⓒ Ⓓ Ⓔ
38.	5200-5599 Pine	38. Ⓐ Ⓑ Ⓒ Ⓓ Ⓔ
39.	5900-6399 Ward	39. Ⓐ Ⓑ Ⓒ Ⓓ Ⓔ
40.	7000-7599 Ward	40. Ⓐ Ⓑ Ⓒ Ⓓ Ⓔ
41.	2300-2499 Main	41. Ⓐ Ⓑ Ⓒ Ⓓ Ⓔ
42.	Linda	42. Ⓐ Ⓑ Ⓒ Ⓓ Ⓔ
43.	Mosca	43. Ⓐ Ⓑ Ⓒ Ⓓ Ⓔ
44.	3200-3699 Main	44. Ⓐ Ⓑ Ⓒ Ⓓ Ⓔ
45.	5100-5199 Pine	45. Ⓐ Ⓑ Ⓒ Ⓓ Ⓔ
46.	Front	46. Ⓐ Ⓑ Ⓒ Ⓓ Ⓔ
47.	5600-5899 Pine	47. Ⓐ Ⓑ Ⓒ Ⓓ Ⓔ
48.	1200-1799 Main	48. Ⓐ Ⓑ Ⓒ Ⓓ Ⓔ
49.	2300-2499 Main	49. Ⓐ Ⓑ Ⓒ Ⓓ Ⓔ
50.	4700-5099 Pine	50. Ⓐ Ⓑ Ⓒ Ⓓ Ⓔ

51. 6400-6999 Ward
52. 5900-6399 Ward
53. Front
54. London
55. 5200-5599 Pine
56. 4700-5099 Pine
57. 2300-2499 Main
58. Mosca
59. Rivera
60. 1200-1799 Main
61. 4500-4699 Pine
62. 5300-5699 Ward
63. 1800-2299 Main
64. 2500-3199 Main
65. Coral
66. China
67. Linda
68. 5100-5199 Pine
69. 5600-5899 Pine
70. 7000-7599 Ward
71. Smith
72. 5700-5899 Ward
73. 3200-3699 Main
74. Post
75. Boca
76. 4500-4699 Pine
77. 5700-5899 Ward
78. 5200-5599 Pine
79. 1200-1799 Main
80. London
81. Coral
82. 2300-2499 Main
83. 7000-7599 Ward
84. Linda
85. Mosca
86. 5900-6399 Ward
87. 5600-5899 Pine
88. 3200-3699 Main

	A	B	C	D	E
51.	Ⓐ	Ⓑ	Ⓒ	Ⓓ	Ⓔ
52.	Ⓐ	Ⓑ	Ⓒ	Ⓓ	Ⓔ
53.	Ⓐ	Ⓑ	Ⓒ	Ⓓ	Ⓔ
54.	Ⓐ	Ⓑ	Ⓒ	Ⓓ	Ⓔ
55.	Ⓐ	Ⓑ	Ⓒ	Ⓓ	Ⓔ
56.	Ⓐ	Ⓑ	Ⓒ	Ⓓ	Ⓔ
57.	Ⓐ	Ⓑ	Ⓒ	Ⓓ	Ⓔ
58.	Ⓐ	Ⓑ	Ⓒ	Ⓓ	Ⓔ
59.	Ⓐ	Ⓑ	Ⓒ	Ⓓ	Ⓔ
60.	Ⓐ	Ⓑ	Ⓒ	Ⓓ	Ⓔ
61.	Ⓐ	Ⓑ	Ⓒ	Ⓓ	Ⓔ
62.	Ⓐ	Ⓑ	Ⓒ	Ⓓ	Ⓔ
63.	Ⓐ	Ⓑ	Ⓒ	Ⓓ	Ⓔ
64.	Ⓐ	Ⓑ	Ⓒ	Ⓓ	Ⓔ
65.	Ⓐ	Ⓑ	Ⓒ	Ⓓ	Ⓔ
66.	Ⓐ	Ⓑ	Ⓒ	Ⓓ	Ⓔ
67.	Ⓐ	Ⓑ	Ⓒ	Ⓓ	Ⓔ
68.	Ⓐ	Ⓑ	Ⓒ	Ⓓ	Ⓔ
69.	Ⓐ	Ⓑ	Ⓒ	Ⓓ	Ⓔ
70.	Ⓐ	Ⓑ	Ⓒ	Ⓓ	Ⓔ
71.	Ⓐ	Ⓑ	Ⓒ	Ⓓ	Ⓔ
72.	Ⓐ	Ⓑ	Ⓒ	Ⓓ	Ⓔ
73.	Ⓐ	Ⓑ	Ⓒ	Ⓓ	Ⓔ
74.	Ⓐ	Ⓑ	Ⓒ	Ⓓ	Ⓔ
75.	Ⓐ	Ⓑ	Ⓒ	Ⓓ	Ⓔ
76.	Ⓐ	Ⓑ	Ⓒ	Ⓓ	Ⓔ
77.	Ⓐ	Ⓑ	Ⓒ	Ⓓ	Ⓔ
78.	Ⓐ	Ⓑ	Ⓒ	Ⓓ	Ⓔ
79.	Ⓐ	Ⓑ	Ⓒ	Ⓓ	Ⓔ
80.	Ⓐ	Ⓑ	Ⓒ	Ⓓ	Ⓔ
81.	Ⓐ	Ⓑ	Ⓒ	Ⓓ	Ⓔ
82.	Ⓐ	Ⓑ	Ⓒ	Ⓓ	Ⓔ
83.	Ⓐ	Ⓑ	Ⓒ	Ⓓ	Ⓔ
84.	Ⓐ	Ⓑ	Ⓒ	Ⓓ	Ⓔ
85.	Ⓐ	Ⓑ	Ⓒ	Ⓓ	Ⓔ
86.	Ⓐ	Ⓑ	Ⓒ	Ⓓ	Ⓔ
87.	Ⓐ	Ⓑ	Ⓒ	Ⓓ	Ⓔ
88.	Ⓐ	Ⓑ	Ⓒ	Ⓓ	Ⓔ

Respuestas al primer grupo:

1. C	12. E	23. D	34. E	45. B	56. C	67. E	78. C
2. A	13. D	24. C	35. E	46. A	57. B	68. B	79. B
3. E	14. A	25. B	36. B	47. B	58. E	69. A	80. E
4. C	15. D	26. A	37. D	48. C	59. C	70. A	81. A
5. B	16. B	27. E	38. D	49. E	60. A	71. A	82. D
6. E	17. B	28. A	39. C	50. B	61. D	72. D	83. B
7. D	18. C	29. B	40. D	51. E	62. C	73. E	84. D
8. B	19. D	30. E	41. E	52. D	63. B	74. E	85. E
9. C	20. A	31. A	42. B	53. B	64. B	75. C	86. E
10. A	21. E	32. D	43. A	54. A	65. E	76. D	87. A
11. E	22. C	33. B	44. A	55. E	66. B	77. A	88. A

Respuestas al segundo grupo:

1. C	12. D	23. A	34. C	45. C	56. E	67. A	78. D
2. E	13. C	24. B	35. C	46. C	57. A	68. C	79. B
3. A	14. C	25. D	36. B	47. B	58. E	69. B	80. C
4. B	15. A	26. D	37. B	48. B	59. B	70. A	81. E
5. D	16. E	27. D	38. D	49. A	60. B	71. B	82. A
6. A	17. A	28. E	39. D	50. E	61. A	72. E	83. A
7. B	18. E	29. E	40. A	51. B	62. C	73. D	84. A
8. C	19. B	30. A	41. A	52. D	63. C	74. A	85. E
9. B	20. D	31. A	42. A	53. C	64. E	75. D	86. D
10. E	21. E	32. B	43. E	54. C	65. E	76. A	87. B
11. E	22. C	33. B	44. D	55. D	66. D	77. E	88. D

A medida que avanza en el libro, recuerde todas las técnicas y trucos que ha aprendido y aplíquelos. Trate también de desarrollar su propio método de memorización. Deje suficiente tiempo entre cada examen de manera que su memorización de un grupo de recuadros no interfiera con la siguiente. Vuelva a consultar este capítulo siempre que lo crea necesario. Vuelva a leer el capítulo el día anterior al examen, pero NO haga el examen modelo ese día. El día en que haga el examen verdadero, su mente necesita estar completamente despeja. El da a fin de poder aprender el método de clasificación.

AVISO IMPORTANTE: En años pasados, los exámenes de Cartero han suplido al menos dos exámenes de práctica para familiarizarlo con el examen de Memorización de Direcciones. Estos exámenes de práctica sirven sólo para ayudar a los aspirantes a aprender cómo responder a las preguntas de Memorización de Direcciones y no se califican. Si usted ha hecho todos los ejercicios en este libro, ya estará familiarizado con la manera de responder a preguntas de Memorización de Direcciones y puede utilizar parte del plazo de tiempo del examen de práctica para memorizar los cajones en lugar de responder a las preguntas de práctica. De esta manera, usted puede ganar cinco ó diez minutos adicionales de tiempo para la memorización, lo que puede añadir puntos valiosos a su resultado.

ANSWER SHEET FOR FOURTH MODEL EXAM

ADDRESS CHECKING

1 Ⓐ Ⓓ	20 Ⓐ Ⓓ	39 Ⓐ Ⓓ	58 Ⓐ Ⓓ	77 Ⓐ Ⓓ
2 Ⓐ Ⓓ	21 Ⓐ Ⓓ	40 Ⓐ Ⓓ	59 Ⓐ Ⓓ	78 Ⓐ Ⓓ
3 Ⓐ Ⓓ	22 Ⓐ Ⓓ	41 Ⓐ Ⓓ	60 Ⓐ Ⓓ	79 Ⓐ Ⓓ
4 Ⓐ Ⓓ	23 Ⓐ Ⓓ	42 Ⓐ Ⓓ	61 Ⓐ Ⓓ	80 Ⓐ Ⓓ
5 Ⓐ Ⓓ	24 Ⓐ Ⓓ	43 Ⓐ Ⓓ	62 Ⓐ Ⓓ	81 Ⓐ Ⓓ
6 Ⓐ Ⓓ	25 Ⓐ Ⓓ	44 Ⓐ Ⓓ	63 Ⓐ Ⓓ	82 Ⓐ Ⓓ
7 Ⓐ Ⓓ	26 Ⓐ Ⓓ	45 Ⓐ Ⓓ	64 Ⓐ Ⓓ	83 Ⓐ Ⓓ
8 Ⓐ Ⓓ	27 Ⓐ Ⓓ	46 Ⓐ Ⓓ	65 Ⓐ Ⓓ	84 Ⓐ Ⓓ
9 Ⓐ Ⓓ	28 Ⓐ Ⓓ	47 Ⓐ Ⓓ	66 Ⓐ Ⓓ	85 Ⓐ Ⓓ
10 Ⓐ Ⓓ	29 Ⓐ Ⓓ	48 Ⓐ Ⓓ	67 Ⓐ Ⓓ	86 Ⓐ Ⓓ
11 Ⓐ Ⓓ	30 Ⓐ Ⓓ	49 Ⓐ Ⓓ	68 Ⓐ Ⓓ	87 Ⓐ Ⓓ
12 Ⓐ Ⓓ	31 Ⓐ Ⓓ	50 Ⓐ Ⓓ	69 Ⓐ Ⓓ	88 Ⓐ Ⓓ
13 Ⓐ Ⓓ	32 Ⓐ Ⓓ	51 Ⓐ Ⓓ	70 Ⓐ Ⓓ	89 Ⓐ Ⓓ
14 Ⓐ Ⓓ	33 Ⓐ Ⓓ	52 Ⓐ Ⓓ	71 Ⓐ Ⓓ	90 Ⓐ Ⓓ
15 Ⓐ Ⓓ	34 Ⓐ Ⓓ	53 Ⓐ Ⓓ	72 Ⓐ Ⓓ	91 Ⓐ Ⓓ
16 Ⓐ Ⓓ	35 Ⓐ Ⓓ	54 Ⓐ Ⓓ	73 Ⓐ Ⓓ	92 Ⓐ Ⓓ
17 Ⓐ Ⓓ	36 Ⓐ Ⓓ	55 Ⓐ Ⓓ	74 Ⓐ Ⓓ	93 Ⓐ Ⓓ
18 Ⓐ Ⓓ	37 Ⓐ Ⓓ	56 Ⓐ Ⓓ	75 Ⓐ Ⓓ	94 Ⓐ Ⓓ
19 Ⓐ Ⓓ	38 Ⓐ Ⓓ	57 Ⓐ Ⓓ	76 Ⓐ Ⓓ	95 Ⓐ Ⓓ

TEAR HERE

MEMORY FOR ADDRESSES

PRACTICE I

1 Ⓐ Ⓑ Ⓒ Ⓓ Ⓔ	23 Ⓐ Ⓑ Ⓒ Ⓓ Ⓔ	45 Ⓐ Ⓑ Ⓒ Ⓓ Ⓔ	67 Ⓐ Ⓑ Ⓒ Ⓓ Ⓔ
2 Ⓐ Ⓑ Ⓒ Ⓓ Ⓔ	24 Ⓐ Ⓑ Ⓒ Ⓓ Ⓔ	46 Ⓐ Ⓑ Ⓒ Ⓓ Ⓔ	68 Ⓐ Ⓑ Ⓒ Ⓓ Ⓔ
3 Ⓐ Ⓑ Ⓒ Ⓓ Ⓔ	25 Ⓐ Ⓑ Ⓒ Ⓓ Ⓔ	47 Ⓐ Ⓑ Ⓒ Ⓓ Ⓔ	69 Ⓐ Ⓑ Ⓒ Ⓓ Ⓔ
4 Ⓐ Ⓑ Ⓒ Ⓓ Ⓔ	26 Ⓐ Ⓑ Ⓒ Ⓓ Ⓔ	48 Ⓐ Ⓑ Ⓒ Ⓓ Ⓔ	70 Ⓐ Ⓑ Ⓒ Ⓓ Ⓔ
5 Ⓐ Ⓑ Ⓒ Ⓓ Ⓔ	27 Ⓐ Ⓑ Ⓒ Ⓓ Ⓔ	49 Ⓐ Ⓑ Ⓒ Ⓓ Ⓔ	71 Ⓐ Ⓑ Ⓒ Ⓓ Ⓔ
6 Ⓐ Ⓑ Ⓒ Ⓓ Ⓔ	28 Ⓐ Ⓑ Ⓒ Ⓓ Ⓔ	50 Ⓐ Ⓑ Ⓒ Ⓓ Ⓔ	72 Ⓐ Ⓑ Ⓒ Ⓓ Ⓔ
7 Ⓐ Ⓑ Ⓒ Ⓓ Ⓔ	29 Ⓐ Ⓑ Ⓒ Ⓓ Ⓔ	51 Ⓐ Ⓑ Ⓒ Ⓓ Ⓔ	73 Ⓐ Ⓑ Ⓒ Ⓓ Ⓔ
8 Ⓐ Ⓑ Ⓒ Ⓓ Ⓔ	30 Ⓐ Ⓑ Ⓒ Ⓓ Ⓔ	52 Ⓐ Ⓑ Ⓒ Ⓓ Ⓔ	74 Ⓐ Ⓑ Ⓒ Ⓓ Ⓔ
9 Ⓐ Ⓑ Ⓒ Ⓓ Ⓔ	31 Ⓐ Ⓑ Ⓒ Ⓓ Ⓔ	53 Ⓐ Ⓑ Ⓒ Ⓓ Ⓔ	75 Ⓐ Ⓑ Ⓒ Ⓓ Ⓔ
10 Ⓐ Ⓑ Ⓒ Ⓓ Ⓔ	32 Ⓐ Ⓑ Ⓒ Ⓓ Ⓔ	54 Ⓐ Ⓑ Ⓒ Ⓓ Ⓔ	76 Ⓐ Ⓑ Ⓒ Ⓓ Ⓔ
11 Ⓐ Ⓑ Ⓒ Ⓓ Ⓔ	33 Ⓐ Ⓑ Ⓒ Ⓓ Ⓔ	55 Ⓐ Ⓑ Ⓒ Ⓓ Ⓔ	77 Ⓐ Ⓑ Ⓒ Ⓓ Ⓔ
12 Ⓐ Ⓑ Ⓒ Ⓓ Ⓔ	34 Ⓐ Ⓑ Ⓒ Ⓓ Ⓔ	56 Ⓐ Ⓑ Ⓒ Ⓓ Ⓔ	78 Ⓐ Ⓑ Ⓒ Ⓓ Ⓔ
13 Ⓐ Ⓑ Ⓒ Ⓓ Ⓔ	35 Ⓐ Ⓑ Ⓒ Ⓓ Ⓔ	57 Ⓐ Ⓑ Ⓒ Ⓓ Ⓔ	79 Ⓐ Ⓑ Ⓒ Ⓓ Ⓔ
14 Ⓐ Ⓑ Ⓒ Ⓓ Ⓔ	36 Ⓐ Ⓑ Ⓒ Ⓓ Ⓔ	58 Ⓐ Ⓑ Ⓒ Ⓓ Ⓔ	80 Ⓐ Ⓑ Ⓒ Ⓓ Ⓔ
15 Ⓐ Ⓑ Ⓒ Ⓓ Ⓔ	37 Ⓐ Ⓑ Ⓒ Ⓓ Ⓔ	59 Ⓐ Ⓑ Ⓒ Ⓓ Ⓔ	81 Ⓐ Ⓑ Ⓒ Ⓓ Ⓔ
16 Ⓐ Ⓑ Ⓒ Ⓓ Ⓔ	38 Ⓐ Ⓑ Ⓒ Ⓓ Ⓔ	60 Ⓐ Ⓑ Ⓒ Ⓓ Ⓔ	82 Ⓐ Ⓑ Ⓒ Ⓓ Ⓔ
17 Ⓐ Ⓑ Ⓒ Ⓓ Ⓔ	39 Ⓐ Ⓑ Ⓒ Ⓓ Ⓔ	61 Ⓐ Ⓑ Ⓒ Ⓓ Ⓔ	83 Ⓐ Ⓑ Ⓒ Ⓓ Ⓔ
18 Ⓐ Ⓑ Ⓒ Ⓓ Ⓔ	40 Ⓐ Ⓑ Ⓒ Ⓓ Ⓔ	62 Ⓐ Ⓑ Ⓒ Ⓓ Ⓔ	84 Ⓐ Ⓑ Ⓒ Ⓓ Ⓔ
19 Ⓐ Ⓑ Ⓒ Ⓓ Ⓔ	41 Ⓐ Ⓑ Ⓒ Ⓓ Ⓔ	63 Ⓐ Ⓑ Ⓒ Ⓓ Ⓕ	85 Ⓐ Ⓑ Ⓒ Ⓓ Ⓔ
20 Ⓐ Ⓑ Ⓒ Ⓓ Ⓔ	42 Ⓐ Ⓑ Ⓒ Ⓓ Ⓔ	64 Ⓐ Ⓑ Ⓒ Ⓓ Ⓔ	86 Ⓐ Ⓑ Ⓒ Ⓓ Ⓔ
21 Ⓐ Ⓑ Ⓒ Ⓓ Ⓔ	43 Ⓐ Ⓑ Ⓒ Ⓓ Ⓔ	65 Ⓐ Ⓑ Ⓒ Ⓓ Ⓔ	87 Ⓐ Ⓑ Ⓒ Ⓓ Ⓔ
22 Ⓐ Ⓑ Ⓒ Ⓓ Ⓔ	44 Ⓐ Ⓑ Ⓒ Ⓓ Ⓔ	66 Ⓐ Ⓑ Ⓒ Ⓓ Ⓔ	88 Ⓐ Ⓑ Ⓒ Ⓓ Ⓔ

PRACTICE II

1 Ⓐ Ⓑ Ⓒ Ⓓ Ⓔ   23 Ⓐ Ⓑ Ⓒ Ⓓ Ⓔ   45 Ⓐ Ⓑ Ⓒ Ⓓ Ⓔ   67 Ⓐ Ⓑ Ⓒ Ⓓ Ⓔ

2 Ⓐ Ⓑ Ⓒ Ⓓ Ⓔ   24 Ⓐ Ⓑ Ⓒ Ⓓ Ⓔ   46 Ⓐ Ⓑ Ⓒ Ⓓ Ⓔ   68 Ⓐ Ⓑ Ⓒ Ⓓ Ⓔ

3 Ⓐ Ⓑ Ⓒ Ⓓ Ⓔ   25 Ⓐ Ⓑ Ⓒ Ⓓ Ⓔ   47 Ⓐ Ⓑ Ⓒ Ⓓ Ⓔ   69 Ⓐ Ⓑ Ⓒ Ⓓ Ⓔ

4 Ⓐ Ⓑ Ⓒ Ⓓ Ⓔ   26 Ⓐ Ⓑ Ⓒ Ⓓ Ⓔ   48 Ⓐ Ⓑ Ⓒ Ⓓ Ⓔ   70 Ⓐ Ⓑ Ⓒ Ⓓ Ⓔ

5 Ⓐ Ⓑ Ⓒ Ⓓ Ⓔ   27 Ⓐ Ⓑ Ⓒ Ⓓ Ⓔ   49 Ⓐ Ⓑ Ⓒ Ⓓ Ⓔ   71 Ⓐ Ⓑ Ⓒ Ⓓ Ⓔ

6 Ⓐ Ⓑ Ⓒ Ⓓ Ⓔ   28 Ⓐ Ⓑ Ⓒ Ⓓ Ⓔ   50 Ⓐ Ⓑ Ⓒ Ⓓ Ⓔ   72 Ⓐ Ⓑ Ⓒ Ⓓ Ⓔ

7 Ⓐ Ⓑ Ⓒ Ⓓ Ⓔ   29 Ⓐ Ⓑ Ⓒ Ⓓ Ⓔ   51 Ⓐ Ⓑ Ⓒ Ⓓ Ⓔ   73 Ⓐ Ⓑ Ⓒ Ⓓ Ⓔ

8 Ⓐ Ⓑ Ⓒ Ⓓ Ⓔ   30 Ⓐ Ⓑ Ⓒ Ⓓ Ⓔ   52 Ⓐ Ⓑ Ⓒ Ⓓ Ⓔ   74 Ⓐ Ⓑ Ⓒ Ⓓ Ⓔ

9 Ⓐ Ⓑ Ⓒ Ⓓ Ⓔ   31 Ⓐ Ⓑ Ⓒ Ⓓ Ⓔ   53 Ⓐ Ⓑ Ⓒ Ⓓ Ⓔ   75 Ⓐ Ⓑ Ⓒ Ⓓ Ⓔ

10 Ⓐ Ⓑ Ⓒ Ⓓ Ⓔ   32 Ⓐ Ⓑ Ⓒ Ⓓ Ⓔ   54 Ⓐ Ⓑ Ⓒ Ⓓ Ⓔ   76 Ⓐ Ⓑ Ⓒ Ⓓ Ⓔ

11 Ⓐ Ⓑ Ⓒ Ⓓ Ⓔ   33 Ⓐ Ⓑ Ⓒ Ⓓ Ⓔ   55 Ⓐ Ⓑ Ⓒ Ⓓ Ⓔ   77 Ⓐ Ⓑ Ⓒ Ⓓ Ⓔ

12 Ⓐ Ⓑ Ⓒ Ⓓ Ⓔ   34 Ⓐ Ⓑ Ⓒ Ⓓ Ⓔ   56 Ⓐ Ⓑ Ⓒ Ⓓ Ⓔ   78 Ⓐ Ⓑ Ⓒ Ⓓ Ⓔ

13 Ⓐ Ⓑ Ⓒ Ⓓ Ⓔ   35 Ⓐ Ⓑ Ⓒ Ⓓ Ⓔ   57 Ⓐ Ⓑ Ⓒ Ⓓ Ⓔ   79 Ⓐ Ⓑ Ⓒ Ⓓ Ⓔ

14 Ⓐ Ⓑ Ⓒ Ⓓ Ⓔ   36 Ⓐ Ⓑ Ⓒ Ⓓ Ⓔ   58 Ⓐ Ⓑ Ⓒ Ⓓ Ⓔ   80 Ⓐ Ⓑ Ⓒ Ⓓ Ⓔ

15 Ⓐ Ⓑ Ⓒ Ⓓ Ⓔ   37 Ⓐ Ⓑ Ⓒ Ⓓ Ⓔ   59 Ⓐ Ⓑ Ⓒ Ⓓ Ⓔ   81 Ⓐ Ⓑ Ⓒ Ⓓ Ⓔ

16 Ⓐ Ⓑ Ⓒ Ⓓ Ⓔ   38 Ⓐ Ⓑ Ⓒ Ⓓ Ⓔ   60 Ⓐ Ⓑ Ⓒ Ⓓ Ⓔ   82 Ⓐ Ⓑ Ⓒ Ⓓ Ⓔ

17 Ⓐ Ⓑ Ⓒ Ⓓ Ⓔ   39 Ⓐ Ⓑ Ⓒ Ⓓ Ⓔ   61 Ⓐ Ⓑ Ⓒ Ⓓ Ⓔ   83 Ⓐ Ⓑ Ⓒ Ⓓ Ⓔ

18 Ⓐ Ⓑ Ⓒ Ⓓ Ⓔ   40 Ⓐ Ⓑ Ⓒ Ⓓ Ⓔ   62 Ⓐ Ⓑ Ⓒ Ⓓ Ⓔ   84 Ⓐ Ⓑ Ⓒ Ⓓ Ⓔ

19 Ⓐ Ⓑ Ⓒ Ⓓ Ⓔ   41 Ⓐ Ⓑ Ⓒ Ⓓ Ⓔ   63 Ⓐ Ⓑ Ⓒ Ⓓ Ⓔ   85 Ⓐ Ⓑ Ⓒ Ⓓ Ⓔ

20 Ⓐ Ⓑ Ⓒ Ⓓ Ⓔ   42 Ⓐ Ⓑ Ⓒ Ⓓ Ⓔ   64 Ⓐ Ⓑ Ⓒ Ⓓ Ⓔ   86 Ⓐ Ⓑ Ⓒ Ⓓ Ⓔ

21 Ⓐ Ⓑ Ⓒ Ⓓ Ⓔ   43 Ⓐ Ⓑ Ⓒ Ⓓ Ⓔ   65 Ⓐ Ⓑ Ⓒ Ⓓ Ⓔ   87 Ⓐ Ⓑ Ⓒ Ⓓ Ⓔ

22 Ⓐ Ⓑ Ⓒ Ⓓ Ⓔ   44 Ⓐ Ⓑ Ⓒ Ⓓ Ⓔ   66 Ⓐ Ⓑ Ⓒ Ⓓ Ⓔ   88 Ⓐ Ⓑ Ⓒ Ⓓ Ⓔ

PRACTICE III

1 Ⓐ Ⓑ Ⓒ Ⓓ Ⓔ	23 Ⓐ Ⓑ Ⓒ Ⓓ Ⓔ	45 Ⓐ Ⓑ Ⓒ Ⓓ Ⓔ	67 Ⓐ Ⓑ Ⓒ Ⓓ Ⓔ
2 Ⓐ Ⓑ Ⓒ Ⓓ Ⓔ	24 Ⓐ Ⓑ Ⓒ Ⓓ Ⓔ	46 Ⓐ Ⓑ Ⓒ Ⓓ Ⓔ	68 Ⓐ Ⓑ Ⓒ Ⓓ Ⓔ
3 Ⓐ Ⓑ Ⓒ Ⓓ Ⓔ	25 Ⓐ Ⓑ Ⓒ Ⓓ Ⓔ	47 Ⓐ Ⓑ Ⓒ Ⓓ Ⓔ	69 Ⓐ Ⓑ Ⓒ Ⓓ Ⓔ
4 Ⓐ Ⓑ Ⓒ Ⓓ Ⓔ	26 Ⓐ Ⓑ Ⓒ Ⓓ Ⓔ	48 Ⓐ Ⓑ Ⓒ Ⓓ Ⓔ	70 Ⓐ Ⓑ Ⓒ Ⓓ Ⓔ
5 Ⓐ Ⓑ Ⓒ Ⓓ Ⓔ	27 Ⓐ Ⓑ Ⓒ Ⓓ Ⓔ	49 Ⓐ Ⓑ Ⓒ Ⓓ Ⓔ	71 Ⓐ Ⓑ Ⓒ Ⓓ Ⓔ
6 Ⓐ Ⓑ Ⓒ Ⓓ Ⓔ	28 Ⓐ Ⓑ Ⓒ Ⓓ Ⓔ	50 Ⓐ Ⓑ Ⓒ Ⓓ Ⓔ	72 Ⓐ Ⓑ Ⓒ Ⓓ Ⓔ
7 Ⓐ Ⓑ Ⓒ Ⓓ Ⓔ	29 Ⓐ Ⓑ Ⓒ Ⓓ Ⓔ	51 Ⓐ Ⓑ Ⓒ Ⓓ Ⓔ	73 Ⓐ Ⓑ Ⓒ Ⓓ Ⓔ
8 Ⓐ Ⓑ Ⓒ Ⓓ Ⓔ	30 Ⓐ Ⓑ Ⓒ Ⓓ Ⓔ	52 Ⓐ Ⓑ Ⓒ Ⓓ Ⓔ	74 Ⓐ Ⓑ Ⓒ Ⓓ Ⓔ
9 Ⓐ Ⓑ Ⓒ Ⓓ Ⓔ	31 Ⓐ Ⓑ Ⓒ Ⓓ Ⓔ	53 Ⓐ Ⓑ Ⓒ Ⓓ Ⓔ	75 Ⓐ Ⓑ Ⓒ Ⓓ Ⓔ
10 Ⓐ Ⓑ Ⓒ Ⓓ Ⓔ	32 Ⓐ Ⓑ Ⓒ Ⓓ Ⓔ	54 Ⓐ Ⓑ Ⓒ Ⓓ Ⓔ	76 Ⓐ Ⓑ Ⓒ Ⓓ Ⓔ
11 Ⓐ Ⓑ Ⓒ Ⓓ Ⓔ	33 Ⓐ Ⓑ Ⓒ Ⓓ Ⓔ	55 Ⓐ Ⓑ Ⓒ Ⓓ Ⓔ	77 Ⓐ Ⓑ Ⓒ Ⓓ Ⓔ
12 Ⓐ Ⓑ Ⓒ Ⓓ Ⓔ	34 Ⓐ Ⓑ Ⓒ Ⓓ Ⓔ	56 Ⓐ Ⓑ Ⓒ Ⓓ Ⓔ	78 Ⓐ Ⓑ Ⓒ Ⓓ Ⓔ
13 Ⓐ Ⓑ Ⓒ Ⓓ Ⓔ	35 Ⓐ Ⓑ Ⓒ Ⓓ Ⓔ	57 Ⓐ Ⓑ Ⓒ Ⓓ Ⓔ	79 Ⓐ Ⓑ Ⓒ Ⓓ Ⓔ
14 Ⓐ Ⓑ Ⓒ Ⓓ Ⓔ	36 Ⓐ Ⓑ Ⓒ Ⓓ Ⓔ	58 Ⓐ Ⓑ Ⓒ Ⓓ Ⓔ	80 Ⓐ Ⓑ Ⓒ Ⓓ Ⓔ
15 Ⓐ Ⓑ Ⓒ Ⓓ Ⓔ	37 Ⓐ Ⓑ Ⓒ Ⓓ Ⓔ	59 Ⓐ Ⓑ Ⓒ Ⓓ Ⓔ	81 Ⓐ Ⓑ Ⓒ Ⓓ Ⓔ
16 Ⓐ Ⓑ Ⓒ Ⓓ Ⓔ	38 Ⓐ Ⓑ Ⓒ Ⓓ Ⓔ	60 Ⓐ Ⓑ Ⓒ Ⓓ Ⓔ	82 Ⓐ Ⓑ Ⓒ Ⓓ Ⓔ
17 Ⓐ Ⓑ Ⓒ Ⓓ Ⓔ	39 Ⓐ Ⓑ Ⓒ Ⓓ Ⓔ	61 Ⓐ Ⓑ Ⓒ Ⓓ Ⓔ	83 Ⓐ Ⓑ Ⓒ Ⓓ Ⓔ
18 Ⓐ Ⓑ Ⓒ Ⓓ Ⓔ	40 Ⓐ Ⓑ Ⓒ Ⓓ Ⓔ	62 Ⓐ Ⓑ Ⓒ Ⓓ Ⓔ	84 Ⓐ Ⓑ Ⓒ Ⓓ Ⓔ
19 Ⓐ Ⓑ Ⓒ Ⓓ Ⓔ	41 Ⓐ Ⓑ Ⓒ Ⓓ Ⓔ	63 Ⓐ Ⓑ Ⓒ Ⓓ Ⓕ	85 Ⓐ Ⓑ Ⓒ Ⓓ Ⓔ
20 Ⓐ Ⓑ Ⓒ Ⓓ Ⓔ	42 Ⓐ Ⓑ Ⓒ Ⓓ Ⓔ	64 Ⓐ Ⓑ Ⓒ Ⓓ Ⓔ	86 Ⓐ Ⓑ Ⓒ Ⓓ Ⓔ
21 Ⓐ Ⓑ Ⓒ Ⓓ Ⓔ	43 Ⓐ Ⓑ Ⓒ Ⓓ Ⓔ	65 Ⓐ Ⓑ Ⓒ Ⓓ Ⓔ	87 Ⓐ Ⓑ Ⓒ Ⓓ Ⓔ
22 Ⓐ Ⓑ Ⓒ Ⓓ Ⓔ	44 Ⓐ Ⓑ Ⓒ Ⓓ Ⓔ	66 Ⓐ Ⓑ Ⓒ Ⓓ Ⓔ	88 Ⓐ Ⓑ Ⓒ Ⓓ Ⓔ

MEMORY FOR ADDRESSES TEST

1 Ⓐ Ⓑ Ⓒ Ⓓ Ⓔ 23 Ⓐ Ⓑ Ⓒ Ⓓ Ⓔ 45 Ⓐ Ⓑ Ⓒ Ⓓ Ⓔ 67 Ⓐ Ⓑ Ⓒ Ⓓ Ⓔ

2 Ⓐ Ⓑ Ⓒ Ⓓ Ⓔ 24 Ⓐ Ⓑ Ⓒ Ⓓ Ⓔ 46 Ⓐ Ⓑ Ⓒ Ⓓ Ⓔ 68 Ⓐ Ⓑ Ⓒ Ⓓ Ⓔ

3 Ⓐ Ⓑ Ⓒ Ⓓ Ⓔ 25 Ⓐ Ⓑ Ⓒ Ⓓ Ⓔ 47 Ⓐ Ⓑ Ⓒ Ⓓ Ⓔ 69 Ⓐ Ⓑ Ⓒ Ⓓ Ⓔ

4 Ⓐ Ⓑ Ⓒ Ⓓ Ⓔ 26 Ⓐ Ⓑ Ⓒ Ⓓ Ⓔ 48 Ⓐ Ⓑ Ⓒ Ⓓ Ⓔ 70 Ⓐ Ⓑ Ⓒ Ⓓ Ⓔ

5 Ⓐ Ⓑ Ⓒ Ⓓ Ⓔ 27 Ⓐ Ⓑ Ⓒ Ⓓ Ⓔ 49 Ⓐ Ⓑ Ⓒ Ⓓ Ⓔ 71 Ⓐ Ⓑ Ⓒ Ⓓ Ⓔ

6 Ⓐ Ⓑ Ⓒ Ⓓ Ⓔ 28 Ⓐ Ⓑ Ⓒ Ⓓ Ⓔ 50 Ⓐ Ⓑ Ⓒ Ⓓ Ⓔ 72 Ⓐ Ⓑ Ⓒ Ⓓ Ⓔ

7 Ⓐ Ⓑ Ⓒ Ⓓ Ⓔ 29 Ⓐ Ⓑ Ⓒ Ⓓ Ⓔ 51 Ⓐ Ⓑ Ⓒ Ⓓ Ⓔ 73 Ⓐ Ⓑ Ⓒ Ⓓ Ⓔ

8 Ⓐ Ⓑ Ⓒ Ⓓ Ⓔ 30 Ⓐ Ⓑ Ⓒ Ⓓ Ⓔ 52 Ⓐ Ⓑ Ⓒ Ⓓ Ⓔ 74 Ⓐ Ⓑ Ⓒ Ⓓ Ⓔ

9 Ⓐ Ⓑ Ⓒ Ⓓ Ⓔ 31 Ⓐ Ⓑ Ⓒ Ⓓ Ⓔ 53 Ⓐ Ⓑ Ⓒ Ⓓ Ⓔ 75 Ⓐ Ⓑ Ⓒ Ⓓ Ⓔ

10 Ⓐ Ⓑ Ⓒ Ⓓ Ⓔ 32 Ⓐ Ⓑ Ⓒ Ⓓ Ⓔ 54 Ⓐ Ⓑ Ⓒ Ⓓ Ⓔ 76 Ⓐ Ⓑ Ⓒ Ⓓ Ⓔ

11 Ⓐ Ⓑ Ⓒ Ⓓ Ⓔ 33 Ⓐ Ⓑ Ⓒ Ⓓ Ⓔ 55 Ⓐ Ⓑ Ⓒ Ⓓ Ⓔ 77 Ⓐ Ⓑ Ⓒ Ⓓ Ⓔ

12 Ⓐ Ⓑ Ⓒ Ⓓ Ⓔ 34 Ⓐ Ⓑ Ⓒ Ⓓ Ⓔ 56 Ⓐ Ⓑ Ⓒ Ⓓ Ⓔ 78 Ⓐ Ⓑ Ⓒ Ⓓ Ⓔ

13 Ⓐ Ⓑ Ⓒ Ⓓ Ⓔ 35 Ⓐ Ⓑ Ⓒ Ⓓ Ⓔ 57 Ⓐ Ⓑ Ⓒ Ⓓ Ⓔ 79 Ⓐ Ⓑ Ⓒ Ⓓ Ⓔ

14 Ⓐ Ⓑ Ⓒ Ⓓ Ⓔ 36 Ⓐ Ⓑ Ⓒ Ⓓ Ⓔ 58 Ⓐ Ⓑ Ⓒ Ⓓ Ⓔ 80 Ⓐ Ⓑ Ⓒ Ⓓ Ⓔ

15 Ⓐ Ⓑ Ⓒ Ⓓ Ⓔ 37 Ⓐ Ⓑ Ⓒ Ⓓ Ⓔ 59 Ⓐ Ⓑ Ⓒ Ⓓ Ⓔ 81 Ⓐ Ⓑ Ⓒ Ⓓ Ⓔ

16 Ⓐ Ⓑ Ⓒ Ⓓ Ⓔ 38 Ⓐ Ⓑ Ⓒ Ⓓ Ⓔ 60 Ⓐ Ⓑ Ⓒ Ⓓ Ⓔ 82 Ⓐ Ⓑ Ⓒ Ⓓ Ⓔ

17 Ⓐ Ⓑ Ⓒ Ⓓ Ⓔ 39 Ⓐ Ⓑ Ⓒ Ⓓ Ⓔ 61 Ⓐ Ⓑ Ⓒ Ⓓ Ⓔ 83 Ⓐ Ⓑ Ⓒ Ⓓ Ⓔ

18 Ⓐ Ⓑ Ⓒ Ⓓ Ⓔ 40 Ⓐ Ⓑ Ⓒ Ⓓ Ⓔ 62 Ⓐ Ⓑ Ⓒ Ⓓ Ⓔ 84 Ⓐ Ⓑ Ⓒ Ⓓ Ⓔ

19 Ⓐ Ⓑ Ⓒ Ⓓ Ⓔ 41 Ⓐ Ⓑ Ⓒ Ⓓ Ⓔ 63 Ⓐ Ⓑ Ⓒ Ⓓ Ⓔ 85 Ⓐ Ⓑ Ⓒ Ⓓ Ⓔ

20 Ⓐ Ⓑ Ⓒ Ⓓ Ⓔ 42 Ⓐ Ⓑ Ⓒ Ⓓ Ⓔ 64 Ⓐ Ⓑ Ⓒ Ⓓ Ⓔ 86 Ⓐ Ⓑ Ⓒ Ⓓ Ⓔ

21 Ⓐ Ⓑ Ⓒ Ⓓ Ⓔ 43 Ⓐ Ⓑ Ⓒ Ⓓ Ⓔ 65 Ⓐ Ⓑ Ⓒ Ⓓ Ⓔ 87 Ⓐ Ⓑ Ⓒ Ⓓ Ⓔ

22 Ⓐ Ⓑ Ⓒ Ⓓ Ⓔ 44 Ⓐ Ⓑ Ⓒ Ⓓ Ⓔ 66 Ⓐ Ⓑ Ⓒ Ⓓ Ⓔ 88 Ⓐ Ⓑ Ⓒ Ⓓ Ⓔ

SCORE SHEET FOR FOURTH MODEL EXAM

ADDRESS CHECKING TEST

Number Right minus Number Wrong equals   Score

_____   –   _____   =   _____

MEMORY FOR ADDRESSES TEST

Number Right minus (Number Wrong ÷ 4) equals   Score

_____   –   _____   =   _____

PROGRESS GRAPH

Blacken the bars for Model Exam 4 to the scores you earned.

Score					
95					
90					
85					
80					
75					
70					
65					
60					
55					
50					
45					
40					
35					
30					
25					
20					
15					
10					
5					
0					

Test Model Exam	AC | M Diag.	AC | M 1	AC | M 2	AC | M 3	AC | M 4

AC = Address Checking   M = Memory for Addresses

FOURTH MODEL EXAM

ADDRESS CHECKING TEST

TIME: 6 Minutes. 95 Questions.

DIRECTIONS: For each question, compare the address in the left column with the address in the right column. If the two addresses are ALIKE IN EVERY WAY, blacken space Ⓐ on your answer sheet. If the two addresses are DIFFERENT IN ANY WAY, blacken space Ⓓ on your answer sheet. Correct answers for this test are on page 141.

1	1038 Nutgrove St	1038 Nutgrove St
2	4830 Schroeder Ave	4380 Schroeder Ave
3	2343 Martine Ave	2343 Martini Ave
4	Winkelman AZ 85292	Winkelman AZ 85292
5	298 Chatterton Pky	298 Chatterton Pky
6	3798 Hillandale Ave	3798 Hillanddale Ave
7	7683 Fountain Pl	7863 Fountain Pl
8	1862 W 164th St	1864 W 164th St
9	Scarborough NY 10510	Scarbourough NY 10510
10	1734 N Highland Ave	1734 W Highland Ave
11	1385 Queens Blvd	1385 Queens Blvd
12	6742 Mendota Ave	6742 Mendota Ave
13	8496 E 245th St	8496 E 254th St
14	2010 Wyndcliff Rd	2010 Wyndecliff Rd
15	4098 Gramatan Ave	4098 Gramatan Ave
16	Denver CO 80236	Denver CO 80236
17	3778 N Broadway	3778 N Broadway
18	532 Broadhollow Rd	532 Broadhollow Rd
19	1386 Carriage House Ln	1386 Carriage House Ln
20	3284 S 10th St	2384 S 10th St
21	2666 Dunwoodie Rd	266 Dunwoodie Rd
22	Pontiac MI 48054	Pontiac MI 48054
23	1080 Nine Acres Ln	1080 Nine Acres Ln
24	2699 Quaker Church Rd	2669 Quaker Church Rd
25	7232 S 45th Ave	7232 S 45th Ave
26	1588 Grand Boulevard	1588 Grand Boulevard

27	2093 S Waverly Rd	2093 S Waverley Rd
28	Las Vegas NV 89112	Las Vegas NM 89112
29	116 Cottage Pl Gdns	116 Cottage Pl Gdns
30	1203 E Lakeview Ave	1203 E Lakeside Ave
31	3446 E Westchester Ave	3446 E Westchester Ave
32	7482 Horseshoe Hill Rd	7482 Horseshoe Hill Rd
33	Waimanalo HI 96795	Waimanale HI 96795
34	9138 McGuire Ave	9138 MacGuire Ave
35	7438 Meadway	7348 Meadway
36	2510 Maryland Ave NW	2510 Maryland Ave NW
37	1085 S 83rd Rd	1085 S 83rd Rd
38	5232 Maplewood Wy	523 Maplewood Wy
39	Kansas City MO 64108	Kansas City MO 61408
40	1063 Valentine Ln	1063 Valentine Ln
41	1066 Furnace Dock Rd	1606 Furnace Dock Rd
42	2121 Rosedale Rd	2121 Rosedale Rd
43	1396 Orawapum St	1396 Orawampum St
44	3004 Palisade Ave	3004 Palisades Ave
45	1776 Independence St	1776 Independence St
46	Canton OH 44707	Canton OH 44707
47	1515 Geoga Cir	1515 Geogia Cir
48	1583 Central Ave	1583 Central Ave
49	4096 Valley Terr	4096 Valley Terr
50	2075 Boston Post Rd	2075 Boston Post Rd
51	1016 Frost Ln	1016 Frost La
52	2186 Ashford Ave	2186 Ashford Ave
53	Battle Mountain NV 89820	Battle Mountain NV 89820
54	6634 Weber Pl	6634 Webber Pl
55	6832 Halycon Terr	6832 Halcyon Terr
56	198 Gedney Esplnde	198 Gedney Esplnde
57	8954 Horsechestnut Rd	8954 Horsechestnut Rd
58	1926 S 283rd Wy	1926 S 283rd Wy
59	Hartsdale NY 10530	Hartsdale NY 15030
60	1569 Ritchy Pl	1569 Ritchy Pl
61	423 S Columbia Ave	423 S Colombia Ave
62	2466 Linette Ct	2466 Linnette Ct
63	2970 Rockledge Ave	2970 Rockridge Ave
64	5764 Guion Blvd	5764 Guion Blvd
65	6976 SW 5th Ave	6976 SE 5th Ave
66	Milwaukie OR 97222	Milwaukee OR 97222
67	2243 Hudson View Ests	2234 Hudson View Ests
68	7743 S 3rd Ave	7743 S 3rd Ave
69	2869 Romaine Ave	2869 Romaine Ave
70	2943 Windermere Dr	2943 Windemere Dr
71	5117 Balmoral Crsnt	5117 Balmoral Crsnt
72	3797 Wappanocca Ave	3797 Wappannocca Ave
73	Arkabutla MS 38602	Arkabutla MS 38602
74	2275 Greenway Terr	2275 Greenaway Terr
75	7153 Taymil Rd	7153 Taymil Rd
76	3864 W 248th St	3864 W 284th St
77	2032 Central Park S	2023 Central Park S
78	1803 Pinewood Rd	1803 Pineywood Rd

79 . . . New York NY 10023	New York NY 10023
80 . . . 1555 E 19th St	1555 E 19th St
81 . . . 3402 Gomer Cir	3402 Comer Ct
82 . . . 9416 Lakeshore Dr	9416 Lakeshore Dr
83 . . . 1576 Kimball Ave	1576 Kimbell Ave
84 . . . 2015 W 51st Ln	2015 W 51st Ln
85 . . . Silver Springs NV 89429	Silver Springs NV 89429
86 . . . 2354 N Washington St	2354 N Washington St
87 . . . 8528 Convent Pl	8258 Convent Pl
88 . . . 1911 Downer Ave	1911 Downer Ave
89 . . . 6108 Woodstock Rd	6108 Woodstock St
90 . . . Akron OH 44308	Akron OK 44308
91 . . . 4548 College Pt Ave	4548 College Pk Ave
92 . . . 8194 Great Oak Ln	8194 Great Oak Ln
93 . . . 280 SW Collins Ave	280 SW Collins Ave
94 . . . 8276 Abbott Mews	8726 Abbott Mews
95 . . . 4717 Deerfield Blvd	4717 Deerfield Blvd

END OF ADDRESS CHECKING TEST

If you finish this test before time is up, use the remaining time to check over your work. Do not turn the page until you are told to do so.

PRACTICE FOR
MEMORY FOR ADDRESSES TEST

DIRECTIONS: The five boxes below are labelled A, B, C, D, and E. In each box are three sets of number spans with names and two names which are not associated with numbers. In the next THREE MINUTES, you must try to memorize the box location of each name and number span. The position of a name or number span within its box is not important. You need only remember the letter of the box in which the item is to be found. You will use these names and numbers to answer three sets of practice questions which are NOT scored and one actual test which is scored. Correct answers are on pages 141 and 142.

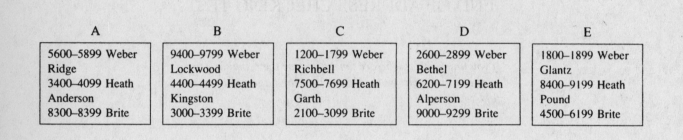

A	B	C	D	E
5600–5899 Weber	9400–9799 Weber	1200–1799 Weber	2600–2899 Weber	1800–1899 Weber
Ridge	Lockwood	Richbell	Bethel	Glantz
3400–4099 Heath	4400–4499 Heath	7500–7699 Heath	6200–7199 Heath	8400–9199 Heath
Anderson	Kingston	Garth	Alperson	Pound
8300–8399 Brite	3000–3399 Brite	2100–3099 Brite	9000–9299 Brite	4500–6199 Brite

PRACTICE I

DIRECTIONS: Use the next THREE MINUTES to mark on your answer sheet the letter of the box in which each item that follows is to be found. Try to mark each item without looking back at the boxes. If, however, you get stuck, you may refer to the boxes during this practice exercise. If you find that you must look at the boxes, try to memorize as you do so. This test is for practice only. It will not be scored.

1. 4400–4499 Heath
2. 2100–3099 Brite
3. Alperson
4. Ridge A
5. 1800–1899 Weber
6. 8300–8399 Brite
7. 9400–9799 Weber
8. 7500–7699 Heath
9. Anderson
10. Bethel
11. Richbell
12. 3000–3399 Brite

13. 8400–9199 Heath
14. 9000–9299 Brite
15. 6200–7199 Heath
16. 5600–5899 Weber
17. Ridge △
18. Glantz
19. 3400–4099 Heath
20. 2600–2899 Weber
21. Garth
22. 2100–3099 Brite
23. Lockwood
24. 4500–6199 Brite
25. 1200–1799 Weber
26. Kingston
27. Pound
28. 6200–7199 Heath
29. 5600–5899 Weber
30. 8300–8399 Brite
31. 1200–1799 Weber
32. 6200–7199 Heath
33. 4500–6199 Brite
34. Anderson
35. Alperson
36. Glantz
37. 2600–2899 Weber
38. 9400–9799 Weber
39. 8400–9199 Heath
40. 2100–3099 Brite
41. Richbell
42. Bethel
43. Ridge
44. 1200–1799 Weber
45. 8400–9199 Heath
46. 2600–2899 Weber
47. 8300–8399 Brite
48. 3000–3399 Brite
49. Pound
50. Garth

51. 9400–9799 Weber
52. 3400–4099 Heath
53. Lockwood
54. 2600–2899 Weber
55. 6200–7199 Heath
56. 8300–8399 Brite
57. Ridge
58. Kingston
59. 1200–1799 Weber
60. 8400–9199 Heath
61. 4500–6199 Brite
62. 3400–4099 Heath
63. Lockwood
64. Richbell
65. 5600–5899 Weber
66. 3000–3399 Brite
67. 2100–3099 Brite
68. 2600–2899 Weber
69. 6200–7199 Heath
70. Anderson
71. Pound
72. Ridge
73. 9400–9799 Weber
74. 2600–2899 Weber
75. 4500–6199 Brite
76. 1800–1899 Weber
77. Glantz
78. 9000–9299 Brite
79. 3400–4099 Heath
80. 8400–9199 Heath
81. Alperson
82. Pound
83. Garth
84. Kingston
85. 9400–9799 Weber
86. 7500–7699 Heath
87. 4500–6199 Brite
88. Lockwood

PRACTICE II

DIRECTIONS: The next 88 questions constitute another practice exercise. Again, you should mark your answers on your answer sheet. Again, the time limit is THREE MINUTES. This time, however, you must NOT look at the boxes while answering the questions. You must rely on your memory in marking the box location of each item. This practice test will not be scored.

1. 6200–7199 Heath
2. Pound
3. 2100–3099 Brite
4. 4400–4499 Heath
5. 9400–9799 Weber
6. Ridge
7. 3000–3399 Brite
8. 8400–9199 Heath
9. 5600–5899 Weber
10. Lockwood
11. 7500–7699 Heath
12. 2600–2899 Weber
13. Alperson
14. 9000–9299 Brite
15. 9400–9799 Weber
16. 2100–3099 Brite
17. 8400–9199 Heath
18. 3400–4099 Heath
19. Anderson
20. Glantz
21. 8300–8399 Brite
22. 1200–1799 Weber
23. 9000–9299 Brite
24. Alperson
25. Richbell
26. Lockwood
27. 4400–4499 Heath
28. 4500–6199 Brite
29. 5600–5899 Weber
30. 2600–2899 Weber
31. Ridge
32. Pound
33. 3000–3399 Brite
34. 7500–7699 Heath
35. 6200–7199 Heath
36. 1800–1899 Weber
37. 4500–6199 Brite
38. Kingston
39. Garth
40. Bethel
41. 3400–4099 Heath
42. 3000–3399 Brite
43. 2100–3099 Brite
44. 2600–2899 Weber

45. 5600–5899 Weber
46. 8300–8399 Brite
47. Anderson
48. 1800–1899 Weber
49. 6200–7199 Heath
50. Alperson
51. Pound
52. 2100–3099 Brite
53. 8400–9199 Heath
54. Glantz
55. 4400–4499 Heath
56. 9400–9799 Weber
57. 8300–8399 Brite
58. 3000–3399 Brite
59. 7500–7699 Heath
60. 2600–2899 Weber
61. Richbell
62. Ridge
63. Bethel
64. 6200–7199 Heath
65. 4400–4499 Heath
66. 9000–9299 Brite
67. 2100–3099 Brite
68. 5600–5899 Weber
69. Kingston
70. Lockwood
71. Garth
72. 1800–1899 Weber
73. 8400–9199 Heath
74. 5600–5899 Weber
75. 4400–4499 Heath
76. Richbell
77. 2100–3099 Brite
78. 1800–1899 Weber
79. Bethel
80. Anderson
81. 9400–9799 Weber
82. 8300–8399 Brite
83. 6200–7199 Heath
84. Lockwood
85. Garth
86. Glantz
87. 9000–9299 Brite
88. 8400–9199 Heath

PRACTICE III

DIRECTIONS: The names and addresses are repeated for you in the boxes below. Each name and each number span is in the same box in which you found it in the original set. You will now be allowed FIVE MINUTES to study the locations again. Do your best to memorize the letter of the box in which each item is located. This is your last chance to see the boxes.

A	B	C	D	E
5600–5899 Weber Ridge 3400–4099 Heath Anderson 8300–8399 Brite	9400–9799 Weber Lockwood 4400–4499 Heath Kingston 3000–3399 Brite	1200–1799 Weber Richbell 7500–7699 Heath Garth 2100–3099 Brite	2600–2899 Weber Bethel 6200–7199 Heath Alperson 9000–9299 Brite	1800–1899 Weber Glantz 8400–9199 Heath Pound 4500–6199 Brite

DIRECTIONS: This is your last practice test. Mark the location of each of the 88 items on your answer sheet. You will have FIVE MINUTES to answer these questions. Do NOT look back at the boxes. This practice test will not be scored.

1. 2100–3099 Brite
2. 4400–4499 Heath
3. Pound
4. 2600–2899 Weber
5. 8300–8399 Brite
6. Lockwood
7. Alperson
8. 9400–9799 Weber
9. 8400–9199 Heath
10. 9000–9299 Brite
11. Kingston
12. Glantz
13. Richbell
14. 3400–4099 Heath
15. 4500–6199 Brite
16. 2600–2899 Weber
17. 7500–7699 Heath
18. 4500–6199 Brite
19. Anderson
20. Pound
21. 5600–5899 Weber
22. 1800–1899 Weber
23. 3000–3399 Brite
24. 8400–9199 Heath
25. Bethel
26. 3400–4099 Heath
27. 2600–2899 Weber
28. 4400–4499 Heath
29. 2100–3099 Brite
30. Garth
31. Kingston
32. Lockwood
33. 9400–9799 Weber
34. 6200–7199 Heath
35. 8300–8399 Brite
36. 4500–6199 Brite
37. Ridge
38. Alperson
39. 3000–3399 Brite
40. 7500–7699 Heath
41. 5600–5899 Weber
42. Richbell
43. Glantz
44. 8400–9199 Heath

45. 9000–9299 Brite
46. Bethel
47. Pound
48. Anderson
49. 1200–1799 Weber
50. 1800–1899 Weber
51. 3400–4099 Heath
52. 4500–6199 Brite
53. 2600–2899 Weber
54. Kingston
55. Pound
56. 5600–5899 Weber
57. 6200–7199 Heath
58. 9000–9299 Brite
59. 8400–9199 Heath
60. Richbell
61. Glantz
62. 8300–8399 Brite
63. 7500–7699 Heath
64. 4400–4499 Heath
65. 8400–9199 Heath
66. 4500–6199 Brite

67. Bethel
68. Ridge
69. Lockwood
70. 2100–3099 Brite
71. 3000–3399 Brite
72. Alperson
73. Garth
74. 1200–1799 Weber
75. 2600–2899 Weber
76. 2100–3099 Brite
77. 1800–1899 Weber
78. Bethel
79. Anderson
80. Glantz
81. 2600–2899 Weber
82. 9000–9299 Brite
83. 3400–4099 Heath
84. 6200–7199 Heath
85. 5600–5899 Weber
86. 4400–4499 Heath
87. Ridge
88. Kingston

MEMORY FOR ADDRESSES TEST

TIME: 5 Minutes. 88 Questions.

DIRECTIONS: Mark your answers on the answer sheet in the section headed "MEMORY FOR ADDRESSES TEST." This test will be scored. You are NOT permitted to look at the boxes. Work from memory, as quickly and as accurately as you can. Correct answers are on page 142.

1. Kingston
2. 8400–9199 Heath
3. 9000–9299 Brite
4. 2600–2899 Weber
5. 3400–4099 Heath
6. Richbell
7. Alperson
8. 4500–6199 Brite
9. 9400–9799 Weber
10. 7500–7699 Heath
11. 5600–5899 Weber
12. 4500–6199 Brite
13. Anderson
14. Glantz
15. Lockwood
16. 8300–8399 Brite
17. 1200–1799 Weber
18. 1800–1899 Weber
19. 8400–9199 Heath
20. 4500–6199 Brite
21. Bethel
22. Richbell
23. 9400–9799 Weber
24. 2100–3099 Brite
25. 2600–2899 Weber
26. 3400–4099 Heath
27. Ridge
28. Kingston
29. 7500–7699 Heath
30. 9000–9299 Brite
31. 6200–7199 Heath
32. Lockwood
33. Glantz
34. Pound
35. 5600–5899 Weber
36. 4400–4499 Heath
37. 2100–3099 Brite
38. Bethel
39. Garth
40. 9000–9299 Brite
41. 8400–9199 Heath
42. 1800–1899 Weber
43. 3400–4099 Heath
44. 9400–9799 Weber
45. 7500–7699 Heath
46. Richbell
47. Bethel
48. 1800–1899 Weber
49. 3400–4099 Heath
50. 3000–3399 Brite
51. 2100–3099 Brite
52. 1800–1899 Weber
53. Anderson
54. Alperson
55. 5600–5899 Weber
56. 4400–4499 Heath
57. 9000–9299 Brite
58. 8400–9199 Heath
59. Glantz
60. 7500–7699 Heath
61. Garth
62. Pound
63. 2600–2899 Weber
64. 7500–7699 Heath

65. 3000–3399 Brite
66. 6200–7199 Heath
67. 2600–2899 Weber
68. 8400–9199 Heath
69. 3000–3399 Brite
70. 7500–7699 Heath
71. Ridge
72. Bethel
73. 5600–5899 Weber
74. 6200–7199 Heath
75. 9000–9299 Brite
76. Lockwood

77. Richbell
78. 2600–2899 Weber
79. 4400–4499 Heath
80. 9400–9799 Weber
81. 2100–3099 Brite
82. Glantz
83. Anderson
84. 9400–9799 Weber
85. 4500–6199 Brite
86. 3400–4099 Heath
87. 1200–1799 Weber
88. Pound

END OF EXAM

ADDRESS CHECKING ERROR ANALYSIS CHART

Type of Error	Tally	Total Number
Number of addresses which were alike and you incorrectly marked "different"		
Number of addresses which were different and you incorrectly marked "alike"		
Number of addresses in which you missed a difference in NUMBERS		
Number of addresses in which you missed a difference in ABBREVIA-TIONS		
Number of addresses in which you missed a difference in NAMES		

SELF-EVALUATION CHART

Test	Excellent	Good	Average	Fair	Poor
Address Checking	80–95	65–79	50–64	35–49	1–34
Memory for Addresses	75–88	60–74	45–59	30–44	1–29

CORRECT ANSWERS FOR FOURTH MODEL EXAM

ADDRESS CHECKING TEST

1. A	13. D	25. A	37. A	49. A	61. D	73. A	85. A
2. D	14. D	26. A	38. D	50. A	62. D	74. D	86. A
3. D	15. A	27. D	39. D	51. D	63. D	75. A	87. D
4. A	16. A	28. D	40. A	52. A	64. A	76. D	88. A
5. A	17. A	29. A	41. D	53. A	65. D	77. D	89. D
6. D	18. A	30. D	42. A	54. D	66. D	78. D	90. D
7. D	19. A	31. A	43. D	55. D	67. D	79. A	91. D
8. D	20. D	32. A	44. D	56. A	68. A	80. A	92. A
9. D	21. D	33. D	45. A	57. A	69. A	81. D	93. A
10. D	22. A	34. D	46. A	58. A	70. D	82. A	94. D
11. A	23. A	35. D	47. D	59. D	71. A	83. D	95. A
12. A	24. D	36. A	48. A	60. A	72. D	84. A	

MEMORY FOR ADDRESSES—PRACTICE I

1. B	12. B	23. B	34. A	45. E	56. A	67. C	78. D
2. C	13. E	24. E	35. D	46. D	57. A	68. D	79. A
3. D	14. D	25. C	36. E	47. A	58. B	69. D	80. E
4. A	15. D	26. B	37. D	48. B	59. C	70. A	81. D
5. E	16. A	27. E	38. B	49. E	60. E	71. E	82. E
6. A	17. A	28. D	39. E	50. C	61. E	72. A	83. C
7. B	18. E	29. A	40. C	51. B	62. A	73. B	84. B
8. C	19. A	30. A	41. C	52. A	63. B	74. D	85. B
9. A	20. D	31. C	42. D	53. B	64. C	75. E	86. C
10. D	21. C	32. D	43. A	54. D	65. A	76. E	87. E
11. C	22. C	33. E	44. C	55. D	66. B	77. E	88. B

MEMORY FOR
ADDRESSES—PRACTICE II

1. D	12. D	23. D	34. C	45. A	56. B	67. C	78. E
2. E	13. D	24. D	35. D	46. A	57. A	68. A	79. D
3. C	14. D	25. C	36. E	47. A	58. B	69. B	80. A
4. B	15. B	26. B	37. E	48. E	59. C	70. B	81. B
5. B	16. C	27. B	38. B	49. D	60. D	71. C	82. A
6. A	17. E	28. E	39. C	50. D	61. C	72. E	83. D
7. B	18. A	29. A	40. D	51. E	62. A	73. E	84. B
8. E	19. A	30. D	41. A	52. C	63. D	74. A	85. C
9. A	20. E	31. A	42. B	53. E	64. D	75. B	86. E
10. B	21. A	32. E	43. C	54. E	65. B	76. C	87. D
11. C	22. C	33. B	44. D	55. B	66. D	77. C	88. E

MEMORY FOR
ADDRESSES—PRACTICE III

1. C	12. E	23. B	34. D	45. D	56. A	67. D	78. D
2. B	13. C	24. E	35. A	46. D	57. D	68. A	79. A
3. E	14. A	25. D	36. E	47. E	58. D	69. B	80. E
4. D	15. E	26. A	37. A	48. A	59. E	70. C	81. D
5. A	16. D	27. D	38. D	49. C	60. C	71. B	82. D
6. B	17. C	28. B	39. B	50. E	61. E	72. D	83. A
7. D	18. E	29. C	40. C	51. A	62. A	73. C	84. D
8. B	19. A	30. C	41. A	52. E	63. C	74. C	85. A
9. E	20. E	31. B	42. C	53. D	64. B	75. D	86. B
10. D	21. A	32. B	43. E	54. B	65. E	76. C	87. A
11. B	22. E	33. B	44. E	55. E	66. E	77. E	88. B

MEMORY FOR ADDRESSES TEST

1. B	12. E	23. B	34. E	45. C	56. B	67. D	78. D
2. E	13. A	24. C	35. A	46. C	57. D	68. E	79. B
3. D	14. E	25. D	36. B	47. D	58. E	69. B	80. B
4. D	15. B	26. A	37. C	48. E	59. E	70. C	81. C
5. A	16. A	27. A	38. D	49. A	60. C	71. A	82. E
6. C	17. C	28. B	39. C	50. B	61. C	72. D	83. A
7. D	18. E	29. C	40. D	51. C	62. E	73. A	84. B
8. E	19. E	30. D	41. E	52. E	63. D	74. D	85. E
9. B	20. E	31. D	42. E	53. A	64. C	75. D	86. A
10. C	21. D	32. B	43. A	54. D	65. B	76. B	87. C
11. A	22. C	33. E	44. B	55. A	66. D	77. C	88. E

ANSWER SHEET FOR FIFTH MODEL EXAM

ADDRESS CHECKING

1 Ⓐ Ⓓ	20 Ⓐ Ⓓ	39 Ⓐ Ⓓ	58 Ⓐ Ⓓ	77 Ⓐ Ⓓ
2 Ⓐ Ⓓ	21 Ⓐ Ⓓ	40 Ⓐ Ⓓ	59 Ⓐ Ⓓ	78 Ⓐ Ⓓ
3 Ⓐ Ⓓ	22 Ⓐ Ⓓ	41 Ⓐ Ⓓ	60 Ⓐ Ⓓ	79 Ⓐ Ⓓ
4 Ⓐ Ⓓ	23 Ⓐ Ⓓ	42 Ⓐ Ⓓ	61 Ⓐ Ⓓ	80 Ⓐ Ⓓ
5 Ⓐ Ⓓ	24 Ⓐ Ⓓ	43 Ⓐ Ⓓ	62 Ⓐ Ⓓ	81 Ⓐ Ⓓ
6 Ⓐ Ⓓ	25 Ⓐ Ⓓ	44 Ⓐ Ⓓ	63 Ⓐ Ⓓ	82 Ⓐ Ⓓ
7 Ⓐ Ⓓ	26 Ⓐ Ⓓ	45 Ⓐ Ⓓ	64 Ⓐ Ⓓ	83 Ⓐ Ⓓ
8 Ⓐ Ⓓ	27 Ⓐ Ⓓ	46 Ⓐ Ⓓ	65 Ⓐ Ⓓ	84 Ⓐ Ⓓ
9 Ⓐ Ⓓ	28 Ⓐ Ⓓ	47 Ⓐ Ⓓ	66 Ⓐ Ⓓ	85 Ⓐ Ⓓ
10 Ⓐ Ⓓ	29 Ⓐ Ⓓ	48 Ⓐ Ⓓ	67 Ⓐ Ⓓ	86 Ⓐ Ⓓ
11 Ⓐ Ⓓ	30 Ⓐ Ⓓ	49 Ⓐ Ⓓ	68 Ⓐ Ⓓ	87 Ⓐ Ⓓ
12 Ⓐ Ⓓ	31 Ⓐ Ⓓ	50 Ⓐ Ⓓ	69 Ⓐ Ⓓ	88 Ⓐ Ⓓ
13 Ⓐ Ⓓ	32 Ⓐ Ⓓ	51 Ⓐ Ⓓ	70 Ⓐ Ⓓ	89 Ⓐ Ⓓ
14 Ⓐ Ⓓ	33 Ⓐ Ⓓ	52 Ⓐ Ⓓ	71 Ⓐ Ⓓ	90 Ⓐ Ⓓ
15 Ⓐ Ⓓ	34 Ⓐ Ⓓ	53 Ⓐ Ⓓ	72 Ⓐ Ⓓ	91 Ⓐ Ⓓ
16 Ⓐ Ⓓ	35 Ⓐ Ⓓ	54 Ⓐ Ⓓ	73 Ⓐ Ⓓ	92 Ⓐ Ⓓ
17 Ⓐ Ⓓ	36 Ⓐ Ⓓ	55 Ⓐ Ⓓ	74 Ⓐ Ⓓ	93 Ⓐ Ⓓ
18 Ⓐ Ⓓ	37 Ⓐ Ⓓ	56 Ⓐ Ⓓ	75 Ⓐ Ⓓ	94 Ⓐ Ⓓ
19 Ⓐ Ⓓ	38 Ⓐ Ⓓ	57 Ⓐ Ⓓ	76 Ⓐ Ⓓ	95 Ⓐ Ⓓ

MEMORY FOR ADDRESSES

PRACTICE I

1 Ⓐ Ⓑ Ⓒ Ⓓ Ⓔ
2 Ⓐ Ⓑ Ⓒ Ⓓ Ⓔ
3 Ⓐ Ⓑ Ⓒ Ⓓ Ⓔ
4 Ⓐ Ⓑ Ⓒ Ⓓ Ⓔ
5 Ⓐ Ⓑ Ⓒ Ⓓ Ⓔ
6 Ⓐ Ⓑ Ⓒ Ⓓ Ⓔ
7 Ⓐ Ⓑ Ⓒ Ⓓ Ⓔ
8 Ⓐ Ⓑ Ⓒ Ⓓ Ⓔ
9 Ⓐ Ⓑ Ⓒ Ⓓ Ⓔ
10 Ⓐ Ⓑ Ⓒ Ⓓ Ⓔ
11 Ⓐ Ⓑ Ⓒ Ⓓ Ⓔ
12 Ⓐ Ⓑ Ⓒ Ⓓ Ⓔ
13 Ⓐ Ⓑ Ⓒ Ⓓ Ⓔ
14 Ⓐ Ⓑ Ⓒ Ⓓ Ⓔ
15 Ⓐ Ⓑ Ⓒ Ⓓ Ⓔ
16 Ⓐ Ⓑ Ⓒ Ⓓ Ⓔ
17 Ⓐ Ⓑ Ⓒ Ⓓ Ⓔ
18 Ⓐ Ⓑ Ⓒ Ⓓ Ⓔ
19 Ⓐ Ⓑ Ⓒ Ⓓ Ⓔ
20 Ⓐ Ⓑ Ⓒ Ⓓ Ⓔ
21 Ⓐ Ⓑ Ⓒ Ⓓ Ⓔ
22 Ⓐ Ⓑ Ⓒ Ⓓ Ⓔ

23 Ⓐ Ⓑ Ⓒ Ⓓ Ⓔ
24 Ⓐ Ⓑ Ⓒ Ⓓ Ⓔ
25 Ⓐ Ⓑ Ⓒ Ⓓ Ⓔ
26 Ⓐ Ⓑ Ⓒ Ⓓ Ⓔ
27 Ⓐ Ⓑ Ⓒ Ⓓ Ⓔ
28 Ⓐ Ⓑ Ⓒ Ⓓ Ⓔ
29 Ⓐ Ⓑ Ⓒ Ⓓ Ⓔ
30 Ⓐ Ⓑ Ⓒ Ⓓ Ⓔ
31 Ⓐ Ⓑ Ⓒ Ⓓ Ⓔ
32 Ⓐ Ⓑ Ⓒ Ⓓ Ⓔ
33 Ⓐ Ⓑ Ⓒ Ⓓ Ⓔ
34 Ⓐ Ⓑ Ⓒ Ⓓ Ⓔ
35 Ⓐ Ⓑ Ⓒ Ⓓ Ⓔ
36 Ⓐ Ⓑ Ⓒ Ⓓ Ⓔ
37 Ⓐ Ⓑ Ⓒ Ⓓ Ⓔ
38 Ⓐ Ⓑ Ⓒ Ⓓ Ⓔ
39 Ⓐ Ⓑ Ⓒ Ⓓ Ⓔ
40 Ⓐ Ⓑ Ⓒ Ⓓ Ⓔ
41 Ⓐ Ⓑ Ⓒ Ⓓ Ⓔ
42 Ⓐ Ⓑ Ⓒ Ⓓ Ⓔ
43 Ⓐ Ⓑ Ⓒ Ⓓ Ⓔ
44 Ⓐ Ⓑ Ⓒ Ⓓ Ⓔ

45 Ⓐ Ⓑ Ⓒ Ⓓ Ⓔ
46 Ⓐ Ⓑ Ⓒ Ⓓ Ⓔ
47 Ⓐ Ⓑ Ⓒ Ⓓ Ⓔ
48 Ⓐ Ⓑ Ⓒ Ⓓ Ⓔ
49 Ⓐ Ⓑ Ⓒ Ⓓ Ⓔ
50 Ⓐ Ⓑ Ⓒ Ⓓ Ⓔ
51 Ⓐ Ⓑ Ⓒ Ⓓ Ⓔ
52 Ⓐ Ⓑ Ⓒ Ⓓ Ⓔ
53 Ⓐ Ⓑ Ⓒ Ⓓ Ⓔ
54 Ⓐ Ⓑ Ⓒ Ⓓ Ⓔ
55 Ⓐ Ⓑ Ⓒ Ⓓ Ⓔ
56 Ⓐ Ⓑ Ⓒ Ⓓ Ⓔ
57 Ⓐ Ⓑ Ⓒ Ⓓ Ⓔ
58 Ⓐ Ⓑ Ⓒ Ⓓ Ⓔ
59 Ⓐ Ⓑ Ⓒ Ⓓ Ⓔ
60 Ⓐ Ⓑ Ⓒ Ⓓ Ⓔ
61 Ⓐ Ⓑ Ⓒ Ⓓ Ⓔ
62 Ⓐ Ⓑ Ⓒ Ⓓ Ⓔ
63 Ⓐ Ⓑ Ⓒ Ⓓ Ⓕ
64 Ⓐ Ⓑ Ⓒ Ⓓ Ⓔ
65 Ⓐ Ⓑ Ⓒ Ⓓ Ⓔ
66 Ⓐ Ⓑ Ⓒ Ⓓ Ⓔ

67 Ⓐ Ⓑ Ⓒ Ⓓ Ⓔ
68 Ⓐ Ⓑ Ⓒ Ⓓ Ⓔ
69 Ⓐ Ⓑ Ⓒ Ⓓ Ⓔ
70 Ⓐ Ⓑ Ⓒ Ⓕ Ⓔ
71 Ⓐ Ⓑ Ⓒ Ⓓ Ⓔ
72 Ⓐ Ⓑ Ⓒ Ⓓ Ⓔ
73 Ⓐ Ⓑ Ⓒ Ⓓ Ⓔ
74 Ⓐ Ⓑ Ⓒ Ⓓ Ⓔ
75 Ⓐ Ⓑ Ⓒ Ⓓ Ⓔ
76 Ⓐ Ⓑ Ⓒ Ⓓ Ⓔ
77 Ⓐ Ⓑ Ⓒ Ⓓ Ⓔ
78 Ⓐ Ⓑ Ⓒ Ⓓ Ⓔ
79 Ⓐ Ⓑ Ⓒ Ⓓ Ⓔ
80 Ⓐ Ⓑ Ⓒ Ⓓ Ⓔ
81 Ⓐ Ⓑ Ⓒ Ⓓ Ⓔ
82 Ⓐ Ⓑ Ⓒ Ⓓ Ⓔ
83 Ⓐ Ⓑ Ⓒ Ⓓ Ⓔ
84 Ⓐ Ⓑ Ⓒ Ⓓ Ⓔ
85 Ⓐ Ⓑ Ⓒ Ⓓ Ⓔ
86 Ⓐ Ⓑ Ⓒ Ⓓ Ⓔ
87 Ⓐ Ⓑ Ⓒ Ⓓ Ⓔ
88 Ⓐ Ⓑ Ⓒ Ⓓ Ⓔ

PRACTICE II

1 Ⓐ Ⓑ Ⓒ Ⓓ Ⓔ
2 Ⓐ Ⓑ Ⓒ Ⓓ Ⓔ
3 Ⓐ Ⓑ Ⓒ Ⓓ Ⓔ
4 Ⓐ Ⓑ Ⓒ Ⓓ Ⓔ
5 Ⓐ Ⓑ Ⓒ Ⓓ Ⓔ
6 Ⓐ Ⓑ Ⓒ Ⓓ Ⓔ
7 Ⓐ Ⓑ Ⓒ Ⓓ Ⓔ
8 Ⓐ Ⓑ Ⓒ Ⓓ Ⓔ
9 Ⓐ Ⓑ Ⓒ Ⓓ Ⓔ
10 Ⓐ Ⓑ Ⓒ Ⓓ Ⓔ
11 Ⓐ Ⓑ Ⓒ Ⓓ Ⓔ
12 Ⓐ Ⓑ Ⓒ Ⓓ Ⓔ
13 Ⓐ Ⓑ Ⓒ Ⓓ Ⓔ
14 Ⓐ Ⓑ Ⓒ Ⓓ Ⓔ
15 Ⓐ Ⓑ Ⓒ Ⓓ Ⓔ
16 Ⓐ Ⓑ Ⓒ Ⓓ Ⓔ
17 Ⓐ Ⓑ Ⓒ Ⓓ Ⓔ
18 Ⓐ Ⓑ Ⓒ Ⓓ Ⓔ
19 Ⓐ Ⓑ Ⓒ Ⓓ Ⓔ
20 Ⓐ Ⓑ Ⓒ Ⓓ Ⓔ
21 Ⓐ Ⓑ Ⓒ Ⓓ Ⓔ
22 Ⓐ Ⓑ Ⓒ Ⓓ Ⓔ

23 Ⓐ Ⓑ Ⓒ Ⓓ Ⓔ
24 Ⓐ Ⓑ Ⓒ Ⓓ Ⓔ
25 Ⓐ Ⓑ Ⓒ Ⓓ Ⓔ
26 Ⓐ Ⓑ Ⓒ Ⓓ Ⓔ
27 Ⓐ Ⓑ Ⓒ Ⓓ Ⓔ
28 Ⓐ Ⓑ Ⓒ Ⓓ Ⓔ
29 Ⓐ Ⓑ Ⓒ Ⓓ Ⓔ
30 Ⓐ Ⓑ Ⓒ Ⓓ Ⓔ
31 Ⓐ Ⓑ Ⓒ Ⓓ Ⓔ
32 Ⓐ Ⓑ Ⓒ Ⓓ Ⓔ
33 Ⓐ Ⓑ Ⓒ Ⓓ Ⓔ
34 Ⓐ Ⓑ Ⓒ Ⓓ Ⓔ
35 Ⓐ Ⓑ Ⓒ Ⓓ Ⓔ
36 Ⓐ Ⓑ Ⓒ Ⓓ Ⓔ
37 Ⓐ Ⓑ Ⓒ Ⓓ Ⓔ
38 Ⓐ Ⓑ Ⓒ Ⓓ Ⓔ
39 Ⓐ Ⓑ Ⓒ Ⓓ Ⓔ
40 Ⓐ Ⓑ Ⓒ Ⓓ Ⓔ
41 Ⓐ Ⓑ Ⓒ Ⓓ Ⓔ
42 Ⓐ Ⓑ Ⓒ Ⓓ Ⓔ
43 Ⓐ Ⓑ Ⓒ Ⓓ Ⓔ
44 Ⓐ Ⓑ Ⓒ Ⓓ Ⓔ

45 Ⓐ Ⓑ Ⓒ Ⓓ Ⓔ
46 Ⓐ Ⓑ Ⓒ Ⓓ Ⓔ
47 Ⓐ Ⓑ Ⓒ Ⓓ Ⓔ
48 Ⓐ Ⓑ Ⓒ Ⓓ Ⓔ
49 Ⓐ Ⓑ Ⓒ Ⓓ Ⓔ
50 Ⓐ Ⓑ Ⓒ Ⓓ Ⓔ
51 Ⓐ Ⓑ Ⓒ Ⓓ Ⓔ
52 Ⓐ Ⓑ Ⓒ Ⓓ Ⓔ
53 Ⓐ Ⓑ Ⓒ Ⓓ Ⓔ
54 Ⓐ Ⓑ Ⓒ Ⓓ Ⓔ
55 Ⓐ Ⓑ Ⓒ Ⓓ Ⓔ
56 Ⓐ Ⓑ Ⓒ Ⓓ Ⓔ
57 Ⓐ Ⓑ Ⓒ Ⓓ Ⓔ
58 Ⓐ Ⓑ Ⓒ Ⓓ Ⓔ
59 Ⓐ Ⓑ Ⓒ Ⓓ Ⓔ
60 Ⓐ Ⓑ Ⓒ Ⓓ Ⓔ
61 Ⓐ Ⓑ Ⓒ Ⓓ Ⓔ
62 Ⓐ Ⓑ Ⓒ Ⓓ Ⓔ
63 Ⓐ Ⓑ Ⓒ Ⓓ Ⓔ
64 Ⓐ Ⓑ Ⓒ Ⓓ Ⓔ
65 Ⓐ Ⓑ Ⓒ Ⓓ Ⓔ
66 Ⓐ Ⓑ Ⓒ Ⓓ Ⓔ

67 Ⓐ Ⓑ Ⓒ Ⓓ Ⓔ
68 Ⓐ Ⓑ Ⓒ Ⓓ Ⓔ
69 Ⓐ Ⓑ Ⓒ Ⓓ Ⓔ
70 Ⓐ Ⓑ Ⓒ Ⓓ Ⓔ
71 Ⓐ Ⓑ Ⓒ Ⓓ Ⓔ
72 Ⓐ Ⓑ Ⓒ Ⓓ Ⓔ
73 Ⓐ Ⓑ Ⓒ Ⓓ Ⓔ
74 Ⓐ Ⓑ Ⓒ Ⓓ Ⓔ
75 Ⓐ Ⓑ Ⓒ Ⓓ Ⓔ
76 Ⓐ Ⓑ Ⓒ Ⓓ Ⓔ
77 Ⓐ Ⓑ Ⓒ Ⓓ Ⓔ
78 Ⓐ Ⓑ Ⓒ Ⓓ Ⓔ
79 Ⓐ Ⓑ Ⓒ Ⓓ Ⓔ
80 Ⓐ Ⓑ Ⓒ Ⓓ Ⓔ
81 Ⓐ Ⓑ Ⓒ Ⓓ Ⓔ
82 Ⓐ Ⓑ Ⓒ Ⓓ Ⓔ
83 Ⓐ Ⓑ Ⓒ Ⓓ Ⓔ
84 Ⓐ Ⓑ Ⓒ Ⓓ Ⓔ
85 Ⓐ Ⓑ Ⓒ Ⓓ Ⓔ
86 Ⓐ Ⓑ Ⓒ Ⓓ Ⓔ
87 Ⓐ Ⓑ Ⓒ Ⓓ Ⓔ
88 Ⓐ Ⓑ Ⓒ Ⓓ Ⓔ

PRACTICE III

1 Ⓐ Ⓑ Ⓒ Ⓓ Ⓔ   23 Ⓐ Ⓑ Ⓒ Ⓓ Ⓔ   45 Ⓐ Ⓑ Ⓒ Ⓓ Ⓔ   67 Ⓐ Ⓑ Ⓒ Ⓓ Ⓔ

2 Ⓐ Ⓑ Ⓒ Ⓓ Ⓔ   24 Ⓐ Ⓑ Ⓒ Ⓓ Ⓔ   46 Ⓐ Ⓑ Ⓒ Ⓓ Ⓔ   68 Ⓐ Ⓑ Ⓒ Ⓓ Ⓔ

3 Ⓐ Ⓑ Ⓒ Ⓓ Ⓔ   25 Ⓐ Ⓑ Ⓒ Ⓓ Ⓔ   47 Ⓐ Ⓑ Ⓒ Ⓓ Ⓔ   69 Ⓐ Ⓑ Ⓒ Ⓓ Ⓔ

4 Ⓐ Ⓑ Ⓒ Ⓓ Ⓔ   26 Ⓐ Ⓑ Ⓒ Ⓓ Ⓔ   48 Ⓐ Ⓑ Ⓒ Ⓓ Ⓔ   70 Ⓐ Ⓑ Ⓒ Ⓓ Ⓔ

5 Ⓐ Ⓑ Ⓒ Ⓓ Ⓔ   27 Ⓐ Ⓑ Ⓒ Ⓓ Ⓔ   49 Ⓐ Ⓑ Ⓒ Ⓓ Ⓔ   71 Ⓐ Ⓑ Ⓒ Ⓓ Ⓔ

6 Ⓐ Ⓑ Ⓒ Ⓓ Ⓔ   28 Ⓐ Ⓑ Ⓒ Ⓓ Ⓔ   50 Ⓐ Ⓑ Ⓒ Ⓓ Ⓔ   72 Ⓐ Ⓑ Ⓒ Ⓓ Ⓔ

7 Ⓐ Ⓑ Ⓒ Ⓓ Ⓔ   29 Ⓐ Ⓑ Ⓒ Ⓓ Ⓔ   51 Ⓐ Ⓑ Ⓒ Ⓓ Ⓔ   73 Ⓐ Ⓑ Ⓒ Ⓓ Ⓔ

8 Ⓐ Ⓑ Ⓒ Ⓓ Ⓔ   30 Ⓐ Ⓑ Ⓒ Ⓓ Ⓔ   52 Ⓐ Ⓑ Ⓒ Ⓓ Ⓔ   74 Ⓐ Ⓑ Ⓒ Ⓓ Ⓔ

9 Ⓐ Ⓑ Ⓒ Ⓓ Ⓔ   31 Ⓐ Ⓑ Ⓒ Ⓓ Ⓔ   53 Ⓐ Ⓑ Ⓒ Ⓓ Ⓔ   75 Ⓐ Ⓑ Ⓒ Ⓓ Ⓔ

10 Ⓐ Ⓑ Ⓒ Ⓓ Ⓔ   32 Ⓐ Ⓑ Ⓒ Ⓓ Ⓔ   54 Ⓐ Ⓑ Ⓒ Ⓓ Ⓔ   76 Ⓐ Ⓑ Ⓒ Ⓓ Ⓔ

11 Ⓐ Ⓑ Ⓒ Ⓓ Ⓔ   33 Ⓐ Ⓑ Ⓒ Ⓓ Ⓔ   55 Ⓐ Ⓑ Ⓒ Ⓓ Ⓔ   77 Ⓐ Ⓑ Ⓒ Ⓓ Ⓔ

12 Ⓐ Ⓑ Ⓒ Ⓓ Ⓔ   34 Ⓐ Ⓑ Ⓒ Ⓓ Ⓔ   56 Ⓐ Ⓑ Ⓒ Ⓓ Ⓔ   78 Ⓐ Ⓑ Ⓒ Ⓓ Ⓔ

13 Ⓐ Ⓑ Ⓒ Ⓓ Ⓔ   35 Ⓐ Ⓑ Ⓒ Ⓓ Ⓔ   57 Ⓐ Ⓑ Ⓒ Ⓓ Ⓔ   79 Ⓐ Ⓑ Ⓒ Ⓓ Ⓔ

14 Ⓐ Ⓑ Ⓒ Ⓓ Ⓔ   36 Ⓐ Ⓑ Ⓒ Ⓓ Ⓔ   58 Ⓐ Ⓑ Ⓒ Ⓓ Ⓔ   80 Ⓐ Ⓑ Ⓒ Ⓓ Ⓔ

15 Ⓐ Ⓑ Ⓒ Ⓓ Ⓔ   37 Ⓐ Ⓑ Ⓒ Ⓓ Ⓔ   59 Ⓐ Ⓑ Ⓒ Ⓓ Ⓔ   81 Ⓐ Ⓑ Ⓒ Ⓓ Ⓔ

16 Ⓐ Ⓑ Ⓒ Ⓓ Ⓔ   38 Ⓐ Ⓑ Ⓒ Ⓓ Ⓔ   60 Ⓐ Ⓑ Ⓒ Ⓓ Ⓔ   82 Ⓐ Ⓑ Ⓒ Ⓓ Ⓔ

17 Ⓐ Ⓑ Ⓒ Ⓓ Ⓔ   39 Ⓐ Ⓑ Ⓒ Ⓓ Ⓔ   61 Ⓐ Ⓑ Ⓒ Ⓓ Ⓔ   83 Ⓐ Ⓑ Ⓒ Ⓓ Ⓔ

18 Ⓐ Ⓑ Ⓒ Ⓓ Ⓔ   40 Ⓐ Ⓑ Ⓒ Ⓓ Ⓔ   62 Ⓐ Ⓑ Ⓒ Ⓓ Ⓔ   84 Ⓐ Ⓑ Ⓒ Ⓓ Ⓔ

19 Ⓐ Ⓑ Ⓒ Ⓓ Ⓔ   41 Ⓐ Ⓑ Ⓒ Ⓓ Ⓔ   63 Ⓐ Ⓑ Ⓒ Ⓓ Ⓔ   85 Ⓐ Ⓑ Ⓒ Ⓓ Ⓔ

20 Ⓐ Ⓑ Ⓒ Ⓓ Ⓔ   42 Ⓐ Ⓑ Ⓒ Ⓓ Ⓔ   64 Ⓐ Ⓑ Ⓒ Ⓓ Ⓔ   86 Ⓐ Ⓑ Ⓒ Ⓓ Ⓔ

21 Ⓐ Ⓑ Ⓒ Ⓓ Ⓔ   43 Ⓐ Ⓑ Ⓒ Ⓓ Ⓔ   65 Ⓐ Ⓑ Ⓒ Ⓓ Ⓔ   87 Ⓐ Ⓑ Ⓒ Ⓓ Ⓔ

22 Ⓐ Ⓑ Ⓒ Ⓓ Ⓔ   44 Ⓐ Ⓑ Ⓒ Ⓓ Ⓔ   66 Ⓐ Ⓑ Ⓒ Ⓓ Ⓔ   88 Ⓐ Ⓑ Ⓒ Ⓓ Ⓔ

MEMORY FOR ADDRESSES TEST

1 Ⓐ Ⓑ Ⓒ Ⓓ Ⓔ
2 Ⓐ Ⓑ Ⓒ Ⓓ Ⓔ
3 Ⓐ Ⓑ Ⓒ Ⓓ Ⓔ
4 Ⓐ Ⓑ Ⓒ Ⓓ Ⓔ
5 Ⓐ Ⓑ Ⓒ Ⓓ Ⓔ
6 Ⓐ Ⓑ Ⓒ Ⓓ Ⓔ
7 Ⓐ Ⓑ Ⓒ Ⓓ Ⓔ
8 Ⓐ Ⓑ Ⓒ Ⓓ Ⓔ
9 Ⓐ Ⓑ Ⓒ Ⓓ Ⓔ
10 Ⓐ Ⓑ Ⓒ Ⓓ Ⓔ
11 Ⓐ Ⓑ Ⓒ Ⓓ Ⓔ
12 Ⓐ Ⓑ Ⓒ Ⓓ Ⓔ
13 Ⓐ Ⓑ Ⓒ Ⓓ Ⓔ
14 Ⓐ Ⓑ Ⓒ Ⓓ Ⓔ
15 Ⓐ Ⓑ Ⓒ Ⓓ Ⓔ
16 Ⓐ Ⓑ Ⓒ Ⓓ Ⓔ
17 Ⓐ Ⓑ Ⓒ Ⓓ Ⓔ
18 Ⓐ Ⓑ Ⓒ Ⓓ Ⓔ
19 Ⓐ Ⓑ Ⓒ Ⓓ Ⓔ
20 Ⓐ Ⓑ Ⓒ Ⓓ Ⓔ
21 Ⓐ Ⓑ Ⓒ Ⓓ Ⓔ
22 Ⓐ Ⓑ Ⓒ Ⓓ Ⓔ

23 Ⓐ Ⓑ Ⓒ Ⓓ Ⓔ
24 Ⓐ Ⓑ Ⓒ Ⓓ Ⓔ
25 Ⓐ Ⓑ Ⓒ Ⓓ Ⓔ
26 Ⓐ Ⓑ Ⓒ Ⓓ Ⓔ
27 Ⓐ Ⓑ Ⓒ Ⓓ Ⓔ
28 Ⓐ Ⓑ Ⓒ Ⓓ Ⓔ
29 Ⓐ Ⓑ Ⓒ Ⓓ Ⓔ
30 Ⓐ Ⓑ Ⓒ Ⓓ Ⓔ
31 Ⓐ Ⓑ Ⓒ Ⓓ Ⓔ
32 Ⓐ Ⓑ Ⓒ Ⓓ Ⓔ
33 Ⓐ Ⓑ Ⓒ Ⓓ Ⓔ
34 Ⓐ Ⓑ Ⓒ Ⓓ Ⓔ
35 Ⓐ Ⓑ Ⓒ Ⓓ Ⓔ
36 Ⓐ Ⓑ Ⓒ Ⓓ Ⓔ
37 Ⓐ Ⓑ Ⓒ Ⓓ Ⓔ
38 Ⓐ Ⓑ Ⓒ Ⓓ Ⓔ
39 Ⓐ Ⓑ Ⓒ Ⓓ Ⓔ
40 Ⓐ Ⓑ Ⓒ Ⓓ Ⓔ
41 Ⓐ Ⓑ Ⓒ Ⓓ Ⓔ
42 Ⓐ Ⓑ Ⓒ Ⓓ Ⓔ
43 Ⓐ Ⓑ Ⓒ Ⓓ Ⓔ
44 Ⓐ Ⓑ Ⓒ Ⓓ Ⓔ

45 Ⓐ Ⓑ Ⓒ Ⓓ Ⓔ
46 Ⓐ Ⓑ Ⓒ Ⓓ Ⓔ
47 Ⓐ Ⓑ Ⓒ Ⓓ Ⓔ
48 Ⓐ Ⓑ Ⓒ Ⓓ Ⓔ
49 Ⓐ Ⓑ Ⓒ Ⓓ Ⓔ
50 Ⓐ Ⓑ Ⓒ Ⓓ Ⓔ
51 Ⓐ Ⓑ Ⓒ Ⓓ Ⓔ
52 Ⓐ Ⓑ Ⓒ Ⓓ Ⓔ
53 Ⓐ Ⓑ Ⓒ Ⓓ Ⓔ
54 Ⓐ Ⓑ Ⓒ Ⓓ Ⓔ
55 Ⓐ Ⓑ Ⓒ Ⓓ Ⓔ
56 Ⓐ Ⓑ Ⓒ Ⓓ Ⓔ
57 Ⓐ Ⓑ Ⓒ Ⓓ Ⓔ
58 Ⓐ Ⓑ Ⓒ Ⓓ Ⓔ
59 Ⓐ Ⓑ Ⓒ Ⓓ Ⓔ
60 Ⓐ Ⓑ Ⓒ Ⓓ Ⓔ
61 Ⓐ Ⓑ Ⓒ Ⓓ Ⓔ
62 Ⓐ Ⓑ Ⓒ Ⓓ Ⓔ
63 Ⓐ Ⓑ Ⓒ Ⓓ Ⓔ
64 Ⓐ Ⓑ Ⓒ Ⓓ Ⓔ
65 Ⓐ Ⓑ Ⓒ Ⓓ Ⓔ
66 Ⓐ Ⓑ Ⓒ Ⓓ Ⓔ

67 Ⓐ Ⓑ Ⓒ Ⓓ Ⓔ
68 Ⓐ Ⓑ Ⓒ Ⓓ Ⓔ
69 Ⓐ Ⓑ Ⓒ Ⓒ Ⓔ
70 Ⓐ Ⓑ Ⓒ Ⓓ Ⓔ
71 Ⓐ Ⓑ Ⓒ Ⓓ Ⓔ
72 Ⓐ Ⓑ Ⓒ Ⓓ Ⓔ
73 Ⓐ Ⓑ Ⓒ Ⓓ Ⓔ
74 Ⓐ Ⓑ Ⓒ Ⓓ Ⓔ
75 Ⓐ Ⓑ Ⓒ Ⓓ Ⓔ
76 Ⓐ Ⓑ Ⓒ Ⓓ Ⓔ
77 Ⓐ Ⓑ Ⓒ Ⓓ Ⓔ
78 Ⓐ Ⓑ Ⓒ Ⓓ Ⓔ
79 Ⓐ Ⓑ Ⓒ Ⓓ Ⓔ
80 Ⓐ Ⓑ Ⓒ Ⓓ Ⓔ
81 Ⓐ Ⓑ Ⓒ Ⓓ Ⓔ
82 Ⓐ Ⓑ Ⓒ Ⓓ Ⓔ
83 Ⓐ Ⓑ Ⓒ Ⓓ Ⓔ
84 Ⓐ Ⓑ Ⓒ Ⓓ Ⓔ
85 Ⓐ Ⓑ Ⓒ Ⓓ Ⓔ
86 Ⓐ Ⓑ Ⓒ Ⓓ Ⓔ
87 Ⓐ Ⓑ Ⓒ Ⓓ Ⓔ
88 Ⓐ Ⓑ Ⓒ Ⓓ Ⓔ

SCORE SHEET FOR FIFTH MODEL EXAM

ADDRESS CHECKING TEST

Number Right minus Number Wrong equals   Score

_____   –   _____   =   _____

MEMORY FOR ADDRESSES TEST

Number Right minus (Number Wrong ÷ 4) equals   Score

_____   –   _____   =   _____

PROGRESS GRAPH

Blacken the bars for Model Exam 5 to the scores you earned.

Score						
95						
90						
85						
80						
75						
70						
65						
60						
55						
50						
45						
40						
35						
30						
25						
20						
15						
10						
5						
0						
Test	AC| M	AC| M	AC| M	AC| M	AC| M	AC| M
Model Exam	Diag.	1	2	3	4	5

AC = Address Checking   M = Memory for Addresses

FIFTH MODEL EXAM

ADDRESS CHECKING TEST

TIME: 6 Minutes. 95 Questions.

DIRECTIONS: For each question, compare the address in the left column with the address in the right column. If the two addresses are ALIKE IN EVERY WAY, blacken space Ⓐ on your answer sheet. If the two addresses are DIFFERENT IN ANY WAY, blacken space Ⓓ on your answer sheet. Correct answers for this test are on page 159.

1	8472 Elizabeth Pl	8472 Elisabeth Pl
2	2418 W 79th Ave	2418 W 79th Ave
3	New Rochelle NY 10804	New Rochelle NY 10804
4	3721 Stuyvesant Plz	3721 Stuyvestant Plz
5	3270 Summit Cir	3720 Summit Cir
6	919 Father Finian Dr	919 Father Finian Dr
7	8562 Coachlight Sq	8562 Coachlight Sq
8	Spartansburg PA 16434	Spartansburg PA 16343
9	1351 S Lexington Ave	1351 S Lexington Ave
10	1947 E 147th Pl	1947 E 174th Pl
11	Kimmswick MO 63053	Kimsswick MO 63053
12	8541 Wyndover Ln	8541 Wyndover Ln
13	6687 Timpson St	6687 Timpson St
14	6338 Black Birch Rd	6338 Black Birch Rd
15	7345 Valerie Dr	7345 Valerie Dr
16	7787 Moseman Ave	7787 Mosemen Ave
17	1828 NW 248th St	1828 NW 148th Rd
18	Pinconning MI 48650	Pinconning MI 48650
19	4650 Hungerford Rd	4650 Hungerford Rd
20	5947 Morrow Ave	5974 Morrow Ave
21	1954 Lincoln Pt	1954 Lincoln Pt
22	3657 Browning Ln	3567 Browning Ln
23	380 S Highland Ave	3800 S Highland Ave
24	Hewlett Bay Park NY 11557	Hewlett Bay Park NY 11577
25	1806 Fox Wood Ln	1806 Foxwood Ln
26	1846 Lockwood Ave	1846 E Lockwood Ave

27 . . . 2481 Copper Beech Rd	2481 Copper Beach Rd
28 . . . 2203 Elissa Ln	2203 Elissa Ln
29 . . . 6713 Oakridge Dr	6713 Oakridge Dr
30 . . . 1291 Raleigh Rd	1291 Raleigh Rd
31 . . . Shuqualak MS 39361	Shuqualak MS 39361
32 . . . 2823 Walker Dr	2823 Walker Dr
33 . . . 7394 Ardsley Rd	7394 Ardsley Ave
34 . . . 1324 N 5th Ave	1324 N 5th Ave
35 . . . 3461 Cecil Crest Rd	3641 Cecil Crest Rd
36 . . . 1689 Beekman Ave	1689 Beekman Ave
37 . . . Defiance IA 51527	Defiance IA 51527
38 . . . 2023 John Jay Pl	2023 John Jay Pl
39 . . . 4286 W 257th Rd	4286 W 275th Rd
40 . . . 464 Campus Brook Rd	464 Canopus Brook Rd
41 . . . 1228 Elliott Ave	1228 Elliot Ave
42 . . . 2624 Flagg Pl	2624 Flagg Pl
43 . . . 1514 E Prospect Ave	1541 E Prospect Ave
44 . . . 6238 Railroad Ave	6238 S Railroad Ave
45 . . . 6575 Iriquois Rd	6575 Iroquois Rd
46 . . . Sublimity OR 97385	Sublimity OR 93785
47 . . . Kosciusko MS 39090	Kocsiusko MS 39090
48 . . . 8129 Leewood Cir	8129 Leewood Cir
49 . . . 6130 Williamson St	6310 Williamson St
50 . . . 1012 S Division St	1012 S Division St
51 . . . 4989 Pugsley Pk	4989 Pugsley Pk
52 . . . 2713 W 375th Rd	2713 W 375th Rd
53 . . . 9412 Otsego Rd	9412 Otsego Rd
54 . . . 5523 Nordica Dr	5523 Nordica Dr
55 . . . 2780 Barrymore Ln	2780 Barrymore Ln
56 . . . 2431 Millington Rd	2341 Millington Rd
57 . . . 7326 Eastchester Rd	7362 Eastchester Rd
58 . . . Linneus MO 64653	Linneaus MO 64653
59 . . . 3975 Concord Pk	3975 Concord Pk
60 . . . 9355 Tanglewood Rd	9335 Tanglewood Rd
61 . . . 8461 S 67th Dr	8461 S 67th Dr
62 . . . 9236 Bajart Pl	9236 Bajarti Pl
63 . . . 1664 Intervale Blvd	1664 Intervale Blvd
64 . . . 8421 Glendella Ave	8421 Glenellda Ave
65 . . . Woodmere NY 11598	Woodmere NJ 11598
66 . . . 858 Fuller Gdns	858 Feller Gdns
67 . . . 6609 Davenport Ave	6690 Davenport Ave
68 . . . 154 Storm King Mtn	154 Storm King Mtn
69 . . . 3492 Trinity Pl	3492 Trinity Plz
70 . . . 2070 Allenby Ave	2070 Allanby Ave
71 . . . 606 Albany Post Rd N	606 Albany Post Rd N
72 . . . 2336 Oliphant Ave	2336 Oliphent Ave
73 . . . 1106 Burhns Ave	1106 Buhrns Ave
74 . . . Chalybeate MS 38684	Chalybeate MS 38684
75 . . . 5238 Chamberlin Ave	5238 Chamberlain Ave
76 . . . 782 E 59th St	782 E 59th St
77 . . . 5273 Wisconsin Ave NE	5237 Wisconsin Ave NE
78 . . . 4982 Loehr Pl	4982 Loehr Pl

79	Toccopola MS 38874	Toccopola MS 38774
80	5399 Pemart Ave	5399 Penmart Ave
81	4968 S Bedford Rd	4986 S Bedford Rd
82	2790 Lincolndale Ave	2790 Lincolndale Ave
83	9056 W 101st St	9056 W 101st Rd
84	5583 Mulberry Ln	5583 Mullberry Ln
85	West Palm Beach FL 33409	West Palm Beach FL 33904
86	4947 Carolyn Wy	4947 Caroline Wy
87	749 Glenville Ave	749 Glenville Ave
88	9047 W Alston St	9047 W Allston St
89	6573 Babbitt Rd	6573 Rabbitt Rd
90	Fontanelle IA 50846	Fontanella IA 50846
91	6938 W Devon Ct	6983 W Devon Ct
92	3988 Kirby Cl	3998 Kirby Cl
93	9071 Peekskill Hollow Rd	9017 Peekskill Hollow Rd
94	659A Richbell Rd	695A Richbell Rd
95	4518 Franklin Ave	4518 Franklin Ave

END OF ADDRESS CHECKING TEST

If you finish this test before time is up, use the remaining time to check over your work. Do not turn the page until you are told to do so.

PRACTICE FOR
MEMORY FOR ADDRESSES TEST

DIRECTIONS: The five boxes below are labelled A, B, C, D, and E. In each box are three sets of number spans with names and two names which are not associated with numbers. In the next THREE MINUTES, you must try to memorize the box location of each name and number span. The position of a name or number span within its box is not important. You need only remember the letter of the box in which the item is to be found. You will use these names and numbers to answer three sets of practice questions which are NOT scored and one actual test which is scored. Correct answers are on pages 159 and 160.

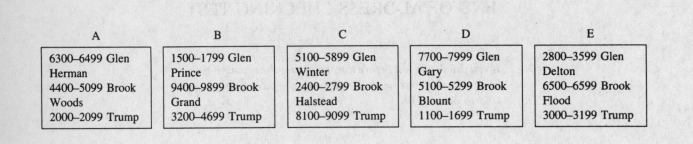

A	B	C	D	E
6300–6499 Glen	1500–1799 Glen	5100–5899 Glen	7700–7999 Glen	2800–3599 Glen
Herman	Prince	Winter	Gary	Delton
4400–5099 Brook	9400–9899 Brook	2400–2799 Brook	5100–5299 Brook	6500–6599 Brook
Woods	Grand	Halstead	Blount	Flood
2000–2099 Trump	3200–4699 Trump	8100–9099 Trump	1100–1699 Trump	3000–3199 Trump

PRACTICE I

DIRECTIONS: Use the next THREE MINUTES to mark on your answer sheet the letter of the box in which each item that follows is to be found. Try to mark each item without looking back at the boxes. If, however, you get stuck, you may refer to the boxes during this practice exercise. If you find that you must look at the boxes, try to memorize as you do so. This test is for practice only. It will not be scored.

1. 1100–1699 Trump
2. 4400–5099 Brook
3. 1500–1799 Glen
4. 2400–2799 Brook
5. 3000–3199 Trump
6. Halstead

7. Blount
8. 6300–6499 Glen
9. 2800–3599 Glen
10. Delton
11. 2400–2799 Brook
12. 2000–2099 Trump

13. 9400–9899 Brook
14. Prince
15. Herman
16. Flood
17. 3200–4699 Trump
18. 8100–9099 Trump
19. 7700–7999 Glen
20. 6300–6499 Glen
21. Woods
22. Grand
23. 5100–5299 Brook
24. 6500–6599 Brook
25. Gary
26. 5100–5899 Glen
27. Flood
28. Winter
29. 9400–9899 Brook
30. 6300–6499 Glen
31. 5100–5299 Brook
32. 8100–9099 Trump
33. 4400–5099 Brook
34. 1500–1799 Glen
35. Winter
36. Halstead
37. 3200–4699 Trump
38. 7700–7999 Glen
39. 6500–6599 Brook
40. 1100–1699 Trump
41. Herman
42. Delton
43. Gary
44. 1500–1799 Glen
45. 2400–2799 Brook
46. 6500–6599 Brook
47. Grand
48. Woods
49. 9400–9899 Brook
50. 5100–5899 Glen

51. 2800–3599 Glen
52. 3000–3199 Trump
53. 3200–4699 Trump
54. Prince
55. Blount
56. Flood
57. 1100–1699 Trump
58. 5100–5299 Brook
59. 5100–5899 Glen
60. Prince
61. Delton
62. 8100–9099 Trump
63. 4400–5099 Brook
64. 7700–7999 Glen
65. 1100–1699 Trump
66. 6500–6599 Brook
67. 3200–4699 Trump
68. Herman
69. Woods
70. 2800–3599 Glen
71. 9400–9899 Brook
72. 6300–6499 Glen
73. 3000–3199 Trump
74. Halstead
75. Blount
76. Flood
77. 4400–5099 Brook
78. 5100–5299 Brook
79. 2800–3599 Glen
80. 8100–9099 Trump
81. 3200–4699 Trump
82. Gary
83. Winter
84. 2000–2099 Trump
85. 1500–1799 Glen
86. 2400–2799 Brook
87. Herman
88. 6500–6599 Brook

PRACTICE II

DIRECTIONS: The next 88 questions constitute another practice exercise. Again, you should mark your answers on your answer sheet. Again, the time limit is THREE MINUTES. This time, however, you must NOT look at the boxes while answering the questions. You must rely on your memory in marking the box location of each item. This practice test will not be scored.

1. 5100–5299 Brook
2. 2800–3599 Glen
3. 2000–2099 Trump
4. 9400–9899 Brook
5. Halstead
6. Flood
7. 3000–3199 Trump
8. 6300–6499 Glen
9. 2400–2799 Brook
10. Herman
11. 8100–9099 Trump
12. Delton
13. 5100–5899 Glen
14. 7700–7999 Glen
15. 6500–6599 Brook
16. 2000–2099 Trump
17. 5100–5899 Glen
18. Prince
19. Blount
20. 6300–6499 Glen
21. 3200–4699 Trump
22. 9400–9899 Brook
23. 5100–5299 Brook
24. 1500–1799 Glen
25. Woods
26. Gary
27. Flood
28. 3000–3199 Trump
29. 2400–2799 Brook
30. 7700–7999 Glen
31. 2800–3599 Glen
32. Halstead
33. Delton
34. 4400–5099 Brook
35. 8100–9099 Trump
36. 1100–1699 Trump
37. Herman
38. Winter
39. Grand
40. 4400–5099 Brook
41. 1500–1799 Glen
42. 5100–5899 Glen
43. 3000–3199 Trump
44. 9400–9899 Brook

45. 1100–1699 Trump
46. 4400–5099 Brook
47. 8100–9099 Trump
48. 7700–7999 Glen
49. Grand
50. Delton
51. Halstead
52. 6300–6499 Glen
53. 2400–2799 Brook
54. 2800–3599 Glen
55. Woods
56. Gary
57. 5100–5899 Glen
58. 6500–6599 Brook
59. 3000–3199 Trump
60. Herman
61. 7700–7999 Glen
62. 2400–2799 Brook
63. 2000–2099 Trump
64. Prince
65. Winter
66. 3200–4699 Trump
67. Flood
68. 3000–3199 Trump
69. 4400–5099 Brook
70. 5100–5299 Brook
71. 6300–6499 Glen
72. Blount
73. 2400–2799 Brook
74. 1500–1799 Glen
75. 2000–2099 Trump
76. Delton
77. Winter
78. 4400–5099 Brook
79. 7700–7999 Glen
80. Blount
81. Halstead
82. 3000–3199 Trump
83. 9400–9899 Brook
84. 5100–5299 Brook
85. 5100–5899 Glen
86. Grand
87. Prince
88. Gary

PRACTICE III

DIRECTIONS: The names and addresses are repeated for you in the boxes below. Each name and each number span is in the same box in which you found it in the original set. You will now be allowed FIVE MINUTES to study the locations again. Do your best to memorize the letter of the box in which each item is located. This is your last chance to see the boxes.

A	B	C	D	E
6300–6499 Glen Herman 4400–5099 Brook Woods 2000–2099 Trump	1500–1799 Glen Prince 9400–9899 Brook Grand 3200–4699 Trump	5100–5899 Glen Winter 2400–2799 Brook Halstead 8100–9099 Trump	7700–7999 Glen Gary 5100–5299 Brook Blount 1100–1699 Trump	2800–3599 Glen Delton 6500–6599 Brook Flood 3000–3199 Trump

DIRECTIONS: This is your last practice test. Mark the location of each of the 88 items on your answer sheet. You will have FIVE MINUTES to answer these questions. Do NOT look back at the boxes. This practice test will not be scored.

1. 9400–9899 Brook
2. 3000–3199 Trump
3. 7700–7999 Glen
4. 4400–5099 Brook
5. 3200–4699 Trump
6. Halstead
7. Delton
8. Prince
9. 6300–6499 Glen
10. 6500–6599 Brook
11. 2800–3599 Glen
12. 8100–9099 Trump
13. Blount
14. Winter
15. Woods
16. 1500–1799 Glen
17. 5100–5299 Brook
18. 5100–5899 Glen
19. 3000–3199 Trump
20. 2000–2099 Trump
21. Herman
22. Gary
23. Flood
24. 7700–7999 Glen
25. 9400–9899 Brook
26. 5100–5899 Glen
27. 1100–1699 Trump
28. 1500–1799 Glen
29. Flood
30. Grand
31. Prince
32. 4400–5099 Brook
33. 7700–7999 Glen
34. 2400–2799 Brook
35. 3200–4699 Trump
36. 6300–6499 Glen
37. Herman
38. Delton
39. Winter
40. 5100–5299 Brook
41. 8100–9099 Trump
42. 2000–2099 Trump
43. 2800–3599 Glen
44. Woods

45. Gary
46. 3000–3199 Trump
47. 9400–9899 Brook
48. Blount
49. Halstead
50. 6500–6599 Brook
51. 7700–7999 Glen
52. 5100–5899 Glen
53. 2000–2099 Trump
54. 4400–5099 Brook
55. 1500–1799 Glen
56. Prince
57. Flood
58. 9400–9899 Brook
59. 6300–6499 Glen
60. 8100–9099 Trump
61. 1100–1699 Trump
62. Blount
63. Winter
64. Herman
65. 3200–4699 Trump
66. 2400–2799 Brook

67. 5100–5299 Brook
68. 2800–3599 Glen
69. 3000–3199 Trump
70. Delton
71. Woods
72. Halstead
73. 6500–6599 Brook
74. 2000–2099 Trump
75. 9400–9899 Brook
76. Grand
77. Gary
78. 5100–5899 Glen
79. 2400–2799 Brook
80. Winter
81. 3200–4699 Trump
82. 5100–5299 Brook
83. 8100–9099 Trump
84. Blount
85. Flood
86. Herman
87. 1500–1799 Glen
88. 1100–1699 Trump

MEMORY FOR ADDRESSES TEST

TIME: 5 Minutes. 88 Questions.

DIRECTIONS: Mark your answers on the answer sheet in the section headed "MEMORY FOR ADDRESSES TEST." This test will be scored. You are NOT permitted to look at the boxes. Work from memory, as quickly and as accurately as you can. Correct answers are on page 160.

1. 1500–1799 Glen
2. 8100–9099 Trump
3. Blount
4. 4400–5099 Brook
5. 3000–3199 Trump
6. 6300–6499 Glen
7. Delton
8. Winter
9. 2000–2099 Trump
10. 2800–3599 Glen
11. 3200–4699 Trump
12. 5100–5299 Brook
13. 3200–4699 Trump
14. Gary
15. Herman
16. Flood
17. 7700–7999 Glen
18. 9400–9899 Brook
19. 2400–2799 Brook
20. 2800–3599 Glen
21. Delton
22. Halstead
23. 2000–2099 Trump
24. 5100–5299 Brook
25. 2800–3599 Glen
26. 9400–9899 Brook
27. 3200–4699 Trump
28. Flood
29. Woods
30. 4400–5099 Brook
31. 7700–7999 Glen
32. Blount
33. Delton
34. 3000–3199 Trump
35. 2400–2799 Brook
36. 6300–6499 Glen
37. 1500–1799 Glen
38. Prince
39. Halstead
40. 6500–6599 Brook
41. 3200–4699 Trump
42. Grand
43. Delton
44. 2000–2099 Trump
45. 5100–5899 Glen
46. 4400–5099 Brook
47. 8100–9099 Trump
48. 7700–7999 Glen
49. 9400–9899 Brook
50. Herman
51. Flood
52. 2000–2099 Trump
53. 2800–3599 Glen
54. Grand
55. Winter
56. Gary
57. 6300–6499 Glen
58. 5100–5299 Brook
59. 3000–3199 Trump
60. 1500–1799 Glen
61. 3200–4699 Trump
62. Woods
63. Blount
64. Grand

65. 9400–9899 Brook
66. Halstead
67. 2400–2799 Brook
68. 2800–3599 Glen
69. 5100–5899 Glen
70. Delton
71. Winter
72. 2000–2099 Trump
73. 5100–5299 Brook
74. 7700–7999 Glen
75. 1100–1699 Trump
76. 9400–9899 Brook

77. 8100–9099 Trump
78. Herman
79. Halstead
80. Prince
81. 6500–6599 Brook
82. 6300–6499 Glen
83. 1500–1799 Glen
84. 4400–5099 Brook
85. Woods
86. Grand
87. Blount
88. Flood

END OF EXAM

ADDRESS CHECKING ERROR ANALYSIS CHART

Type of Error	Tally	Total Number
Number of addresses which were alike and you incorrectly marked "different"		
Number of addresses which were different and you incorrectly marked "alike"		
Number of addresses in which you missed a difference in NUMBERS		
Number of addresses in which you missed a difference in ABBREVIATIONS		
Number of addresses in which you missed a difference in NAMES		

SELF-EVALUATION CHART

Test	Excellent	Good	Average	Fair	Poor
Address Checking	80–95	65–79	50–64	35–49	1–34
Memory for Addresses	75–88	60–74	45–59	30–44	1–29

CORRECT ANSWERS FOR FIFTH MODEL EXAM

ADDRESS CHECKING TEST

1. D	13. A	25. D	37. A	49. D	61. A	73. D	85. D
2. A	14. A	26. D	38. A	50. A	62. D	74. A	86. D
3. A	15. A	27. D	39. D	51. A	63. A	75. D	87. A
4. D	16. D	28. A	40. D	52. A	64. D	76. A	88. D
5. D	17. D	29. A	41. D	53. A	65. E	77. D	89. D
6. A	18. A	30. A	42. A	54. A	66. D	78. A	90. D
7. A	19. A	31. A	43. D	55. A	67. D	79. D	91. D
8. D	20. D	32. A	44. D	56. D	68. A	80. D	92. D
9. A	21. A	33. D	45. D	57. D	69. D	81. D	93. D
10. D	22. D	34. A	46. D	58. D	70. D	82. A	94. D
11. D	23. D	35. D	47. D	59. A	71. A	83. D	95. A
12. A	24. D	36. A	48. A	60. D	72. D	84. D	

MEMORY FOR ADDRESSES—PRACTICE I

1. D	12. A	23. D	34. B	45. C	56. E	67. B	78. D
2. A	13. B	24. E	35. C	46. E	57. D	68. A	79. E
3. B	14. B	25. D	36. C	47. B	58. D	69. A	80. C
4. C	15. A	26. C	37. B	48. A	59. C	70. E	81. B
5. E	16. E	27. E	38. D	49. B	60. B	71. B	82. D
6. C	17. B	28. C	39. E	50. C	61. E	72. A	83. C
7. D	18. C	29. B	40. D	51. E	62. C	73. E	84. A
8. A	19. D	30. A	41. A	52. E	63. A	74. C	85. B
9. E	20. A	31. D	42. E	53. B	64. D	75. D	86. C
10. E	21. A	32. C	43. D	54. B	65. D	76. E	87. A
11. C	22. B	33. A	44. B	55. D	66. E	77. A	88. E

MEMORY FOR
ADDRESSES—PRACTICE II

1. D	12. E	23. D	34. A	45. D	56. D	67. E	78. A
2. E	13. C	24. B	35. C	46. A	57. C	68. E	79. D
3. A	14. D	25. A	36. D	47. C	58. E	69. A	80. D
4. B	15. E	26. D	37. A	48. D	59. E	70. D	81. C
5. C	16. A	27. E	38. C	49. B	60. A	71. A	82. E
6. E	17. C	28. E	39. B	50. E	61. D	72. D	83. B
7. E	18. B	29. C	40. A	51. C	62. C	73. C	84. D
8. A	19. D	30. D	41. B	52. A	63. A	74. B	85. C
9. C	20. A	31. E	42. C	53. C	64. B	75. A	86. B
10. A	21. B	32. C	43. E	54. E	65. C	76. E	87. B
11. C	22. B	33. E	44. B	55. A	66. B	77. C	88. D

MEMORY FOR
ADDRESSES—PRACTICE III

1. B	12. C	23. E	34. C	45. D	56. B	67. D	78. C
2. E	13. D	24. D	35. B	46. E	57. E	68. E	79. C
3. D	14. C	25. B	36. A	47. B	58. B	69. E	80. C
4. A	15. A	26. C	37. A	48. D	59. A	70. E	81. B
5. B	16. B	27. D	38. E	49. C	60. C	71. A	82. D
6. C	17. D	28. B	39. C	50. E	61. D	72. C	83. C
7. E	18. C	29. E	40. D	51. D	62. D	73. E	84. D
8. B	19. E	30. B	41. C	52. C	63. C	74. A	85. E
9. A	20. A	31. B	42. A	53. A	64. A	75. B	86. A
10. E	21. A	32. A	43. E	54. A	65. B	76. B	87. B
11. E	22. D	33. D	44. A	55. B	66. C	77. D	88. D

MEMORY FOR ADDRESSES TEST

1. B	12. D	23. A	34. E	45. C	56. D	67. C	78. A
2. C	13. B	24. D	35. C	46. A	57. A	68. E	79. C
3. D	14. D	25. E	36. A	47. C	58. D	69. C	80. B
4. A	15. A	26. B	37. B	48. D	59. E	70. E	81. E
5. E	16. E	27. B	38. B	49. A	60. B	71. C	82. A
6. A	17. D	28. E	39. C	50. A	61. B	72. A	83. B
7. E	18. B	29. A	40. E	51. E	62. A	73. D	84. A
8. C	19. C	30. A	41. B	52. A	63. D	74. D	85. A
9. A	20. E	31. D	42. B	53. E	64. B	75. D	86. B
10. E	21. E	32. D	43. E	54. B	65. B	76. B	87. D
11. B	22. C	33. E	44. A	55. C	66. C	77. C	88. E

ANSWER SHEET FOR SIXTH MODEL EXAM

ADDRESS CHECKING

TEAR HERE

1 Ⓐ Ⓓ	20 Ⓐ Ⓓ	39 Ⓐ Ⓓ	58 Ⓐ Ⓓ	77 Ⓐ Ⓓ
2 Ⓐ Ⓓ	21 Ⓐ Ⓓ	40 Ⓐ Ⓓ	59 Ⓐ Ⓓ	78 Ⓐ Ⓓ
3 Ⓐ Ⓓ	22 Ⓐ Ⓓ	41 Ⓐ Ⓓ	60 Ⓐ Ⓓ	79 Ⓐ Ⓓ
4 Ⓐ Ⓓ	23 Ⓐ Ⓓ	42 Ⓐ Ⓓ	61 Ⓐ Ⓓ	80 Ⓐ Ⓓ
5 Ⓐ Ⓓ	24 Ⓐ Ⓓ	43 Ⓐ Ⓓ	62 Ⓐ Ⓓ	81 Ⓐ Ⓓ
6 Ⓐ Ⓓ	25 Ⓐ Ⓓ	44 Ⓐ Ⓓ	63 Ⓐ Ⓓ	82 Ⓐ Ⓓ
7 Ⓐ Ⓓ	26 Ⓐ Ⓓ	45 Ⓐ Ⓓ	64 Ⓐ Ⓓ	83 Ⓐ Ⓓ
8 Ⓐ Ⓓ	27 Ⓐ Ⓓ	46 Ⓐ Ⓓ	65 Ⓐ Ⓓ	84 Ⓐ Ⓓ
9 Ⓐ Ⓓ	28 Ⓐ Ⓓ	47 Ⓐ Ⓓ	66 Ⓐ Ⓓ	85 Ⓐ Ⓓ
10 Ⓐ Ⓓ	29 Ⓐ Ⓓ	48 Ⓐ Ⓓ	67 Ⓐ Ⓓ	86 Ⓐ Ⓓ
11 Ⓐ Ⓓ	30 Ⓐ Ⓓ	49 Ⓐ Ⓓ	68 Ⓐ Ⓓ	87 Ⓐ Ⓓ
12 Ⓐ Ⓓ	31 Ⓐ Ⓓ	50 Ⓐ Ⓓ	69 Ⓐ Ⓓ	88 Ⓐ Ⓓ
13 Ⓐ Ⓓ	32 Ⓐ Ⓓ	51 Ⓐ Ⓓ	70 Ⓐ Ⓓ	89 Ⓐ Ⓓ
14 Ⓐ Ⓓ	33 Ⓐ Ⓓ	52 Ⓐ Ⓓ	71 Ⓐ Ⓓ	90 Ⓐ Ⓓ
15 Ⓐ Ⓓ	34 Ⓐ Ⓓ	53 Ⓐ Ⓓ	72 Ⓐ Ⓓ	91 Ⓐ Ⓓ
16 Ⓐ Ⓓ	35 Ⓐ Ⓓ	54 Ⓐ Ⓓ	73 Ⓐ Ⓓ	92 Ⓐ Ⓓ
17 Ⓐ Ⓓ	36 Ⓐ Ⓓ	55 Ⓐ Ⓓ	74 Ⓐ Ⓓ	93 Ⓐ Ⓓ
18 Ⓐ Ⓓ	37 Ⓐ Ⓓ	56 Ⓐ Ⓓ	75 Ⓐ Ⓓ	94 Ⓐ Ⓓ
19 Ⓐ Ⓓ	38 Ⓐ Ⓓ	57 Ⓐ Ⓓ	76 Ⓐ Ⓓ	95 Ⓐ Ⓓ

MEMORY FOR ADDRESSES

PRACTICE I

1 Ⓐ Ⓑ Ⓒ Ⓓ Ⓔ	23 Ⓐ Ⓑ Ⓒ Ⓓ Ⓔ	45 Ⓐ Ⓑ Ⓒ Ⓓ Ⓔ	67 Ⓐ Ⓑ Ⓒ Ⓓ Ⓔ
2 Ⓐ Ⓑ Ⓒ Ⓓ Ⓔ	24 Ⓐ Ⓑ Ⓒ Ⓓ Ⓔ	46 Ⓐ Ⓑ Ⓒ Ⓓ Ⓔ	68 Ⓐ Ⓑ Ⓒ Ⓓ Ⓔ
3 Ⓐ Ⓑ Ⓒ Ⓓ Ⓔ	25 Ⓐ Ⓑ Ⓒ Ⓓ Ⓔ	47 Ⓐ Ⓑ Ⓒ Ⓓ Ⓔ	69 Ⓐ Ⓑ Ⓒ Ⓓ Ⓔ
4 Ⓐ Ⓑ Ⓒ Ⓓ Ⓔ	26 Ⓐ Ⓑ Ⓒ Ⓓ Ⓔ	48 Ⓐ Ⓑ Ⓒ Ⓓ Ⓔ	70 Ⓐ Ⓑ Ⓒ Ⓓ Ⓔ
5 Ⓐ Ⓑ Ⓒ Ⓓ Ⓔ	27 Ⓐ Ⓑ Ⓒ Ⓓ Ⓔ	49 Ⓐ Ⓑ Ⓒ Ⓓ Ⓔ	71 Ⓐ Ⓑ Ⓒ Ⓓ Ⓔ
6 Ⓐ Ⓑ Ⓒ Ⓓ Ⓔ	28 Ⓐ Ⓑ Ⓒ Ⓓ Ⓔ	50 Ⓐ Ⓑ Ⓒ Ⓓ Ⓔ	72 Ⓐ Ⓑ Ⓒ Ⓓ Ⓔ
7 Ⓐ Ⓑ Ⓒ Ⓓ Ⓔ	29 Ⓐ Ⓑ Ⓒ Ⓓ Ⓔ	51 Ⓐ Ⓑ Ⓒ Ⓓ Ⓔ	73 Ⓐ Ⓑ Ⓒ Ⓓ Ⓔ
8 Ⓐ Ⓑ Ⓒ Ⓓ Ⓔ	30 Ⓐ Ⓑ Ⓒ Ⓓ Ⓔ	52 Ⓐ Ⓑ Ⓒ Ⓓ Ⓔ	74 Ⓐ Ⓑ Ⓒ Ⓓ Ⓔ
9 Ⓐ Ⓑ Ⓒ Ⓓ Ⓔ	31 Ⓐ Ⓑ Ⓒ Ⓓ Ⓔ	53 Ⓐ Ⓑ Ⓒ Ⓓ Ⓔ	75 Ⓐ Ⓑ Ⓒ Ⓓ Ⓔ
10 Ⓐ Ⓑ Ⓒ Ⓓ Ⓔ	32 Ⓐ Ⓑ Ⓒ Ⓓ Ⓔ	54 Ⓐ Ⓑ Ⓒ Ⓓ Ⓔ	76 Ⓐ Ⓑ Ⓒ Ⓓ Ⓔ
11 Ⓐ Ⓑ Ⓒ Ⓓ Ⓔ	33 Ⓐ Ⓑ Ⓒ Ⓓ Ⓔ	55 Ⓐ Ⓑ Ⓒ Ⓓ Ⓔ	77 Ⓐ Ⓑ Ⓒ Ⓓ Ⓔ
12 Ⓐ Ⓑ Ⓒ Ⓓ Ⓔ	34 Ⓐ Ⓑ Ⓒ Ⓓ Ⓔ	56 Ⓐ Ⓑ Ⓒ Ⓓ Ⓔ	78 Ⓐ Ⓑ Ⓒ Ⓓ Ⓔ
13 Ⓐ Ⓑ Ⓒ Ⓓ Ⓔ	35 Ⓐ Ⓑ Ⓒ Ⓓ Ⓔ	57 Ⓐ Ⓑ Ⓒ Ⓓ Ⓔ	79 Ⓐ Ⓑ Ⓒ Ⓓ Ⓔ
14 Ⓐ Ⓑ Ⓒ Ⓓ Ⓔ	36 Ⓐ Ⓑ Ⓒ Ⓓ Ⓔ	58 Ⓐ Ⓑ Ⓒ Ⓓ Ⓔ	80 Ⓐ Ⓑ Ⓒ Ⓓ Ⓔ
15 Ⓐ Ⓑ Ⓒ Ⓓ Ⓔ	37 Ⓐ Ⓑ Ⓒ Ⓓ Ⓔ	59 Ⓐ Ⓑ Ⓒ Ⓓ Ⓔ	81 Ⓐ Ⓑ Ⓒ Ⓓ Ⓔ
16 Ⓐ Ⓑ Ⓒ Ⓓ Ⓔ	38 Ⓐ Ⓑ Ⓒ Ⓓ Ⓔ	60 Ⓐ Ⓑ Ⓒ Ⓓ Ⓔ	82 Ⓐ Ⓑ Ⓒ Ⓓ Ⓔ
17 Ⓐ Ⓑ Ⓒ Ⓓ Ⓔ	39 Ⓐ Ⓑ Ⓒ Ⓓ Ⓔ	61 Ⓐ Ⓑ Ⓒ Ⓓ Ⓔ	83 Ⓐ Ⓑ Ⓒ Ⓓ Ⓔ
18 Ⓐ Ⓑ Ⓒ Ⓓ Ⓔ	40 Ⓐ Ⓑ Ⓒ Ⓓ Ⓔ	62 Ⓐ Ⓑ Ⓒ Ⓓ Ⓔ	84 Ⓐ Ⓑ Ⓒ Ⓓ Ⓔ
19 Ⓐ Ⓑ Ⓒ Ⓓ Ⓔ	41 Ⓐ Ⓑ Ⓒ Ⓓ Ⓔ	63 Ⓐ Ⓑ Ⓒ Ⓓ Ⓔ	85 Ⓐ Ⓑ Ⓒ Ⓓ Ⓔ
20 Ⓐ Ⓑ Ⓒ Ⓓ Ⓔ	42 Ⓐ Ⓑ Ⓒ Ⓓ Ⓔ	64 Ⓐ Ⓑ Ⓒ Ⓓ Ⓔ	86 Ⓐ Ⓑ Ⓒ Ⓓ Ⓔ
21 Ⓐ Ⓑ Ⓒ Ⓓ Ⓔ	43 Ⓐ Ⓑ Ⓒ Ⓓ Ⓔ	65 Ⓐ Ⓑ Ⓒ Ⓓ Ⓔ	87 Ⓐ Ⓑ Ⓒ Ⓓ Ⓔ
22 Ⓐ Ⓑ Ⓒ Ⓓ Ⓔ	44 Ⓐ Ⓑ Ⓒ Ⓓ Ⓔ	66 Ⓐ Ⓑ Ⓒ Ⓓ Ⓔ	88 Ⓐ Ⓑ Ⓒ Ⓓ Ⓔ

PRACTICE II

1 Ⓐ Ⓑ Ⓒ Ⓓ Ⓔ	23 Ⓐ Ⓑ Ⓒ Ⓓ Ⓔ	45 Ⓐ Ⓑ Ⓒ Ⓓ Ⓔ	67 Ⓐ Ⓑ Ⓒ Ⓓ Ⓔ
2 Ⓐ Ⓑ Ⓒ Ⓓ Ⓔ	24 Ⓐ Ⓑ Ⓒ Ⓓ Ⓔ	46 Ⓐ Ⓑ Ⓒ Ⓓ Ⓔ	68 Ⓐ Ⓑ Ⓒ Ⓓ Ⓔ
3 Ⓐ Ⓑ Ⓒ Ⓓ Ⓔ	25 Ⓐ Ⓑ Ⓒ Ⓓ Ⓔ	47 Ⓐ Ⓑ Ⓒ Ⓓ Ⓔ	69 Ⓐ Ⓑ Ⓒ Ⓓ Ⓔ
4 Ⓐ Ⓑ Ⓒ Ⓓ Ⓔ	26 Ⓐ Ⓑ Ⓒ Ⓓ Ⓔ	48 Ⓐ Ⓑ Ⓒ Ⓓ Ⓔ	70 Ⓐ Ⓑ Ⓒ Ⓓ Ⓔ
5 Ⓐ Ⓑ Ⓒ Ⓓ Ⓔ	27 Ⓐ Ⓑ Ⓒ Ⓓ Ⓔ	49 Ⓐ Ⓑ Ⓒ Ⓓ Ⓔ	71 Ⓐ Ⓑ Ⓒ Ⓓ Ⓔ
6 Ⓐ Ⓑ Ⓒ Ⓓ Ⓔ	28 Ⓐ Ⓑ Ⓒ Ⓓ Ⓔ	50 Ⓐ Ⓑ Ⓒ Ⓓ Ⓔ	72 Ⓐ Ⓑ Ⓒ Ⓓ Ⓔ
7 Ⓐ Ⓑ Ⓒ Ⓓ Ⓔ	29 Ⓐ Ⓑ Ⓒ Ⓓ Ⓔ	51 Ⓐ Ⓑ Ⓒ Ⓓ Ⓔ	73 Ⓐ Ⓑ Ⓒ Ⓓ Ⓔ
8 Ⓐ Ⓑ Ⓒ Ⓓ Ⓔ	30 Ⓐ Ⓑ Ⓒ Ⓓ Ⓔ	52 Ⓐ Ⓑ Ⓒ Ⓓ Ⓔ	74 Ⓐ Ⓑ Ⓒ Ⓓ Ⓔ
9 Ⓐ Ⓑ Ⓒ Ⓓ Ⓔ	31 Ⓐ Ⓑ Ⓒ Ⓓ Ⓔ	53 Ⓐ Ⓑ Ⓒ Ⓓ Ⓔ	75 Ⓐ Ⓑ Ⓒ Ⓓ Ⓔ
10 Ⓐ Ⓑ Ⓒ Ⓓ Ⓔ	32 Ⓐ Ⓑ Ⓒ Ⓓ Ⓔ	54 Ⓐ Ⓑ Ⓒ Ⓓ Ⓔ	76 Ⓐ Ⓑ Ⓒ Ⓓ Ⓔ
11 Ⓐ Ⓑ Ⓒ Ⓓ Ⓔ	33 Ⓐ Ⓑ Ⓒ Ⓓ Ⓔ	55 Ⓐ Ⓑ Ⓒ Ⓓ Ⓔ	77 Ⓐ Ⓑ Ⓒ Ⓓ Ⓔ
12 Ⓐ Ⓑ Ⓒ Ⓓ Ⓔ	34 Ⓐ Ⓑ Ⓒ Ⓓ Ⓔ	56 Ⓐ Ⓑ Ⓒ Ⓓ Ⓔ	78 Ⓐ Ⓑ Ⓒ Ⓓ Ⓔ
13 Ⓐ Ⓑ Ⓒ Ⓓ Ⓔ	35 Ⓐ Ⓑ Ⓒ Ⓓ Ⓔ	57 Ⓐ Ⓑ Ⓒ Ⓓ Ⓔ	79 Ⓐ Ⓑ Ⓒ Ⓓ Ⓔ
14 Ⓐ Ⓑ Ⓒ Ⓓ Ⓔ	36 Ⓐ Ⓑ Ⓒ Ⓓ Ⓔ	58 Ⓐ Ⓑ Ⓒ Ⓓ Ⓔ	80 Ⓐ Ⓑ Ⓒ Ⓓ Ⓔ
15 Ⓐ Ⓑ Ⓒ Ⓓ Ⓔ	37 Ⓐ Ⓑ Ⓒ Ⓓ Ⓔ	59 Ⓐ Ⓑ Ⓒ Ⓓ Ⓔ	81 Ⓐ Ⓑ Ⓒ Ⓓ Ⓔ
16 Ⓐ Ⓑ Ⓒ Ⓓ Ⓔ	38 Ⓐ Ⓑ Ⓒ Ⓓ Ⓔ	60 Ⓐ Ⓑ Ⓒ Ⓓ Ⓔ	82 Ⓐ Ⓑ Ⓒ Ⓓ Ⓔ
17 Ⓐ Ⓑ Ⓒ Ⓓ Ⓔ	39 Ⓐ Ⓑ Ⓒ Ⓓ Ⓔ	61 Ⓐ Ⓑ Ⓒ Ⓓ Ⓔ	83 Ⓐ Ⓑ Ⓒ Ⓓ Ⓔ
18 Ⓐ Ⓑ Ⓒ Ⓓ Ⓔ	40 Ⓐ Ⓑ Ⓒ Ⓓ Ⓔ	62 Ⓐ Ⓑ Ⓒ Ⓓ Ⓔ	84 Ⓐ Ⓑ Ⓒ Ⓓ Ⓔ
19 Ⓐ Ⓑ Ⓒ Ⓓ Ⓔ	41 Ⓐ Ⓑ Ⓒ Ⓓ Ⓔ	63 Ⓐ Ⓑ Ⓒ Ⓓ Ⓔ	85 Ⓐ Ⓑ Ⓒ Ⓓ Ⓔ
20 Ⓐ Ⓑ Ⓒ Ⓓ Ⓔ	42 Ⓐ Ⓑ Ⓒ Ⓓ Ⓔ	64 Ⓐ Ⓑ Ⓒ Ⓓ Ⓔ	86 Ⓐ Ⓑ Ⓒ Ⓓ Ⓔ
21 Ⓐ Ⓑ Ⓒ Ⓓ Ⓔ	43 Ⓐ Ⓑ Ⓒ Ⓓ Ⓔ	65 Ⓐ Ⓑ Ⓒ Ⓓ Ⓔ	87 Ⓐ Ⓑ Ⓒ Ⓓ Ⓔ
22 Ⓐ Ⓑ Ⓒ Ⓓ Ⓔ	44 Ⓐ Ⓑ Ⓒ Ⓓ Ⓔ	66 Ⓐ Ⓑ Ⓒ Ⓓ Ⓔ	88 Ⓐ Ⓑ Ⓒ Ⓓ Ⓔ

PRACTICE III

1 Ⓐ Ⓑ Ⓒ Ⓓ Ⓔ	23 Ⓐ Ⓑ Ⓒ Ⓓ Ⓔ	45 Ⓐ Ⓑ Ⓒ Ⓓ Ⓔ	67 Ⓐ Ⓑ Ⓒ Ⓓ Ⓔ
2 Ⓐ Ⓑ Ⓒ Ⓓ Ⓔ	24 Ⓐ Ⓑ Ⓒ Ⓓ Ⓔ	46 Ⓐ Ⓑ Ⓒ Ⓓ Ⓔ	68 Ⓐ Ⓑ Ⓒ Ⓓ Ⓔ
3 Ⓐ Ⓑ Ⓒ Ⓓ Ⓔ	25 Ⓐ Ⓑ Ⓒ Ⓓ Ⓔ	47 Ⓐ Ⓑ Ⓒ Ⓓ Ⓔ	69 Ⓐ Ⓑ Ⓒ Ⓓ Ⓔ
4 Ⓐ Ⓑ Ⓒ Ⓓ Ⓔ	26 Ⓐ Ⓑ Ⓒ Ⓓ Ⓔ	48 Ⓐ Ⓑ Ⓒ Ⓓ Ⓔ	70 Ⓐ Ⓑ Ⓒ Ⓓ Ⓔ
5 Ⓐ Ⓑ Ⓒ Ⓓ Ⓔ	27 Ⓐ Ⓑ Ⓒ Ⓓ Ⓔ	49 Ⓐ Ⓑ Ⓒ Ⓓ Ⓔ	71 Ⓐ Ⓑ Ⓒ Ⓓ Ⓔ
6 Ⓐ Ⓑ Ⓒ Ⓓ Ⓔ	28 Ⓐ Ⓑ Ⓒ Ⓓ Ⓔ	50 Ⓐ Ⓑ Ⓒ Ⓓ Ⓔ	72 Ⓐ Ⓑ Ⓒ Ⓓ Ⓔ
7 Ⓐ Ⓑ Ⓒ Ⓓ Ⓔ	29 Ⓐ Ⓑ Ⓒ Ⓓ Ⓔ	51 Ⓐ Ⓑ Ⓒ Ⓓ Ⓔ	73 Ⓐ Ⓑ Ⓒ Ⓓ Ⓔ
8 Ⓐ Ⓑ Ⓒ Ⓓ Ⓔ	30 Ⓐ Ⓑ Ⓒ Ⓓ Ⓔ	52 Ⓐ Ⓑ Ⓒ Ⓓ Ⓔ	74 Ⓐ Ⓑ Ⓒ Ⓓ Ⓔ
9 Ⓐ Ⓑ Ⓒ Ⓓ Ⓔ	31 Ⓐ Ⓑ Ⓒ Ⓓ Ⓔ	53 Ⓐ Ⓑ Ⓒ Ⓓ Ⓔ	75 Ⓐ Ⓑ Ⓒ Ⓓ Ⓔ
10 Ⓐ Ⓑ Ⓒ Ⓓ Ⓔ	32 Ⓐ Ⓑ Ⓒ Ⓓ Ⓔ	54 Ⓐ Ⓑ Ⓒ Ⓓ Ⓔ	76 Ⓐ Ⓑ Ⓒ Ⓓ Ⓔ
11 Ⓐ Ⓑ Ⓒ Ⓓ Ⓔ	33 Ⓐ Ⓑ Ⓒ Ⓓ Ⓔ	55 Ⓐ Ⓑ Ⓒ Ⓓ Ⓔ	77 Ⓐ Ⓑ Ⓒ Ⓓ Ⓔ
12 Ⓐ Ⓑ Ⓒ Ⓓ Ⓔ	34 Ⓐ Ⓑ Ⓒ Ⓓ Ⓔ	56 Ⓐ Ⓑ Ⓒ Ⓓ Ⓔ	78 Ⓐ Ⓑ Ⓒ Ⓓ Ⓔ
13 Ⓐ Ⓑ Ⓒ Ⓓ Ⓔ	35 Ⓐ Ⓑ Ⓒ Ⓓ Ⓔ	57 Ⓐ Ⓑ Ⓒ Ⓓ Ⓔ	79 Ⓐ Ⓑ Ⓒ Ⓓ Ⓔ
14 Ⓐ Ⓑ Ⓒ Ⓓ Ⓔ	36 Ⓐ Ⓑ Ⓒ Ⓓ Ⓔ	58 Ⓐ Ⓑ Ⓒ Ⓓ Ⓔ	80 Ⓐ Ⓑ Ⓒ Ⓓ Ⓔ
15 Ⓐ Ⓑ Ⓒ Ⓓ Ⓔ	37 Ⓐ Ⓑ Ⓒ Ⓓ Ⓔ	59 Ⓐ Ⓑ Ⓒ Ⓓ Ⓔ	81 Ⓐ Ⓑ Ⓒ Ⓓ Ⓔ
16 Ⓐ Ⓑ Ⓒ Ⓓ Ⓔ	38 Ⓐ Ⓑ Ⓒ Ⓓ Ⓔ	60 Ⓐ Ⓑ Ⓒ Ⓓ Ⓔ	82 Ⓐ Ⓑ Ⓒ Ⓓ Ⓔ
17 Ⓐ Ⓑ Ⓒ Ⓓ Ⓔ	39 Ⓐ Ⓑ Ⓒ Ⓓ Ⓔ	61 Ⓐ Ⓑ Ⓒ Ⓓ Ⓔ	83 Ⓐ Ⓑ Ⓒ Ⓓ Ⓔ
18 Ⓐ Ⓑ Ⓒ Ⓓ Ⓔ	40 Ⓐ Ⓑ Ⓒ Ⓓ Ⓔ	62 Ⓐ Ⓑ Ⓒ Ⓓ Ⓔ	84 Ⓐ Ⓑ Ⓒ Ⓓ Ⓔ
19 Ⓐ Ⓑ Ⓒ Ⓓ Ⓔ	41 Ⓐ Ⓑ Ⓒ Ⓓ Ⓔ	63 Ⓐ Ⓑ Ⓒ Ⓓ Ⓔ	85 Ⓐ Ⓑ Ⓒ Ⓓ Ⓔ
20 Ⓐ Ⓑ Ⓒ Ⓓ Ⓔ	42 Ⓐ Ⓑ Ⓒ Ⓓ Ⓔ	64 Ⓐ Ⓑ Ⓒ Ⓓ Ⓔ	86 Ⓐ Ⓑ Ⓒ Ⓓ Ⓔ
21 Ⓐ Ⓑ Ⓒ Ⓓ Ⓔ	43 Ⓐ Ⓑ Ⓒ Ⓓ Ⓔ	65 Ⓐ Ⓑ Ⓒ Ⓓ Ⓔ	87 Ⓐ Ⓑ Ⓒ Ⓓ Ⓔ
22 Ⓐ Ⓑ Ⓒ Ⓓ Ⓔ	44 Ⓐ Ⓑ Ⓒ Ⓓ Ⓔ	66 Ⓐ Ⓑ Ⓒ Ⓓ Ⓔ	88 Ⓐ Ⓑ Ⓒ Ⓓ Ⓔ

MEMORY FOR ADDRESSES TEST

1 Ⓐ Ⓑ Ⓒ Ⓓ Ⓔ	23 Ⓐ Ⓑ Ⓒ Ⓓ Ⓔ	45 Ⓐ Ⓑ Ⓒ Ⓓ Ⓔ	67 Ⓐ Ⓑ Ⓒ Ⓓ Ⓔ
2 Ⓐ Ⓑ Ⓒ Ⓓ Ⓔ	24 Ⓐ Ⓑ Ⓒ Ⓓ Ⓔ	46 Ⓐ Ⓑ Ⓒ Ⓓ Ⓔ	68 Ⓐ Ⓑ Ⓒ Ⓓ Ⓔ
3 Ⓐ Ⓑ Ⓒ Ⓓ Ⓔ	25 Ⓐ Ⓑ Ⓒ Ⓓ Ⓔ	47 Ⓐ Ⓑ Ⓒ Ⓓ Ⓔ	69 Ⓐ Ⓑ Ⓒ Ⓓ Ⓔ
4 Ⓐ Ⓑ Ⓒ Ⓓ Ⓔ	26 Ⓐ Ⓑ Ⓒ Ⓓ Ⓔ	48 Ⓐ Ⓑ Ⓒ Ⓓ Ⓔ	70 Ⓐ Ⓑ Ⓒ Ⓓ Ⓔ
5 Ⓐ Ⓑ Ⓒ Ⓓ Ⓔ	27 Ⓐ Ⓑ Ⓒ Ⓓ Ⓔ	49 Ⓐ Ⓑ Ⓒ Ⓓ Ⓔ	71 Ⓐ Ⓑ Ⓒ Ⓓ Ⓔ
6 Ⓐ Ⓑ Ⓒ Ⓓ Ⓔ	28 Ⓐ Ⓑ Ⓒ Ⓓ Ⓔ	50 Ⓐ Ⓑ Ⓒ Ⓓ Ⓔ	72 Ⓐ Ⓑ Ⓒ Ⓓ Ⓔ
7 Ⓐ Ⓑ Ⓒ Ⓓ Ⓔ	29 Ⓐ Ⓑ Ⓒ Ⓓ Ⓔ	51 Ⓐ Ⓑ Ⓒ Ⓓ Ⓔ	73 Ⓐ Ⓑ Ⓒ Ⓓ Ⓔ
8 Ⓐ Ⓑ Ⓒ Ⓓ Ⓔ	30 Ⓐ Ⓑ Ⓒ Ⓓ Ⓔ	52 Ⓐ Ⓑ Ⓒ Ⓓ Ⓔ	74 Ⓐ Ⓑ Ⓒ Ⓓ Ⓔ
9 Ⓐ Ⓑ Ⓒ Ⓓ Ⓔ	31 Ⓐ Ⓑ Ⓒ Ⓓ Ⓔ	53 Ⓐ Ⓑ Ⓒ Ⓓ Ⓔ	75 Ⓐ Ⓑ Ⓒ Ⓓ Ⓔ
10 Ⓐ Ⓑ Ⓒ Ⓓ Ⓔ	32 Ⓐ Ⓑ Ⓒ Ⓓ Ⓔ	54 Ⓐ Ⓑ Ⓒ Ⓓ Ⓔ	76 Ⓐ Ⓑ Ⓒ Ⓓ Ⓔ
11 Ⓐ Ⓑ Ⓒ Ⓓ Ⓔ	33 Ⓐ Ⓑ Ⓒ Ⓓ Ⓔ	55 Ⓐ Ⓑ Ⓒ Ⓓ Ⓔ	77 Ⓐ Ⓑ Ⓒ Ⓓ Ⓔ
12 Ⓐ Ⓑ Ⓒ Ⓓ Ⓔ	34 Ⓐ Ⓑ Ⓒ Ⓓ Ⓔ	56 Ⓐ Ⓑ Ⓒ Ⓓ Ⓔ	78 Ⓐ Ⓑ Ⓒ Ⓓ Ⓔ
13 Ⓐ Ⓑ Ⓒ Ⓓ Ⓔ	35 Ⓐ Ⓑ Ⓒ Ⓓ Ⓔ	57 Ⓐ Ⓑ Ⓒ Ⓓ Ⓔ	79 Ⓐ Ⓑ Ⓒ Ⓓ Ⓔ
14 Ⓐ Ⓑ Ⓒ Ⓓ Ⓔ	36 Ⓐ Ⓑ Ⓒ Ⓓ Ⓔ	58 Ⓐ Ⓑ Ⓒ Ⓓ Ⓔ	80 Ⓐ Ⓑ Ⓒ Ⓓ Ⓔ
15 Ⓐ Ⓑ Ⓒ Ⓓ Ⓔ	37 Ⓐ Ⓑ Ⓒ Ⓓ Ⓔ	59 Ⓐ Ⓑ Ⓒ Ⓓ Ⓔ	81 Ⓐ Ⓑ Ⓒ Ⓓ Ⓔ
16 Ⓐ Ⓑ Ⓒ Ⓓ Ⓔ	38 Ⓐ Ⓑ Ⓒ Ⓓ Ⓔ	60 Ⓐ Ⓑ Ⓒ Ⓓ Ⓔ	82 Ⓐ Ⓑ Ⓒ Ⓓ Ⓔ
17 Ⓐ Ⓑ Ⓒ Ⓓ Ⓔ	39 Ⓐ Ⓑ Ⓒ Ⓓ Ⓔ	61 Ⓐ Ⓑ Ⓒ Ⓓ Ⓔ	83 Ⓐ Ⓑ Ⓒ Ⓓ Ⓔ
18 Ⓐ Ⓑ Ⓒ Ⓓ Ⓔ	40 Ⓐ Ⓑ Ⓒ Ⓓ Ⓔ	62 Ⓐ Ⓑ Ⓒ Ⓓ Ⓔ	84 Ⓐ Ⓑ Ⓒ Ⓓ Ⓔ
19 Ⓐ Ⓑ Ⓒ Ⓓ Ⓔ	41 Ⓐ Ⓑ Ⓒ Ⓓ Ⓔ	63 Ⓐ Ⓑ Ⓒ Ⓓ Ⓔ	85 Ⓐ Ⓑ Ⓒ Ⓓ Ⓔ
20 Ⓐ Ⓑ Ⓒ Ⓓ Ⓔ	42 Ⓐ Ⓑ Ⓒ Ⓓ Ⓔ	64 Ⓐ Ⓑ Ⓒ Ⓓ Ⓔ	86 Ⓐ Ⓑ Ⓒ Ⓓ Ⓔ
21 Ⓐ Ⓑ Ⓒ Ⓓ Ⓔ	43 Ⓐ Ⓑ Ⓒ Ⓓ Ⓔ	65 Ⓐ Ⓑ Ⓒ Ⓓ Ⓔ	87 Ⓐ Ⓑ Ⓒ Ⓓ Ⓔ
22 Ⓐ Ⓑ Ⓒ Ⓓ Ⓔ	44 Ⓐ Ⓑ Ⓒ Ⓓ Ⓔ	66 Ⓐ Ⓑ Ⓒ Ⓓ Ⓔ	88 Ⓐ Ⓑ Ⓒ Ⓓ Ⓔ

SCORE SHEET FOR SIXTH MODEL EXAM

ADDRESS CHECKING TEST

Number Right minus Number Wrong equals   Score

_____ – _____ = _____

MEMORY FOR ADDRESSES TEST

Number Right minus (Number Wrong ÷ 4) equals   Score

_____ – _____ = _____

PROGRESS GRAPH

Blacken the bars for Model Exam 6 to the scores you earned.

Score							
95							
90							
85							
80							
75							
70							
65							
60							
55							
50							
45							
40							
35							
30							
25							
20							
15							
10							
5							
0							

Test	AC|M	AC|M	AC|M	AC|M	AC|M	AC|M	AC|M
Model Exam	Diag.	1	2	3	4	5	6

AC = Address Checking   M = Memory for Addresses

SIXTH MODEL EXAM

ADDRESS CHECKING TEST

TIME: 6 Minutes. 95 Questions.

DIRECTIONS: For each question, compare the address in the left column with the address in the right column. If the two addresses are ALIKE IN EVERY WAY, blacken space Ⓐ on your answer sheet. If the two addresses are DIFFERENT IN ANY WAY, blacken space Ⓓ on your answer sheet. Correct answers for this test are on page 177.

1 . . .	1596 Century Vill	1956 Century Vill
2 . . .	W Hempstead NY 11552	W Hempstead NY 11522
3 . . .	2465 Chappaquidik Rd	2465 Chappaquidik Rd
4 . . .	2591 Wiltshire Pl	2591 Wittshire Pl
5 . . .	7251 Chalmers Blvd	7251 Chalmers Blvd
6 . . .	1444 Croton Dam Rd	144 Croton Dam Rd
7 . . .	2679 Windmill Dr	2697 Windmill Dr
8 . . .	921 S 129th St	921 S 129th St
9 . . .	Luebbering MO 63061	Luebbering MO 63061
10 . . .	7159 W Eastway	7159 E Westway
11 . . .	2405 E Tremont Ave	2504 E Tremont Ave
12 . . .	6774 Hutchinson Ave	6774 Hutchinson Blvd
13 . . .	8487 Leighton Ave	8487 Lieghton Ave
14 . . .	7663 Hildreth Pl	7663 Hildreth Pl
15 . . .	781 W Pershing Ave	781 W Pershing Ave
16 . . .	Charlvoix MI 49720	Charlvoix HI 49720
17 . . .	6351 Smith Ridge Rd	6531 Smith Ridge Rd
18 . . .	7292 Sickletown Rd	7292 Sickeltown Rd
19 . . .	8592 Wainright Ave	8592 Wainright Ave
20 . . .	5095 Thornbury Rd	5095 Thornbery Rd
21 . . .	2829 E 169th St	2829 E 169th St
22 . . .	1120 Mile Square Rd	1120 Mile Square Rd
23 . . .	Aredale IA 50605	Airedale IA 50605
24 . . .	4740 Concordia Rd	4740 Concordia Rd
25 . . .	6390 Depeyster St	6390 Depeyster St
26 . . .	8002 Floradan Rd	8002 Floridan Rd
27 . . .	8767 Davis Ave	8767 David Ave

28	. . . 2119 Farragut Pky	2119 Farragut Pky
29	. . . 836 Tewkesbury Rd	836 Twekesbury Rd
30	. . . Mohegan Lake NY 10547	Mohecan Lake NY 10547
31	. . . 9248 Saginaw Rd	9248 Saginaw Rd
32	. . . 9458 Upperhook Rd	9458 Upperhook Rd
33	. . . 6443 Blackberry Dr	6334 Blackberry Dr
34	. . . 9279 Martling Ave	9279 Martling Ave
35	. . . 4879 Pearsall Dr	4879 Piersall Dr
36	. . . 4977 Duxbury Rd	4799 Duxbury Rd
37	. . . 1281 Clymer Pky	1281 Clymer Pkwy
38	. . . 7117 SW 117th St	717 SW 117th St
39	. . . 3687 Alta Vista Dr	3687 Alta Vista Rd
40	. . . Otter Rock OR 97369	Otter Rock OR 97639
41	. . . 3607 Hessian Hills Rd	3067 Hessian Hills Rd
42	. . . 8988 Cassilis Ave	8988 Cassillis Ave
43	. . . 3541 W Mt Airy Rd	3541 W Mt Airy Rd
44	. . . 1885 Winnetou Rd	1885 Winnetou Rd
45	. . . 9647 E 59th St	9467 E 59th St
46	. . . 2392 Tecumsah Ave	2392 Tecumsah Ave
47	. . . 7248 Loomis Ave	7284 Loomis Ave
48	. . . Yorktown Heights NY 10598	Yorktown Hieghts NY 10598
49	. . . 2555 Greenhaven Rd	2255 Greenhaven Rd
50	. . . 4378 N Barry Ave	4378 N Barry Ave
51	. . . 4872 W 174th Ave	4872 W 174th Ave
52	. . . 2107 Warwick Ave	2107 Warwick Ave
53	. . . 1219 Academy Pl	1219 Academy Pl
54	. . . 7632 Winding Wood Rd S	7362 Winding Wood Rd S
55	. . . Bellefontaine MS 39737	Bellafontaine MS 39737
56	. . . 4611 Poningo Pt	4611 Poningo Pt
57	. . . 4978 VanTassel Apts	4978 VanTassle Apts
58	. . . 6508 Pengilly Dr	6085 Pengilly Dr
59	. . . 4186 N 342nd St	4186 N 432nd St
60	. . . 198 Witherbee Rd	198 Witherbee Rd
61	. . . 3558 Atherstone Rd	3558 Atherstone Rd
62	. . . 4338 Mechanics Ave	4338 Mechanic Ave
63	. . . 7387 Old State Rd	7837 Old State Rd
64	. . . 8289 Moquet Rd	8289 Mocquet Rd
65	. . . 8836 Bonefoy Pl	8836 Bonefoy Pl
66	. . . Amawalk NY 10501	Amawak NY 10501
67	. . . 9204 Juana Rw	9204 Juana Rw
68	. . . 3433 S 2nd Ave	3433 S 2nd Ave
69	. . . 547 Don Bosco Pl	574 Don Bosco Pl
70	. . . 7693 Amberland Apts	7693 Amberlands Apts
71	. . . 3510 Eldridge Ave	3510 Eldridge Ave
72	. . . 3152 Colonial Ct	3125 Colonial Ct
73	. . . 4849 Tonetta Lake Dr	4849 Tonneta Lake Dr
74	. . . 3309 Anderson Hill Rd	3309 Andersen Hill Rd
75	. . . Cheboygan MI 48650	Cheboygan MI 48650
76	. . . 1174 Devonshire Rd	1174 Devonshire Rd
77	. . . 8024 S Buckhout St	8024 S Buckout St
78	. . . 6158 Calhoun Ave	6185 Calhoun Ave
79	. . . 1826 W 153rd Ln	1826 W 153rd Ln

80 . . . 9423 Firenze St   9423 Firenze St
81 . . . 2591 Gregory Ln   2591 Gregory Wy
82 . . . 2756 W Beekman Rd   2756 W Beekman Rd
83 . . . Goldens Bridge NY 10526   Goldens Bridge NY 15026
84 . . . 1683 Glengary Rd   1683 Glengarry Rd
85 . . . 4361 Sloe Hidden Rd   3461 Sloe Hidden Rd
86 . . . 5990 Sadore Ln   5990 Sadore Ln
87 . . . 4360 S Nimitz Rd   4630 S Nimitz Rd
88 . . . 5137 Titicus Rd   5137 Titicus Rd
89 . . . 9847 Industrial Hwy   9487 Industrial Hwy
90 . . . 2536 Heritage Hls   2536 Heritage Hls
91 . . . 3237 Farrington Rd   3237 Farington Rd
92 . . . Tillamook OR 97141   Tillamock OR 97141
93 . . . 686 Watchhill Rd   6886 Watchhill Rd
94 . . . 1879 Crompond Rd   1879 Crompound Rd
95 . . . 2104 LaVoie Ct   2014 LaVoie Ct

END OF ADDRESS CHECKING TEST

If you finish this test before time is up, use the remaining time to check over your work. Do not turn the page until you are told to do so.

PRACTICE FOR
MEMORY FOR ADDRESSES TEST

DIRECTIONS: The five boxes below are labelled A, B, C, D, and E. In each box are three sets of number spans with names and two names which are not associated with numbers. In the next THREE MINUTES, you must try to memorize the box location of each name and number span. The position of a name or number span within its box is not important. You need only remember the letter of the box in which the item is to be found. You will use these names and numbers to answer three sets of practice questions which are NOT scored and one actual test which is scored. Correct answers are on pages 177 and 178.

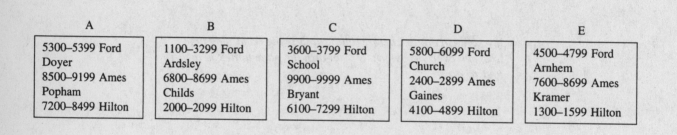

A	B	C	D	E
5300–5399 Ford	1100–3299 Ford	3600–3799 Ford	5800–6099 Ford	4500–4799 Ford
Doyer	Ardsley	School	Church	Arnhem
8500–9199 Ames	6800–8699 Ames	9900–9999 Ames	2400–2899 Ames	7600–8699 Ames
Popham	Childs	Bryant	Gaines	Kramer
7200–8499 Hilton	2000–2099 Hilton	6100–7299 Hilton	4100–4899 Hilton	1300–1599 Hilton

PRACTICE I

DIRECTIONS: Use the next THREE MINUTES to mark on your answer sheet the letter of the box in which each item that follows is to be found. Try to mark each item without looking back at the boxes. If, however, you get stuck, you may refer to the boxes during this practice exercise. If you find that you must look at the boxes, try to memorize as you do so. This test is for practice only. It will not be scored.

1. 2000–2099 Hilton
2. 4500–4799 Ford
3. 8500–9199 Ames
4. Gaines
5. Kramer
6. 1100–3299 Ford

7. 9900–9999 Ames
8. 1300–1599 Hilton
9. 5300–5399 Ford
10. 7200–8499 Hilton
11. Popham
12. Bryant

13. Arnhem
14. 5800–6099 Ford
15. 7600–8699 Ames
16. 6100–7299 Hilton
17. School
18. Childs
19. 2400–2899 Ames
20. 6800–8699 Ames
21. Church
22. Doyer
23. 3600–3799 Ford
24. 4100–4899 Hilton
25. Ardsley
26. 7200–8499 Hilton
27. 9900–9999 Ames
28. 3600–3799 Ford
29. 5800–6099 Ford
30. 1100–3299 Ford
31. 4100–4899 Hilton
32. Doyer
33. Kramer
34. Bryant
35. 5800–6099 Ford
36. 7600–8699 Ames
37. 5300–5399 Ford
38. 2000–2099 Hilton
39. 1300–1599 Hilton
40. 8500–9199 Ames
41. Popham
42. Church
43. Childs
44. 6800–8699 Ames
45. 4500–4799 Ford
46. 7200–8499 Hilton
47. Gaines
48. Arnhem
49. 3600–3799 Ford
50. 9900–9999 Ames

51. 6100–7299 Hilton
52. 5300–5399 Ford
53. 2400–2899 Ames
54. School
55. Ardsley
56. 1100–3299 Ford
57. 7200–8499 Hilton
58. 7600–8699 Ames
59. 1300–1599 Hilton
60. 9900–9999 Ames
61. 5800–6099 Ford
62. 1300–1599 Hilton
63. 7200–8499 Hilton
64. Ardsley
65. Kramer
66. 1100–3299 Ford
67. 2400–2899 Ames
68. 6100–7299 Hilton
69. 2000–2099 Hilton
70. 7600–8699 Ames
71. Gaines
72. Arnhem
73. Bryant
74. 1100–3299 Ford
75. 6100–7299 Hilton
76. 2400–2899 Ames
77. 4100–4899 Hilton
78. Doyer
79. School
80. Popham
81. 1300–1599 Hilton
82. 4500–4799 Ford
83. 8500–9199 Ames
84. 7200–8499 Hilton
85. 6800–8699 Ames
86. 5800–6099 Ford
87. Childs
88. Church

PRACTICE II

DIRECTIONS: *The next 88 questions constitute another practice exercise. Again, you should mark your answers on your answer sheet. Again, the time limit is THREE MINUTES. This time, however, you must NOT look at the boxes while answering the questions. You must rely on your memory in marking the box location of each time. This practice test will not be scored.*

1. 2400–2899 Ames
2. 4500–4799 Ford
3. 2000–2099 Hilton
4. 9900–9999 Ames
5. 5300–5399 Ford
6. 6100–7299 Hilton
7. 1300–1599 Hilton
8. 5800–6099 Ford
9. 8500–9199 Ames
10. Gaines
11. Doyer
12. Ardsley
13. Bryant
14. Popham
15. 4100–4899 Hilton
16. 7600–8699 Ames
17. 1100–3299 Ford
18. 9900–9999 Ames
19. Gaines
20. 1300–1599 Hilton
21. 8500–9199 Ames
22. 2000–2099 Hilton
23. Bryant
24. Arnhem
25. 5800–6099 Ford
26. 3600–3799 Ford
27. 4100–4899 Hilton
28. 6800–8699 Ames
29. Kramer
30. Doyer
31. School
32. 6100–7299 Hilton
33. 4500–4799 Ford
34. 2400–2899 Ames
35. 7600–8699 Ames
36. Church
37. Popham
38. 5300–5399 Ford
39. 7200–8499 Hilton
40. Childs
41. Ardsley
42. 9900–9999 Ames
43. 2000–2099 Hilton
44. 1100–3299 Ford

45. 4100–4899 Hilton
46. 8500–9199 Ames
47. 4500–4799 Ford
48. 6100–7299 Hilton
49. Kramer
50. Gaines
51. Doyer
52. 6800–8699 Ames
53. 5800–6099 Ford
54. 5300–5399 Ford
55. 8500–9199 Ames
56. 1300–1599 Hilton
57. Popham
58. Bryant
59. Arnhem
60. 7200–8499 Hilton
61. 9900–9999 Ames
62. 2000–2099 Hilton
63. 1100–3299 Ford
64. Ardsley
65. School
66. 2400–2899 Ames
67. 5300–5399 Ford
68. 6100–7299 Hilton
69. 4100–4899 Hilton
70. Church
71. Kramer
72. 7200–8499 Hilton
73. 1100–3299 Ford
74. 1300–1599 Hilton
75. 2000–2099 Hilton
76. 4500–4799 Ford
77. 8500–9199 Ames
78. 9900–9999 Ames
79. Childs
80. Arnhem
81. 7600–8699 Ames
82. 5800–6099 Ford
83. 2400–2899 Ames
84. 5300–5399 Ford
85. 6100–7299 Hilton
86. Ardsley
87. Doyer
88. 7200–8499 Hilton

PRACTICE III

DIRECTIONS: The names and addresses are repeated for you in the boxes below. Each name and each number span is in the same box in which you found it in the original set. You will now be allowed FIVE MINUTES to study the locations again. Do your best to memorize the letter of the box in which each item is located. This is your last chance to see the boxes.

A	B	C	D	E
5300–5399 Ford Doyer 8500–9199 Ames Popham 7200–8499 Hilton	1100–3299 Ford Ardsley 6800–8699 Ames Childs 2000–2099 Hilton	3600–3799 Ford School 9900–9999 Ames Bryant 6100–7299 Hilton	5800–6099 Ford Church 2400–2899 Ames Gaines 4100–4899 Hilton	4500–4799 Ford Arnhem 7600–8699 Ames Kramer 1300–1599 Hilton

DIRECTIONS: This is your last practice test. Mark the location of each of the 88 items on your answer sheet. You will have FIVE MINUTES to answer these questions. Do NOT look back at the boxes. This practice test will not be scored.

1. 1100–3299 Ford
2. 1300–1599 Hilton
3. Gaines
4. Bryant
5. 2400–2899 Ames
6. 8500–9199 Ames
7. 4500–4799 Ford
8. 6100–7299 Hilton
9. 5300–5399 Ford
10. Ardsley
11. Arnhem
12. Popham
13. 7200–8499 Hilton
14. 9900–9999 Ames
15. 5800–6099 Ford
16. 6800–8699 Ames
17. 2000–2099 Hilton
18. Church
19. School
20. Doyer
21. 3600–3799 Ford
22. 4100–4899 Hilton

23. 7600–8699 Ames
24. Childs
25. Kramer
26. 7200–8499 Hilton
27. 6800–8699 Ames
28. 3600–3799 Ford
29. 6100–7299 Hilton
30. 7600–8699 Ames
31. Church
32. Doyer
33. 5300–5399 Ford
34. 4500–4799 Ford
35. 9900–9999 Ames
36. 4100–4899 Hilton
37. Popham
38. Bryant
39. 1100–3299 Ford
40. Kramer
41. 2400–2899 Ames
42. 2000–2099 Hilton
43. 1300–1599 Hilton
44. Ardsley

45. Arnhem
46. School
47. 8500–9199 Ames
48. 5800–6099 Ford
49. Childs
50. Gaines
51. 5800–6099 Ford
52. 6800–8699 Ames
53. 7200–8499 Hilton
54. Bryant
55. Arnhem
56. 8500–9199 Amcs
57. 6100–7299 Hilton
58. 4500–4799 Ford
59. 2000–2099 Hilton
60. 1100–3299 Ford
61. Popham
62. School
63. Kramer
64. 7600–8699 Ames
65. 1300–1599 Hilton
66. 9900–9999 Ames

67. 3600–3799 Ford
68. Childs
69. Gaines
70. 5300–5399 Ford
71. 7200–8499 Hilton
72. 2400–2899 Ames
73. Kramer
74. School
75. 9900–9999 Ames
76. 4100–4899 Hilton
77. 8500–9199 Ames
78. Gaines
79. Popham
80. Arnhem
81. 6800–8699 Ames
82. 4500–4799 Ford
83. 3600–3799 Ford
84. 2000–2099 Hilton
85. 5800–6099 Ford
86. 7600–8699 Ames
87. Ardsley
88. Bryant

MEMORY FOR ADDRESSES TEST

TIME: 5 Minutes. 88 Questions.

DIRECTIONS: Mark your answers on the answer sheet in the section headed "MEMORY FOR ADDRESSES TEST." This test will be scored. You are NOT permitted to look at the boxes. Work from memory, as quickly and as accurately as you can. Correct answers are on page 178.

1. 9900–9999 Ames
2. 1300–1599 Hilton
3. 7200–8499 Hilton
4. 1100–3299 Ford
5. Childs
6. Kramer
7. 6100–7299 Hilton
8. 2400–2899 Ames
9. 4500–4799 Ford
10. School
11. Gaines
12. 5300–5399 Ford
13. 7600–8699 Ames
14. 8500–9199 Ames
15. 5800–6099 Ford
16. 2000–2099 Hilton
17. Popham
18. Doyer
19. 3600–3799 Ford
20. 4100–4899 Hilton
21. 6800–8699 Ames
22. Ardsley
23. Arnhem
24. Bryant
25. 8500–9199 Ames
26. 1300–1599 Hilton
27. 5800–6099 Ford
28. Church
29. 5300–5399 Ford
30. 9900–9999 Ames
31. 3600–3799 Ford
32. 6100–7299 Hilton
33. School
34. Childs
35. 2000–2099 Hilton
36. 2400–2899 Ames
37. 7600–8699 Ames
38. 7200–8499 Hilton
39. 1100–3299 Ford
40. Kramer
41. Popham
42. 6800–8699 Ames
43. 4100–4899 Hilton
44. 5800–6099 Ford
45. Doyer
46. Ardsley
47. Gaines
48. 4500–4799 Ford
49. 2000–2099 Hilton
50. 9900–9999 Ames
51. 1300–1599 Hilton
52. 5300–5399 Ford
53. Bryant
54. Church
55. 7600–8699 Ames
56. 8500–9199 Ames
57. 1100–3299 Ford
58. 2400–2899 Ames
59. 6100–7299 Hilton
60. Arnhem
61. Popham
62. Kramer
63. 7200–8499 Hilton
64. 6800–8699 Ames

65. 4100–4899 Hilton
66. 5800–6099 Ford
67. 3600–3799 Ford
68. 6100–7299 Hilton
69. 8500–9199 Ames
70. Gaines
71. Doyer
72. 7600–8699 Ames
73. 5300–5399 Ford
74. 4100–4899 Hilton
75. Popham
76. Ardsley

77. 9900–9999 Ames
78. 4500–4799 Ford
79. 7200–8499 Hilton
80. 5800–6099 Ford
81. Church
82. Bryant
83. Kramer
84. 1100–3299 Ford
85. 2400–2899 Ames
86. 2000–2099 Hilton
87. 1300–1599 Hilton
88. 3600–3799 Ford

END OF EXAM

ADDRESS CHECKING ERROR ANALYSIS CHART

Type of Error	Tally	Total Number
Number of addresses which were alike and you incorrectly marked "different"		
Number of addresses which were different and you incorrectly marked "alike"		
Number of addresses in which you missed a difference in NUMBERS		
Number of addresses in which you missed a difference in ABBREVIATIONS		
Number of addresses in which you missed a difference in NAMES		

SELF-EVALUATION CHART

Test	Excellent	Good	Average	Fair	Poor
Address Checking	80–95	65–79	50–64	35–49	1–34
Memory for Addresses	75–88	60–74	45–59	30–44	1–29

CORRECT ANSWERS FOR SIXTH MODEL EXAM

ADDRESS CHECKING TEST

1. D	13. D	25. A	37. D	49. D	61. A	73. D	85. D
2. D	14. A	26. D	38. D	50. A	62. D	74. D	86. A
3. A	15. A	27. D	39. D	51. A	63. D	75. A	87. D
4. D	16. D	28. A	40. D	52. A	64. D	76. A	88. A
5. A	17. D	29. D	41. D	53. A	65. A	77. D	89. D
6. D	18. D	30. D	42. D	54. D	66. D	78. D	90. A
7. D	19. A	31. A	43. A	55. D	67. A	79. A	91. D
8. A	20. D	32. A	44. A	56. A	68. A	80. A	92. D
9. A	21. A	33. D	45. D	57. D	69. D	81. D	93. D
10. D	22. A	34. A	46. A	58. D	70. D	82. A	94. D
11. D	23. D	35. D	47. D	59. D	71. A	83. D	95. D
12. D	24. A	36. D	48. D	60. A	72. D	84. D	

MEMORY FOR ADDRESSES—PRACTICE I

1. B	12. C	23. C	34. C	45. E	56. B	67. D	78. A
2. E	13. E	24. D	35. D	46. A	57. A	68. C	79. C
3. A	14. D	25. B	36. E	47. D	58. E	69. B	80. A
4. D	15. E	26. A	37. A	48. E	59. E	70. E	81. E
5. E	16. C	27. C	38. B	49. C	60. C	71. D	82. E
6. B	17. C	28. C	39. E	50. C	61. D	72. E	83. A
7. C	18. B	29. D	40. A	51. C	62. E	73. C	84. A
8. E	19. D	30. B	41. A	52. A	63. A	74. B	85. B
9. A	20. B	31. D	42. D	53. D	64. B	75. C	86. D
10. A	21. D	32. A	43. B	54. C	65. E	76. D	87. B
11. A	22. A	33. E	44. B	55. B	66. B	77. D	88. D

MEMORY FOR ADDRESSES—PRACTICE II

1. D	12. B	23. C	34. D	45. D	56. E	67. A	78. C
2. E	13. C	24. E	35. E	46. A	57. A	68. C	79. B
3. B	14. A	25. D	36. D	47. E	58. C	69. D	80. E
4. C	15. D	26. C	37. A	48. C	59. E	70. D	81. E
5. A	16. E	27. D	38. A	49. E	60. A	71. E	82. D
6. C	17. B	28. B	39. A	50. D	61. C	72. A	83. D
7. E	18. C	29. E	40. B	51. A	62. B	73. B	84. A
8. D	19. D	30. A	41. B	52. B	63. B	74. E	85. C
9. A	20. E	31. C	42. C	53. D	64. B	75. B	86. B
10. D	21. A	32. C	43. B	54. A	65. C	76. E	87. A
11. A	22. B	33. E	44. B	55. A	66. D	77. A	88. A

MEMORY FOR ADDRESSES—PRACTICE III

1. B	12. A	23. E	34. E	45. E	56. A	67. C	78. D
2. E	13. A	24. B	35. C	46. C	57. C	68. B	79. A
3. D	14. C	25. E	36. D	47. A	58. E	69. D	80. E
4. C	15. D	26. A	37. A	48. D	59. B	70. A	81. B
5. D	16. B	27. B	38. C	49. B	60. B	71. A	82. E
6. A	17. B	28. C	39. B	50. D	61. A	72. D	83. C
7. E	18. D	29. C	40. E	51. D	62. C	73. E	84. B
8. C	19. C	30. E	41. D	52. B	63. E	74. C	85. D
9. A	20. A	31. D	42. B	53. A	64. E	75. C	86. E
10. B	21. C	32. A	43. E	54. C	65. E	76. D	87. B
11. E	22. D	33. A	44. B	55. E	66. C	77. A	88. C

MEMORY FOR ADDRESSES TEST

1. C	12. A	23. E	34. B	45. A	56. A	67. C	78. E
2. E	13. E	24. C	35. B	46. B	57. B	68. C	79. A
3. A	14. A	25. A	36. D	47. D	58. D	69. A	80. D
4. B	15. D	26. E	37. E	48. E	59. C	70. D	81. D
5. B	16. B	27. D	38. A	49. B	60. E	71. A	82. C
6. E	17. A	28. D	39. B	50. C	61. A	72. E	83. E
7. C	18. A	29. A	40. E	51. E	62. E	73. A	84. B
8. D	19. C	30. C	41. A	52. A	63. A	74. D	85. D
9. E	20. D	31. C	42. B	53. C	64. B	75. A	86. B
10. C	21. B	32. C	43. D	54. D	65. D	76. B	87. E
11. D	22. B	33. C	44. D	55. E	66. D	77. C	88. C

ANSWER SHEET FOR SEVENTH MODEL EXAM

ADDRESS CHECKING

1 Ⓐ Ⓓ	20 Ⓐ Ⓓ	39 Ⓐ Ⓓ	58 Ⓐ Ⓓ	77 Ⓐ Ⓓ
2 Ⓐ Ⓓ	21 Ⓐ Ⓓ	40 Ⓐ Ⓓ	59 Ⓐ Ⓓ	78 Ⓐ Ⓓ
3 Ⓐ Ⓓ	22 Ⓐ Ⓓ	41 Ⓐ Ⓓ	60 Ⓐ Ⓓ	79 Ⓐ Ⓓ
4 Ⓐ Ⓓ	23 Ⓐ Ⓓ	42 Ⓐ Ⓓ	61 Ⓐ Ⓓ	80 Ⓐ Ⓓ
5 Ⓐ Ⓓ	24 Ⓐ Ⓓ	43 Ⓐ Ⓓ	62 Ⓐ Ⓓ	81 Ⓐ Ⓓ
6 Ⓐ Ⓓ	25 Ⓐ Ⓓ	44 Ⓐ Ⓓ	63 Ⓐ Ⓓ	82 Ⓐ Ⓓ
7 Ⓐ Ⓓ	26 Ⓐ Ⓓ	45 Ⓐ Ⓓ	64 Ⓐ Ⓓ	83 Ⓐ Ⓓ
8 Ⓐ Ⓓ	27 Ⓐ Ⓓ	46 Ⓐ Ⓓ	65 Ⓐ Ⓓ	84 Ⓐ Ⓓ
9 Ⓐ Ⓓ	28 Ⓐ Ⓓ	47 Ⓐ Ⓓ	66 Ⓐ Ⓓ	85 Ⓐ Ⓓ
10 Ⓐ Ⓓ	29 Ⓐ Ⓓ	48 Ⓐ Ⓓ	67 Ⓐ Ⓓ	86 Ⓐ Ⓓ
11 Ⓐ Ⓓ	30 Ⓐ Ⓓ	49 Ⓐ Ⓓ	68 Ⓐ Ⓓ	87 Ⓐ Ⓓ
12 Ⓐ Ⓓ	31 Ⓐ Ⓓ	50 Ⓐ Ⓓ	69 Ⓐ Ⓓ	88 Ⓐ Ⓓ
13 Ⓐ Ⓓ	32 Ⓐ Ⓓ	51 Ⓐ Ⓓ	70 Ⓐ Ⓓ	89 Ⓐ Ⓓ
14 Ⓐ Ⓓ	33 Ⓐ Ⓓ	52 Ⓐ Ⓓ	71 Ⓐ Ⓓ	90 Ⓐ Ⓓ
15 Ⓐ Ⓓ	34 Ⓐ Ⓓ	53 Ⓐ Ⓓ	72 Ⓐ Ⓓ	91 Ⓐ Ⓓ
16 Ⓐ Ⓓ	35 Ⓐ Ⓓ	54 Ⓐ Ⓓ	73 Ⓐ Ⓓ	92 Ⓐ Ⓓ
17 Ⓐ Ⓓ	36 Ⓐ Ⓓ	55 Ⓐ Ⓓ	74 Ⓐ Ⓓ	93 Ⓐ Ⓓ
18 Ⓐ Ⓓ	37 Ⓐ Ⓓ	56 Ⓐ Ⓓ	75 Ⓐ Ⓓ	94 Ⓐ Ⓓ
19 Ⓐ Ⓓ	38 Ⓐ Ⓓ	57 Ⓐ Ⓓ	76 Ⓐ Ⓓ	95 Ⓐ Ⓓ

MEMORY FOR ADDRESSES

PRACTICE I

1 Ⓐ Ⓑ Ⓒ Ⓓ Ⓔ 23 Ⓐ Ⓑ Ⓒ Ⓓ Ⓔ 45 Ⓐ Ⓑ Ⓒ Ⓓ Ⓔ 67 Ⓐ Ⓑ Ⓒ Ⓓ Ⓔ

2 Ⓐ Ⓑ Ⓒ Ⓓ Ⓔ 24 Ⓐ Ⓑ Ⓒ Ⓓ Ⓔ 46 Ⓐ Ⓑ Ⓒ Ⓓ Ⓔ 68 Ⓐ Ⓑ Ⓒ Ⓓ Ⓔ

3 Ⓐ Ⓑ Ⓒ Ⓓ Ⓔ 25 Ⓐ Ⓑ Ⓒ Ⓓ Ⓔ 47 Ⓐ Ⓑ Ⓒ Ⓓ Ⓔ 69 Ⓐ Ⓑ Ⓒ Ⓓ Ⓔ

4 Ⓐ Ⓑ Ⓒ Ⓓ Ⓔ 26 Ⓐ Ⓑ Ⓒ Ⓓ Ⓔ 48 Ⓐ Ⓑ Ⓒ Ⓓ Ⓔ 70 Ⓐ Ⓑ Ⓒ Ⓓ Ⓔ

5 Ⓐ Ⓑ Ⓒ Ⓓ Ⓔ 27 Ⓐ Ⓑ Ⓒ Ⓓ Ⓔ 49 Ⓐ Ⓑ Ⓒ Ⓓ Ⓔ 71 Ⓐ Ⓑ Ⓒ Ⓓ Ⓔ

6 Ⓐ Ⓑ Ⓒ Ⓓ Ⓔ 28 Ⓐ Ⓑ Ⓒ Ⓓ Ⓔ 50 Ⓐ Ⓑ Ⓒ Ⓓ Ⓔ 72 Ⓐ Ⓑ Ⓒ Ⓓ Ⓔ

7 Ⓐ Ⓑ Ⓒ Ⓓ Ⓔ 29 Ⓐ Ⓑ Ⓒ Ⓓ Ⓔ 51 Ⓐ Ⓑ Ⓒ Ⓓ Ⓔ 73 Ⓐ Ⓑ Ⓒ Ⓓ Ⓔ

8 Ⓐ Ⓑ Ⓒ Ⓓ Ⓔ 30 Ⓐ Ⓑ Ⓒ Ⓓ Ⓔ 52 Ⓐ Ⓑ Ⓒ Ⓓ Ⓔ 74 Ⓐ Ⓑ Ⓒ Ⓓ Ⓔ

9 Ⓐ Ⓑ Ⓒ Ⓓ Ⓔ 31 Ⓐ Ⓑ Ⓒ Ⓓ Ⓔ 53 Ⓐ Ⓑ Ⓒ Ⓓ Ⓔ 75 Ⓐ Ⓑ Ⓒ Ⓓ Ⓔ

10 Ⓐ Ⓑ Ⓒ Ⓓ Ⓔ 32 Ⓐ Ⓑ Ⓒ Ⓓ Ⓔ 54 Ⓐ Ⓑ Ⓒ Ⓓ Ⓔ 76 Ⓐ Ⓑ Ⓒ Ⓓ Ⓔ

11 Ⓐ Ⓑ Ⓒ Ⓓ Ⓔ 33 Ⓐ Ⓑ Ⓒ Ⓓ Ⓔ 55 Ⓐ Ⓑ Ⓒ Ⓓ Ⓔ 77 Ⓐ Ⓑ Ⓒ Ⓓ Ⓔ

12 Ⓐ Ⓑ Ⓒ Ⓓ Ⓔ 34 Ⓐ Ⓑ Ⓒ Ⓓ Ⓔ 56 Ⓐ Ⓑ Ⓒ Ⓓ Ⓔ 78 Ⓐ Ⓑ Ⓒ Ⓓ Ⓔ

13 Ⓐ Ⓑ Ⓒ Ⓓ Ⓔ 35 Ⓐ Ⓑ Ⓒ Ⓓ Ⓔ 57 Ⓐ Ⓑ Ⓒ Ⓓ Ⓔ 79 Ⓐ Ⓑ Ⓒ Ⓓ Ⓔ

14 Ⓐ Ⓑ Ⓒ Ⓓ Ⓔ 36 Ⓐ Ⓑ Ⓒ Ⓓ Ⓔ 58 Ⓐ Ⓑ Ⓒ Ⓓ Ⓔ 80 Ⓐ Ⓑ Ⓒ Ⓓ Ⓔ

15 Ⓐ Ⓑ Ⓒ Ⓓ Ⓔ 37 Ⓐ Ⓑ Ⓒ Ⓓ Ⓔ 59 Ⓐ Ⓑ Ⓒ Ⓓ Ⓔ 81 Ⓐ Ⓑ Ⓒ Ⓓ Ⓔ

16 Ⓐ Ⓑ Ⓒ Ⓓ Ⓔ 38 Ⓐ Ⓑ Ⓒ Ⓓ Ⓔ 60 Ⓐ Ⓑ Ⓒ Ⓓ Ⓔ 82 Ⓐ Ⓑ Ⓒ Ⓓ Ⓔ

17 Ⓐ Ⓑ Ⓒ Ⓓ Ⓔ 39 Ⓐ Ⓑ Ⓒ Ⓓ Ⓔ 61 Ⓐ Ⓑ Ⓒ Ⓓ Ⓔ 83 Ⓐ Ⓑ Ⓒ Ⓓ Ⓔ

18 Ⓐ Ⓑ Ⓒ Ⓓ Ⓔ 40 Ⓐ Ⓑ Ⓒ Ⓓ Ⓔ 62 Ⓐ Ⓑ Ⓒ Ⓓ Ⓔ 84 Ⓐ Ⓑ Ⓒ Ⓓ Ⓔ

19 Ⓐ Ⓑ Ⓒ Ⓓ Ⓔ 41 Ⓐ Ⓑ Ⓒ Ⓓ Ⓔ 63 Ⓐ Ⓑ Ⓒ Ⓓ Ⓔ 85 Ⓐ Ⓑ Ⓒ Ⓓ Ⓔ

20 Ⓐ Ⓑ Ⓒ Ⓓ Ⓔ 42 Ⓐ Ⓑ Ⓒ Ⓓ Ⓔ 64 Ⓐ Ⓑ Ⓒ Ⓓ Ⓔ 86 Ⓐ Ⓑ Ⓒ Ⓓ Ⓔ

21 Ⓐ Ⓑ Ⓒ Ⓓ Ⓔ 43 Ⓐ Ⓑ Ⓒ Ⓓ Ⓔ 65 Ⓐ Ⓑ Ⓒ Ⓓ Ⓔ 87 Ⓐ Ⓑ Ⓒ Ⓓ Ⓔ

22 Ⓐ Ⓑ Ⓒ Ⓓ Ⓔ 44 Ⓐ Ⓑ Ⓒ Ⓓ Ⓔ 66 Ⓐ Ⓑ Ⓒ Ⓓ Ⓔ 88 Ⓐ Ⓑ Ⓒ Ⓓ Ⓔ

PRACTICE II

1 Ⓐ Ⓑ Ⓒ Ⓓ Ⓔ   23 Ⓐ Ⓑ Ⓒ Ⓓ Ⓔ   45 Ⓐ Ⓑ Ⓒ Ⓓ Ⓔ   67 Ⓐ Ⓑ Ⓒ Ⓓ Ⓔ

2 Ⓐ Ⓑ Ⓒ Ⓓ Ⓔ   24 Ⓐ Ⓑ Ⓒ Ⓓ Ⓔ   46 Ⓐ Ⓑ Ⓒ Ⓓ Ⓔ   68 Ⓐ Ⓑ Ⓒ Ⓓ Ⓔ

3 Ⓐ Ⓑ Ⓒ Ⓓ Ⓔ   25 Ⓐ Ⓑ Ⓒ Ⓓ Ⓔ   47 Ⓐ Ⓑ Ⓒ Ⓓ Ⓔ   69 Ⓐ Ⓑ Ⓒ Ⓓ Ⓔ

4 Ⓐ Ⓑ Ⓒ Ⓓ Ⓔ   26 Ⓐ Ⓑ Ⓒ Ⓓ Ⓔ   48 Ⓐ Ⓑ Ⓒ Ⓓ Ⓔ   70 Ⓐ Ⓑ Ⓒ Ⓓ Ⓔ

5 Ⓐ Ⓑ Ⓒ Ⓓ Ⓔ   27 Ⓐ Ⓑ Ⓒ Ⓓ Ⓔ   49 Ⓐ Ⓑ Ⓒ Ⓓ Ⓔ   71 Ⓐ Ⓑ Ⓒ Ⓓ Ⓔ

6 Ⓐ Ⓑ Ⓒ Ⓓ Ⓔ   28 Ⓐ Ⓑ Ⓒ Ⓓ Ⓔ   50 Ⓐ Ⓑ Ⓒ Ⓓ Ⓔ   72 Ⓐ Ⓑ Ⓒ Ⓓ Ⓔ

7 Ⓐ Ⓑ Ⓒ Ⓓ Ⓔ   29 Ⓐ Ⓑ Ⓒ Ⓓ Ⓔ   51 Ⓐ Ⓑ Ⓒ Ⓓ Ⓔ   73 Ⓐ Ⓑ Ⓒ Ⓓ Ⓔ

8 Ⓐ Ⓑ Ⓒ Ⓓ Ⓔ   30 Ⓐ Ⓑ Ⓒ Ⓓ Ⓔ   52 Ⓐ Ⓑ Ⓒ Ⓓ Ⓔ   74 Ⓐ Ⓑ Ⓒ Ⓓ Ⓔ

9 Ⓐ Ⓑ Ⓒ Ⓓ Ⓔ   31 Ⓐ Ⓑ Ⓒ Ⓓ Ⓔ   53 Ⓐ Ⓑ Ⓒ Ⓓ Ⓔ   75 Ⓐ Ⓑ Ⓒ Ⓓ Ⓔ

10 Ⓐ Ⓑ Ⓒ Ⓓ Ⓔ   32 Ⓐ Ⓑ Ⓒ Ⓓ Ⓔ   54 Ⓐ Ⓑ Ⓒ Ⓓ Ⓔ   76 Ⓐ Ⓑ Ⓒ Ⓓ Ⓔ

11 Ⓐ Ⓑ Ⓒ Ⓓ Ⓔ   33 Ⓐ Ⓑ Ⓒ Ⓓ Ⓔ   55 Ⓐ Ⓑ Ⓒ Ⓓ Ⓔ   77 Ⓐ Ⓑ Ⓒ Ⓓ Ⓔ

12 Ⓐ Ⓑ Ⓒ Ⓓ Ⓔ   34 Ⓐ Ⓑ Ⓒ Ⓓ Ⓔ   56 Ⓐ Ⓑ Ⓒ Ⓓ Ⓔ   78 Ⓐ Ⓑ Ⓒ Ⓓ Ⓔ

13 Ⓐ Ⓑ Ⓒ Ⓓ Ⓔ   35 Ⓐ Ⓑ Ⓒ Ⓓ Ⓔ   57 Ⓐ Ⓑ Ⓒ Ⓓ Ⓔ   79 Ⓐ Ⓑ Ⓒ Ⓓ Ⓔ

14 Ⓐ Ⓑ Ⓒ Ⓓ Ⓔ   36 Ⓐ Ⓑ Ⓒ Ⓓ Ⓔ   58 Ⓐ Ⓑ Ⓒ Ⓓ Ⓔ   80 Ⓐ Ⓑ Ⓒ Ⓓ Ⓔ

15 Ⓐ Ⓑ Ⓒ Ⓓ Ⓔ   37 Ⓐ Ⓑ Ⓒ Ⓓ Ⓔ   59 Ⓐ Ⓑ Ⓒ Ⓓ Ⓔ   81 Ⓐ Ⓑ Ⓒ Ⓓ Ⓔ

16 Ⓐ Ⓑ Ⓒ Ⓓ Ⓔ   38 Ⓐ Ⓑ Ⓒ Ⓓ Ⓔ   60 Ⓐ Ⓑ Ⓒ Ⓓ Ⓔ   82 Ⓐ Ⓑ Ⓒ Ⓓ Ⓔ

17 Ⓐ Ⓑ Ⓒ Ⓓ Ⓔ   39 Ⓐ Ⓑ Ⓒ Ⓓ Ⓔ   61 Ⓐ Ⓑ Ⓒ Ⓓ Ⓔ   83 Ⓐ Ⓑ Ⓒ Ⓓ Ⓔ

18 Ⓐ Ⓑ Ⓒ Ⓓ Ⓔ   40 Ⓐ Ⓑ Ⓒ Ⓓ Ⓔ   62 Ⓐ Ⓑ Ⓒ Ⓓ Ⓔ   84 Ⓐ Ⓑ Ⓒ Ⓓ Ⓔ

19 Ⓐ Ⓑ Ⓒ Ⓓ Ⓔ   41 Ⓐ Ⓑ Ⓒ Ⓓ Ⓔ   63 Ⓐ Ⓑ Ⓒ Ⓓ Ⓔ   85 Ⓐ Ⓑ Ⓒ Ⓓ Ⓔ

20 Ⓐ Ⓑ Ⓒ Ⓓ Ⓔ   42 Ⓐ Ⓑ Ⓒ Ⓓ Ⓔ   64 Ⓐ Ⓑ Ⓒ Ⓓ Ⓔ   86 Ⓐ Ⓑ Ⓒ Ⓓ Ⓔ

21 Ⓐ Ⓑ Ⓒ Ⓓ Ⓔ   43 Ⓐ Ⓑ Ⓒ Ⓓ Ⓔ   65 Ⓐ Ⓑ Ⓒ Ⓓ Ⓔ   87 Ⓐ Ⓑ Ⓒ Ⓓ Ⓔ

22 Ⓐ Ⓑ Ⓒ Ⓓ Ⓔ   44 Ⓐ Ⓑ Ⓒ Ⓓ Ⓔ   66 Ⓐ Ⓑ Ⓒ Ⓓ Ⓔ   88 Ⓐ Ⓑ Ⓒ Ⓓ Ⓔ

PRACTICE III

1 Ⓐ Ⓑ Ⓒ Ⓓ Ⓔ	23 Ⓐ Ⓑ Ⓒ Ⓓ Ⓔ	45 Ⓐ Ⓑ Ⓒ Ⓓ Ⓔ	67 Ⓐ Ⓑ Ⓒ Ⓓ Ⓔ
2 Ⓐ Ⓑ Ⓒ Ⓓ Ⓔ	24 Ⓐ Ⓑ Ⓒ Ⓓ Ⓔ	46 Ⓐ Ⓑ Ⓒ Ⓓ Ⓔ	68 Ⓐ Ⓑ Ⓒ Ⓓ Ⓔ
3 Ⓐ Ⓑ Ⓒ Ⓓ Ⓔ	25 Ⓐ Ⓑ Ⓒ Ⓓ Ⓔ	47 Ⓐ Ⓑ Ⓒ Ⓓ Ⓔ	69 Ⓐ Ⓑ Ⓒ Ⓓ Ⓔ
4 Ⓐ Ⓑ Ⓒ Ⓓ Ⓔ	26 Ⓐ Ⓑ Ⓒ Ⓓ Ⓔ	48 Ⓐ Ⓑ Ⓒ Ⓓ Ⓔ	70 Ⓐ Ⓑ Ⓒ Ⓓ Ⓔ
5 Ⓐ Ⓑ Ⓒ Ⓓ Ⓔ	27 Ⓐ Ⓑ Ⓒ Ⓓ Ⓔ	49 Ⓐ Ⓑ Ⓒ Ⓓ Ⓔ	71 Ⓐ Ⓑ Ⓒ Ⓓ Ⓔ
6 Ⓐ Ⓑ Ⓒ Ⓓ Ⓔ	28 Ⓐ Ⓑ Ⓒ Ⓓ Ⓔ	50 Ⓐ Ⓑ Ⓒ Ⓓ Ⓔ	72 Ⓐ Ⓑ Ⓒ Ⓓ Ⓔ
7 Ⓐ Ⓑ Ⓒ Ⓓ Ⓔ	29 Ⓐ Ⓑ Ⓒ Ⓓ Ⓔ	51 Ⓐ Ⓑ Ⓒ Ⓓ Ⓔ	73 Ⓐ Ⓑ Ⓒ Ⓓ Ⓔ
8 Ⓐ Ⓑ Ⓒ Ⓓ Ⓔ	30 Ⓐ Ⓑ Ⓒ Ⓓ Ⓔ	52 Ⓐ Ⓑ Ⓒ Ⓓ Ⓔ	74 Ⓐ Ⓑ Ⓒ Ⓓ Ⓔ
9 Ⓐ Ⓑ Ⓒ Ⓓ Ⓔ	31 Ⓐ Ⓑ Ⓒ Ⓓ Ⓔ	53 Ⓐ Ⓑ Ⓒ Ⓓ Ⓔ	75 Ⓐ Ⓑ Ⓒ Ⓓ Ⓔ
10 Ⓐ Ⓑ Ⓒ Ⓓ Ⓔ	32 Ⓐ Ⓑ Ⓒ Ⓓ Ⓔ	54 Ⓐ Ⓑ Ⓒ Ⓓ Ⓔ	76 Ⓐ Ⓑ Ⓒ Ⓓ Ⓔ
11 Ⓐ Ⓑ Ⓒ Ⓓ Ⓔ	33 Ⓐ Ⓑ Ⓒ Ⓓ Ⓔ	55 Ⓐ Ⓑ Ⓒ Ⓓ Ⓔ	77 Ⓐ Ⓑ Ⓒ Ⓓ Ⓔ
12 Ⓐ Ⓑ Ⓒ Ⓓ Ⓔ	34 Ⓐ Ⓑ Ⓒ Ⓓ Ⓔ	56 Ⓐ Ⓑ Ⓒ Ⓓ Ⓔ	78 Ⓐ Ⓑ Ⓒ Ⓓ Ⓔ
13 Ⓐ Ⓑ Ⓒ Ⓓ Ⓔ	35 Ⓐ Ⓑ Ⓒ Ⓓ Ⓔ	57 Ⓐ Ⓑ Ⓒ Ⓓ Ⓔ	79 Ⓐ Ⓑ Ⓒ Ⓓ Ⓔ
14 Ⓐ Ⓑ Ⓒ Ⓓ Ⓔ	36 Ⓐ Ⓑ Ⓒ Ⓓ Ⓔ	58 Ⓐ Ⓑ Ⓒ Ⓓ Ⓔ	80 Ⓐ Ⓑ Ⓒ Ⓓ Ⓔ
15 Ⓐ Ⓑ Ⓒ Ⓓ Ⓔ	37 Ⓐ Ⓑ Ⓒ Ⓓ Ⓔ	59 Ⓐ Ⓑ Ⓒ Ⓓ Ⓔ	81 Ⓐ Ⓑ Ⓒ Ⓓ Ⓔ
16 Ⓐ Ⓑ Ⓒ Ⓓ Ⓔ	38 Ⓐ Ⓑ Ⓒ Ⓓ Ⓔ	60 Ⓐ Ⓑ Ⓒ Ⓓ Ⓔ	82 Ⓐ Ⓑ Ⓒ Ⓓ Ⓔ
17 Ⓐ Ⓑ Ⓒ Ⓓ Ⓔ	39 Ⓐ Ⓑ Ⓒ Ⓓ Ⓔ	61 Ⓐ Ⓑ Ⓒ Ⓓ Ⓔ	83 Ⓐ Ⓑ Ⓒ Ⓓ Ⓔ
18 Ⓐ Ⓑ Ⓒ Ⓓ Ⓔ	40 Ⓐ Ⓑ Ⓒ Ⓓ Ⓔ	62 Ⓐ Ⓑ Ⓒ Ⓓ Ⓔ	84 Ⓐ Ⓑ Ⓒ Ⓓ Ⓔ
19 Ⓐ Ⓑ Ⓒ Ⓓ Ⓔ	41 Ⓐ Ⓑ Ⓒ Ⓓ Ⓔ	63 Ⓐ Ⓑ Ⓒ Ⓓ Ⓔ	85 Ⓐ Ⓑ Ⓒ Ⓓ Ⓔ
20 Ⓐ Ⓑ Ⓒ Ⓓ Ⓔ	42 Ⓐ Ⓑ Ⓒ Ⓓ Ⓔ	64 Ⓐ Ⓑ Ⓒ Ⓓ Ⓔ	86 Ⓐ Ⓑ Ⓒ Ⓓ Ⓔ
21 Ⓐ Ⓑ Ⓒ Ⓓ Ⓔ	43 Ⓐ Ⓑ Ⓒ Ⓓ Ⓔ	65 Ⓐ Ⓑ Ⓒ Ⓓ Ⓔ	87 Ⓐ Ⓑ Ⓒ Ⓓ Ⓔ
22 Ⓐ Ⓑ Ⓒ Ⓓ Ⓔ	44 Ⓐ Ⓑ Ⓒ Ⓓ Ⓔ	66 Ⓐ Ⓑ Ⓒ Ⓓ Ⓔ	88 Ⓐ Ⓑ Ⓒ Ⓓ Ⓔ

MEMORY FOR ADDRESSES TEST

1 Ⓐ Ⓑ Ⓒ Ⓓ Ⓔ   23 Ⓐ Ⓑ Ⓒ Ⓓ Ⓔ   45 Ⓐ Ⓑ Ⓒ Ⓓ Ⓔ   67 Ⓐ Ⓑ Ⓒ Ⓓ Ⓔ

2 Ⓐ Ⓑ Ⓒ Ⓓ Ⓔ   24 Ⓐ Ⓑ Ⓒ Ⓓ Ⓔ   46 Ⓐ Ⓑ Ⓒ Ⓓ Ⓔ   68 Ⓐ Ⓑ Ⓒ Ⓓ Ⓔ

3 Ⓐ Ⓑ Ⓒ Ⓓ Ⓔ   25 Ⓐ Ⓑ Ⓒ Ⓓ Ⓔ   47 Ⓐ Ⓑ Ⓒ Ⓓ Ⓔ   69 Ⓐ Ⓑ Ⓒ Ⓓ Ⓔ

4 Ⓐ Ⓑ Ⓒ Ⓓ Ⓔ   26 Ⓐ Ⓑ Ⓒ Ⓓ Ⓔ   48 Ⓐ Ⓑ Ⓒ Ⓓ Ⓔ   70 Ⓐ Ⓑ Ⓒ Ⓓ Ⓔ

5 Ⓐ Ⓑ Ⓒ Ⓓ Ⓔ   27 Ⓐ Ⓑ Ⓒ Ⓓ Ⓔ   49 Ⓐ Ⓑ Ⓒ Ⓓ Ⓔ   71 Ⓐ Ⓑ Ⓒ Ⓓ Ⓔ

6 Ⓐ Ⓑ Ⓒ Ⓓ Ⓔ   28 Ⓐ Ⓑ Ⓒ Ⓓ Ⓔ   50 Ⓐ Ⓑ Ⓒ Ⓓ Ⓔ   72 Ⓐ Ⓑ Ⓒ Ⓓ Ⓔ

7 Ⓐ Ⓑ Ⓒ Ⓓ Ⓔ   29 Ⓐ Ⓑ Ⓒ Ⓓ Ⓔ   51 Ⓐ Ⓑ Ⓒ Ⓓ Ⓔ   73 Ⓐ Ⓑ Ⓒ Ⓓ Ⓔ

8 Ⓐ Ⓑ Ⓒ Ⓓ Ⓔ   30 Ⓐ Ⓑ Ⓒ Ⓓ Ⓔ   52 Ⓐ Ⓑ Ⓒ Ⓓ Ⓔ   74 Ⓐ Ⓑ Ⓒ Ⓓ Ⓔ

9 Ⓐ Ⓑ Ⓒ Ⓓ Ⓔ   31 Ⓐ Ⓑ Ⓒ Ⓓ Ⓔ   53 Ⓐ Ⓑ Ⓒ Ⓓ Ⓔ   75 Ⓐ Ⓑ Ⓒ Ⓓ Ⓔ

10 Ⓐ Ⓑ Ⓒ Ⓓ Ⓔ   32 Ⓐ Ⓑ Ⓒ Ⓓ Ⓔ   54 Ⓐ Ⓑ Ⓒ Ⓓ Ⓔ   76 Ⓐ Ⓑ Ⓒ Ⓓ Ⓔ

11 Ⓐ Ⓑ Ⓒ Ⓓ Ⓔ   33 Ⓐ Ⓑ Ⓒ Ⓓ Ⓔ   55 Ⓐ Ⓑ Ⓒ Ⓓ Ⓔ   77 Ⓐ Ⓑ Ⓒ Ⓓ Ⓔ

12 Ⓐ Ⓑ Ⓒ Ⓓ Ⓔ   34 Ⓐ Ⓑ Ⓒ Ⓓ Ⓔ   56 Ⓐ Ⓑ Ⓒ Ⓓ Ⓔ   78 Ⓐ Ⓑ Ⓒ Ⓓ Ⓔ

13 Ⓐ Ⓑ Ⓒ Ⓓ Ⓔ   35 Ⓐ Ⓑ Ⓒ Ⓓ Ⓔ   57 Ⓐ Ⓑ Ⓒ Ⓓ Ⓔ   79 Ⓐ Ⓑ Ⓒ Ⓓ Ⓔ

14 Ⓐ Ⓑ Ⓒ Ⓓ Ⓔ   36 Ⓐ Ⓑ Ⓒ Ⓓ Ⓔ   58 Ⓐ Ⓑ Ⓒ Ⓓ Ⓔ   80 Ⓐ Ⓑ Ⓒ Ⓓ Ⓔ

15 Ⓐ Ⓑ Ⓒ Ⓓ Ⓔ   37 Ⓐ Ⓑ Ⓒ Ⓓ Ⓔ   59 Ⓐ Ⓑ Ⓒ Ⓓ Ⓔ   81 Ⓐ Ⓑ Ⓒ Ⓓ Ⓔ

16 Ⓐ Ⓑ Ⓒ Ⓓ Ⓔ   38 Ⓐ Ⓑ Ⓒ Ⓓ Ⓔ   60 Ⓐ Ⓑ Ⓒ Ⓓ Ⓔ   82 Ⓐ Ⓑ Ⓒ Ⓓ Ⓔ

17 Ⓐ Ⓑ Ⓒ Ⓓ Ⓔ   39 Ⓐ Ⓑ Ⓒ Ⓓ Ⓔ   61 Ⓐ Ⓑ Ⓒ Ⓓ Ⓔ   83 Ⓐ Ⓑ Ⓒ Ⓓ Ⓔ

18 Ⓐ Ⓑ Ⓒ Ⓓ Ⓔ   40 Ⓐ Ⓑ Ⓒ Ⓓ Ⓔ   62 Ⓐ Ⓑ Ⓒ Ⓓ Ⓔ   84 Ⓐ Ⓑ Ⓒ Ⓓ Ⓔ

19 Ⓐ Ⓑ Ⓒ Ⓓ Ⓔ   41 Ⓐ Ⓑ Ⓒ Ⓓ Ⓔ   63 Ⓐ Ⓑ Ⓒ Ⓓ Ⓔ   85 Ⓐ Ⓑ Ⓒ Ⓓ Ⓔ

20 Ⓐ Ⓑ Ⓒ Ⓓ Ⓔ   42 Ⓐ Ⓑ Ⓒ Ⓓ Ⓔ   64 Ⓐ Ⓑ Ⓒ Ⓓ Ⓔ   86 Ⓐ Ⓑ Ⓒ Ⓓ Ⓔ

21 Ⓐ Ⓑ Ⓒ Ⓓ Ⓔ   43 Ⓐ Ⓑ Ⓒ Ⓓ Ⓔ   65 Ⓐ Ⓑ Ⓒ Ⓓ Ⓔ   87 Ⓐ Ⓑ Ⓒ Ⓓ Ⓔ

22 Ⓐ Ⓑ Ⓒ Ⓓ Ⓔ   44 Ⓐ Ⓑ Ⓒ Ⓓ Ⓔ   66 Ⓐ Ⓑ Ⓒ Ⓓ Ⓔ   88 Ⓐ Ⓑ Ⓒ Ⓓ Ⓔ

SCORE SHEET FOR SEVENTH MODEL EXAM

ADDRESS CHECKING TEST

Number Right minus Number Wrong equals   Score

_____ – _____ = _____

MEMORY FOR ADDRESSES TEST

Number Right minus (Number Wrong ÷ 4) equals   Score

_____ – _____ = _____

PROGRESS GRAPH

Blacken the bars for Model Exam 7 to the scores you earned.

Score
95
90
85
80
75
70
65
60
55
50
45
40
35
30
25
20
15
10
5
0

Test Model Exam	AC	M	AC	M	AC	M	AC	M	AC	M	AC	M	AC	M	AC	M
	Diag.		1		2		3		4		5		6		7	

AC = Address Checking   M = Memory for Addresses

SEVENTH MODEL EXAM

ADDRESS CHECKING TEST

TIME: 6 Minutes. 95 Questions.

DIRECTIONS: For each question, compare the address in the left column with the address in the right column. If the two addresses are ALIKE IN EVERY WAY, blacken space Ⓐ on your answer sheet. If the two addresses are DIFFERENT IN ANY WAY. blacken space Ⓓ on your answer sheet. Correct answers for this test are on page 195.

1	4623 Grand Concourse	4623 Grand Concourse
2	6179 RidgecroftRd	6719 Ridgecroft Rd
3	5291 Hanover Cir	5291 Hangover Cir
4	2333 Palmer Ave	233 Palmer Ave
5	1859 SE 148th St	1859 SE 148th St
6	Dowagiac MI 49047	Dowagiac MI 49047
7	4147 Wykagyl Terr	4147 Wykagyl Terr
8	1504 N 10th Ave	1504 N 10th St
9	2967 Montross Ave	2967 Montrose Ave
10	Chicago IL 60601	Chicago IL 60601
11	2073 Defoe Ct	2073 Dcfoc Ct
12	2433 Westchester Plz	2343 Westchester Plz
13	6094 Carpenter Ave	6094 Charpenter Ave
14	5677 Bolman Twrs	5677 Bolman Twrs
15	Chappaqua NY 10514	Chappaqua NY 10541
16	3428 Constantine Ave	3248 Constantine Ave
17	847 S 147th Rd	847 S 147th Rd
18	6676 Harwood Ct	6676 Hardwood Ct
19	3486 Mosholu Pky	3486 Mosholu Pkwy
20	Mindenmines MO 64769	Mindenmines MO 64679
21	816 Oscawana Lake Rd	816 Ocsawana Lake Rd
22	9159 Battle Hill Rd	9195 Battle Hill Rd
23	7558 Winston Ln	7558 Winston Ln
24	3856 W 385th St	3856 W 386th St
25	3679 W Alpine Pl	3679 W Alpine Pl
26	Hartford CT 06115	Hartford CN 06115

27 . . . 6103 Locust Hill Wy	6013 Locust Hill Wy
28 . . . 4941 Annrock Dr	4941 Annrock Dr
29 . . . 2018 N St Andrews Pl	2018 N St Andrews Pl
30 . . . 8111 Drewville Rd	8111 Drewsville Rd
31 . . . 463 Peaceable Hill Rd	463 Peaceable Hill Rd
32 . . . Biloxi MS 39532	Biloxi MS 39532
33 . . . 3743 Point Dr S	3734 Point Dr S
34 . . . 5665 Barnington Rd	5665 Barnington Rd
35 . . . 2246 E Sheldrake Ave	2246 W Sheldrake Ave
36 . . . 1443 Bloomingdale Rd	1443 Bloomingdales Rd
37 . . . 2064 Chalford Ln	2064 Chalford Ln
38 . . . McMinnville OR 97128	McMinville OR 97128
39 . . . 6160 Shadybrook Ln	6160 Shadybrook Ln
40 . . . 2947 E Lake Blvd	2947 E Lake Blvd
41 . . . 3907 Evergreen Row	3907 Evergreen Row
42 . . . 2192 SE Hotel Dr	2192 SE Hotel Dr
43 . . . 8844 Fremont St	8844 Fremont Rd
44 . . . 8487 Wolfshead Rd	8487 Wolfshead Rd
45 . . . Anamosa IA 52205	Anamoosa IA 52205
46 . . . 4055 Katonah Ave	4055 Katonah Ave
47 . . . 1977 Buckingham Apts	1979 Buckingham Apts
48 . . . 983 W 139th Way	983 W 139th Wy
49 . . . 7822 Bayliss Ln	7822 Bayliss Ln
50 . . . 8937 Banksville Rd	8937 Banksville Rd
51 . . . 4759 Strathmore Rd	4579 Strathmore Rd
52 . . . 2221 E Main St	221 E Main St
53 . . . South Orange NJ 07079	South Orange NJ 07079
54 . . . 4586 Sylvia Wy	4586 Sylvan Wy
55 . . . 6335 Soundview Ave	6335 SoundView Ave
56 . . . 3743 Popham Rd	3743 Poppam Rd
57 . . . 2845 Brookfield Dr	2485 Brookfield Dr
58 . . . 3845 Fort Slocum Rd	3845 Fort Slocum St
59 . . . 9268 Jochum Ave	9268 Jochum Ave
60 . . . Bloomington MN 55437	Bloomington MN 54537
61 . . . 6903 S 184th St	6903 S 184th St
62 . . . 7486 Rossmor Rd	7486 Rosemor Rd
63 . . . 4176 Whitlockville Rd	4176 Whitlockville Wy
64 . . . 4286 Megquire Ln	4286 Megquire Ln
65 . . . 6270 Tamarock Rd	6270 Tammarock Rd
66 . . . 3630 Bulkley Mnr	3630 Bulkley Mnr
67 . . . 7158 Scarswold Apts	7185 Scarswold Apts
68 . . . Brooklyn NY 11218	Brooklyn NY 11128
69 . . . 9598 Prince Edward Rd	9598 Prince Edward Rd
70 . . . 8439 S 145th St	8439 S 154th St
71 . . . 9795 Shady Glen Ct	9795 Shady Grove Ct
72 . . . 7614 Ganung St	7614 Ganung St
73 . . . Teaneck NJ 07666	Teaneck NH 07666
74 . . . 6359 Dempster Rd	6359 Dumpster Rd
75 . . . 1065 Colchester Hl	1065 Colchester Hl
76 . . . 5381 Phillipse Pl	5381 Philipse Pl
77 . . . 6484 Rochester Terr	6484 Rochester Terr
78 . . . 2956 Quinin St	2956 Quinin St

79 . . . Tarzana CA 91356   Tarzana CA 91536
80 . . . 7558 Winston Ln   7558 Whinston Ln
81 . . . 1862 W 293rd St   1862 W 393rd St
82 . . . 8534 S Huntington Ave   8534 N Huntington Ave
83 . . . 9070 Wild Oaks Vlg   9070 Wild Oakes Vlg
84 . . . 4860 Smadbeck Ave   4680 Smadbeck Ave
85 . . . 8596 E Commonwealth Ave 8596 E Commonwealth Ave
86 . . . Ridgefield NJ 07657   Ridgefield NJ 07657
87 . . . 1478 Charter Cir   1478 W Charter Cir
88 . . . 3963 Priscilla Ave   3963 Pricsilla Ave
89 . . . 4897 Winding Ln   4897 Winding Ln
90 . . . 847 Windmill Terr   847 Windmill Terr
91 . . . 1662 Wixon St W   1662 Wixon St W
92 . . . West Hartford CT 06107 West Hartford CT 06107
93 . . . 6494 Rochelle Terr   9464 Rochelle Terr
94 . . . 4228 Pocantico Rd   4228 Pocantico Rd
95 . . . 1783 S 486th Ave   1783 S 486th Ave

END OF ADDRESS CHECKING TEST

If you finish this test before time is up, use the remaining time to check over your work. Do not turn to the next page until you are told to do so.

PRACTICE FOR
MEMORY FOR ADDRESSES TEST

DIRECTIONS: The five boxes below are labelled A, B, C, D, and E. In each box are three sets of number spans with names and two names which are not associated with numbers. In the next THREE MINUTES, you must try to memorize the box location of each name and number span. The position of a name or number span within its box is not important. You need only remember the letter of the box in which the item is to be found. You will use these names and numbers to answer three sets of practice questions which are NOT scored and one actual test which is scored. Correct answers are on pages 195 and 196.

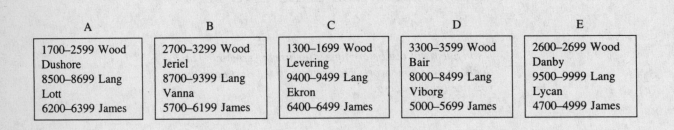

A	B	C	D	E
1700–2599 Wood	2700–3299 Wood	1300–1699 Wood	3300–3599 Wood	2600–2699 Wood
Dushore	Jeriel	Levering	Bair	Danby
8500–8699 Lang	8700–9399 Lang	9400–9499 Lang	8000–8499 Lang	9500–9999 Lang
Lott	Vanna	Ekron	Viborg	Lycan
6200–6399 James	5700–6199 James	6400–6499 James	5000–5699 James	4700–4999 James

PRACTICE I

DIRECTIONS: Use the next THREE MINUTES to mark on your answer sheet the letter of the box in which each item that follows is to be found. Try to mark each item without looking back at the boxes. If, however, you get stuck, you may refer to the boxes during this practice exercise. If you find that you must look at the boxes, try to memorize as you do so. This test is for practice only. It will not be scored.

1. Jeriel
2. Dushore
3. 5000–5699 James
4. 1300–1699 Wood
5. 8500–8699 Lang
6. Bair
7. 5700–6199 James
8. Levering
9. Danby
10. Viborg
11. 8000–8499 Lang
12. 2700–3299 Wood

13. 9400–9499 Lang
14. 3300–3599 Wood
15. 4700–4999 James
16. 9500–9999 Lang
17. Ekron
18. 1300–1699 Wood
19. Vanna
20. Lycan
21. 8700–9399 Lang
22. Dushore
23. 6200–6399 James
24. Lott
25. 2700–3299 Wood
26. 5700–6199 James
27. Levering
28. 9500–9999 Lang
29. 2600–2699 Wood
30. 3300–3599 Wood
31. Viborg
32. 9400–9499 Lang
33. Jeriel
34. Bair
35. 8500–8699 Lang
36. 1700–2599 Wood
37. 8000–8499 Lang
38. Danby
39. Ekron
40. 4700–4999 James
41. Dushore
42. Vanna
43. 5000–5699 James
44. Lott
45. 1300–1699 Wood
46. Levering
47. 5700–6199 James
48. 9500–9999 Lang
49. Bair
50. 8700–9399 Lang

51. 6200–6399 James
52. 9400–9499 Lang
53. Viborg
54. 8000–8499 Lang
55. 4700–4999 James
56. Lycan
57. Vanna
58. Danby
59. 5700–6199 James
60. Lott
61. 2700–3299 Wood
62. 5000–5699 James
63. 1700–2599 Wood
64. 8000–8499 Lang
65. 9400–9499 Lang
66. Jeriel
67. 9500–9999 Lang
68. Dushore
69. 2600–2699 Wood
70. 8500–8699 Lang
71. Levering
72. 5000–5699 James
73. Dushore
74. 8000–8499 Lang
75. Bair
76. Ekron
77. 6200–6399 James
78. 3300–3599 Wood
79. 8700–9399 Lang
80. Viborg
81. 4700–4999 James
82. Lycan
83. 1700–2599 Wood
84. 8500–8699 Lang
85. 1300–1699 Wood
86. Jeriel
87. Danby
88. 6400–6499 James

PRACTICE II

DIRECTIONS: The next 88 questions constitute another practice exercise. Again, you should mark your answers on your answer sheet. Again, the time limit is THREE MINUTES. This time, however, you must NOT look at the boxes while answering the questions. You must rely on your memory in marking the box location of each item. This practice test will not be scored.

1. 6200–6399 James
2. 1700–2599 Wood
3. Bair
4. 1700–2599 Wood
5. Ekron
6. Viborg
7. Danby
8. 8500–8699 Lang
9. Lycan
10. 8000–8499 Lang
11. 4700–4999 James
12. 9400–9499 Lang
13. 2700–3299 Wood
14. Jeriel
15. 9500–9999 Lang
16. 1300–1699 Wood
17. 8700–9399 Lang
18. Levering
19. Vanna
20. 6400–6499 James
21. 3300–3599 Wood
22. Dushore
23. Lycan
24. 5700–6199 James
25. Lott
26. Viborg
27. Jeriel
28. 5000–5699 James
29. 2600–2699 Wood
30. 4700–4999 James
31. 2700–3299 Wood
32. 8000–8499 Lang
33. Ekron
34. 3300–3599 Wood
35. 9400–9499 Lang
36. 6200–6399 James
37. 2600–2699 Wood
38. 8500–8699 Lang
39. Levering
40. Lott
41. Bair
42. 1700–2599 Wood
43. 6400–6499 James
44. 9500–9999 Lang

45. Jeriel
46. 4700–4999 James
47. Dushore
48. Lycan
49. 1700–2599 Wood
50. 6200–6399 James
51. Vanna
52. Ekron
53. 8700–9399 Long
54. Bair
55. 2600–2699 Wood
56. Dushore
57. 5700–6199 James
58. 1300–1699 Wood
59. Levering
60. Lott
61. Jeriel
62. 2600–2699 Wood
63. Lott
64. 4700–4999 James
65. Dushore
66. Danby
67. 8500–8699 Lang
68. Vanna
69. 2700–3299 Wood
70. 9500–9999 Lang
71. Viborg
72. Ekron
73. 6200–6399 James
74. 2600–2699 Wood
75. Levering
76. Lott
77. 1300–1699 Wood
78. Bair
79. Lycan
80. 5700–6199 James
81. Levering
82. 8700–9399 Lang
83. 5000–5699 James
84. 1700–2599 Wood
85. Jeriel
86. 6200–6399 James
87. Ekron
88. 2700–3299 Wood

PRACTICE III

DIRECTIONS: The names and addresses are repeated for you in the boxes below. Each name and each number span is in the same box in which you found it in the original set. You will now be allowed FIVE MINUTES to study the locations again. Do your best to memorize the letter of the box in which each item is located. This is your last chance to see the boxes.

A	B	C	D	E
1700–2599 Wood Dushore 8500–8699 Lang Lott 6200–6399 James	2700–3299 Wood Jeriel 8700–9399 Lang Vanna 5700–6199 James	1300–1699 Wood Levering 9400–9499 Lang Ekron 6400–6499 James	3300–3599 Wood Bair 8000–8499 Lang Viborg 5000–5699 James	2600–2699 Wood Danby 9500–9999 Lang Lycan 4700–4999 James

DIRECTIONS: This is your last practice test. Mark the location of each of the 88 items on your answer sheet. You will have FIVE MINUTES to answer these questions. Do NOT look back at the boxes. This practice test will not be scored.

1. 8000–8499 Lang
2. 4700–4999 James
3. 1700–2599 Wood
4. Vanna
5. Bair
6. Dushore
7. 2700–3299 Wood
8. 5700–6199 James
9. Ekron
10. 3300–3599 Wood
11. 8500–8699 Lang
12. 5000–5999 James
13. Lott
14. Viborg
15. 2600–2699 Wood
16. 6200–6399 James
17. 8700–9399 Lang
18. Ekron
19. 1300–1699 Wood
20. 9400–9499 Lang
21. 8000–8499 Lang
22. 6400–6499 James
23. Dushore
24. Jeriel
25. Danby
26. 5700–6199 James
27. 2600–2699 Wood
28. 6200–6399 James
29. 5000–5699 James
30. 2700–3299 Wood
31. Lott
32. Lycan
33. Viborg
34. 1700–2599 Wood
35. 8700–9399 Lang
36. 6400–6499 James
37. 8000–8499 Lang
38. 2600–2699 Wood
39. Dushore
40. Danby
41. Bair
42. Jeriel
43. 4700–4999 James
44. 3300–3599 Wood

45. 6400–6499 James
46. Levering
47. Ekron
48. 2700–3299 Wood
49. 6200–6399 James
50. 8500–8699 Lang
51. Vanna
52. Jeriel
53. 9400–9499 Lang
54. 9500–9999 Lang
55. 1300–1699 Wood
56. 8700–9399 Lang
57. Lott
58. 6200–6399 James
59. 2600–2699 Wood
60. 8000–8499 Lang
61. 1700–2599 Wood
62. 5700–6199 James
63. 1300–1699 Wood
64. 8000–8499 Lang
65. Viborg
66. Danby

67. Bair
68. Ekron
69. 6200–6399 James
70. 8700–9399 Lang
71. Dushore
72. Levering
73. 3300–3599 Wood
74. 9500–9999 Lang
75. 8500–8699 Lang
76. 6400–6499 James
77. 2600–2699 Wood
78. Lott
79. Lycan
80. 6200–6399 James
81. 2700–3299 Wood
82. 5700–6199 James
83. 8000–8499 Lang
84. 4700–4999 James
85. 3300–3599 Wood
86. Dushore
87. Ekron
88. Danby

MEMORY FOR ADDRESSES TEST

TIME: 5 Minutes. 88 Questions.

DIRECTIONS: Mark your answers on the answer sheet in the section headed "MEMORY FOR ADDRESSES TEST." This test will be scored. You are NOT permitted to look at the boxes. Work from memory, as quickly and as accurately as you can. Correct answers are on page 196.

1. 9400–9499 Lang
2. 6200–6399 James
3. Dushore
4. 2700–3299 Wood
5. 3300–3599 Wood
6. 5000–5699 James
7. Viborg
8. 2600–2699 Wood
9. 9500–9999 Lang
10. 5000–5699 James
11. Vanna
12. Levering
13. Lott
14. 1700–2599 Wood
15. 8700–9399 Lang
16. 1300–1699 Wood
17. 6400–6499 James
18. Jeriel
19. Ekron
20. 8000–8499 Lang
21. 8500–8699 Lang
22. 4700–4999 James
23. 9500–9999 Lang
24. 2700–3299 Wood
25. Dushore
26. Bair
27. 9400–9499 Lang
28. 8500–8699 Lang
29. 1700–2599 Wood
30. 6200–6399 James
31. 8000–8499 Lang
32. Lott

33. 5700–6199 James
34. 6400–6499 James
35. Vanna
36. Jeriel
37. 2600–2699 Wood
38. 8700–9399 Lang
39. Viborg
40. Levering
41. 1300–1699 Wood
42. 3300–3599 Wood
43. 5000–5699 James
44. 9500–9999 Lang
45. 4700–4999 James
46. Ekron
47. Danby
48. Lycan
49. 2700–3299 Wood
50. 9400–9499 Lang
51. 4700–4999 James
52. 8500–8699 Lang
53. 1300–1699 Wood
54. 8000–8499 Lang
55. Dushore
56. 1700–2599 Wood
57. Viborg
58. Lott
59. Levering
60. 3300–3599 Wood
61. 9500–9999 Lang
62. 5700–6199 James
63. Ekron
64. Jeriel

65. 9400–9499 Lang
66. 5000–5699 James
67. 2700–3299 Wood
68. 8500–8699 Lang
69. 3300–3599 Wood
70. 6200–6399 James
71. 5000–5699 James
72. Danby
73. Levering
74. Dushore
75. 6400–6499 James
76. 1700–2599 Wood

77. 4700–4999 James
78. Vanna
79. Ekron
80. 1300–1699 Wood
81. 5000–5699 James
82. 8700–9399 Lang
83. 9500–9999 Lang
84. Jeriel
85. Lycan
86. Bair
87. 5700–6199 James
88. 8000–8499 Lang

END OF EXAM

ADDRESS CHECKING ERROR ANALYSIS CHART

Type of Error	Tally	Total Number
Number of addresses which were alike and you incorrectly marked "different"		
Number of addresses which were different and you incorrectly marked "alike"		
Number of addresses in which you missed a difference in NUMBERS		
Number of addresses in which you missed a difference in ABBREVIATIONS		
Number of addresses in which you missed a difference in NAMES		

SELF-EVALUATION CHART

Test	Excellent	Good	Average	Fair	Poor
Address Checking	80–95	65–79	50–64	35–49	1–34
Memory for Addresses	75–88	60–74	45–59	30–44	1–29

CORRECT ANSWERS FOR SEVENTH MODEL EXAM

ADDRESS CHECKING TEST

1. A	13. D	25. A	37. A	49. A	61. A	73. D	85. A
2. D	14. A	26. D	38. D	50. A	62. D	74. D	86. A
3. D	15. D	27. D	39. A	51. D	63. D	75. A	87. D
4. D	16. D	28. A	40. A	52. D	64. A	76. D	88. D
5. A	17. A	29. A	41. A	53. D	65. D	77. A	89. A
6. A	18. D	30. D	42. A	54. D	66. A	78. A	90. A
7. A	19. D	31. A	43. D	55. D	67. D	79. D	91. A
8. D	20. D	32. A	44. A	56. D	68. D	80. D	92. A
9. D	21. D	33. D	45. D	57. D	69. A	81. D	93. D
10. A	22. D	34. A	46. A	58. D	70. D	82. D	94. A
11. A	23. A	35. D	47. D	59. A	71. D	83. D	95. A
12. D	24. D	36. D	48. D	60. D	72. A	84. D	

MEMORY FOR ADDRESSES—PRACTICE I

1. B	12. B	23. A	34. D	45. C	56. E	67. E	78. D
2. A	13. C	24. A	35. A	46. C	57. B	68. A	79. B
3. D	14. D	25. B	36. A	47. B	58. E	69. E	80. D
4. C	15. E	26. B	37. D	48. E	59. B	70. A	81. E
5. A	16. E	27. C	38. E	49. D	60. A	71. C	82. E
6. D	17. C	28. E	39. C	50. B	61. B	72. D	83. A
7. B	18. C	29. E	40. E	51. A	62. D	73. A	84. A
8. C	19. B	30. D	41. A	52. C	63. A	74. D	85. C
9. E	20. E	31. D	42. B	53. D	64. D	75. D	86. B
10. D	21. B	32. C	43. D	54. D	65. C	76. C	87. E
11. D	22. A	33. B	44. A	55. E	66. B	77. A	88. C

MEMORY FOR
ADDRESSES—PRACTICE II

1. A	12. C	23. E	34. D	45. B	56. A	67. A	78. D
2. A	13. B	24. B	35. C	46. E	57. B	68. B	79. E
3. D	14. B	25. A	36. A	47. A	58. C	69. B	80. B
4. A	15. E	26. D	37. E	48. E	59. C	70. E	81. C
5. C	16. C	27. B	38. A	49. A	60. A	71. D	82. B
6. D	17. B	28. D	39. C	50. A	61. B	72. C	83. D
7. E	18. C	29. E	40. A	51. B	62. E	73. A	84. A
8. A	19. B	30. E	41. D	52. C	63. A	74. E	85. B
9. E	20. C	31. B	42. A	53. B	64. E	75. C	86. A
10. D	21. D	32. D	43. C	54. D	65. A	76. A	87. C
11. E	22. A	33. C	44. E	55. E	66. E	77. C	88. B

MEMORY FOR
ADDRESSES—PRACTICE III

1. D	12. D	23. A	34. A	45. C	56. B	67. D	78. A
2. E	13. A	24. B	35. B	46. C	57. A	68. C	79. E
3. A	14. D	25. E	36. C	47. C	58. A	69. A	80. A
4. B	15. E	26. B	37. D	48. B	59. E	70. B	81. B
5. D	16. A	27. E	38. E	49. A	60. D	71. A	82. B
6. A	17. B	28. A	39. A	50. A	61. A	72. C	83. D
7. B	18. C	29. D	40. E	51. B	62. B	73. D	84. E
8. B	19. C	30. B	41. D	52. B	63. C	74. E	85. D
9. C	20. C	31. A	42. B	53. C	64. D	75. A	86. A
10. D	21. D	32. E	43. E	54. E	65. D	76. C	87. C
11. A	22. C	33. D	44. D	55. C	66. E	77. E	88. E

MEMORY FOR ADDRESSES TEST

1. C	12. C	23. E	34. C	45. E	56. A	67. B	78. B
2. A	13. A	24. B	35. B	46. C	57. D	68. A	79. C
3. A	14. A	25. A	36. B	47. E	58. A	69. D	80. C
4. B	15. B	26. D	37. E	48. E	59. C	70. A	81. D
5. D	16. C	27. C	38. B	49. B	60. D	71. D	82. B
6. D	17. C	28. A	39. D	50. C	61. E	72. E	83. E
7. D	18. B	29. A	40. C	51. E	62. B	73. C	84. B
8. E	19. C	30. A	41. C	52. A	63. C	74. A	85. E
9. E	20. D	31. D	42. D	53. C	64. B	75. C	86. D
10. D	21. A	32. A	43. D	54. D	65. C	76. A	87. B
11. B	22. E	33. B	44. E	55. A	66. D	77. E	88. D

ANSWER SHEET FOR EIGHTH MODEL EXAM

ADDRESS CHECKING

1 Ⓐ Ⓓ	20 Ⓐ Ⓓ	39 Ⓐ Ⓓ	58 Ⓐ Ⓓ	77 Ⓐ Ⓓ
2 Ⓐ Ⓓ	21 Ⓐ Ⓓ	40 Ⓐ Ⓓ	59 Ⓐ Ⓓ	78 Ⓐ Ⓓ
3 Ⓐ Ⓓ	22 Ⓐ Ⓓ	41 Ⓐ Ⓓ	60 Ⓐ Ⓓ	79 Ⓐ Ⓓ
4 Ⓐ Ⓓ	23 Ⓐ Ⓓ	42 Ⓐ Ⓓ	61 Ⓐ Ⓓ	80 Ⓐ Ⓓ
5 Ⓐ Ⓓ	24 Ⓐ Ⓓ	43 Ⓐ Ⓓ	62 Ⓐ Ⓓ	81 Ⓐ Ⓓ
6 Ⓐ Ⓓ	25 Ⓐ Ⓓ	44 Ⓐ Ⓓ	63 Ⓐ Ⓓ	82 Ⓐ Ⓓ
7 Ⓐ Ⓓ	26 Ⓐ Ⓓ	45 Ⓐ Ⓓ	64 Ⓐ Ⓓ	83 Ⓐ Ⓓ
8 Ⓐ Ⓓ	27 Ⓐ Ⓓ	46 Ⓐ Ⓓ	65 Ⓐ Ⓓ	84 Ⓐ Ⓓ
9 Ⓐ Ⓓ	28 Ⓐ Ⓓ	47 Ⓐ Ⓓ	66 Ⓐ Ⓓ	85 Ⓐ Ⓓ
10 Ⓐ Ⓓ	29 Ⓐ Ⓓ	48 Ⓐ Ⓓ	67 Ⓐ Ⓓ	86 Ⓐ Ⓓ
11 Ⓐ Ⓓ	30 Ⓐ Ⓓ	49 Ⓐ Ⓓ	68 Ⓐ Ⓓ	87 Ⓐ Ⓓ
12 Ⓐ Ⓓ	31 Ⓐ Ⓓ	50 Ⓐ Ⓓ	69 Ⓐ Ⓓ	88 Ⓐ Ⓓ
13 Ⓐ Ⓓ	32 Ⓐ Ⓓ	51 Ⓐ Ⓓ	70 Ⓐ Ⓓ	89 Ⓐ Ⓓ
14 Ⓐ Ⓓ	33 Ⓐ Ⓓ	52 Ⓐ Ⓓ	71 Ⓐ Ⓓ	90 Ⓐ Ⓓ
15 Ⓐ Ⓓ	34 Ⓐ Ⓓ	53 Ⓐ Ⓓ	72 Ⓐ Ⓓ	91 Ⓐ Ⓓ
16 Ⓐ Ⓓ	35 Ⓐ Ⓓ	54 Ⓐ Ⓓ	73 Ⓐ Ⓓ	92 Ⓐ Ⓓ
17 Ⓐ Ⓓ	36 Ⓐ Ⓓ	55 Ⓐ Ⓓ	74 Ⓐ Ⓓ	93 Ⓐ Ⓓ
18 Ⓐ Ⓓ	37 Ⓐ Ⓓ	56 Ⓐ Ⓓ	75 Ⓐ Ⓓ	94 Ⓐ Ⓓ
19 Ⓐ Ⓓ	38 Ⓐ Ⓓ	57 Ⓐ Ⓓ	76 Ⓐ Ⓓ	95 Ⓐ Ⓓ

MEMORY FOR ADDRESSES

PRACTICE I

1 Ⓐ Ⓑ Ⓒ Ⓓ Ⓔ	23 Ⓐ Ⓑ Ⓒ Ⓓ Ⓔ	45 Ⓐ Ⓑ Ⓒ Ⓓ Ⓔ	67 Ⓐ Ⓑ Ⓒ Ⓓ Ⓔ
2 Ⓐ Ⓑ Ⓒ Ⓓ Ⓔ	24 Ⓐ Ⓑ Ⓒ Ⓓ Ⓔ	46 Ⓐ Ⓑ Ⓒ Ⓓ Ⓔ	68 Ⓐ Ⓑ Ⓒ Ⓓ Ⓔ
3 Ⓐ Ⓑ Ⓒ Ⓓ Ⓔ	25 Ⓐ Ⓑ Ⓒ Ⓓ Ⓔ	47 Ⓐ Ⓑ Ⓒ Ⓓ Ⓔ	69 Ⓐ Ⓑ Ⓒ Ⓕ Ⓔ
4 Ⓐ Ⓑ Ⓒ Ⓓ Ⓔ	26 Ⓐ Ⓑ Ⓒ Ⓓ Ⓔ	48 Ⓐ Ⓑ Ⓒ Ⓓ Ⓔ	70 Ⓐ Ⓑ Ⓒ Ⓓ Ⓔ
5 Ⓐ Ⓑ Ⓒ Ⓓ Ⓔ	27 Ⓐ Ⓑ Ⓒ Ⓓ Ⓔ	49 Ⓐ Ⓑ Ⓒ Ⓓ Ⓔ	71 Ⓐ Ⓑ Ⓒ Ⓓ Ⓔ
6 Ⓐ Ⓑ Ⓒ Ⓓ Ⓔ	28 Ⓐ Ⓑ Ⓒ Ⓓ Ⓔ	50 Ⓐ Ⓑ Ⓒ Ⓓ Ⓔ	72 Ⓐ Ⓑ Ⓒ Ⓓ Ⓔ
7 Ⓐ Ⓑ Ⓒ Ⓓ Ⓔ	29 Ⓐ Ⓑ Ⓒ Ⓓ Ⓔ	51 Ⓐ Ⓑ Ⓒ Ⓓ Ⓔ	73 Ⓐ Ⓑ Ⓒ Ⓓ Ⓔ
8 Ⓐ Ⓑ Ⓒ Ⓓ Ⓔ	30 Ⓐ Ⓑ Ⓒ Ⓓ Ⓔ	52 Ⓐ Ⓑ Ⓒ Ⓓ Ⓔ	74 Ⓐ Ⓑ Ⓒ Ⓓ Ⓔ
9 Ⓐ Ⓑ Ⓒ Ⓓ Ⓔ	31 Ⓐ Ⓑ Ⓒ Ⓓ Ⓔ	53 Ⓐ Ⓑ Ⓒ Ⓓ Ⓔ	75 Ⓐ Ⓑ Ⓒ Ⓓ Ⓔ
10 Ⓐ Ⓑ Ⓒ Ⓓ Ⓔ	32 Ⓐ Ⓑ Ⓒ Ⓓ Ⓔ	54 Ⓐ Ⓑ Ⓒ Ⓓ Ⓔ	76 Ⓐ Ⓑ Ⓒ Ⓓ Ⓔ
11 Ⓐ Ⓑ Ⓒ Ⓓ Ⓔ	33 Ⓐ Ⓑ Ⓒ Ⓓ Ⓔ	55 Ⓐ Ⓑ Ⓒ Ⓓ Ⓔ	77 Ⓐ Ⓑ Ⓒ Ⓓ Ⓔ
12 Ⓐ Ⓑ Ⓒ Ⓓ Ⓔ	34 Ⓐ Ⓑ Ⓒ Ⓓ Ⓔ	56 Ⓐ Ⓑ Ⓒ Ⓓ Ⓔ	78 Ⓐ Ⓑ Ⓒ Ⓓ Ⓔ
13 Ⓐ Ⓑ Ⓒ Ⓓ Ⓔ	35 Ⓐ Ⓑ Ⓒ Ⓓ Ⓔ	57 Ⓐ Ⓑ Ⓒ Ⓓ Ⓔ	79 Ⓐ Ⓑ Ⓒ Ⓓ Ⓔ
14 Ⓐ Ⓑ Ⓒ Ⓓ Ⓔ	36 Ⓐ Ⓑ Ⓒ Ⓓ Ⓔ	58 Ⓐ Ⓑ Ⓒ Ⓓ Ⓔ	80 Ⓐ Ⓑ Ⓒ Ⓓ Ⓔ
15 Ⓐ Ⓑ Ⓒ Ⓓ Ⓔ	37 Ⓐ Ⓑ Ⓒ Ⓓ Ⓔ	59 Ⓐ Ⓑ Ⓒ Ⓓ Ⓔ	81 Ⓐ Ⓑ Ⓒ Ⓓ Ⓔ
16 Ⓐ Ⓑ Ⓒ Ⓓ Ⓔ	38 Ⓐ Ⓑ Ⓒ Ⓓ Ⓔ	60 Ⓐ Ⓑ Ⓒ Ⓓ Ⓔ	82 Ⓐ Ⓑ Ⓒ Ⓓ Ⓔ
17 Ⓐ Ⓑ Ⓒ Ⓓ Ⓔ	39 Ⓐ Ⓑ Ⓒ Ⓓ Ⓔ	61 Ⓐ Ⓑ Ⓒ Ⓓ Ⓔ	83 Ⓐ Ⓑ Ⓒ Ⓓ Ⓔ
18 Ⓐ Ⓑ Ⓒ Ⓓ Ⓔ	40 Ⓐ Ⓑ Ⓒ Ⓓ Ⓔ	62 Ⓐ Ⓑ Ⓒ Ⓓ Ⓔ	84 Ⓐ Ⓑ Ⓒ Ⓓ Ⓔ
19 Ⓐ Ⓑ Ⓒ Ⓓ Ⓔ	41 Ⓐ Ⓑ Ⓒ Ⓓ Ⓔ	63 Ⓐ Ⓑ Ⓒ Ⓓ Ⓔ	85 Ⓐ Ⓑ Ⓒ Ⓓ Ⓔ
20 Ⓐ Ⓑ Ⓒ Ⓓ Ⓔ	42 Ⓐ Ⓑ Ⓒ Ⓓ Ⓔ	64 Ⓐ Ⓑ Ⓒ Ⓓ Ⓔ	86 Ⓐ Ⓑ Ⓒ Ⓓ Ⓔ
21 Ⓐ Ⓑ Ⓒ Ⓓ Ⓔ	43 Ⓐ Ⓑ Ⓒ Ⓓ Ⓔ	65 Ⓐ Ⓑ Ⓒ Ⓓ Ⓔ	87 Ⓐ Ⓑ Ⓒ Ⓓ Ⓔ
22 Ⓐ Ⓑ Ⓒ Ⓓ Ⓔ	44 Ⓐ Ⓑ Ⓒ Ⓓ Ⓔ	66 Ⓐ Ⓑ Ⓒ Ⓓ Ⓔ	88 Ⓐ Ⓑ Ⓒ Ⓓ Ⓔ

PRACTICE II

1 Ⓐ Ⓑ Ⓒ Ⓓ Ⓔ   23 Ⓐ Ⓑ Ⓒ Ⓓ Ⓔ   45 Ⓐ Ⓑ Ⓒ Ⓓ Ⓔ   67 Ⓐ Ⓑ Ⓒ Ⓓ Ⓔ

2 Ⓐ Ⓑ Ⓒ Ⓓ Ⓔ   24 Ⓐ Ⓑ Ⓒ Ⓓ Ⓔ   46 Ⓐ Ⓑ Ⓒ Ⓓ Ⓔ   68 Ⓐ Ⓑ Ⓒ Ⓓ Ⓔ

3 Ⓐ Ⓑ Ⓒ Ⓓ Ⓔ   25 Ⓐ Ⓑ Ⓒ Ⓓ Ⓔ   47 Ⓐ Ⓑ Ⓒ Ⓓ Ⓔ   69 Ⓐ Ⓑ Ⓒ Ⓓ Ⓔ

4 Ⓐ Ⓑ Ⓒ Ⓓ Ⓔ   26 Ⓐ Ⓑ Ⓒ Ⓓ Ⓔ   48 Ⓐ Ⓑ Ⓒ Ⓓ Ⓔ   70 Ⓐ Ⓑ Ⓒ Ⓓ Ⓔ

5 Ⓐ Ⓑ Ⓒ Ⓓ Ⓔ   27 Ⓐ Ⓑ Ⓒ Ⓓ Ⓔ   49 Ⓐ Ⓑ Ⓒ Ⓓ Ⓔ   71 Ⓐ Ⓑ Ⓒ Ⓓ Ⓔ

6 Ⓐ Ⓑ Ⓒ Ⓓ Ⓔ   28 Ⓐ Ⓑ Ⓒ Ⓓ Ⓔ   50 Ⓐ Ⓑ Ⓒ Ⓓ Ⓔ   72 Ⓐ Ⓑ Ⓒ Ⓓ Ⓔ

7 Ⓐ Ⓑ Ⓒ Ⓓ Ⓔ   29 Ⓐ Ⓑ Ⓒ Ⓓ Ⓔ   51 Ⓐ Ⓑ Ⓒ Ⓓ Ⓔ   73 Ⓐ Ⓑ Ⓒ Ⓓ Ⓔ

8 Ⓐ Ⓑ Ⓒ Ⓓ Ⓔ   30 Ⓐ Ⓑ Ⓒ Ⓓ Ⓔ   52 Ⓐ Ⓑ Ⓒ Ⓓ Ⓔ   74 Ⓐ Ⓑ Ⓒ Ⓓ Ⓔ

9 Ⓐ Ⓑ Ⓒ Ⓓ Ⓔ   31 Ⓐ Ⓑ Ⓒ Ⓓ Ⓔ   53 Ⓐ Ⓑ Ⓒ Ⓓ Ⓔ   75 Ⓐ Ⓑ Ⓒ Ⓓ Ⓔ

10 Ⓐ Ⓑ Ⓒ Ⓓ Ⓔ   32 Ⓐ Ⓑ Ⓒ Ⓓ Ⓔ   54 Ⓐ Ⓑ Ⓒ Ⓓ Ⓔ   76 Ⓐ Ⓑ Ⓒ Ⓓ Ⓔ

11 Ⓐ Ⓑ Ⓒ Ⓓ Ⓔ   33 Ⓐ Ⓑ Ⓒ Ⓓ Ⓔ   55 Ⓐ Ⓑ Ⓒ Ⓓ Ⓔ   77 Ⓐ Ⓑ Ⓒ Ⓓ Ⓔ

12 Ⓐ Ⓑ Ⓒ Ⓓ Ⓔ   34 Ⓐ Ⓑ Ⓒ Ⓓ Ⓔ   56 Ⓐ Ⓑ Ⓒ Ⓓ Ⓔ   78 Ⓐ Ⓑ Ⓒ Ⓓ Ⓔ

13 Ⓐ Ⓑ Ⓒ Ⓓ Ⓔ   35 Ⓐ Ⓑ Ⓒ Ⓓ Ⓔ   57 Ⓐ Ⓑ Ⓒ Ⓓ Ⓔ   79 Ⓐ Ⓑ Ⓒ Ⓓ Ⓔ

14 Ⓐ Ⓑ Ⓒ Ⓓ Ⓔ   36 Ⓐ Ⓑ Ⓒ Ⓓ Ⓔ   58 Ⓐ Ⓑ Ⓒ Ⓓ Ⓔ   80 Ⓐ Ⓑ Ⓒ Ⓓ Ⓔ

15 Ⓐ Ⓑ Ⓒ Ⓓ Ⓔ   37 Ⓐ Ⓑ Ⓒ Ⓓ Ⓔ   59 Ⓐ Ⓑ Ⓒ Ⓓ Ⓔ   81 Ⓐ Ⓑ Ⓒ Ⓓ Ⓔ

16 Ⓐ Ⓑ Ⓒ Ⓓ Ⓔ   38 Ⓐ Ⓑ Ⓒ Ⓓ Ⓔ   60 Ⓐ Ⓑ Ⓒ Ⓓ Ⓔ   82 Ⓐ Ⓑ Ⓒ Ⓓ Ⓔ

17 Ⓐ Ⓑ Ⓒ Ⓓ Ⓔ   39 Ⓐ Ⓑ Ⓒ Ⓓ Ⓔ   61 Ⓐ Ⓑ Ⓒ Ⓓ Ⓔ   83 Ⓐ Ⓑ Ⓒ Ⓓ Ⓔ

18 Ⓐ Ⓑ Ⓒ Ⓓ Ⓔ   40 Ⓐ Ⓑ Ⓒ Ⓓ Ⓔ   62 Ⓐ Ⓑ Ⓒ Ⓓ Ⓔ   84 Ⓐ Ⓑ Ⓒ Ⓓ Ⓔ

19 Ⓐ Ⓑ Ⓒ Ⓓ Ⓔ   41 Ⓐ Ⓑ Ⓒ Ⓓ Ⓔ   63 Ⓐ Ⓑ Ⓒ Ⓓ Ⓔ   85 Ⓐ Ⓑ Ⓒ Ⓓ Ⓔ

20 Ⓐ Ⓑ Ⓒ Ⓓ Ⓔ   42 Ⓐ Ⓑ Ⓒ Ⓓ Ⓔ   64 Ⓐ Ⓑ Ⓒ Ⓓ Ⓔ   86 Ⓐ Ⓑ Ⓒ Ⓓ Ⓔ

21 Ⓐ Ⓑ Ⓒ Ⓓ Ⓔ   43 Ⓐ Ⓑ Ⓒ Ⓓ Ⓔ   65 Ⓐ Ⓑ Ⓒ Ⓓ Ⓔ   87 Ⓐ Ⓑ Ⓒ Ⓓ Ⓔ

22 Ⓐ Ⓑ Ⓒ Ⓓ Ⓔ   44 Ⓐ Ⓑ Ⓒ Ⓓ Ⓔ   66 Ⓐ Ⓑ Ⓒ Ⓓ Ⓔ   88 Ⓐ Ⓑ Ⓒ Ⓓ Ⓔ

PRACTICE III

1 Ⓐ Ⓑ Ⓒ Ⓓ Ⓔ   23 Ⓐ Ⓑ Ⓒ Ⓓ Ⓔ   45 Ⓐ Ⓑ Ⓒ Ⓓ Ⓔ   67 Ⓐ Ⓑ Ⓒ Ⓓ Ⓔ

2 Ⓐ Ⓑ Ⓒ Ⓓ Ⓔ   24 Ⓐ Ⓑ Ⓒ Ⓓ Ⓔ   46 Ⓐ Ⓑ Ⓒ Ⓓ Ⓔ   68 Ⓐ Ⓑ Ⓒ Ⓓ Ⓔ

3 Ⓐ Ⓑ Ⓒ Ⓓ Ⓔ   25 Ⓐ Ⓑ Ⓒ Ⓓ Ⓔ   47 Ⓐ Ⓑ Ⓒ Ⓓ Ⓔ   69 Ⓐ Ⓑ Ⓒ Ⓓ Ⓔ

4 Ⓐ Ⓑ Ⓒ Ⓓ Ⓔ   26 Ⓐ Ⓑ Ⓒ Ⓓ Ⓔ   48 Ⓐ Ⓑ Ⓒ Ⓓ Ⓔ   70 Ⓐ Ⓑ Ⓒ Ⓓ Ⓔ

5 Ⓐ Ⓑ Ⓒ Ⓓ Ⓔ   27 Ⓐ Ⓑ Ⓒ Ⓓ Ⓔ   49 Ⓐ Ⓑ Ⓒ Ⓓ Ⓔ   71 Ⓐ Ⓑ Ⓒ Ⓓ Ⓔ

6 Ⓐ Ⓑ Ⓒ Ⓓ Ⓔ   28 Ⓐ Ⓑ Ⓒ Ⓓ Ⓔ   50 Ⓐ Ⓑ Ⓒ Ⓓ Ⓔ   72 Ⓐ Ⓑ Ⓒ Ⓓ Ⓔ

7 Ⓐ Ⓑ Ⓒ Ⓓ Ⓔ   29 Ⓐ Ⓑ Ⓒ Ⓓ Ⓔ   51 Ⓐ Ⓑ Ⓒ Ⓓ Ⓔ   73 Ⓐ Ⓑ Ⓒ Ⓓ Ⓔ

8 Ⓐ Ⓑ Ⓒ Ⓓ Ⓔ   30 Ⓐ Ⓑ Ⓒ Ⓓ Ⓔ   52 Ⓐ Ⓑ Ⓒ Ⓓ Ⓔ   74 Ⓐ Ⓑ Ⓒ Ⓓ Ⓔ

9 Ⓐ Ⓑ Ⓒ Ⓓ Ⓔ   31 Ⓐ Ⓑ Ⓒ Ⓓ Ⓔ   53 Ⓐ Ⓑ Ⓒ Ⓓ Ⓔ   75 Ⓐ Ⓑ Ⓒ Ⓓ Ⓔ

10 Ⓐ Ⓑ Ⓒ Ⓓ Ⓔ   32 Ⓐ Ⓑ Ⓒ Ⓓ Ⓔ   54 Ⓐ Ⓑ Ⓒ Ⓓ Ⓔ   76 Ⓐ Ⓑ Ⓒ Ⓓ Ⓔ

11 Ⓐ Ⓑ Ⓒ Ⓓ Ⓔ   33 Ⓐ Ⓑ Ⓒ Ⓓ Ⓔ   55 Ⓐ Ⓑ Ⓒ Ⓓ Ⓔ   77 Ⓐ Ⓑ Ⓒ Ⓓ Ⓔ

12 Ⓐ Ⓑ Ⓒ Ⓓ Ⓔ   34 Ⓐ Ⓑ Ⓒ Ⓓ Ⓔ   56 Ⓐ Ⓑ Ⓒ Ⓓ Ⓔ   78 Ⓐ Ⓑ Ⓒ Ⓓ Ⓔ

13 Ⓐ Ⓑ Ⓒ Ⓓ Ⓔ   35 Ⓐ Ⓑ Ⓒ Ⓓ Ⓔ   57 Ⓐ Ⓑ Ⓒ Ⓓ Ⓔ   79 Ⓐ Ⓑ Ⓒ Ⓓ Ⓔ

14 Ⓐ Ⓑ Ⓒ Ⓓ Ⓔ   36 Ⓐ Ⓑ Ⓒ Ⓓ Ⓔ   58 Ⓐ Ⓑ Ⓒ Ⓓ Ⓔ   80 Ⓐ Ⓑ Ⓒ Ⓓ Ⓔ

15 Ⓐ Ⓑ Ⓒ Ⓓ Ⓔ   37 Ⓐ Ⓑ Ⓒ Ⓓ Ⓔ   59 Ⓐ Ⓑ Ⓒ Ⓓ Ⓔ   81 Ⓐ Ⓑ Ⓒ Ⓓ Ⓔ

16 Ⓐ Ⓑ Ⓒ Ⓓ Ⓔ   38 Ⓐ Ⓑ Ⓒ Ⓓ Ⓔ   60 Ⓐ Ⓑ Ⓒ Ⓓ Ⓔ   82 Ⓐ Ⓑ Ⓒ Ⓓ Ⓔ

17 Ⓐ Ⓑ Ⓒ Ⓓ Ⓔ   39 Ⓐ Ⓑ Ⓒ Ⓓ Ⓔ   61 Ⓐ Ⓑ Ⓒ Ⓓ Ⓔ   83 Ⓐ Ⓑ Ⓒ Ⓓ Ⓔ

18 Ⓐ Ⓑ Ⓒ Ⓓ Ⓔ   40 Ⓐ Ⓑ Ⓒ Ⓓ Ⓔ   62 Ⓐ Ⓑ Ⓒ Ⓓ Ⓔ   84 Ⓐ Ⓑ Ⓒ Ⓓ Ⓔ

19 Ⓐ Ⓑ Ⓒ Ⓓ Ⓔ   41 Ⓐ Ⓑ Ⓒ Ⓓ Ⓔ   63 Ⓐ Ⓑ Ⓒ Ⓓ Ⓔ   85 Ⓐ Ⓑ Ⓒ Ⓓ Ⓔ

20 Ⓐ Ⓑ Ⓒ Ⓓ Ⓔ   42 Ⓐ Ⓑ Ⓒ Ⓓ Ⓔ   64 Ⓐ Ⓑ Ⓒ Ⓓ Ⓔ   86 Ⓐ Ⓑ Ⓒ Ⓓ Ⓔ

21 Ⓐ Ⓑ Ⓒ Ⓓ Ⓔ   43 Ⓐ Ⓑ Ⓒ Ⓓ Ⓔ   65 Ⓐ Ⓑ Ⓒ Ⓓ Ⓔ   87 Ⓐ Ⓑ Ⓒ Ⓓ Ⓔ

22 Ⓐ Ⓑ Ⓒ Ⓓ Ⓔ   44 Ⓐ Ⓑ Ⓒ Ⓓ Ⓔ   66 Ⓐ Ⓑ Ⓒ Ⓓ Ⓔ   88 Ⓐ Ⓑ Ⓒ Ⓓ Ⓔ

MEMORY FOR ADDRESSES TEST

1 Ⓐ Ⓑ Ⓒ Ⓓ Ⓔ   23 Ⓐ Ⓑ Ⓒ Ⓓ Ⓔ   45 Ⓐ Ⓑ Ⓒ Ⓓ Ⓔ   67 Ⓐ Ⓑ Ⓒ Ⓓ Ⓔ
2 Ⓐ Ⓑ Ⓒ Ⓓ Ⓔ   24 Ⓐ Ⓑ Ⓒ Ⓓ Ⓔ   46 Ⓐ Ⓑ Ⓒ Ⓓ Ⓔ   68 Ⓐ Ⓑ Ⓒ Ⓓ Ⓔ
3 Ⓐ Ⓑ Ⓒ Ⓓ Ⓔ   25 Ⓐ Ⓑ Ⓒ Ⓓ Ⓔ   47 Ⓐ Ⓑ Ⓒ Ⓓ Ⓔ   69 Ⓐ Ⓑ Ⓒ Ⓓ Ⓔ
4 Ⓐ Ⓑ Ⓒ Ⓓ Ⓔ   26 Ⓐ Ⓑ Ⓒ Ⓓ Ⓔ   48 Ⓐ Ⓑ Ⓒ Ⓓ Ⓔ   70 Ⓐ Ⓑ Ⓒ Ⓓ Ⓔ
5 Ⓐ Ⓑ Ⓒ Ⓓ Ⓔ   27 Ⓐ Ⓑ Ⓒ Ⓓ Ⓔ   49 Ⓐ Ⓑ Ⓒ Ⓓ Ⓔ   71 Ⓐ Ⓑ Ⓒ Ⓓ Ⓔ
6 Ⓐ Ⓑ Ⓒ Ⓓ Ⓔ   28 Ⓐ Ⓑ Ⓒ Ⓓ Ⓔ   50 Ⓐ Ⓑ Ⓒ Ⓓ Ⓔ   72 Ⓐ Ⓑ Ⓒ Ⓓ Ⓔ
7 Ⓐ Ⓑ Ⓒ Ⓓ Ⓔ   29 Ⓐ Ⓑ Ⓒ Ⓓ Ⓔ   51 Ⓐ Ⓑ Ⓒ Ⓓ Ⓔ   73 Ⓐ Ⓑ Ⓒ Ⓓ Ⓔ
8 Ⓐ Ⓑ Ⓒ Ⓓ Ⓔ   30 Ⓐ Ⓑ Ⓒ Ⓓ Ⓔ   52 Ⓐ Ⓑ Ⓒ Ⓓ Ⓔ   74 Ⓐ Ⓑ Ⓒ Ⓓ Ⓔ
9 Ⓐ Ⓑ Ⓒ Ⓓ Ⓔ   31 Ⓐ Ⓑ Ⓒ Ⓓ Ⓔ   53 Ⓐ Ⓑ Ⓒ Ⓓ Ⓔ   75 Ⓐ Ⓑ Ⓒ Ⓓ Ⓔ
10 Ⓐ Ⓑ Ⓒ Ⓓ Ⓔ   32 Ⓐ Ⓑ Ⓒ Ⓓ Ⓔ   54 Ⓐ Ⓑ Ⓒ Ⓓ Ⓔ   76 Ⓐ Ⓑ Ⓒ Ⓓ Ⓔ
11 Ⓐ Ⓑ Ⓒ Ⓓ Ⓔ   33 Ⓐ Ⓑ Ⓒ Ⓓ Ⓔ   55 Ⓐ Ⓑ Ⓒ Ⓓ Ⓔ   77 Ⓐ Ⓑ Ⓒ Ⓓ Ⓔ
12 Ⓐ Ⓑ Ⓒ Ⓓ Ⓔ   34 Ⓐ Ⓑ Ⓒ Ⓓ Ⓔ   56 Ⓐ Ⓑ Ⓒ Ⓓ Ⓔ   78 Ⓐ Ⓑ Ⓒ Ⓓ Ⓔ
13 Ⓐ Ⓑ Ⓒ Ⓓ Ⓔ   35 Ⓐ Ⓑ Ⓒ Ⓓ Ⓔ   57 Ⓐ Ⓑ Ⓒ Ⓓ Ⓔ   79 Ⓐ Ⓑ Ⓒ Ⓓ Ⓔ
14 Ⓐ Ⓑ Ⓒ Ⓓ Ⓔ   36 Ⓐ Ⓑ Ⓒ Ⓓ Ⓔ   58 Ⓐ Ⓑ Ⓒ Ⓓ Ⓔ   80 Ⓐ Ⓑ Ⓒ Ⓓ Ⓔ
15 Ⓐ Ⓑ Ⓒ Ⓓ Ⓔ   37 Ⓐ Ⓑ Ⓒ Ⓓ Ⓔ   59 Ⓐ Ⓑ Ⓒ Ⓓ Ⓔ   81 Ⓐ Ⓑ Ⓒ Ⓓ Ⓔ
16 Ⓐ Ⓑ Ⓒ Ⓓ Ⓔ   38 Ⓐ Ⓑ Ⓒ Ⓓ Ⓔ   60 Ⓐ Ⓑ Ⓒ Ⓓ Ⓔ   82 Ⓐ Ⓑ Ⓒ Ⓓ Ⓔ
17 Ⓐ Ⓑ Ⓒ Ⓓ Ⓔ   39 Ⓐ Ⓑ Ⓒ Ⓓ Ⓔ   61 Ⓐ Ⓑ Ⓒ Ⓓ Ⓔ   83 Ⓐ Ⓑ Ⓒ Ⓓ Ⓔ
18 Ⓐ Ⓑ Ⓒ Ⓓ Ⓔ   40 Ⓐ Ⓑ Ⓒ Ⓓ Ⓔ   62 Ⓐ Ⓑ Ⓒ Ⓓ Ⓔ   84 Ⓐ Ⓑ Ⓒ Ⓓ Ⓔ
19 Ⓐ Ⓑ Ⓒ Ⓓ Ⓔ   41 Ⓐ Ⓑ Ⓒ Ⓓ Ⓔ   63 Ⓐ Ⓑ Ⓒ Ⓓ Ⓔ   85 Ⓐ Ⓑ Ⓒ Ⓓ Ⓔ
20 Ⓐ Ⓑ Ⓒ Ⓓ Ⓔ   42 Ⓐ Ⓑ Ⓒ Ⓓ Ⓔ   64 Ⓐ Ⓑ Ⓒ Ⓓ Ⓔ   86 Ⓐ Ⓑ Ⓒ Ⓓ Ⓔ
21 Ⓐ Ⓑ Ⓒ Ⓓ Ⓔ   43 Ⓐ Ⓑ Ⓒ Ⓓ Ⓔ   65 Ⓐ Ⓑ Ⓒ Ⓓ Ⓔ   87 Ⓐ Ⓑ Ⓒ Ⓓ Ⓔ
22 Ⓐ Ⓑ Ⓒ Ⓓ Ⓔ   44 Ⓐ Ⓑ Ⓒ Ⓓ Ⓔ   66 Ⓐ Ⓑ Ⓒ Ⓓ Ⓔ   88 Ⓐ Ⓑ Ⓒ Ⓓ Ⓔ

SCORE SHEET FOR EIGHTH MODEL EXAM

ADDRESS CHECKING TEST

Number Right minus Number Wrong equals   Score

_____ – _____ = _____

MEMORY FOR ADDRESSES TEST

Number Right minus (Number Wrong ÷ 4) equals   Score

_____ – _____ = _____

PROGRESS GRAPH

Blacken the bars for Model Exam 8 to the scores you earned.

Score
95
90
85
80
75
70
65
60
55
50
45
40
35
30
25
20
15
10
5
0

Test Model Exam	AC M Diag.	AC M 1	AC M 2	AC M 3	AC M 4	AC M 5	AC M 6	AC M 7	AC M 8

AC = Address Checking   M = Memory for Addresses

EIGHTH MODEL EXAM

ADDRESS CHECKING TEST

TIME: 6 Minutes. 95 Questions.

DIRECTIONS: For each question, compare the address in the left column with the address in the right column. If the two addresses are ALIKE IN EVERY WAY, blacken space Ⓐ on your answer sheet. If the two addresses are DIFFERENT IN ANY WAY, blacken space Ⓓ on your answer sheet. Correct answers for this test are on page 213.

1	. . . 3684 E Woodlawn Ave	3864 E Woodlawn Ave
2	. . . 1948 Southern Artery	1948 Southern Artery
3	. . . 3852 W 257th St	3852 W 257th St
4	. . . Newfoundland PA 18445	Newfoundland PN 18445
5	. . . 9583 Hillcrest Ave	9583 Hillside Ave
6	. . . 4275 Lake Isle Dr	4725 Lake Isle Dr
7	. . . 735 W Englewood Wy	735 W Englewood Way
8	. . . 5396 Broadhurst Sta	5396 Broadherst Sta
9	. . . Sudbury MA 01776	Sudbury MA 10776
10	. . . 7423 Valedosta Wy	7423 Valedosta Wy
11	. . . 1223 Stephenson Blvd	1223 Stephenson Blvd
12	. . . 4674 Udell Ct	4674 Udell Ct
13	. . . 1584 S 136th Rd	1584 S 136th Rd
14	. . . 9637 Ressique Ln	9637 Ressique Wy
15	. . . 2042 Canopus Hlw	2042 Canopus Hlw
16	. . . 3885 Ettman St	3885 Ettnam St
17	. . . 2136 Buena Vista Ave	2136 Buena Vista Ave
18	. . . Bronx NY 10548	Bronx NY 10548
19	. . . 3012 Quinlan Rd	3012 Quinlan Dr
20	. . . 1811 Barnhart Ave	1811 Barnhardt Ave
21	. . . 4023 Inverness Rd	4023 Inverness Rd
22	. . . Darien CT 06820	Darein CT 06820
23	. . . 4188 Fahnestock Pky	4188 Fahnestock Pky
24	. . . 3684 NE 479th Ave	3684 NE 479th Ave
25	. . . 7287 Haverstraw Hl	7287 Havestraw Hl
26	. . . 2020 Kitchawan Wds	2020 Kitchawan Wds

27 . . . 3965 Valhalla Sta Pl	3695 Valhalla Sta Pl
28 . . . 958 Teatown Blvd	958 Teetown Blvd
29 . . . Allentown PA 18104	Allentown PA 18104
30 . . . 1482 S 15th St	1482 S 15th St
31 . . . 722 Verplanck Rd	7222 Verplanck Rd
32 . . . 1992 Wiccopee Dr	1992 Wicoppee Dr
33 . . . 7374 Oscawana Cor	7374 Oscawana Cors
34 . . . Baltimore MD 21218	Baltimore MD 21218
35 . . . 6116 Belle Haven Rd	6116 Belle Haven Rd
36 . . . 1899 W Boutonville Wy	1899 W Boutonville Wy
37 . . . 1721 W 212th St	1721 W 112th St
38 . . . Great Barrington MA 01230	Great Barrington MA 01230
39 . . . 2071 Dunwoodie Wy	2071 Dunwoodie Wy
40 . . . 4531 Worthington Blvd	4531 Worthington Blvd
41 . . . 7642 Kentucky Ave NE	7642 Kentuckey Ave NE
42 . . . 4328 Manursing Ct	4328 Manursing Ct
43 . . . 7359 Granite Springs Ln	7539 Granite Springs Ln
44 . . . Clifton NJ 07012	Clifton NM 07012
45 . . . 3930 S Tighe Rd	3930 S Tighe Rd
46 . . . 2244 Old Knollwood Rd	2244 Old Knolwood Rd
47 . . . 9642 Christie Pl	9462 Christie Pl
48 . . . 6198 Emmett Burke Gdns	6198 Emmett Burke Gdns
49 . . . Provo UT 84601	Provo UT 84601
50 . . . 1989 S Maple Hl	1989 S Maple Hl
51 . . . 9871 W South St	9871 S West St
52 . . . 4661 Coligni Ave	4661 Coligni Ave
53 . . . 3479 The Farm Rd	3479 The Farm Rd
54 . . . 8160 Banksville Rd	8160 Bankville Rd
55 . . . Providence RI 02912	Providence RI 02912
56 . . . 4691 Manchester Rd	4619 Manchester Rd
57 . . . 6285 Dahlia Dr	6285 Dalhia Dr
58 . . . 5378 Bonnie Brae Ct	5378 Bonnie Brae Ct
59 . . . 5618 Upper Shad Rd	5618 Upper Shag Rd
60 . . . 5653 Beechdale Dr	5653 Beachdale Dr
61 . . . 4557 Whittington Wy	4557 Whittington Wy
62 . . . Franklin Lakes NJ 07417	Franklin Lake NJ 07417
63 . . . 3195 Travis Cors Rd	3159 Travis Cors Rd
64 . . . 4914 S 59th Ave	4914 S 59th Ave
65 . . . 8693 The Crossway	6893 The Crossway
66 . . . 3520 Tanglewylde Rd	352 Tanglewylde Rd
67 . . . 7160 S Larchmont Ave	7160 S Larchmount Ave
68 . . . 1737 Sheridan Pl	1737 Sheridan Pl
69 . . . Los Angeles CA 90049	Los Angeles CA 90049
70 . . . 7242 Farmington Blvd	7242 E Farmington Blvd
71 . . . 9086 Sunrise Hwy	9086 Sunrise Hwy
72 . . . 1601 Hanover Ct	1601 Hanover Ct
73 . . . 5743 S Consulate Dr	5743 N Consulate Dr
74 . . . 2759 E 169th Wy	2795 E 169th Wy
75 . . . Bryn Mawr PA 19010	Bryn Mawr PA 10910
76 . . . 1768 McDougall Dr	1768 McDougall Dr
77 . . . 8163 Roccoco Blvd	8163 Rococco Blvd
78 . . . 2407 Romantic Wy	2407 Romantic Ln

79	. . . 1884 W 476th Rd	1884 W 467th Rd
80	. . . Baltimore MD 21208	Baltimore MD 21208
81	. . . 2392 Vredenburgh Ave	2392 Vredenburgh Ave
82	. . . 1520 Baroque St	1520 Baroque St
83	. . . 5130 Cantito Rd E	5130 Cantito Rd E
84	. . . 232 S Bleecker St	2320 S Bleecker St
85	. . . 5494 Charlotte Pl	5494 Charlotte Pl
86	. . . Fayetteville NY 13066	Fayetteville NY 13606
87	. . . 4325 W Nepera Pl	4325 W Nepera Pl
88	. . . 6740 Pasadena Rd	6740 Pasadena Rd
89	. . . 5881 Hazelton Cir	5881 Hazeltine Cir
90	. . . 3624 N 274th St	3624 N 274th Rd
91	. . . 1515 Bruckner Blvd	1515 Bruckner Blvd
92	. . . 6258 W Cedar St	6258 W Cedar St
93	. . . 9374 Averill Dr	9374 Averill Dr
94	. . . New Haven CT 06520	New Haven Ct 06502
95	. . . 8687 Deerman Ave	9687 Dearman Ave

END OF ADDRESS CHECKING TEST

If you finish this test before time is up, use the remaining time to check over your work. Do not turn the page until you are told to do so.

PRACTICE FOR
MEMORY FOR ADDRESSES TEST

DIRECTIONS: The five boxes below are labelled A, B, C, D, and E. In each box are three sets of number spans with names and two names which are not associated with numbers. In the next THREE MINUTES, you must try to memorize the box location of each name and number span. The position of a name or number span within its box is not important. You need only remember the letter of the box in which the item is to be found. You will use these names and numbers to answer three sets of practice questions which are NOT scored and one actual test which is scored. Correct answers are on pages 213 and 214.

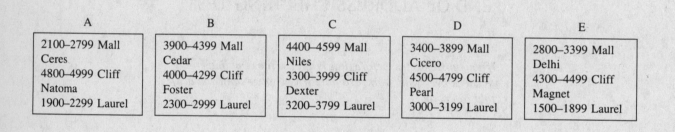

A	B	C	D	E
2100–2799 Mall	3900–4399 Mall	4400–4599 Mall	3400–3899 Mall	2800–3399 Mall
Ceres	Cedar	Niles	Cicero	Delhi
4800–4999 Cliff	4000–4299 Cliff	3300–3999 Cliff	4500–4799 Cliff	4300–4499 Cliff
Natoma	Foster	Dexter	Pearl	Magnet
1900–2299 Laurel	2300–2999 Laurel	3200–3799 Laurel	3000–3199 Laurel	1500–1899 Laurel

PRACTICE I

DIRECTIONS: Use the next THREE MINUTES to mark on your answer sheet the letter of the box in which each item that follows is to be found. Try to mark each item without looking back at the boxes. If, however, you get stuck, you may refer to the boxes during this practice exercise. If you find that you must look at the boxes, try to memorize as you do so. This test is for practice only. It will not be scored.

1. Cedar
2. 4300–4499 Cliff
3. 4400–4599 Mall
4. Natoma
5. 2300–2999 Laurel
6. 4500–4799 Cliff
7. Ceres
8. 3400–3899 Mall
9. Delhi
10. Dexter
11. 1900–2299 Laurel
12. 3300–3999 Cliff

13. Cicero
14. 4000–4299 Cliff
15. 2100–2799 Mall
16. Foster
17. Magnet
18. Ceres
19. 2800–3399 Mall
20. 3200–3799 Laurel
21. 4300–4499 Cliff
22. Pearl
23. 3900–4399 Mall
24. Natoma
25. 4800–4999 Cliff
26. 1500–1899 Laurel
27. Cedar
28. 4400–4599 Mall
29. 4500–4799 Cliff
30. Dexter
31. 3000–3199 Laurel
32. Niles
33. Delhi
34. 3900–4399 Mall
35. Cicero
36. Dexter
37. 4800–4999 Cliff
38. 2300–2999 Laurel
39. 2100–2799 Mall
40. 3300–3999 Cliff
41. 3400–3899 Mall
42. 4300–4499 Cliff
43. Ceres
44. Foster
45. Magnet
46. 3200–3799 Laurel
47. Pearl
48. 1500–1899 Laurel
49. 4500–4799 Cliff
50. 1900–2299 Laurel

51. Niles
52. 3300–3999 Cliff
53. 2800–3399 Mall
54. Cicero
55. Delhi
56. 4000–4299 Cliff
57. Dexter
58. Magnet
59. 3000–3199 Laurel
60. 3900–4399 Mall
61. Natoma
62. 3000–3199 Laurel
63. 4300–4499 Cliff
64. Cedar
65. 4400–4599 Mall
66. 1500–1899 Laurel
67. 4800–4999 Cliff
68. Delhi
69. Pearl
70. 2300–2999 Laurel
71. 4500–4799 Cliff
72. Niles
73. 4000–4299 Cliff
74. 3400–3899 Mall
75. 1900–2299 Laurel
76. 2800–3399 Mall
77. Ceres
78. Magnet
79. Cicero
80. 3200–3799 Laurel
81. 3000–3199 Laurel
82. 3900–4399 Mall
83. Natoma
84. 3300–3999 Cliff
85. 3400–3899 Mall
86. Foster
87. 2100–2799 Mall
88. 4300–4499 Cliff

PRACTICE II

DIRECTIONS: *The next 88 questions constitute another practice exercise. Again, you should mark your answers on your answer sheet. Again, the time limit is THREE MINUTES. This time, however, you must NOT look at the boxes while answering the questions. You must rely on your memory in marking the box location of each item. This practice test will not be scored.*

1. Magnet
2. Niles
3. 3400–3899 Mall
4. 1900–2299 Laurel
5. Cicero
6. Dexter
7. 2300–2999 Laurel
8. 3300–3999 Cliff
9. 3200–3799 Laurel
10. 2100–2799 Mall
11. Pearl
12. 3200–3799 Laurel
13. Ceres
14. 4500–4799 Cliff
15. 3900–4399 Mall
16. Delhi
17. 4300–4499 Cliff
18. 3000–3199 Laurel
19. Ceres
20. Foster
21. Natoma
22. 4400–4599 Mall
23. Cedar
24. 2300–2999 Laurel
25. 1500–1899 Laurel
26. 4000–4299 Cliff
27. Dexter
28. Magnet
29. 3300–3999 Cliff
30. 3400–3899 Mall
31. Niles
32. 2100–2799 Mall
33. 1900–2299 Laurel
34. Cedar
35. Pearl
36. 2800–3399 Mall
37. 4800–4999 Cliff
38. 3900–4399 Mall
39. Foster
40. 3000–3199 Laurel
41. Ceres
42. Niles
43. 3400–3899 Mall
44. Delhi
45. 2300–2999 Laurel
46. 4500–4799 Cliff
47. Dexter
48. Magnet
49. 3300–3999 Cliff
50. Cicero
51. 4300–4499 Cliff
52. 3900–4399 Mall
53. Natoma
54. 3200–3799 Laurel
55. Pearl
56. 4000–4299 Cliff
57. 4500–4799 Cliff
58. 2100–2799 Mall
59. Foster
60. 4400–4599 Mall
61. 4800–4999 Cliff
62. Ceres
63. 2800–3399 Mall
64. 1500–1899 Laurel
65. Natoma
66. 3000–3199 Laurel
67. 4000–4299 Cliff
68. Niles
69. 2300–2999 Laurel
70. Magnet
71. Delhi
72. 4400–4599 Mall
73. Cicero
74. Cedar
75. 2800–3399 Mall
76. 1900–2299 Laurel
77. Dexter
78. Pearl
79. 4300–4499 Cliff
80. 3900–4399 Mall
81. Foster
82. 4800–4999 Cliff
83. Delhi
84. Ceres
85. 1500–1899 Laurel
86. Natoma
87. 2800–3399 Mall
88. Niles

PRACTICE III

DIRECTIONS: The names and addresses are repeated for you in the boxes below. Each name and each number span is in the same box in which you found it in the original set. You will now be allowed FIVE MINUTES to study the locations again. Do your best to memorize the letter of the box in which each item is located. This is your last chance to see the boxes.

A	B	C	D	E
2100–2799 Mall Ceres 4800–4999 Cliff Natoma 1900–2299 Laurel	3900–4399 Mall Cedar 4000–4299 Cliff Foster 2300–2999 Laurel	4400–4599 Mall Niles 3300–3999 Cliff Dexter 3200–3799 Laurel	3400–3899 Mall Cicero 4500–4799 Cliff Pearl 3000–3199 Laurel	2800–3399 Mall Delhi 4300–4499 Cliff Magnet 1500–1899 Laurel

DIRECTIONS: This is your last practice test. Mark the location of each of the 88 items on your answer sheet. You will have FIVE MINUTES to answer these questions. Do NOT look back at the boxes. This practice test will not be scored.

1. 4500–4799 Cliff
2. 3200–3799 Laurel
3. 2100–2799 Mall
4. Foster
5. Cicero
6. 4000–4299 Cliff
7. 1900–2299 Laurel
8. 3400–3899 Mall
9. 1500–1899 Laurel
10. 2800–3399 Mall
11. Natoma
12. Magnet
13. Ceres
14. 4400–4599 Mall
15. 4300–4499 Cliff
16. 3900–4399 Mall
17. 4000–4299 Cliff
18. 4500–4799 Cliff
19. 4400–4599 Mall
20. Pearl
21. Delhi
22. Niles

23. 3900–4399 Mall
24. 3000–3199 Laurel
25. 2300–2999 Laurel
26. Magnet
27. Dexter
28. 3300–3999 Cliff
29. Cedar
30. 1900–2299 Laurel
31. 2100–2799 Mall
32. 4300–4499 Cliff
33. 4000–4299 Cliff
34. 3200–3799 Laurel
35. 4300–4499 Cliff
36. Natoma
37. Foster
38. Pearl
39. 4800–4999 Cliff
40. 2800–3399 Mall
41. 3900–4399 Mall
42. 3200–3799 Laurel
43. Ceres
44. Cedar

45. Delhi
46. 1900–2299 Laurel
47. 4400–4599 Mall
48. Magnet
49. 4500–4799 Cliff
50. 2100–2799 Mall
51. 2800–3399 Mall
52. Cicero
53. 3300–3999 Cliff
54. 3000–3199 Laurel
55. Dexter
56. Niles
57. 4300–4499 Cliff
58. 2300–2999 Laurel
59. 3400–3899 Mall
60. 1500–1899 Laurel
61. 2100–2799 Mall
62. 3300–3999 Cliff
63. 2300–2999 Laurel
64. 4800–4999 Cliff
65. 3200–3799 Laurel
66. 2800–3399 Mall

67. Cicero
68. Magnet
69. Natoma
70. 4800–4999 Cliff
71. 1900–2299 Laurel
72. 3900–4399 Mall
73. 4400–4599 Mall
74. Cedar
75. Ceres
76. 4500–4799 Cliff
77. 1500–1899 Laurel
78. Dexter
79. 4000–4299 Cliff
80. Foster
81. Niles
82. 3000–3199 Laurel
83. 2100–2799 Mall
84. 1500–1899 Laurel
85. Delhi
86. Pearl
87. 4400–4599 Mall
88. 4500–4799 Cliff

MEMORY FOR ADDRESSES TEST

TIME: 5 Minutes. 88 Questions.

DIRECTIONS: Mark your answers on the answer sheet in the section headed "MEMORY FOR ADDRESSES TEST." This test will be scored. You are NOT permitted to look at the boxes. Work from memory, as quickly and as accurately as you can. Correct answers are on page 214.

1. 4800–4999 Cliff
2. 3200–3799 Laurel
3. 3400–3899 Mall
4. 2100–2799 Mall
5. 1500–1899 Laurel
6. Natoma
7. Dexter
8. Delhi
9. 4800–4999 Cliff
10. 4500–4799 Cliff
11. 2800–3399 Mall
12. 2300–2999 Laurel
13. Foster
14. Niles
15. Cicero
16. 1900–2299 Laurel
17. 3300–3999 Cliff
18. 3000–3199 Laurel
19. Magnet
20. Ceres
21. 4400–4599 Mall
22. 3900–4399 Mall
23. 4000–4299 Cliff
24. 3400–3899 Mall
25. 4300–4499 Cliff
26. 1900–2299 Laurel
27. Dexter
28. Foster
29. 3300–3999 Cliff
30. 3200–3799 Laurel
31. 4400–4599 Mall
32. Natoma
33. Cedar
34. Delhi
35. 2800–3399 Mall
36. 4500–4799 Cliff
37. 2300–2999 Laurel
38. 2100–2799 Mall
39. Ceres
40. Magnet
41. 3900–4399 Mall
42. 4000–4299 Cliff
43. 3000–3199 Laurel
44. 4800–4999 Cliff
45. 1500–1899 Laurel
46. Niles
47. 4300–4499 Cliff
48. 2300–2999 Laurel
49. 3300–3999 Cliff
50. 3900–4399 Mall
51. Dexter
52. Cicero
53. Magnet
54. 2100–2799 Mall
55. 3200–3799 Laurel
56. 4500–4799 Cliff
57. 4400–4599 Mall
58. Cedar
59. Pearl
60. Delhi
61. 1900–2299 Laurel
62. 3000–3199 Laurel
63. 2800–3399 Mall
64. 4800–4999 Cliff

65. 1500–1899 Laurel
66. 2800–3399 Mall
67. 4400–4599 Mall
68. 4000–4299 Cliff
69. 3000–3199 Laurel
70. 3400–3899 Mall
71. Pearl
72. Foster
73. Niles
74. Cedar
75. 1900–2299 Laurel
76. 4000–4299 Cliff
77. 2300–2999 Laurel
78. 4800–4999 Cliff
79. 2800–3399 Mall
80. 2100–2799 Mall
81. 1500–1899 Laurel
82. Cicero
83. Natoma
84. Dexter
85. 3200–3799 Laurel
86. 3900–4399 Mall
87. 3300–3999 Cliff
88. 4300–4499 Cliff

END OF EXAM

ADDRESS CHECKING ERROR ANALYSIS CHART

Type of Error	Tally	Total Number
Number of addresses which were alike and you incorrectly marked "different"		
Number of addresses which were different and you incorrectly marked "alike"		
Number of addresses in which you missed a difference in NUMBERS		
Number of addresses in which you missed a difference in ABBREVIA-TIONS		
Number of addresses in which you missed a difference in NAMES		

SELF-EVALUATION CHART

Test	Excellent	Good	Average	Fair	Poor
Address Checking	80–95	65–79	50–64	35–49	1–34
Memory for Addresses	75–88	60–74	45–59	30–44	1–29

CORRECT ANSWERS FOR EIGHTH MODEL EXAM

ADDRESS CHECKING TEST

1. D	13. A	25. D	37. D	49. A	61. A	73. D	85. A
2. A	14. D	26. A	38. A	50. A	62. D	74. D	86. D
3. A	15. A	27. D	39. A	51. D	63. D	75. D	87. A
4. D	16. D	28. D	40. A	52. A	64. A	76. A	88. A
5. D	17. A	29. A	41. D	53. A	65. D	77. D	89. D
6. D	18. A	30. A	42. A	54. D	66. D	78. D	90. D
7. D	19. D	31. D	43. D	55. A	67. D	79. D	91. A
8. D	20. D	32. D	44. D	56. D	68. A	80. A	92. A
9. D	21. A	33. D	45. A	57. D	69. A	81. A	93. A
10. A	22. D	34. A	46. D	58. A	70. D	82. A	94. D
11. A	23. A	35. A	47. D	59. D	71. A	83. A	95. D
12. A	24. A	36. A	48. A	60. D	72. A	84. D	

MEMORY FOR ADDRESSES—PRACTICE I

1. B	12. C	23. B	34. B	45. E	56. B	67. A	78. E
2. E	13. D	24. A	35. D	46. C	57. C	68. E	79. D
3. C	14. B	25. A	36. C	47. D	58. E	69. D	80. C
4. A	15. A	26. E	37. A	48. E	59. D	70. B	81. D
5. B	16. B	27. B	38. B	49. D	60. B	71. D	82. B
6. D	17. E	28. C	39. A	50. A	61. A	72. C	83. A
7. A	18. A	29. D	40. C	51. C	62. D	73. B	84. C
8. D	19. E	30. C	41. D	52. C	63. E	74. D	85. D
9. E	20. C	31. D	42. E	53. E	64. B	75. A	86. B
10. C	21. E	32. C	43. A	54. D	65. C	76. E	87. A
11. A	22. D	33. E	44. B	55. E	66. E	77. A	88. E

MEMORY FOR ADDRESSES—PRACTICE II

1. E	12. C	23. B	34. B	45. B	56. B	67. B	78. D
2. C	13. A	24. B	35. D	46. D	57. D	68. C	79. E
3. D	14. D	25. E	36. E	47. C	58. A	69. B	80. B
4. A	15. B	26. B	37. A	48. E	59. B	70. E	81. B
5. D	16. E	27. C	38. B	49. C	60. C	71. E	82. A
6. C	17. E	28. E	39. B	50. D	61. A	72. C	83. E
7. B	18. D	29. C	40. D	51. E	62. A	73. D	84. A
8. C	19. A	30. D	41. A	52. B	63. E	74. B	85. E
9. C	20. B	31. C	42. C	53. A	64. E	75. E	86. A
10. A	21. A	32. A	43. D	54. C	65. A	76. A	87. E
11. D	22. C	33. A	44. E	55. D	66. D	77. C	88. C

MEMORY FOR ADDRESSES—PRACTICE III

1. D	12. E	23. B	34. C	45. E	56. C	67. D	78. C
2. C	13. A	24. D	35. E	46. A	57. E	68. E	79. B
3. A	14. C	25. B	36. A	47. C	58. B	69. A	80. B
4. B	15. E	26. E	37. B	48. E	59. D	70. A	81. C
5. D	16. B	27. C	38. D	49. D	60. E	71. A	82. D
6. B	17. B	28. C	39. A	50. A	61. A	72. B	83. A
7. A	18. D	29. B	40. E	51. E	62. C	73. C	84. E
8. D	19. C	30. A	41. B	52. D	63. B	74. B	85. E
9. E	20. D	31. A	42. C	53. C	64. A	75. A	86. D
10. E	21. E	32. E	43. A	54. D	65. C	76. D	87. C
11. A	22. C	33. B	44. B	55. C	66. E	77. E	88. D

MEMORY FOR ADDRESSES TEST

1. A	12. B	23. B	34. E	45. E	56. D	67. C	78. A
2. C	13. B	24. D	35. E	46. C	57. C	68. B	79. E
3. D	14. C	25. E	36. D	47. E	58. B	69. D	80. A
4. A	15. D	26. A	37. B	48. B	59. D	70. D	81. E
5. E	16. A	27. C	38. A	49. C	60. E	71. D	82. D
6. A	17. C	28. B	39. A	50. B	61. A	72. B	83. A
7. C	18. D	29. C	40. E	51. C	62. D	73. C	84. C
8. E	19. E	30. C	41. B	52. D	63. E	74. B	85. C
9. A	20. A	31. C	42. B	53. E	64. A	75. A	86. B
10. D	21. C	32. A	43. D	54. A	65. E	76. B	87. C
11. E	22. B	33. B	44. A	55. C	66. E	77. B	88. E

ANSWER SHEET FOR NINTH MODEL EXAM

ADDRESS CHECKING

1 Ⓐ Ⓓ	20 Ⓐ Ⓓ	39 Ⓐ Ⓓ	58 Ⓐ Ⓓ	77 Ⓐ Ⓓ
2 Ⓐ Ⓓ	21 Ⓐ Ⓓ	40 Ⓐ Ⓓ	59 Ⓐ Ⓓ	78 Ⓐ Ⓓ
3 Ⓐ Ⓓ	22 Ⓐ Ⓓ	41 Ⓐ Ⓓ	60 Ⓐ Ⓓ	79 Ⓐ Ⓓ
4 Ⓐ Ⓓ	23 Ⓐ Ⓓ	42 Ⓐ Ⓓ	61 Ⓐ Ⓓ	80 Ⓐ Ⓓ
5 Ⓐ Ⓓ	24 Ⓐ Ⓓ	43 Ⓐ Ⓓ	62 Ⓐ Ⓓ	81 Ⓐ Ⓓ
6 Ⓐ Ⓓ	25 Ⓐ Ⓓ	44 Ⓐ Ⓓ	63 Ⓐ Ⓓ	82 Ⓐ Ⓓ
7 Ⓐ Ⓓ	26 Ⓐ Ⓓ	45 Ⓐ Ⓓ	64 Ⓐ Ⓓ	83 Ⓐ Ⓓ
8 Ⓐ Ⓓ	27 Ⓐ Ⓓ	46 Ⓐ Ⓓ	65 Ⓐ Ⓓ	84 Ⓐ Ⓓ
9 Ⓐ Ⓓ	28 Ⓐ Ⓓ	47 Ⓐ Ⓓ	66 Ⓐ Ⓓ	85 Ⓐ Ⓓ
10 Ⓐ Ⓓ	29 Ⓐ Ⓓ	48 Ⓐ Ⓓ	67 Ⓐ Ⓓ	86 Ⓐ Ⓓ
11 Ⓐ Ⓓ	30 Ⓐ Ⓓ	49 Ⓐ Ⓓ	68 Ⓐ Ⓓ	87 Ⓐ Ⓓ
12 Ⓐ Ⓓ	31 Ⓐ Ⓓ	50 Ⓐ Ⓓ	69 Ⓐ Ⓓ	88 Ⓐ Ⓓ
13 Ⓐ Ⓓ	32 Ⓐ Ⓓ	51 Ⓐ Ⓓ	70 Ⓐ Ⓓ	89 Ⓐ Ⓓ
14 Ⓐ Ⓓ	33 Ⓐ Ⓓ	52 Ⓐ Ⓓ	71 Ⓐ Ⓓ	90 Ⓐ Ⓓ
15 Ⓐ Ⓓ	34 Ⓐ Ⓓ	53 Ⓐ Ⓓ	72 Ⓐ Ⓓ	91 Ⓐ Ⓓ
16 Ⓐ Ⓓ	35 Ⓐ Ⓓ	54 Ⓐ Ⓓ	73 Ⓐ Ⓓ	92 Ⓐ Ⓓ
17 Ⓐ Ⓓ	36 Ⓐ Ⓓ	55 Ⓐ Ⓓ	74 Ⓐ Ⓓ	93 Ⓐ Ⓓ
18 Ⓐ Ⓓ	37 Ⓐ Ⓓ	56 Ⓐ Ⓓ	75 Ⓐ Ⓓ	94 Ⓐ Ⓓ
19 Ⓐ Ⓓ	38 Ⓐ Ⓓ	57 Ⓐ Ⓓ	76 Ⓐ Ⓓ	95 Ⓐ Ⓓ

MEMORY FOR ADDRESSES

PRACTICE I

1 Ⓐ Ⓑ Ⓒ Ⓓ Ⓔ	23 Ⓐ Ⓑ Ⓒ Ⓓ Ⓔ	45 Ⓐ Ⓑ Ⓒ Ⓓ Ⓔ	67 Ⓐ Ⓑ Ⓒ Ⓓ Ⓔ
2 Ⓐ Ⓑ Ⓒ Ⓓ Ⓔ	24 Ⓐ Ⓑ Ⓒ Ⓓ Ⓔ	46 Ⓐ Ⓑ Ⓒ Ⓓ Ⓔ	68 Ⓐ Ⓑ Ⓒ Ⓓ Ⓔ
3 Ⓐ Ⓑ Ⓒ Ⓓ Ⓔ	25 Ⓐ Ⓑ Ⓒ Ⓓ Ⓔ	47 Ⓐ Ⓑ Ⓒ Ⓓ Ⓔ	69 Ⓐ Ⓑ Ⓒ Ⓓ Ⓔ
4 Ⓐ Ⓑ Ⓒ Ⓓ Ⓔ	26 Ⓐ Ⓑ Ⓒ Ⓓ Ⓔ	48 Ⓐ Ⓑ Ⓒ Ⓓ Ⓔ	70 Ⓐ Ⓑ Ⓒ Ⓓ Ⓔ
5 Ⓐ Ⓑ Ⓒ Ⓓ Ⓔ	27 Ⓐ Ⓑ Ⓒ Ⓓ Ⓔ	49 Ⓐ Ⓑ Ⓒ Ⓓ Ⓔ	71 Ⓐ Ⓑ Ⓒ Ⓓ Ⓔ
6 Ⓐ Ⓑ Ⓒ Ⓓ Ⓔ	28 Ⓐ Ⓑ Ⓒ Ⓓ Ⓔ	50 Ⓐ Ⓑ Ⓒ Ⓓ Ⓔ	72 Ⓐ Ⓑ Ⓒ Ⓓ Ⓔ
7 Ⓐ Ⓑ Ⓒ Ⓓ Ⓔ	29 Ⓐ Ⓑ Ⓒ Ⓓ Ⓔ	51 Ⓐ Ⓑ Ⓒ Ⓓ Ⓔ	73 Ⓐ Ⓑ Ⓒ Ⓓ Ⓔ
8 Ⓐ Ⓑ Ⓒ Ⓓ Ⓔ	30 Ⓐ Ⓑ Ⓒ Ⓓ Ⓔ	52 Ⓐ Ⓑ Ⓒ Ⓓ Ⓔ	74 Ⓐ Ⓑ Ⓒ Ⓓ Ⓔ
9 Ⓐ Ⓑ Ⓒ Ⓓ Ⓔ	31 Ⓐ Ⓑ Ⓒ Ⓓ Ⓔ	53 Ⓐ Ⓑ Ⓒ Ⓓ Ⓔ	75 Ⓐ Ⓑ Ⓒ Ⓓ Ⓔ
10 Ⓐ Ⓑ Ⓒ Ⓓ Ⓔ	32 Ⓐ Ⓑ Ⓒ Ⓓ Ⓔ	54 Ⓐ Ⓑ Ⓒ Ⓓ Ⓔ	76 Ⓐ Ⓑ Ⓒ Ⓓ Ⓔ
11 Ⓐ Ⓑ Ⓒ Ⓓ Ⓔ	33 Ⓐ Ⓑ Ⓒ Ⓓ Ⓔ	55 Ⓐ Ⓑ Ⓒ Ⓓ Ⓔ	77 Ⓐ Ⓑ Ⓒ Ⓓ Ⓔ
12 Ⓐ Ⓑ Ⓒ Ⓓ Ⓔ	34 Ⓐ Ⓑ Ⓒ Ⓓ Ⓔ	56 Ⓐ Ⓑ Ⓒ Ⓓ Ⓔ	78 Ⓐ Ⓑ Ⓒ Ⓓ Ⓔ
13 Ⓐ Ⓑ Ⓒ Ⓓ Ⓔ	35 Ⓐ Ⓑ Ⓒ Ⓓ Ⓔ	57 Ⓐ Ⓑ Ⓒ Ⓓ Ⓔ	79 Ⓐ Ⓑ Ⓒ Ⓓ Ⓔ
14 Ⓐ Ⓑ Ⓒ Ⓓ Ⓔ	36 Ⓐ Ⓑ Ⓒ Ⓓ Ⓔ	58 Ⓐ Ⓑ Ⓒ Ⓓ Ⓔ	80 Ⓐ Ⓑ Ⓒ Ⓓ Ⓔ
15 Ⓐ Ⓑ Ⓒ Ⓓ Ⓔ	37 Ⓐ Ⓑ Ⓒ Ⓓ Ⓔ	59 Ⓐ Ⓑ Ⓒ Ⓓ Ⓔ	81 Ⓐ Ⓑ Ⓒ Ⓓ Ⓔ
16 Ⓐ Ⓑ Ⓒ Ⓓ Ⓔ	38 Ⓐ Ⓑ Ⓒ Ⓓ Ⓔ	60 Ⓐ Ⓑ Ⓒ Ⓓ Ⓔ	82 Ⓐ Ⓑ Ⓒ Ⓓ Ⓔ
17 Ⓐ Ⓑ Ⓒ Ⓓ Ⓔ	39 Ⓐ Ⓑ Ⓒ Ⓓ Ⓔ	61 Ⓐ Ⓑ Ⓒ Ⓓ Ⓔ	83 Ⓐ Ⓑ Ⓒ Ⓓ Ⓔ
18 Ⓐ Ⓑ Ⓒ Ⓓ Ⓔ	40 Ⓐ Ⓑ Ⓒ Ⓓ Ⓔ	62 Ⓐ Ⓑ Ⓒ Ⓓ Ⓔ	84 Ⓐ Ⓑ Ⓒ Ⓓ Ⓔ
19 Ⓐ Ⓑ Ⓒ Ⓓ Ⓔ	41 Ⓐ Ⓑ Ⓒ Ⓓ Ⓔ	63 Ⓐ Ⓑ Ⓒ Ⓓ Ⓔ	85 Ⓐ Ⓑ Ⓒ Ⓓ Ⓔ
20 Ⓐ Ⓑ Ⓒ Ⓓ Ⓔ	42 Ⓐ Ⓑ Ⓒ Ⓓ Ⓔ	64 Ⓐ Ⓑ Ⓒ Ⓓ Ⓔ	86 Ⓐ Ⓑ Ⓒ Ⓓ Ⓔ
21 Ⓐ Ⓑ Ⓒ Ⓓ Ⓔ	43 Ⓐ Ⓑ Ⓒ Ⓓ Ⓔ	65 Ⓐ Ⓑ Ⓒ Ⓓ Ⓔ	87 Ⓐ Ⓑ Ⓒ Ⓓ Ⓔ
22 Ⓐ Ⓑ Ⓒ Ⓓ Ⓔ	44 Ⓐ Ⓑ Ⓒ Ⓓ Ⓔ	66 Ⓐ Ⓑ Ⓒ Ⓓ Ⓔ	88 Ⓐ Ⓑ Ⓒ Ⓓ Ⓔ

PRACTICE II

1 Ⓐ Ⓑ Ⓒ Ⓓ Ⓔ   23 Ⓐ Ⓑ Ⓒ Ⓓ Ⓔ   45 Ⓐ Ⓑ Ⓒ Ⓓ Ⓔ   67 Ⓐ Ⓑ Ⓒ Ⓓ Ⓔ
2 Ⓐ Ⓑ Ⓒ Ⓓ Ⓔ   24 Ⓐ Ⓑ Ⓒ Ⓓ Ⓔ   46 Ⓐ Ⓑ Ⓒ Ⓓ Ⓔ   68 Ⓐ Ⓑ Ⓒ Ⓓ Ⓔ
3 Ⓐ Ⓑ Ⓒ Ⓓ Ⓔ   25 Ⓐ Ⓑ Ⓒ Ⓓ Ⓔ   47 Ⓐ Ⓑ Ⓒ Ⓓ Ⓔ   69 Ⓐ Ⓑ Ⓒ Ⓓ Ⓔ
4 Ⓐ Ⓑ Ⓒ Ⓓ Ⓔ   26 Ⓐ Ⓑ Ⓒ Ⓓ Ⓔ   48 Ⓐ Ⓑ Ⓒ Ⓓ Ⓔ   70 Ⓐ Ⓑ Ⓒ Ⓓ Ⓔ
5 Ⓐ Ⓑ Ⓒ Ⓓ Ⓔ   27 Ⓐ Ⓑ Ⓒ Ⓓ Ⓔ   49 Ⓐ Ⓑ Ⓒ Ⓓ Ⓔ   71 Ⓐ Ⓑ Ⓒ Ⓓ Ⓔ
6 Ⓐ Ⓑ Ⓒ Ⓓ Ⓔ   28 Ⓐ Ⓑ Ⓒ Ⓓ Ⓔ   50 Ⓐ Ⓑ Ⓒ Ⓓ Ⓔ   72 Ⓐ Ⓑ Ⓒ Ⓓ Ⓔ
7 Ⓐ Ⓑ Ⓒ Ⓓ Ⓔ   29 Ⓐ Ⓑ Ⓒ Ⓓ Ⓔ   51 Ⓐ Ⓑ Ⓒ Ⓓ Ⓔ   73 Ⓐ Ⓑ Ⓒ Ⓓ Ⓔ
8 Ⓐ Ⓑ Ⓒ Ⓓ Ⓔ   30 Ⓐ Ⓑ Ⓒ Ⓓ Ⓔ   52 Ⓐ Ⓑ Ⓒ Ⓓ Ⓔ   74 Ⓐ Ⓑ Ⓒ Ⓓ Ⓔ
9 Ⓐ Ⓑ Ⓒ Ⓓ Ⓔ   31 Ⓐ Ⓑ Ⓒ Ⓓ Ⓔ   53 Ⓐ Ⓑ Ⓒ Ⓓ Ⓔ   75 Ⓐ Ⓑ Ⓒ Ⓓ Ⓔ
10 Ⓐ Ⓑ Ⓒ Ⓓ Ⓔ   32 Ⓐ Ⓑ Ⓒ Ⓓ Ⓔ   54 Ⓐ Ⓑ Ⓒ Ⓓ Ⓔ   76 Ⓐ Ⓑ Ⓒ Ⓓ Ⓔ
11 Ⓐ Ⓑ Ⓒ Ⓓ Ⓔ   33 Ⓐ Ⓑ Ⓒ Ⓓ Ⓔ   55 Ⓐ Ⓑ Ⓒ Ⓓ Ⓔ   77 Ⓐ Ⓑ Ⓒ Ⓓ Ⓔ
12 Ⓐ Ⓑ Ⓒ Ⓓ Ⓔ   34 Ⓐ Ⓑ Ⓒ Ⓓ Ⓔ   56 Ⓐ Ⓑ Ⓒ Ⓓ Ⓔ   78 Ⓐ Ⓑ Ⓒ Ⓓ Ⓔ
13 Ⓐ Ⓑ Ⓒ Ⓓ Ⓔ   35 Ⓐ Ⓑ Ⓒ Ⓓ Ⓔ   57 Ⓐ Ⓑ Ⓒ Ⓓ Ⓔ   79 Ⓐ Ⓑ Ⓒ Ⓓ Ⓔ
14 Ⓐ Ⓑ Ⓒ Ⓓ Ⓔ   36 Ⓐ Ⓑ Ⓒ Ⓓ Ⓔ   58 Ⓐ Ⓑ Ⓒ Ⓓ Ⓔ   80 Ⓐ Ⓑ Ⓒ Ⓓ Ⓔ
15 Ⓐ Ⓑ Ⓒ Ⓓ Ⓔ   37 Ⓐ Ⓑ Ⓒ Ⓓ Ⓔ   59 Ⓐ Ⓑ Ⓒ Ⓓ Ⓔ   81 Ⓐ Ⓑ Ⓒ Ⓓ Ⓔ
16 Ⓐ Ⓑ Ⓒ Ⓓ Ⓔ   38 Ⓐ Ⓑ Ⓒ Ⓓ Ⓔ   60 Ⓐ Ⓑ Ⓒ Ⓓ Ⓔ   82 Ⓐ Ⓑ Ⓒ Ⓓ Ⓔ
17 Ⓐ Ⓑ Ⓒ Ⓓ Ⓔ   39 Ⓐ Ⓑ Ⓒ Ⓓ Ⓔ   61 Ⓐ Ⓑ Ⓒ Ⓓ Ⓔ   83 Ⓐ Ⓑ Ⓒ Ⓓ Ⓔ
18 Ⓐ Ⓑ Ⓒ Ⓓ Ⓔ   40 Ⓐ Ⓑ Ⓒ Ⓓ Ⓔ   62 Ⓐ Ⓑ Ⓒ Ⓓ Ⓔ   84 Ⓐ Ⓑ Ⓒ Ⓓ Ⓔ
19 Ⓐ Ⓑ Ⓒ Ⓓ Ⓔ   41 Ⓐ Ⓑ Ⓒ Ⓓ Ⓔ   63 Ⓐ Ⓑ Ⓒ Ⓓ Ⓔ   85 Ⓐ Ⓑ Ⓒ Ⓓ Ⓔ
20 Ⓐ Ⓑ Ⓒ Ⓓ Ⓔ   42 Ⓐ Ⓑ Ⓒ Ⓓ Ⓔ   64 Ⓐ Ⓑ Ⓒ Ⓓ Ⓔ   86 Ⓐ Ⓑ Ⓒ Ⓓ Ⓔ
21 Ⓐ Ⓑ Ⓒ Ⓓ Ⓔ   43 Ⓐ Ⓑ Ⓒ Ⓓ Ⓔ   65 Ⓐ Ⓑ Ⓒ Ⓓ Ⓔ   87 Ⓐ Ⓑ Ⓒ Ⓓ Ⓔ
22 Ⓐ Ⓑ Ⓒ Ⓓ Ⓔ   44 Ⓐ Ⓑ Ⓒ Ⓓ Ⓔ   66 Ⓐ Ⓑ Ⓒ Ⓓ Ⓔ   88 Ⓐ Ⓑ Ⓒ Ⓓ Ⓔ

PRACTICE III

1 Ⓐ Ⓑ Ⓒ Ⓓ Ⓔ   23 Ⓐ Ⓑ Ⓒ Ⓓ Ⓔ   45 Ⓐ Ⓑ Ⓒ Ⓓ Ⓔ   67 Ⓐ Ⓑ Ⓒ Ⓓ Ⓔ

2 Ⓐ Ⓑ Ⓒ Ⓓ Ⓔ   24 Ⓐ Ⓑ Ⓒ Ⓓ Ⓔ   46 Ⓐ Ⓑ Ⓒ Ⓓ Ⓔ   68 Ⓐ Ⓑ Ⓒ Ⓓ Ⓔ

3 Ⓐ Ⓑ Ⓒ Ⓓ Ⓔ   25 Ⓐ Ⓑ Ⓒ Ⓓ Ⓔ   47 Ⓐ Ⓑ Ⓒ Ⓓ Ⓔ   69 Ⓐ Ⓑ Ⓒ Ⓓ Ⓔ

4 Ⓐ Ⓑ Ⓒ Ⓓ Ⓔ   26 Ⓐ Ⓑ Ⓒ Ⓓ Ⓔ   48 Ⓐ Ⓑ Ⓒ Ⓓ Ⓔ   70 Ⓐ Ⓑ Ⓒ Ⓓ Ⓔ

5 Ⓐ Ⓑ Ⓒ Ⓓ Ⓔ   27 Ⓐ Ⓑ Ⓒ Ⓓ Ⓔ   49 Ⓐ Ⓑ Ⓒ Ⓓ Ⓔ   71 Ⓐ Ⓑ Ⓒ Ⓓ Ⓔ

6 Ⓐ Ⓑ Ⓒ Ⓓ Ⓔ   28 Ⓐ Ⓑ Ⓒ Ⓓ Ⓔ   50 Ⓐ Ⓑ Ⓒ Ⓓ Ⓔ   72 Ⓐ Ⓑ Ⓒ Ⓓ Ⓔ

7 Ⓐ Ⓑ Ⓒ Ⓓ Ⓔ   29 Ⓐ Ⓑ Ⓒ Ⓓ Ⓔ   51 Ⓐ Ⓑ Ⓒ Ⓓ Ⓔ   73 Ⓐ Ⓑ Ⓒ Ⓓ Ⓔ

8 Ⓐ Ⓑ Ⓒ Ⓓ Ⓔ   30 Ⓐ Ⓑ Ⓒ Ⓓ Ⓔ   52 Ⓐ Ⓑ Ⓒ Ⓓ Ⓔ   74 Ⓐ Ⓑ Ⓒ Ⓓ Ⓔ

9 Ⓐ Ⓑ Ⓒ Ⓓ Ⓔ   31 Ⓐ Ⓑ Ⓒ Ⓓ Ⓔ   53 Ⓐ Ⓑ Ⓒ Ⓓ Ⓔ   75 Ⓐ Ⓑ Ⓒ Ⓓ Ⓔ

10 Ⓐ Ⓑ Ⓒ Ⓓ Ⓔ   32 Ⓐ Ⓑ Ⓒ Ⓓ Ⓔ   54 Ⓐ Ⓑ Ⓒ Ⓓ Ⓔ   76 Ⓐ Ⓑ Ⓒ Ⓓ Ⓔ

11 Ⓐ Ⓑ Ⓒ Ⓓ Ⓔ   33 Ⓐ Ⓑ Ⓒ Ⓓ Ⓔ   55 Ⓐ Ⓑ Ⓒ Ⓓ Ⓔ   77 Ⓐ Ⓑ Ⓒ Ⓓ Ⓔ

12 Ⓐ Ⓑ Ⓒ Ⓓ Ⓔ   34 Ⓐ Ⓑ Ⓒ Ⓓ Ⓔ   56 Ⓐ Ⓑ Ⓒ Ⓓ Ⓔ   78 Ⓐ Ⓑ Ⓒ Ⓓ Ⓔ

13 Ⓐ Ⓑ Ⓒ Ⓓ Ⓔ   35 Ⓐ Ⓑ Ⓒ Ⓓ Ⓔ   57 Ⓐ Ⓑ Ⓒ Ⓓ Ⓔ   79 Ⓐ Ⓑ Ⓒ Ⓓ Ⓔ

14 Ⓐ Ⓑ Ⓒ Ⓓ Ⓔ   36 Ⓐ Ⓑ Ⓒ Ⓓ Ⓔ   58 Ⓐ Ⓑ Ⓒ Ⓓ Ⓔ   80 Ⓐ Ⓑ Ⓒ Ⓓ Ⓔ

15 Ⓐ Ⓑ Ⓒ Ⓓ Ⓔ   37 Ⓐ Ⓑ Ⓒ Ⓓ Ⓔ   59 Ⓐ Ⓑ Ⓒ Ⓓ Ⓔ   81 Ⓐ Ⓑ Ⓒ Ⓓ Ⓔ

16 Ⓐ Ⓑ Ⓒ Ⓓ Ⓔ   38 Ⓐ Ⓑ Ⓒ Ⓓ Ⓔ   60 Ⓐ Ⓑ Ⓒ Ⓓ Ⓔ   82 Ⓐ Ⓑ Ⓒ Ⓓ Ⓔ

17 Ⓐ Ⓑ Ⓒ Ⓓ Ⓔ   39 Ⓐ Ⓑ Ⓒ Ⓓ Ⓔ   61 Ⓐ Ⓑ Ⓒ Ⓓ Ⓔ   83 Ⓐ Ⓑ Ⓒ Ⓓ Ⓔ

18 Ⓐ Ⓑ Ⓒ Ⓓ Ⓔ   40 Ⓐ Ⓑ Ⓒ Ⓓ Ⓔ   62 Ⓐ Ⓑ Ⓒ Ⓓ Ⓔ   84 Ⓐ Ⓑ Ⓒ Ⓓ Ⓔ

19 Ⓐ Ⓑ Ⓒ Ⓓ Ⓔ   41 Ⓐ Ⓑ Ⓒ Ⓓ Ⓔ   63 Ⓐ Ⓑ Ⓒ Ⓓ Ⓔ   85 Ⓐ Ⓑ Ⓒ Ⓓ Ⓔ

20 Ⓐ Ⓑ Ⓒ Ⓓ Ⓔ   42 Ⓐ Ⓑ Ⓒ Ⓓ Ⓔ   64 Ⓐ Ⓑ Ⓒ Ⓓ Ⓔ   86 Ⓐ Ⓑ Ⓒ Ⓓ Ⓔ

21 Ⓐ Ⓑ Ⓒ Ⓓ Ⓔ   43 Ⓐ Ⓑ Ⓒ Ⓓ Ⓔ   65 Ⓐ Ⓑ Ⓒ Ⓓ Ⓔ   87 Ⓐ Ⓑ Ⓒ Ⓓ Ⓔ

22 Ⓐ Ⓑ Ⓒ Ⓓ Ⓔ   44 Ⓐ Ⓑ Ⓒ Ⓓ Ⓔ   66 Ⓐ Ⓑ Ⓒ Ⓓ Ⓔ   88 Ⓐ Ⓑ Ⓒ Ⓓ Ⓔ

MEMORY FOR ADDRESSES TEST

1 Ⓐ Ⓑ Ⓒ Ⓓ Ⓔ	23 Ⓐ Ⓑ Ⓒ Ⓓ Ⓔ	45 Ⓐ Ⓑ Ⓒ Ⓓ Ⓔ	67 Ⓐ Ⓑ Ⓒ Ⓓ Ⓔ
2 Ⓐ Ⓑ Ⓒ Ⓓ Ⓔ	24 Ⓐ Ⓑ Ⓒ Ⓓ Ⓔ	46 Ⓐ Ⓑ Ⓒ Ⓓ Ⓔ	68 Ⓐ Ⓑ Ⓒ Ⓓ Ⓔ
3 Ⓐ Ⓑ Ⓒ Ⓓ Ⓔ	25 Ⓐ Ⓑ Ⓒ Ⓓ Ⓔ	47 Ⓐ Ⓑ Ⓒ Ⓓ Ⓔ	69 Ⓐ Ⓑ Ⓒ Ⓓ Ⓔ
4 Ⓐ Ⓑ Ⓒ Ⓓ Ⓔ	26 Ⓐ Ⓑ Ⓒ Ⓓ Ⓔ	48 Ⓐ Ⓑ Ⓒ Ⓓ Ⓔ	70 Ⓐ Ⓑ Ⓒ Ⓓ Ⓔ
5 Ⓐ Ⓑ Ⓒ Ⓓ Ⓔ	27 Ⓐ Ⓑ Ⓒ Ⓓ Ⓔ	49 Ⓐ Ⓑ Ⓒ Ⓓ Ⓔ	71 Ⓐ Ⓑ Ⓒ Ⓓ Ⓔ
6 Ⓐ Ⓑ Ⓒ Ⓓ Ⓔ	28 Ⓐ Ⓑ Ⓒ Ⓓ Ⓔ	50 Ⓐ Ⓑ Ⓒ Ⓓ Ⓔ	72 Ⓐ Ⓑ Ⓒ Ⓓ Ⓔ
7 Ⓐ Ⓑ Ⓒ Ⓓ Ⓔ	29 Ⓐ Ⓑ Ⓒ Ⓓ Ⓔ	51 Ⓐ Ⓑ Ⓒ Ⓓ Ⓔ	73 Ⓐ Ⓑ Ⓒ Ⓓ Ⓔ
8 Ⓐ Ⓑ Ⓒ Ⓓ Ⓔ	30 Ⓐ Ⓑ Ⓒ Ⓓ Ⓔ	52 Ⓐ Ⓑ Ⓒ Ⓓ Ⓔ	74 Ⓐ Ⓑ Ⓒ Ⓓ Ⓔ
9 Ⓐ Ⓑ Ⓒ Ⓓ Ⓔ	31 Ⓐ Ⓑ Ⓒ Ⓓ Ⓔ	53 Ⓐ Ⓑ Ⓒ Ⓓ Ⓔ	75 Ⓐ Ⓑ Ⓒ Ⓓ Ⓔ
10 Ⓐ Ⓑ Ⓒ Ⓓ Ⓔ	32 Ⓐ Ⓑ Ⓒ Ⓓ Ⓔ	54 Ⓐ Ⓑ Ⓒ Ⓓ Ⓔ	76 Ⓐ Ⓑ Ⓒ Ⓓ Ⓔ
11 Ⓐ Ⓑ Ⓒ Ⓓ Ⓔ	33 Ⓐ Ⓑ Ⓒ Ⓓ Ⓔ	55 Ⓐ Ⓑ Ⓒ Ⓓ Ⓔ	77 Ⓐ Ⓑ Ⓒ Ⓓ Ⓔ
12 Ⓐ Ⓑ Ⓒ Ⓓ Ⓔ	34 Ⓐ Ⓑ Ⓒ Ⓓ Ⓔ	56 Ⓐ Ⓑ Ⓒ Ⓓ Ⓔ	78 Ⓐ Ⓑ Ⓒ Ⓓ Ⓔ
13 Ⓐ Ⓑ Ⓒ Ⓓ Ⓔ	35 Ⓐ Ⓑ Ⓒ Ⓓ Ⓔ	57 Ⓐ Ⓑ Ⓒ Ⓓ Ⓔ	79 Ⓐ Ⓑ Ⓒ Ⓓ Ⓔ
14 Ⓐ Ⓑ Ⓒ Ⓓ Ⓔ	36 Ⓐ Ⓑ Ⓒ Ⓓ Ⓔ	58 Ⓐ Ⓑ Ⓒ Ⓓ Ⓔ	80 Ⓐ Ⓑ Ⓒ Ⓓ Ⓔ
15 Ⓐ Ⓑ Ⓒ Ⓓ Ⓔ	37 Ⓐ Ⓑ Ⓒ Ⓓ Ⓔ	59 Ⓐ Ⓑ Ⓒ Ⓓ Ⓔ	81 Ⓐ Ⓑ Ⓒ Ⓓ Ⓔ
16 Ⓐ Ⓑ Ⓒ Ⓓ Ⓔ	38 Ⓐ Ⓑ Ⓒ Ⓓ Ⓔ	60 Ⓐ Ⓑ Ⓒ Ⓓ Ⓔ	82 Ⓐ Ⓑ Ⓒ Ⓓ Ⓔ
17 Ⓐ Ⓑ Ⓒ Ⓓ Ⓔ	39 Ⓐ Ⓑ Ⓒ Ⓓ Ⓔ	61 Ⓐ Ⓑ Ⓒ Ⓓ Ⓔ	83 Ⓐ Ⓑ Ⓒ Ⓓ Ⓔ
18 Ⓐ Ⓑ Ⓒ Ⓓ Ⓔ	40 Ⓐ Ⓑ Ⓒ Ⓓ Ⓔ	62 Ⓐ Ⓑ Ⓒ Ⓓ Ⓔ	84 Ⓐ Ⓑ Ⓒ Ⓓ Ⓔ
19 Ⓐ Ⓑ Ⓒ Ⓓ Ⓔ	41 Ⓐ Ⓑ Ⓒ Ⓓ Ⓔ	63 Ⓐ Ⓑ Ⓒ Ⓓ Ⓔ	85 Ⓐ Ⓑ Ⓒ Ⓓ Ⓔ
20 Ⓐ Ⓑ Ⓒ Ⓓ Ⓔ	42 Ⓐ Ⓑ Ⓒ Ⓓ Ⓔ	64 Ⓐ Ⓑ Ⓒ Ⓓ Ⓔ	86 Ⓐ Ⓑ Ⓒ Ⓓ Ⓔ
21 Ⓐ Ⓑ Ⓒ Ⓓ Ⓔ	43 Ⓐ Ⓑ Ⓒ Ⓓ Ⓔ	65 Ⓐ Ⓑ Ⓒ Ⓓ Ⓔ	87 Ⓐ Ⓑ Ⓒ Ⓓ Ⓔ
22 Ⓐ Ⓑ Ⓒ Ⓓ Ⓔ	44 Ⓐ Ⓑ Ⓒ Ⓓ Ⓔ	66 Ⓐ Ⓑ Ⓒ Ⓓ Ⓔ	88 Ⓐ Ⓑ Ⓒ Ⓓ Ⓔ

SCORE SHEET FOR NINTH MODEL EXAM

ADDRESS CHECKING TEST

Number Right minus Number Wrong equals   Score

—————————   –   —————————   =   —————————

MEMORY FOR ADDRESSES TEST

Number Right minus (Number Wrong ÷ 4) equals   Score

—————————   –   ———————————————   =   —————————

PROGRESS GRAPH

Blacken the bars for Model Exam 9 to the scores you earned.

Score										
95										
90										
85										
80										
75										
70										
65										
60										
55										
50										
45										
40										
35										
30										
25										
20										
15										
10										
5										
0										
Test	AC M	AC M	AC M	AC M	AC M	AC M	AC M	AC M	AC M	AC M
Model Exam	Diag.	1	2	3	4	5	6	7	8	9

AC = Address Checking   M = Memory for Addresses

NINTH MODEL EXAM

ADDRESS CHECKING TEST

TIME: 6 Minutes. 95 Questions.

DIRECTIONS: For each question, compare the address in the left column with the address in the right column. If the two addresses are ALIKE IN EVERY WAY, blacken space Ⓐ on your answer sheet. If the two addresses are DIF-FERENT IN ANY WAY, blacken space Ⓓ on your answer sheet. Correct answers for this test are on page 231.

1 . . .	1683 S 173rd St	1683 S 173rd St
2 . . .	8387 Michigan Ave NE	8387 Michigan Ave NE
3 . . .	3784 VanMeter Fnwy	3748 VanMeter Fnwy
4 . . .	Upper Montclair NJ 07043	Upper Montclaire NJ 07043
5 . . .	9506 Shady Ln	9605 Shady Ln
6 . . .	4590 W 65th Rd	4950 W 65th Rd
7 . . .	8574 Lansdowne Pl	8574 Landsdowne Pl
8 . . .	Hanover NH 03755	Hanover NH 03755
9 . . .	842 Conshohocken Wy	842 Conshohocken Wy
10 . . .	1486 NW 468th St	1486 NW 486th St
11 . . .	8472 Adrienne Pl	8472 Adrienne Pl
12 . . .	7346 Saxon Woods Rd	7346 Saxon Woods Rd
13 . . .	Washington DC 20016	Washington DC 20016
14 . . .	1221 Sassafras Ln	1221 Sasaffras Ln
15 . . .	3183 Plateau Cir E	3183 Plateau Cir E
16 . . .	5301 N Yerkes Rd	5310 N Yerkes Rd
17 . . .	4191 W Wildway	4191 W Wildeway
18 . . .	Amherst MA 01002	Amherst ME 01002
19 . . .	9499 Yellowstone Blvd	949 Yellowstone Blvd
20 . . .	3508 Mildred Pky	3508 Mildred Pkwy
21 . . .	3273 Greenridge Ave	3273 Greenridge Ave
22 . . .	3286 Toronto Tpke	2386 Toronto Tpke
23 . . .	Tempe AZ 85281	Tempe AZ 85281
24 . . .	2389 Buffington Pl	2389 Buffington Pl
25 . . .	9097 E Scenic Cir	9097 E Scenic Cir
26 . . .	5387 Delancey St	5387 Delaney St

27 . . .	4784 Lounsbury Rd Ext	4748 Lounsbury Rd Ext
28 . . .	1045 Nautilus Ln	1045 Nautilus Ln
29 . . .	Fayetteville AR 72701	Fayetteville AR 72701
30 . . .	3486 W 147th St	3468 W 147th St
31 . . .	9715 Corporate Pk Dr	9715 Corporate Pk Rd
32 . . .	2861 Rutledge Rd	2861 Rutledge Rd
33 . . .	3158 Willoughby Ave	3158 Willowghby Ave
34 . . .	3207 Poplar Rdg	3207 Popular Rdg
35 . . .	Yellow Springs OH 45387	Yellow Springs OH 45378
36 . . .	4707 Copper Beech Cir	4707 Copper Beech Cir
37 . . .	8806 LeCount Blvd	806 LeCount Blvd
38 . . .	1912 Pleasantville Rd	1912 Pleasantville Rd
39 . . .	4856 Chichester Ave	4856 Chichester Ave
40 . . .	Auburn AL 36830	Auburn AL 38630
41 . . .	5475 Meeting House Rd	5475 Meeting House Rd
42 . . .	6121 Fieldstone Dr	6121 Fieldston Dr
43 . . .	5725 Mt Joy Plz	5725 Mt Joy Plz
44 . . .	3697 Anderson Ave	3697 Amberson Ave
45 . . .	6000 Manhattan Ave	6000 Manhatten Ave
46 . . .	Lewiston ME 04240	Lewiston ME 04240
47 . . .	4597 County Center Rd	4597 County Centre Rd
48 . . .	2868 W 153rd Rd	2868 W 153rd Dr
49 . . .	675 Constantinian Pky	675 Constantinian Pky
50 . . .	7343 Sweetfield Cir	7343 Sweetville Cir
51 . . .	4584 Sun Valley Dr	4584 Sun Valley Dr
52 . . .	Baylor TX 76706	Baylor TX 76076
53 . . .	4562 Wixon Pond Rd	5462 Wixon Pond Rd
54 . . .	2820 Dirubbo Dr	2820 Dirubbo Dr
55 . . .	5238 N State Rd	5238 N State Rd
56 . . .	6248 W Jezebel Wy	6248 W Jezebel Wy
57 . . .	1020 Luise Rd	1020 Luisa Rd
58 . . .	Tucson AZ 85721	Tuscon AZ 85721
59 . . .	4825 S 297th Ave	4825 S 297th Ave
60 . . .	1787 Laundry Ln	1787 Laundry Ln
61 . . .	3610 Curry Ct	3601 Curry Ct
62 . . .	2464 Petersburg Blvd	2464 Petersberg Blvd
63 . . .	Bennington VT 05201	Bennington VT 05201
64 . . .	743 Hickory Kingdom Rd	734 Hickory Kingdom Rd
65 . . .	6817 Bellew Rd	6817 Bellew St
66 . . .	4179 Ellendale Ave	4179 Ellendale Ave
67 . . .	4873 N 159th St	4873 N 159th St
68 . . .	2346 Fifth Ave	2346 Firth Ave
69 . . .	Beloit WI 53511	Beliot WI 53511
70 . . .	8003 Lovell Dr	803 Lovell Dr
71 . . .	2569 LaBarranca Apts	2569 LaBarranca Apts
72 . . .	9283 Shadow Ln	9283 Shadowy Ln
73 . . .	8372 N Scarsdale Rd	8372 N Scarsdale Ave
74 . . .	2070 Cohawney Rd	2070 Cohawney Rd
75 . . .	Chestnut Hill MA 02167	Chestnut Hill MA 02167
76 . . .	9372 W Coyle Pl	9732 W Coyle Pl
77 . . .	3083 Slick Shore Dr	3038 Slick Shore Dr
78 . . .	7666 Morsmere Rd	7666 Morsmere Rd

79 . . .	8715 Cardinal Ln	8715 Cardinal Ln
80 . . .	Brunswick ME 04011	Brunswick ME 04011
81 . . .	8643 Dubrovnik Ct	8463 Dubrovnik Ct
82 . . .	1781 W 184th St	1781 W 84th St
83 . . .	5656 Marquardt Ave	5656 Marquardt Ave
84 . . .	707 California Rdg	7077 California Rdg
85 . . .	Bowling Green OH 43403	Bowling Green OH 43403
86 . . .	7285 Madurodam St	7285 Madurodam Pl
87 . . .	9375 W Auditorium Wy	9375 S Auditorium Wy
88 . . .	7315 Queensland Ct	7315 Queenland Ct
89 . . .	9004 Lord Kitchener Blvd	9004 Lord Kitchener Blvd
90 . . .	6589 Arkansas Ave SW	6859 Arkansas Ave SW
91 . . .	Waltham MA 02154	Waltham MA 02154
92 . . .	4681 Torrington CT	4681 Torrington Ct
93 . . .	3846 W Princeton Blvd	3846 W Princeton Blvd
94 . . .	4114 Oneida St	4114 Onieda St
95 . . .	Lewisburg PA 19010	Lewisburg PA 19010

END OF ADDRESS CHECKING TEST

*If you finish this test before time is up, use the remaining time
to check over your work. Do not turn the page until you are
told to do so.*

PRACTICE FOR
MEMORY FOR ADDRESSES TEST

DIRECTIONS: The five boxes below are labelled A, B, C, D, and E. In each box are three sets of number spans with names and two names which are not associated with numbers. In the next THREE MINUTES, you must try to memorize the box location of each name and number span. The position of a name or number span within its box is not important. You need only remember the letter of the box in which the item is to be found. You will use these names and numbers to answer three sets of practice questions which are NOT scored and one actual test which is scored. Correct answers are on pages 231 and 232.

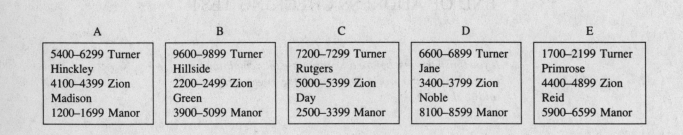

A	B	C	D	E
5400–6299 Turner	9600–9899 Turner	7200–7299 Turner	6600–6899 Turner	1700–2199 Turner
Hinckley	Hillside	Rutgers	Jane	Primrose
4100–4399 Zion	2200–2499 Zion	5000–5399 Zion	3400–3799 Zion	4400–4899 Zion
Madison	Green	Day	Noble	Reid
1200–1699 Manor	3900–5099 Manor	2500–3399 Manor	8100–8599 Manor	5900–6599 Manor

PRACTICE I

DIRECTIONS: Use the next THREE MINUTES to mark on your answer sheet the letter of the box in which each item that follows is to be found. Try to mark each item without looking back at the boxes. If, however, you get stuck, you may refer to the boxes during this practice exercise. If you find that you must look at the boxes, try to memorize as you do so. This test is for practice only. It will not be scored.

1. 2500–3399 Manor
2. 4400–4899 Zion
3. 6600–6899 Turner
4. 5400–6299 Turner
5. Hillside
6. Rutgers
7. Primrose
8. 1200–1699 Manor
9. 2200–2499 Zion
10. 5000–5399 Zion
11. 1700–2199 Turner
12. 3900–5099 Manor

13. Day
14. Hinckley
15. Jane
16. 7200–7299 Turner
17. 2500–3399 Manor
18. 5900–6599 Manor
19. Madison
20. Noble
21. 9600–9899 Turner
22. 3400–3799 Zion
23. Reid
24. 4400–4899 Zion
25. Primrose
26. 9600–9899 Turner
27. 2500–3399 Manor
28. 3400–3799 Zion
29. 1200–1699 Manor
30. 5400–6299 Turner
31. 8100–8599 Manor
32. 4400–4899 Zion
33. Madison
34. Primose
35. Reid
36. 1700–2199 Turner
37. 2200–2499 Zion
38. 2500–3399 Manor
39. 1200–1699 Manor
40. 6600–6899 Turner
41. 3400–3799 Zion
42. Hillside
43. Rutgers
44. Hinckley
45. 9600–9899 Turner
46. 5000–5399 Zion
47. 3900–5099 Manor
48. 7200–7299 Turner
49. Green
50. Day

51. Noble
52. 5900–6599 Manor
53. 4400–4899 Zion
54. Jane
55. 4100–4399 Zion
56. 9600–9899 Turner
57. 2500–3399 Manor
58. 2200–2499 Zion
59. 1700–2199 Turner
60. 8100–8599 Manor
61. Noble
62. Reid
63. 4100–4399 Zion
64. 3400–3799 Zion
65. 3900–5099 Manor
66. Green
67. Hillside
68. Primrose
69. 9600–9899 Turner
70. 1200–1699 Manor
71. 5000–5399 Zion
72. 7200–7299 Turner
73. 5900–6599 Manor
74. Hinckley
75. Rutgers
76. Jane
77. Day
78. 5400–6299 Turner
79. 3400–3799 Zion
80. 8100–8599 Manor
81. 4400–4899 Zion
82. 9600–9899 Turner
83. 5000–5399 Zion
84. Madison
85. Noble
86. Reid
87. 4100–4399 Zion
88. 3900–5099 Manor

PRACTICE II

DIRECTIONS: The next 88 questions constitute another practice exercise. Again, you should mark your answers on your answer sheet. Again, the time limit is THREE MINUTES. This time, however, you must NOT look at the boxes while answering the questions. You must rely on your memory in marking the box location of each item. This practice test will not be scored.

1. Hillside
2. 2500–3399 Manor
3. 4400–4899 Zion
4. Primrose
5. Jane
6. 1700–2199 Turner
7. 8100–8599 Manor
8. 6600–6899 Turner
9. 4100–4399 Zion
10. 3900–5099 Manor
11. 2200–2499 Zion
12. 5400–6299 Turner
13. Green
14. Noble
15. 1200–1699 Manor
16. 5000–5399 Zion
17. 9600–9899 Turner
18. Rutgers
19. Jane
20. Day
21. 6600–6899 Turner
22. 4400–4899 Zion
23. 3900–5099 Manor
24. 8100–8599 Manor
25. Primrose
26. Madison
27. 7200–7299 Turner
28. 3400–3799 Zion
29. 5900–6599 Manor
30. 2500–3399 Manor
31. 5400–6299 Turner
32. Hillside
33. Reid
34. Hinckley
35. 1700–2199 Turner
36. 2200–2499 Zion
37. 4400–4899 Zion
38. Noble
39. Green
40. 6600–6899 Turner
41. 5000–5399 Zion
42. 1700–2199 Turner
43. 1200–1699 Manor
44. Rutgers
45. Madison
46. Jane
47. 4100–4399 Zion
48. 9600–9899 Turner
49. 2500–3399 Manor
50. 5900–6599 Manor
51. 5000–5399 Zion
52. 6600–6899 Turner
53. Hinckley
54. Green
55. 3400–3799 Zion
56. 8100–8599 Manor
57. 1700–2199 Turner
58. Day
59. Primrose
60. 1200–1699 Manor
61. 2200–2499 Zion
62. 5400–6299 Turner
63. 7200–7299 Turner
64. 3900–5099 Manor
65. 4400–4899 Zion
66. Hillside
67. Noble
68. Reid
69. 1200–1699 Manor
70. 2200–2499 Zion
71. 1700–2199 Turner
72. 7200–7299 Turner
73. 3400–3799 Zion
74. 6600–6899 Turner
75. 5900–6599 Manor
76. 4100–4399 Zion
77. Madison
78. Primrose
79. 5000–5399 Zion
80. 2500–3399 Manor
81. 5400–6299 Turner
82. 3900–5099 Manor
83. Hillside
84. Day
85. Reid
86. 6600–6899 Turner
87. 1200–1699 Manor
88. 4400–4899 Zion

PRACTICE III

DIRECTIONS: The names and addresses are repeated for you in the boxes below. Each name and each number span is in the same box in which you found it in the original set. You will now be allowed FIVE MINUTES to study the locations again. Do your best to memorize the letter of the box in which each item is located. This is your last chance to see the boxes.

A	B	C	D	E
5400–6299 Turner Hinckley 4100–4399 Zion Madison 1200–1699 Manor	9600–9899 Turner Hillside 2200–2499 Zion Green 3900–5099 Manor	7200–7299 Turner Rutgers 5000–5399 Zion Day 2500–3399 Manor	6600–6899 Turner Jane 3400–3799 Zion Noble 8100–8599 Manor	1700–2199 Turner Primrose 4400–4899 Zion Reid 5900–6599 Manor

DIRECTIONS: This is your last practice test. Mark the location of each of the 88 items on your answer sheet. You will have FIVE MINUTES to answer these questions. Do NOT look back at the boxes. This practice test will not be scored.

1. 8100–8599 Manor
2. 1700–2199 Turner
3. 4100–4399 Zion
4. Reid
5. Rutgers
6. 1200–1699 Manor
7. 2200–2499 Zion
8. 9600–9899 Turner
9. 5000–5399 Zion
10. Day
11. Hinckley
12. Jane
13. 6600–6899 Turner
14. 5900–6599 Manor
15. 4400–4899 Zion
16. 7200–7299 Turner
17. 2500–3399 Manor
18. Primrose
19. Madison
20. Green
21. 3900–5099 Manor
22. 5400–6299 Turner
23. 3400–3799 Zion
24. Noble
25. Hillside
26. 9600–9899 Turner
27. 2500–3399 Manor
28. Madison
29. 3400–3799 Zion
30. 5900–6599 Manor
31. 1700–2199 Turner
32. Primrose
33. 4100–4399 Zion
34. 3900–5099 Manor
35. 4400–4899 Zion
36. Rutgers
37. Hinckley
38. 6600–6899 Turner
39. 1200–1699 Manor
40. 5000–5399 Zion
41. Green
42. Day
43. Reid
44. 8100–8599 Manor

45. 5400–6299 Turner
46. 7200–7299 Turner
47. 2200–2499 Zion
48. Noble
49. Hillside
50. Jane
51. 5900–6599 Manor
52. 2200–2499 Zion
53. 7200–7299 Turner
54. Madison
55. Green
56. 8100–8599 Manor
57. 6600–6899 Turner
58. 4400–4899 Zion
59. 5000–5399 Zion
60. 1700–2199 Turner
61. 1200–1699 Manor
62. 5400–6299 Turner
63. Day
64. Primrose
65. Green
66. Jane

67. 9600–9899 Turner
68. 3400–3799 Zion
69. 3900–5099 Manor
70. 4100–4399 Zion
71. Rutgers
72. Reid
73. Madison
74. 2500–3399 Manor
75. 7200–7299 Turner
76. 5000–5399 Zion
77. Primrose
78. Hinckley
79. 1200–1699 Manor
80. 9600–9899 Turner
81. Green
82. 2200–2499 Zion
83. 1700–2199 Turner
84. Noble
85. 3400–3799 Zion
86. 3900–5099 Manor
87. Rutgers
88. Jane

MEMORY FOR ADDRESSES TEST

TIME: 5 Minutes. 88 Questions.

DIRECTIONS: Mark your answers on the answer sheet in the section headed "MEMORY FOR ADDRESSES TEST." This test will be scored. You are NOT permitted to look at the boxes. Work from memory, as quickly and as accurately as you can. Correct answers are on page 232.

1. 5000–5399 Zion
2. 1700–2199 Turner
3. 1200–1699 Manor
4. Green
5. Jane
6. 5900–6599 Manor
7. 9600–9899 Turner
8. 3400–3799 Zion
9. 2500–3399 Manor
10. Rutgers
11. Reid
12. Hinckley
13. 5400–6299 Turner
14. 8100–8599 Manor
15. 3900–5099 Manor
16. 3400–3799 Zion
17. Noble
18. Madison
19. 4400–4899 Zion
20. 7200–7299 Turner
21. 4100–4399 Zion
22. Primrose
23. 1700–2199 Turner
24. 3400–3799 Zion
25. 2500–3399 Manor
26. 2200–2499 Zion
27. 5400–6299 Turner
28. Noble
29. Primrose
30. Rutgers
31. 4100–4399 Zion
32. 1200–1699 Manor

33. Madison
34. 3900–5099 Manor
35. 5000–5399 Zion
36. Hinckley
37. Hillside
38. 4400–4899 Zion
39. 8100–8599 Manor
40. 9600–9899 Turner
41. 6600–6899 Turner
42. 5900–6599 Manor
43. Jane
44. Day
45. 7200–7299 Turner
46. Green
47. Reid
48. 2500–3399 Manor
49. 4100–4399 Zion
50. 5400–6299 Turner
51. 9600–9899 Turner
52. 8100–8599 Manor
53. 4400–4899 Zion
54. 1700–2199 Turner
55. Primrose
56. Hinckley
57. Green
58. 5000–5399 Zion
59. 2500–3399 Manor
60. 6600–6899 Turner
61. 3400–3799 Zion
62. Jane
63. Noble
64. Day

65. 5900–6599 Manor
66. 2200–2499 Zion
67. 3900–5099 Manor
68. Primrose
69. Rutgers
70. 1200–1699 Manor
71. Hillside
72. Jane
73. 3900–5099 Manor
74. 3400–3799 Zion
75. 5400–6299 Turner
76. Green

77. Primrose
78. 2500–3399 Manor
79. 9600–9899 Turner
80. 4400–4899 Zion
81. 5000–5399 Zion
82. Hinckley
83. Noble
84. 1700–2199 Turner
85. 8100–8599 Manor
86. 5000–5399 Zion
87. 6600–6899 Turner
88. Madison

END OF EXAM

ADDRESS CHECKING ERROR ANALYSIS CHART

Type of Error	Tally	Total Number
Number of addresses which were alike and you incorrectly marked "different"		
Number of addresses which were different and you incorrectly marked "alike"		
Number of addresses in which you missed a difference in NUMBERS		
Number of addresses in which you missed a difference in ABBREVIATIONS		
Number of addresses in which you missed a difference in NAMES		

SELF-EVALUATION CHART

Test	Excellent	Good	Average	Fair	Poor
Address Checking	80–95	65–79	50–64	35–49	1–34
Memory for Addresses	75–88	60–74	45–59	30–44	1–29

CORRECT ANSWERS FOR NINTH MODEL EXAM

ADDRESS CHECKING TEST

1. A	13. A	25. A	37. D	49. A	61. D	73. D	85. A
2. A	14. D	26. D	38. A	50. D	62. D	74. A	86. D
3. D	15. A	27. D	39. A	51. A	63. A	75. A	87. D
4. D	16. D	28. A	40. D	52. D	64. D	76. D	88. D
5. D	17. D	29. A	41. A	53. D	65. D	77. D	89. A
6. D	18. D	30. D	42. D	54. A	66. A	78. A	90. D
7. D	19. D	31. D	43. A	55. A	67. A	79. A	91. A
8. A	20. D	32. A	44. D	56. A	68. D	80. A	92. A
9. A	21. A	33. D	45. D	57. D	69. D	81. D	93. A
10. D	22. D	34. D	46. A	58. D	70. D	82. D	94. D
11. A	23. A	35. D	47. D	59. A	71. A	83. A	95. A
12. A	24. A	36. A	48. D	60. A	72. D	84. D	

MEMORY FOR ADDRESSES—PRACTICE I

1. C	12. B	23. E	34. E	45. B	56. B	67. B	78. A
2. E	13. C	24. E	35. E	46. C	57. C	68. E	79. D
3. D	14. A	25. E	36. E	47. B	58. B	69. B	80. D
4. A	15. D	26. B	37. B	48. C	59. E	70. A	81. E
5. B	16. C	27. C	38. C	49. B	60. D	71. C	82. B
6. C	17. C	28. D	39. A	50. C	61. D	72. C	83. C
7. E	18. E	29. A	40. D	51. D	62. E	73. E	84. A
8. A	19. A	30. A	41. D	52. E	63. A	74. A	85. D
9. B	20. D	31. D	42. B	53. E	64. D	75. C	86. E
10. C	21. B	32. E	43. C	54. D	65. B	76. D	87. A
11. E	22. D	33. A	44. A	55. A	66. B	77. C	88. B

MEMORY FOR ADDRESSES—PRACTICE II

1. B	12. A	23. B	34. A	45. A	56. D	67. D	78. E
2. C	13. B	24. D	35. E	46. D	57. E	68. E	79. C
3. E	14. D	25. E	36. B	47. A	58. C	69. A	80. C
4. E	15. A	26. A	37. E	48. B	59. E	70. B	81. A
5. D	16. C	27. C	38. D	49. C	60. A	71. E	82. B
6. E	17. B	28. D	39. B	50. E	61. B	72. C	83. B
7. D	18. C	29. E	40. D	51. C	62. A	73. D	84. C
8. D	19. D	30. C	41. C	52. D	63. C	74. D	85. E
9. A	20. C	31. A	42. E	53. A	64. B	75. E	86. D
10. B	21. D	32. B	43. A	54. B	65. E	76. A	87. A
11. B	22. E	33. E	44. C	55. D	66. B	77. A	88. E

MEMORY FOR ADDRESSES—PRACTICE III

1. D	12. D	23. D	34. B	45. A	56. D	67. B	78. A
2. E	13. D	24. D	35. E	46. C	57. D	68. D	79. A
3. A	14. E	25. B	36. C	47. B	58. E	69. B	80. B
4. E	15. E	26. B	37. A	48. D	59. C	70. A	81. B
5. C	16. C	27. C	38. D	49. B	60. E	71. C	82. B
6. A	17. C	28. A	39. A	50. D	61. A	72. E	83. E
7. B	18. E	29. D	40. C	51. E	62. A	73. A	84. D
8. B	19. A	30. E	41. B	52. B	63. C	74. C	85. D
9. C	20. B	31. E	42. C	53. C	64. E	75. C	86. B
10. C	21. B	32. E	43. E	54. A	65. B	76. C	87. C
11. A	22. A	33. A	44. D	55. B	66. D	77. E	88. D

MEMORY FOR ADDRESSES TEST

1. C	12. A	23. E	34. B	45. C	56. A	67. B	78. C
2. E	13. A	24. D	35. C	46. B	57. B	68. E	79. B
3. A	14. D	25. C	36. A	47. E	58. C	69. C	80. E
4. B	15. B	26. B	37. B	48. C	59. C	70. A	81. C
5. D	16. D	27. A	38. E	49. A	60. D	71. B	82. A
6. E	17. D	28. D	39. D	50. A	61. D	72. D	83. D
7. B	18. A	29. E	40. B	51. B	62. D	73. B	84. E
8. D	19. E	30. C	41. D	52. D	63. D	74. D	85. D
9. C	20. C	31. A	42. E	53. E	64. C	75. A	86. C
10. C	21. A	32. A	43. D	54. E	65. E	76. B	87. D
11. E	22. E	33. A	44. C	55. E	66. B	77. E	88. A

ANSWER SHEET FOR TENTH MODEL EXAM

ADDRESS CHECKING

1 Ⓐ Ⓓ	20 Ⓐ Ⓓ	39 Ⓐ Ⓓ	58 Ⓐ Ⓓ	77 Ⓐ Ⓓ
2 Ⓐ Ⓓ	21 Ⓐ Ⓓ	40 Ⓐ Ⓓ	59 Ⓐ Ⓓ	78 Ⓐ Ⓓ
3 Ⓐ Ⓓ	22 Ⓐ Ⓓ	41 Ⓐ Ⓓ	60 Ⓐ Ⓓ	79 Ⓐ Ⓓ
4 Ⓐ Ⓓ	23 Ⓐ Ⓓ	42 Ⓐ Ⓓ	61 Ⓐ Ⓓ	80 Ⓐ Ⓓ
5 Ⓐ Ⓓ	24 Ⓐ Ⓓ	43 Ⓐ Ⓓ	62 Ⓐ Ⓓ	81 Ⓐ Ⓓ
6 Ⓐ Ⓓ	25 Ⓐ Ⓓ	44 Ⓐ Ⓓ	63 Ⓐ Ⓓ	82 Ⓐ Ⓓ
7 Ⓐ Ⓓ	26 Ⓐ Ⓓ	45 Ⓐ Ⓓ	64 Ⓐ Ⓓ	83 Ⓐ Ⓓ
8 Ⓐ Ⓓ	27 Ⓐ Ⓓ	46 Ⓐ Ⓓ	65 Ⓐ Ⓓ	84 Ⓐ Ⓓ
9 Ⓐ Ⓓ	28 Ⓐ Ⓓ	47 Ⓐ Ⓓ	66 Ⓐ Ⓓ	85 Ⓐ Ⓓ
10 Ⓐ Ⓓ	29 Ⓐ Ⓓ	48 Ⓐ Ⓓ	67 Ⓐ Ⓓ	86 Ⓐ Ⓓ
11 Ⓐ Ⓓ	30 Ⓐ Ⓓ	49 Ⓐ Ⓓ	68 Ⓐ Ⓓ	87 Ⓐ Ⓓ
12 Ⓐ Ⓓ	31 Ⓐ Ⓓ	50 Ⓐ Ⓓ	69 Ⓐ Ⓓ	88 Ⓐ Ⓓ
13 Ⓐ Ⓓ	32 Ⓐ Ⓓ	51 Ⓐ Ⓓ	70 Ⓐ Ⓓ	89 Ⓐ Ⓓ
14 Ⓐ Ⓓ	33 Ⓐ Ⓓ	52 Ⓐ Ⓓ	71 Ⓐ Ⓓ	90 Ⓐ Ⓓ
15 Ⓐ Ⓓ	34 Ⓐ Ⓓ	53 Ⓐ Ⓓ	72 Ⓐ Ⓓ	91 Ⓐ Ⓓ
16 Ⓐ Ⓓ	35 Ⓐ Ⓓ	54 Ⓐ Ⓓ	73 Ⓐ Ⓓ	92 Ⓐ Ⓓ
17 Ⓐ Ⓓ	36 Ⓐ Ⓓ	55 Ⓐ Ⓓ	74 Ⓐ Ⓓ	93 Ⓐ Ⓓ
18 Ⓐ Ⓓ	37 Ⓐ Ⓓ	56 Ⓐ Ⓓ	75 Ⓐ Ⓓ	94 Ⓐ Ⓓ
19 Ⓐ Ⓓ	38 Ⓐ Ⓓ	57 Ⓐ Ⓓ	76 Ⓐ Ⓓ	95 Ⓐ Ⓓ

TEAR HERE

MEMORY FOR ADDRESSES

PRACTICE I

1 Ⓐ Ⓑ Ⓒ Ⓓ Ⓔ   23 Ⓐ Ⓑ Ⓒ Ⓓ Ⓔ   45 Ⓐ Ⓑ Ⓒ Ⓓ Ⓔ   67 Ⓐ Ⓑ Ⓒ Ⓓ Ⓔ

2 Ⓐ Ⓑ Ⓒ Ⓓ Ⓔ   24 Ⓐ Ⓑ Ⓒ Ⓓ Ⓔ   46 Ⓐ Ⓑ Ⓒ Ⓓ Ⓔ   68 Ⓐ Ⓑ Ⓒ Ⓓ Ⓔ

3 Ⓐ Ⓑ Ⓒ Ⓓ Ⓔ   25 Ⓐ Ⓑ Ⓒ Ⓓ Ⓔ   47 Ⓐ Ⓑ Ⓒ Ⓓ Ⓔ   69 Ⓐ Ⓑ Ⓒ Ⓓ Ⓔ

4 Ⓐ Ⓑ Ⓒ Ⓓ Ⓔ   26 Ⓐ Ⓑ Ⓒ Ⓓ Ⓔ   48 Ⓐ Ⓑ Ⓒ Ⓓ Ⓔ   70 Ⓐ Ⓑ Ⓒ Ⓕ Ⓔ

5 Ⓐ Ⓑ Ⓒ Ⓓ Ⓔ   27 Ⓐ Ⓑ Ⓒ Ⓓ Ⓔ   49 Ⓐ Ⓑ Ⓒ Ⓓ Ⓔ   71 Ⓐ Ⓑ Ⓒ Ⓓ Ⓔ

6 Ⓐ Ⓑ Ⓒ Ⓓ Ⓔ   28 Ⓐ Ⓑ Ⓒ Ⓓ Ⓔ   50 Ⓐ Ⓑ Ⓒ Ⓓ Ⓔ   72 Ⓐ Ⓑ Ⓒ Ⓓ Ⓔ

7 Ⓐ Ⓑ Ⓒ Ⓓ Ⓔ   29 Ⓐ Ⓑ Ⓒ Ⓓ Ⓔ   51 Ⓐ Ⓑ Ⓒ Ⓓ Ⓔ   73 Ⓐ Ⓑ Ⓒ Ⓓ Ⓔ

8 Ⓐ Ⓑ Ⓒ Ⓓ Ⓔ   30 Ⓐ Ⓑ Ⓒ Ⓓ Ⓔ   52 Ⓐ Ⓑ Ⓒ Ⓓ Ⓔ   74 Ⓐ Ⓑ Ⓒ Ⓓ Ⓔ

9 Ⓐ Ⓑ Ⓒ Ⓓ Ⓔ   31 Ⓐ Ⓑ Ⓒ Ⓓ Ⓔ   53 Ⓐ Ⓑ Ⓒ Ⓓ Ⓔ   75 Ⓐ Ⓑ Ⓒ Ⓓ Ⓔ

10 Ⓐ Ⓑ Ⓒ Ⓓ Ⓔ   32 Ⓐ Ⓑ Ⓒ Ⓓ Ⓔ   54 Ⓐ Ⓑ Ⓒ Ⓓ Ⓔ   76 Ⓐ Ⓑ Ⓒ Ⓓ Ⓔ

11 Ⓐ Ⓑ Ⓒ Ⓓ Ⓔ   33 Ⓐ Ⓑ Ⓒ Ⓓ Ⓔ   55 Ⓐ Ⓑ Ⓒ Ⓓ Ⓔ   77 Ⓐ Ⓑ Ⓒ Ⓓ Ⓔ

12 Ⓐ Ⓑ Ⓒ Ⓓ Ⓔ   34 Ⓐ Ⓑ Ⓒ Ⓓ Ⓔ   56 Ⓐ Ⓑ Ⓒ Ⓓ Ⓔ   78 Ⓐ Ⓑ Ⓒ Ⓓ Ⓔ

13 Ⓐ Ⓑ Ⓒ Ⓓ Ⓔ   35 Ⓐ Ⓑ Ⓒ Ⓓ Ⓔ   57 Ⓐ Ⓑ Ⓒ Ⓓ Ⓔ   79 Ⓐ Ⓑ Ⓒ Ⓓ Ⓔ

14 Ⓐ Ⓑ Ⓒ Ⓓ Ⓔ   36 Ⓐ Ⓑ Ⓒ Ⓓ Ⓔ   58 Ⓐ Ⓑ Ⓒ Ⓓ Ⓔ   80 Ⓐ Ⓑ Ⓒ Ⓓ Ⓔ

15 Ⓐ Ⓑ Ⓒ Ⓓ Ⓔ   37 Ⓐ Ⓑ Ⓒ Ⓓ Ⓔ   59 Ⓐ Ⓑ Ⓒ Ⓓ Ⓔ   81 Ⓐ Ⓑ Ⓒ Ⓓ Ⓔ

16 Ⓐ Ⓑ Ⓒ Ⓓ Ⓔ   38 Ⓐ Ⓑ Ⓒ Ⓓ Ⓔ   60 Ⓐ Ⓑ Ⓒ Ⓓ Ⓔ   82 Ⓐ Ⓑ Ⓒ Ⓓ Ⓔ

17 Ⓐ Ⓑ Ⓒ Ⓓ Ⓔ   39 Ⓐ Ⓑ Ⓒ Ⓓ Ⓔ   61 Ⓐ Ⓑ Ⓒ Ⓓ Ⓔ   83 Ⓐ Ⓑ Ⓒ Ⓓ Ⓔ

18 Ⓐ Ⓑ Ⓒ Ⓓ Ⓔ   40 Ⓐ Ⓑ Ⓒ Ⓓ Ⓔ   62 Ⓐ Ⓑ Ⓒ Ⓓ Ⓔ   84 Ⓐ Ⓑ Ⓒ Ⓓ Ⓔ

19 Ⓐ Ⓑ Ⓒ Ⓓ Ⓔ   41 Ⓐ Ⓑ Ⓒ Ⓓ Ⓔ   63 Ⓐ Ⓑ Ⓒ Ⓓ Ⓕ   85 Ⓐ Ⓑ Ⓒ Ⓓ Ⓔ

20 Ⓐ Ⓑ Ⓒ Ⓓ Ⓔ   42 Ⓐ Ⓑ Ⓒ Ⓓ Ⓔ   64 Ⓐ Ⓑ Ⓒ Ⓓ Ⓔ   86 Ⓐ Ⓑ Ⓒ Ⓓ Ⓔ

21 Ⓐ Ⓑ Ⓒ Ⓓ Ⓔ   43 Ⓐ Ⓑ Ⓒ Ⓓ Ⓔ   65 Ⓐ Ⓑ Ⓒ Ⓓ Ⓔ   87 Ⓐ Ⓑ Ⓒ Ⓓ Ⓔ

22 Ⓐ Ⓑ Ⓒ Ⓓ Ⓔ   44 Ⓐ Ⓑ Ⓒ Ⓓ Ⓔ   66 Ⓐ Ⓑ Ⓒ Ⓓ Ⓔ   88 Ⓐ Ⓑ Ⓒ Ⓓ Ⓔ

PRACTICE II

1 Ⓐ Ⓑ Ⓒ Ⓓ Ⓔ   23 Ⓐ Ⓑ Ⓒ Ⓓ Ⓔ   45 Ⓐ Ⓑ Ⓒ Ⓓ Ⓔ   67 Ⓐ Ⓑ Ⓒ Ⓤ Ⓔ

2 Ⓐ Ⓑ Ⓒ Ⓓ Ⓔ   24 Ⓐ Ⓑ Ⓒ Ⓓ Ⓔ   46 Ⓐ Ⓑ Ⓒ Ⓓ Ⓔ   68 Ⓐ Ⓑ Ⓒ Ⓓ Ⓔ

3 Ⓐ Ⓑ Ⓒ Ⓓ Ⓔ   25 Ⓐ Ⓑ Ⓒ Ⓓ Ⓔ   47 Ⓐ Ⓑ Ⓒ Ⓓ Ⓔ   69 Ⓐ Ⓑ Ⓒ Ⓓ Ⓔ

4 Ⓐ Ⓑ Ⓒ Ⓓ Ⓔ   26 Ⓐ Ⓑ Ⓒ Ⓓ Ⓔ   48 Ⓐ Ⓑ Ⓒ Ⓓ Ⓔ   70 Ⓐ Ⓑ Ⓒ Ⓓ Ⓔ

5 Ⓐ Ⓑ Ⓒ Ⓓ Ⓔ   27 Ⓐ Ⓑ Ⓒ Ⓓ Ⓔ   49 Ⓐ Ⓑ Ⓒ Ⓓ Ⓔ   71 Ⓐ Ⓑ Ⓒ Ⓓ Ⓔ

6 Ⓐ Ⓑ Ⓒ Ⓓ Ⓔ   28 Ⓐ Ⓑ Ⓒ Ⓓ Ⓔ   50 Ⓐ Ⓑ Ⓒ Ⓓ Ⓔ   72 Ⓐ Ⓑ Ⓒ Ⓓ Ⓔ

7 Ⓐ Ⓑ Ⓒ Ⓓ Ⓔ   29 Ⓐ Ⓑ Ⓒ Ⓓ Ⓔ   51 Ⓐ Ⓑ Ⓒ Ⓓ Ⓔ   73 Ⓐ Ⓑ Ⓒ Ⓓ Ⓔ

8 Ⓐ Ⓑ Ⓒ Ⓓ Ⓔ   30 Ⓐ Ⓑ Ⓒ Ⓓ Ⓔ   52 Ⓐ Ⓑ Ⓒ Ⓓ Ⓔ   74 Ⓐ Ⓑ Ⓒ Ⓓ Ⓔ

9 Ⓐ Ⓑ Ⓒ Ⓓ Ⓔ   31 Ⓐ Ⓑ Ⓒ Ⓓ Ⓔ   53 Ⓐ Ⓑ Ⓒ Ⓓ Ⓔ   75 Ⓐ Ⓑ Ⓒ Ⓓ Ⓔ

10 Ⓐ Ⓑ Ⓒ Ⓓ Ⓔ   32 Ⓐ Ⓑ Ⓒ Ⓓ Ⓔ   54 Ⓐ Ⓑ Ⓒ Ⓓ Ⓔ   76 Ⓐ Ⓑ Ⓒ Ⓓ Ⓔ

11 Ⓐ Ⓑ Ⓒ Ⓓ Ⓔ   33 Ⓐ Ⓑ Ⓒ Ⓓ Ⓔ   55 Ⓐ Ⓑ Ⓒ Ⓓ Ⓔ   77 Ⓐ Ⓑ Ⓒ Ⓓ Ⓔ

12 Ⓐ Ⓑ Ⓒ Ⓓ Ⓔ   34 Ⓐ Ⓑ Ⓒ Ⓓ Ⓔ   56 Ⓐ Ⓑ Ⓒ Ⓓ Ⓔ   78 Ⓐ Ⓑ Ⓒ Ⓓ Ⓔ

13 Ⓐ Ⓑ Ⓒ Ⓓ Ⓔ   35 Ⓐ Ⓑ Ⓒ Ⓓ Ⓔ   57 Ⓐ Ⓑ Ⓒ Ⓓ Ⓔ   79 Ⓐ Ⓑ Ⓒ Ⓓ Ⓔ

14 Ⓐ Ⓑ Ⓒ Ⓓ Ⓔ   36 Ⓐ Ⓑ Ⓒ Ⓓ Ⓔ   58 Ⓐ Ⓑ Ⓒ Ⓓ Ⓔ   80 Ⓐ Ⓑ Ⓒ Ⓓ Ⓔ

15 Ⓐ Ⓑ Ⓒ Ⓓ Ⓔ   37 Ⓐ Ⓑ Ⓒ Ⓓ Ⓔ   59 Ⓐ Ⓑ Ⓒ Ⓓ Ⓔ   81 Ⓐ Ⓑ Ⓒ Ⓓ Ⓔ

16 Ⓐ Ⓑ Ⓒ Ⓓ Ⓔ   38 Ⓐ Ⓑ Ⓒ Ⓓ Ⓔ   60 Ⓐ Ⓑ Ⓒ Ⓓ Ⓔ   82 Ⓐ Ⓑ Ⓒ Ⓓ Ⓔ

17 Ⓐ Ⓑ Ⓒ Ⓓ Ⓔ   39 Ⓐ Ⓑ Ⓒ Ⓓ Ⓔ   61 Ⓐ Ⓑ Ⓒ Ⓓ Ⓔ   83 Ⓐ Ⓑ Ⓒ Ⓓ Ⓔ

18 Ⓐ Ⓑ Ⓒ Ⓓ Ⓔ   40 Ⓐ Ⓑ Ⓒ Ⓓ Ⓔ   62 Ⓐ Ⓑ Ⓒ Ⓓ Ⓔ   84 Ⓐ Ⓑ Ⓒ Ⓓ Ⓔ

19 Ⓐ Ⓑ Ⓒ Ⓓ Ⓔ   41 Ⓐ Ⓑ Ⓒ Ⓓ Ⓔ   63 Ⓐ Ⓑ Ⓒ Ⓓ Ⓔ   85 Ⓐ Ⓑ Ⓒ Ⓓ Ⓔ

20 Ⓐ Ⓑ Ⓒ Ⓓ Ⓔ   42 Ⓐ Ⓑ Ⓒ Ⓓ Ⓔ   64 Ⓐ Ⓑ Ⓒ Ⓓ Ⓔ   86 Ⓐ Ⓑ Ⓒ Ⓓ Ⓔ

21 Ⓐ Ⓑ Ⓒ Ⓓ Ⓔ   43 Ⓐ Ⓑ Ⓒ Ⓓ Ⓔ   65 Ⓐ Ⓑ Ⓒ Ⓓ Ⓔ   87 Ⓐ Ⓑ Ⓒ Ⓓ Ⓔ

22 Ⓐ Ⓑ Ⓒ Ⓓ Ⓔ   44 Ⓐ Ⓑ Ⓒ Ⓓ Ⓔ   66 Ⓐ Ⓑ Ⓒ Ⓓ Ⓔ   88 Ⓐ Ⓑ Ⓒ Ⓓ Ⓔ

PRACTICE III

1 Ⓐ Ⓑ Ⓒ Ⓓ Ⓔ   23 Ⓐ Ⓑ Ⓒ Ⓓ Ⓔ   45 Ⓐ Ⓑ Ⓒ Ⓓ Ⓔ   67 Ⓐ Ⓑ Ⓒ Ⓓ Ⓔ

2 Ⓐ Ⓑ Ⓒ Ⓓ Ⓔ   24 Ⓐ Ⓑ Ⓒ Ⓓ Ⓔ   46 Ⓐ Ⓑ Ⓒ Ⓓ Ⓔ   68 Ⓐ Ⓑ Ⓒ Ⓓ Ⓔ

3 Ⓐ Ⓑ Ⓒ Ⓓ Ⓔ   25 Ⓐ Ⓑ Ⓒ Ⓓ Ⓔ   47 Ⓐ Ⓑ Ⓒ Ⓓ Ⓔ   69 Ⓐ Ⓑ Ⓒ Ⓓ Ⓔ

4 Ⓐ Ⓑ Ⓒ Ⓓ Ⓔ   26 Ⓐ Ⓑ Ⓒ Ⓓ Ⓔ   48 Ⓐ Ⓑ Ⓒ Ⓓ Ⓔ   70 Ⓐ Ⓑ Ⓒ Ⓒ Ⓔ

5 Ⓐ Ⓑ Ⓒ Ⓓ Ⓔ   27 Ⓐ Ⓑ Ⓒ Ⓓ Ⓔ   49 Ⓐ Ⓑ Ⓒ Ⓓ Ⓔ   71 Ⓐ Ⓑ Ⓒ Ⓓ Ⓔ

6 Ⓐ Ⓑ Ⓒ Ⓓ Ⓔ   28 Ⓐ Ⓑ Ⓒ Ⓓ Ⓔ   50 Ⓐ Ⓑ Ⓒ Ⓓ Ⓔ   72 Ⓐ Ⓑ Ⓒ Ⓓ Ⓔ

7 Ⓐ Ⓑ Ⓒ Ⓓ Ⓔ   29 Ⓐ Ⓑ Ⓒ Ⓓ Ⓔ   51 Ⓐ Ⓑ Ⓒ Ⓓ Ⓔ   73 Ⓐ Ⓑ Ⓒ Ⓓ Ⓔ

8 Ⓐ Ⓑ Ⓒ Ⓓ Ⓔ   30 Ⓐ Ⓑ Ⓒ Ⓓ Ⓔ   52 Ⓐ Ⓑ Ⓒ Ⓓ Ⓔ   74 Ⓐ Ⓑ Ⓒ Ⓓ Ⓔ

9 Ⓐ Ⓑ Ⓒ Ⓓ Ⓔ   31 Ⓐ Ⓑ Ⓒ Ⓓ Ⓔ   53 Ⓐ Ⓑ Ⓒ Ⓓ Ⓔ   75 Ⓐ Ⓑ Ⓒ Ⓓ Ⓔ

10 Ⓐ Ⓑ Ⓒ Ⓓ Ⓔ   32 Ⓐ Ⓑ Ⓒ Ⓓ Ⓔ   54 Ⓐ Ⓑ Ⓒ Ⓓ Ⓔ   76 Ⓐ Ⓑ Ⓒ Ⓓ Ⓔ

11 Ⓐ Ⓑ Ⓒ Ⓓ Ⓔ   33 Ⓐ Ⓑ Ⓒ Ⓓ Ⓔ   55 Ⓐ Ⓑ Ⓒ Ⓓ Ⓔ   77 Ⓐ Ⓑ Ⓒ Ⓓ Ⓔ

12 Ⓐ Ⓑ Ⓒ Ⓓ Ⓔ   34 Ⓐ Ⓑ Ⓒ Ⓓ Ⓔ   56 Ⓐ Ⓑ Ⓒ Ⓓ Ⓔ   78 Ⓐ Ⓑ Ⓒ Ⓓ Ⓔ

13 Ⓐ Ⓑ Ⓒ Ⓓ Ⓔ   35 Ⓐ Ⓑ Ⓒ Ⓓ Ⓔ   57 Ⓐ Ⓑ Ⓒ Ⓓ Ⓔ   79 Ⓐ Ⓑ Ⓒ Ⓓ Ⓔ

14 Ⓐ Ⓑ Ⓒ Ⓓ Ⓔ   36 Ⓐ Ⓑ Ⓒ Ⓓ Ⓔ   58 Ⓐ Ⓑ Ⓒ Ⓓ Ⓔ   80 Ⓐ Ⓑ Ⓒ Ⓓ Ⓔ

15 Ⓐ Ⓑ Ⓒ Ⓓ Ⓔ   37 Ⓐ Ⓑ Ⓒ Ⓓ Ⓔ   59 Ⓐ Ⓑ Ⓒ Ⓓ Ⓔ   81 Ⓐ Ⓑ Ⓒ Ⓓ Ⓔ

16 Ⓐ Ⓑ Ⓒ Ⓓ Ⓔ   38 Ⓐ Ⓑ Ⓒ Ⓓ Ⓔ   60 Ⓐ Ⓑ Ⓒ Ⓓ Ⓔ   82 Ⓐ Ⓑ Ⓒ Ⓓ Ⓔ

17 Ⓐ Ⓑ Ⓒ Ⓓ Ⓔ   39 Ⓐ Ⓑ Ⓒ Ⓓ Ⓔ   61 Ⓐ Ⓑ Ⓒ Ⓓ Ⓔ   83 Ⓐ Ⓑ Ⓒ Ⓓ Ⓔ

18 Ⓐ Ⓑ Ⓒ Ⓓ Ⓔ   40 Ⓐ Ⓑ Ⓒ Ⓓ Ⓔ   62 Ⓐ Ⓑ Ⓒ Ⓓ Ⓔ   84 Ⓐ Ⓑ Ⓒ Ⓓ Ⓔ

19 Ⓐ Ⓑ Ⓒ Ⓓ Ⓔ   41 Ⓐ Ⓑ Ⓒ Ⓓ Ⓔ   63 Ⓐ Ⓑ Ⓒ Ⓓ Ⓔ   85 Ⓐ Ⓑ Ⓒ Ⓓ Ⓔ

20 Ⓐ Ⓑ Ⓒ Ⓓ Ⓔ   42 Ⓐ Ⓑ Ⓒ Ⓓ Ⓔ   64 Ⓐ Ⓑ Ⓒ Ⓓ Ⓔ   86 Ⓐ Ⓑ Ⓒ Ⓓ Ⓔ

21 Ⓐ Ⓑ Ⓒ Ⓓ Ⓔ   43 Ⓐ Ⓑ Ⓒ Ⓓ Ⓔ   65 Ⓐ Ⓑ Ⓒ Ⓓ Ⓔ   87 Ⓐ Ⓑ Ⓒ Ⓓ Ⓔ

22 Ⓐ Ⓑ Ⓒ Ⓓ Ⓔ   44 Ⓐ Ⓑ Ⓒ Ⓓ Ⓔ   66 Ⓐ Ⓑ Ⓒ Ⓓ Ⓔ   88 Ⓐ Ⓑ Ⓒ Ⓓ Ⓔ

MEMORY FOR ADDRESSES TEST

1 Ⓐ Ⓑ Ⓒ Ⓓ Ⓔ
2 Ⓐ Ⓑ Ⓒ Ⓓ Ⓔ
3 Ⓐ Ⓑ Ⓒ Ⓓ Ⓔ
4 Ⓐ Ⓑ Ⓒ Ⓓ Ⓔ
5 Ⓐ Ⓑ Ⓒ Ⓓ Ⓔ
6 Ⓐ Ⓑ Ⓒ Ⓓ Ⓔ
7 Ⓐ Ⓑ Ⓒ Ⓓ Ⓔ
8 Ⓐ Ⓑ Ⓒ Ⓓ Ⓔ
9 Ⓐ Ⓑ Ⓒ Ⓓ Ⓔ
10 Ⓐ Ⓑ Ⓒ Ⓓ Ⓔ
11 Ⓐ Ⓑ Ⓒ Ⓓ Ⓔ
12 Ⓐ Ⓑ Ⓒ Ⓓ Ⓔ
13 Ⓐ Ⓑ Ⓒ Ⓓ Ⓔ
14 Ⓐ Ⓑ Ⓒ Ⓓ Ⓔ
15 Ⓐ Ⓑ Ⓒ Ⓓ Ⓔ
16 Ⓐ Ⓑ Ⓒ Ⓓ Ⓔ
17 Ⓐ Ⓑ Ⓒ Ⓓ Ⓔ
18 Ⓐ Ⓑ Ⓒ Ⓓ Ⓔ
19 Ⓐ Ⓑ Ⓒ Ⓓ Ⓔ
20 Ⓐ Ⓑ Ⓒ Ⓓ Ⓔ
21 Ⓐ Ⓑ Ⓒ Ⓓ Ⓔ
22 Ⓐ Ⓑ Ⓒ Ⓓ Ⓔ

23 Ⓐ Ⓑ Ⓒ Ⓓ Ⓔ
24 Ⓐ Ⓑ Ⓒ Ⓓ Ⓔ
25 Ⓐ Ⓑ Ⓒ Ⓓ Ⓔ
26 Ⓐ Ⓑ Ⓒ Ⓓ Ⓔ
27 Ⓐ Ⓑ Ⓒ Ⓓ Ⓔ
28 Ⓐ Ⓑ Ⓒ Ⓓ Ⓔ
29 Ⓐ Ⓑ Ⓒ Ⓓ Ⓔ
30 Ⓐ Ⓑ Ⓒ Ⓓ Ⓔ
31 Ⓐ Ⓑ Ⓒ Ⓓ Ⓔ
32 Ⓐ Ⓑ Ⓒ Ⓓ Ⓔ
33 Ⓐ Ⓑ Ⓒ Ⓓ Ⓔ
34 Ⓐ Ⓑ Ⓒ Ⓓ Ⓔ
35 Ⓐ Ⓑ Ⓒ Ⓓ Ⓔ
36 Ⓐ Ⓑ Ⓒ Ⓓ Ⓔ
37 Ⓐ Ⓑ Ⓒ Ⓓ Ⓔ
38 Ⓐ Ⓑ Ⓒ Ⓓ Ⓔ
39 Ⓐ Ⓑ Ⓒ Ⓓ Ⓔ
40 Ⓐ Ⓑ Ⓒ Ⓓ Ⓔ
41 Ⓐ Ⓑ Ⓒ Ⓓ Ⓔ
42 Ⓐ Ⓑ Ⓒ Ⓓ Ⓔ
43 Ⓐ Ⓑ Ⓒ Ⓓ Ⓔ
44 Ⓐ Ⓑ Ⓒ Ⓓ Ⓔ

45 Ⓐ Ⓑ Ⓒ Ⓓ Ⓔ
46 Ⓐ Ⓑ Ⓒ Ⓓ Ⓔ
47 Ⓐ Ⓑ Ⓒ Ⓓ Ⓔ
48 Ⓐ Ⓑ Ⓒ Ⓓ Ⓔ
49 Ⓐ Ⓑ Ⓒ Ⓓ Ⓔ
50 Ⓐ Ⓑ Ⓒ Ⓓ Ⓔ
51 Ⓐ Ⓑ Ⓒ Ⓓ Ⓔ
52 Ⓐ Ⓑ Ⓒ Ⓓ Ⓔ
53 Ⓐ Ⓑ Ⓒ Ⓓ Ⓔ
54 Ⓐ Ⓑ Ⓒ Ⓓ Ⓔ
55 Ⓐ Ⓑ Ⓒ Ⓓ Ⓔ
56 Ⓐ Ⓑ Ⓒ Ⓓ Ⓔ
57 Ⓐ Ⓑ Ⓒ Ⓓ Ⓔ
58 Ⓐ Ⓑ Ⓒ Ⓓ Ⓔ
59 Ⓐ Ⓑ Ⓒ Ⓓ Ⓔ
60 Ⓐ Ⓑ Ⓒ Ⓓ Ⓔ
61 Ⓐ Ⓑ Ⓒ Ⓓ Ⓔ
62 Ⓐ Ⓑ Ⓒ Ⓓ Ⓔ
63 Ⓐ Ⓑ Ⓒ Ⓓ Ⓔ
64 Ⓐ Ⓑ Ⓒ Ⓓ Ⓔ
65 Ⓐ Ⓑ Ⓒ Ⓓ Ⓔ
66 Ⓐ Ⓑ Ⓒ Ⓓ Ⓔ

67 Ⓐ Ⓑ Ⓒ Ⓓ Ⓔ
68 Ⓐ Ⓑ Ⓒ Ⓓ Ⓔ
69 Ⓐ Ⓑ Ⓒ Ⓓ Ⓔ
70 Ⓐ Ⓑ Ⓒ Ⓓ Ⓔ
71 Ⓐ Ⓑ Ⓒ Ⓓ Ⓔ
72 Ⓐ Ⓑ Ⓒ Ⓓ Ⓔ
73 Ⓐ Ⓑ Ⓒ Ⓓ Ⓔ
74 Ⓐ Ⓑ Ⓒ Ⓓ Ⓔ
75 Ⓐ Ⓑ Ⓒ Ⓓ Ⓔ
76 Ⓐ Ⓑ Ⓒ Ⓓ Ⓔ
77 Ⓐ Ⓑ Ⓒ Ⓓ Ⓔ
78 Ⓐ Ⓑ Ⓒ Ⓓ Ⓔ
79 Ⓐ Ⓑ Ⓒ Ⓓ Ⓔ
80 Ⓐ Ⓑ Ⓒ Ⓓ Ⓔ
81 Ⓐ Ⓑ Ⓒ Ⓓ Ⓔ
82 Ⓐ Ⓑ Ⓒ Ⓓ Ⓔ
83 Ⓐ Ⓑ Ⓒ Ⓓ Ⓔ
84 Ⓐ Ⓑ Ⓒ Ⓓ Ⓔ
85 Ⓐ Ⓑ Ⓒ Ⓓ Ⓔ
86 Ⓐ Ⓑ Ⓒ Ⓓ Ⓔ
87 Ⓐ Ⓑ Ⓒ Ⓓ Ⓔ
88 Ⓐ Ⓑ Ⓒ Ⓓ Ⓔ

SCORE SHEET FOR TENTH MODEL EXAM

ADDRESS CHECKING TEST

Number Right minus Number Wrong equals   Score

_____ − _____ = _____

MEMORY FOR ADDRESSES TEST

Number Right minus (Number Wrong ÷ 4) equals   Score

_____ − _____ = _____

PROGRESS GRAPH

Blacken the bars for Model Exam 10 to the scores you earned.

Score										
95										
90										
85										
80										
75										
70										
65										
60										
55										
50										
45										
40										
35										
30										
25										
20										
15										
10										
5										
0										

Test	AC M	AC M	AC M	AC M	AC M	AC M	AC M	AC M	AC M	AC M	AC M
Model Exam	Diag.	1	2	3	4	5	6	7	8	9	10

AC = Address Checking   M = Memory for Addresses

TENTH MODEL EXAM

ADDRESS CHECKING TEST

TIME: 6 Minutes. 95 Questions.

DIRECTIONS: For each question, compare the address in the left column with the address in the right column. If the two addresses are ALIKE IN EVERY WAY, blacken space Ⓐ on your answer sheet. If the two addresses are DIFFERENT IN ANY WAY, blacken space Ⓓ on your answer sheet. Correct answers for this test are on page 249.

1 . . .	4326 NE Ridge Rd	4326 NW Ridge Rd
2 . . .	5182 Sarles Ln	5182 Saries Ln
3 . . .	8490 Roaring Brk Lk	8490 Roaring Brk Lk
4 . . .	2576 Van Cortlandt Pk Ave	2756 Van Cortlandt Pk Ave
5 . . .	5234 Chateau Lorraine	5234 Chateau Larraine
6 . . .	Pocatello ID 83209	Pocatello ID 82309
7 . . .	9081 Siscowit Rd	9081 Siscowit Rd
8 . . .	7585 138th Cir Dr	7585 138th Cir Dr
9 . . .	5159 Coachlight Sq Apts	5159 Coachlight Dr Apts
10 . . .	1869 Sprout Brook Pky	1869 Sprout Brook Rd
11 . . .	1445 Riverview Ave	1455 Riverview Ave
12 . . .	2588 Somerstown Ctr	2588 Somerston Ctr
13 . . .	1864 W Lefurgy Ave	1864 N Lefurgy Ave
14 . . .	8297 Fort Hill Village	8297 Fort Hill Village
15 . . .	6070 Timberland Pass	607 Timberland Pass
16 . . .	3423 Moseman St	3423 Moselman St
17 . . .	5526 Forbes Blvd	5526 Forbes Blvd
18 . . .	La Jolla CA 92093	La Jolla CA 92093
19 . . .	4606 Muchmore Rd	4406 Muchmore Rd
20 . . .	825 Bullet Hole Way	825 Bullet Hole Way
21 . . .	5871 Guion Pl So	5871 Guion Pl No
22 . . .	1027 Rolhus Pt	1027 Rolhus Pt
23 . . .	2182 Buena Vista Dr	2128 Buena Vista Dr
24 . . .	4570 Halstead Ave	4570 Halsted Ave
25 . . .	Poughkeepsie NY 12601	Poughkeeppsie NY 12601
26 . . .	1939 Riverdale Blvd	1939 Riverside Blvd

27 . . .	2275 Jefferson Valley Rd	2257 Jefferson Valley Rd
28 . . .	8719 Shenorock Houses	8719 Shenorock Houses
29 . . .	9426 Elisa Lane	9426 Elissa Lane
30 . . .	7203 Montefiore Pky	7203 Monteforte Pky
31 . . .	Carbondale IL 62901	Carbondale IL 62901
32 . . .	4144 Stonegate Apts	4144 Stonegate Apts
33 . . .	6576 Hortontown Hill Rd	6576 Hortontown Hill Rd
34 . . .	3965 W Palmer Ave	3956 W Palmer Ave
35 . . .	8973 W Mountain Rd S	8973 S Mountain Rd W
36 . . .	2358 Cowles Ave	235A Cowles Ave
37 . . .	Lynchburg VA 24503	Lynchberg VA 24503
38 . . .	3481 Poningo Pt	3481 Poningo Pt
39 . . .	8762 Mile Square Rd	8762 Miles Square Rd
40 . . .	1441 Massachsuetts Ave NE	1441 Massachusetts Ave NW
41 . . .	2214 Quaker Bridge Hwy	2214 Quaker Ridge Hwy
42 . . .	2776 Babbitt Rdg Dr	2776 Babbitt Rdg Dr
43 . . .	Albuquerque NM 87131	Albuquerque NH 87131
44 . . .	8268 Bronxville River Rd	8628 Bronxville River Rd
45 . . .	1100 Ehrbar Ave	1100 Ehrbar Ave
46 . . .	2143 Leather Stocking Ln	2143 Leatherstocking Ln
47 . . .	Gainesville FL 32611	Gainesville FL 23611
48 . . .	6224 Scarborough Manor	6224 Scarborough Manor
49 . . .	6785 Scenic Circle	6785 Scenick Circle
50 . . .	5416 Crossbar Rd	5416 Crossbar Rd
51 . . .	9162 E 145th Crescent Rd	9162 E 145th Crescent Dr
52 . . .	6048 Administration Ave	6048 Administrative Ave
53 . . .	8588 Quintard Dr Pt	8558 Quintad Dr Pt
54 . . .	Bethlehem PA 18015	Bethlehem PA 18015
55 . . .	6456 Attitash Pl	6456 Attitash Pz
56 . . .	135 Sixth No	1355 Sixth No
57 . . .	4461 Doansbridge St	4461 Doonsbridge St
58 . . .	9296 Hollowbrook Ct	9296 Hollowbrook Ct
59 . . .	3907 Middle Patent Val	3097 Middle Patent Val
60 . . .	Lincoln NE 68508	Lincoln NB 68508
61 . . .	2756 Nepperhan Av	2756 Neperhan Av
62 . . .	4365 Cadillac Dr	4365 Cadillac Rd
63 . . .	5176 Tanglewylde Wy	5176 Tanglewood Wy
64 . . .	8429 Grey Rock Terr	8429 Grey Rock Terr
65 . . .	Boulder CO 80302	Boulder CO 80302
66 . . .	852J Depew Dr N	852J Depuw Dr N
67 . . .	1571 Kissam Rd	1571 Kissam Rd
68 . . .	8858 Albany Post Rd	8558 Albany Post Rd
69 . . .	4274 S Winchester Oval	4274 E Winchester Oval
70 . . .	2606 Gleneida Ave	2606 Glenieda Ave
71 . . .	Grinnell IA 50112	Grinnell IA 50122
72 . . .	3125 Lakeshore Dr	3125 Lake Shore Dr
73 . . .	1075 Central Park Ave NW	1075 Central Park Ave NE
74 . . .	6422 Borcher Ave	6422 Borcher Ave
75 . . .	9832 Brooklands Blvd	9832 Brooklands Blvd
76 . . .	352½ Village Green Center	352½ Village Green Centre
77 . . .	3611 W 361st Ave NE	3611 W 361st Ave NE
78 . . .	6368 Woodlea Dr	6368 Woodlea Dr

79	. . . Lawrence KS 66045	Laurence KS 66045
80	. . . 5656 Heritage Hills Dr	5656 Heritage Hills Dr
81	. . . 6579 Olcott Ave	6579 Alcott Ave
82	. . . 7587 Koerner St	7857 Koerner St
83	. . . 222E Skytop Hill Wy	222E Skytop Hill Wy
84	. . . 2271 Old Knollwood Dr	2271 Knollwood Dr
85	. . . Granville OH 43023	Granville OH 43023
86	. . . 4913 Pythian Pl	4913 Phythian Pl
87	. . . 5784 Birch Brk Blvd	7584 Birch Brk Blvd
88	. . . 6276 Dogwood Lk Ln	6276 Dogwood Ln Lk
89	. . . 5083 Ellendale Ave	5083 Ellendale Ave
90	. . . Bronx NY 10458	Bronx NY 10485
91	. . . 5614 Theodore Fremd Ave	5614 Theodore Freud Ave
92	. . . 3798 Augustine Ave So	3798 Augustine Ave So
93	. . . 9421 Reyna Ln	9421 Reyna Ln
94	. . . 8205 Martling Ave Ext	8205 Martting Ave Ext
95	. . . 9278 Sabbathday Hill Rd S	9278 Sabbathday Hill Rd S

END OF ADDRESS CHECKING TEST

If you finish this test before time is up, use the remaining time to check over your work. Do not turn the page until you are told to do so.

PRACTICE FOR
MEMORY FOR ADDRESSES TEST

DIRECTIONS: The five boxes below are labelled A, B, C, D, and E. In each box are three sets of number spans with names and two names which are not associated with numbers. In the next THREE MINUTES, you must try to memorize the box location of each name and number span. The position of a name or number span within its box is not important. You need only remember the letter of the box in which the item is to be found. You will use these names and numbers to answer three sets of practice questions which are NOT scored and one actual test which is scored. Correct answers are on pages 249 and 250.

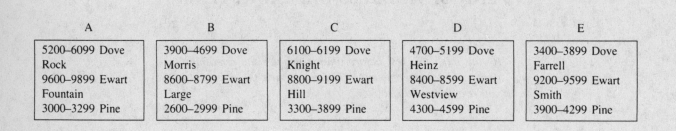

A	B	C	D	E
5200–6099 Dove	3900–4699 Dove	6100–6199 Dove	4700–5199 Dove	3400–3899 Dove
Rock	Morris	Knight	Heinz	Farrell
9600–9899 Ewart	8600–8799 Ewart	8800–9199 Ewart	8400–8599 Ewart	9200–9599 Ewart
Fountain	Large	Hill	Westview	Smith
3000–3299 Pine	2600–2999 Pine	3300–3899 Pine	4300–4599 Pine	3900–4299 Pine

PRACTICE 1

DIRECTIONS: Use the next THREE MINUTES to mark on your answer sheet the letter of the box in which each item that follows is to be found. Try to mark each item without looking back at the boxes. If, however, you get stuck, you may refer to the boxes during this practice exercise. If you find that you must look back, try to memorize as you do so. This test is for practice only. It will not be scored.

1. 8600–8799 Ewart
2. Westview
3. 5200–6099 Dove
4. 6100–6199 Dove
5. 9200–9599 Ewart
6. Smith

7. 3000–3299 Pine
8. Fountain
9. 4700–5199 Dove
10. 9200–9599 Ewart
11. Heinz
12. 4300–4599 Pine

13. 2600–2999 Pine
14. 8800–9199 Ewart
15. Morris
16. Hill
17. 3900–4699 Dove
18. 8400–8599 Ewart
19. Rock
20. Farrell
21. 3900–4299 Pine
22. 2600–2999 Pine
23. Knight
24. 3400–3899 Dove
25. Large
26. 9600–9899 Ewart
27. 3300–3899 Pine
28. 9200–9599 Ewart
29. 4300–4599 Pine
30. Heinz
31. 5200–6099 Dove
32. 3400–3899 Dove
33. Fountain
34. 2600–2999 Pine
35. 8600–8799 Ewart
36. Morris
37. Westview
38. Smith
39. 3000–3299 Pine
40. 6100–6199 Dove
41. 8400–8599 Ewart
42. Rock
43. 4300–4599 Pine
44. 9600–9899 Ewart
45. 3900–4699 Dove
46. Farrell
47. 8800–9199 Ewart
48. 9200–9599 Ewart
49. Knight
50. 4700–5199 Dove

51. 3300–3899 Pine
52. 3900–4299 Pine
53. Large
54. Hill
55. 3900–4699 Dove
56. 8800–9199 Ewart
57. Morris
58. 5200–6099 Dove
59. Heinz
60. 9600–9899 Ewart
61. 3400–3899 Dove
62. 3900–4299 Pine
63. Large
64. Knight
65. 8400–8599 Ewart
66. 3000–3299 Pine
67. 6100–6199 Dove
68. Fountain
69. Rock
70. 4300–4599 Pine
71. 2600–2999 Pine
72. 6100–6199 Dove
73. Hill
74. 9200–9599 Ewart
75. 8800–9199 Ewart
76. Smith
77. 5200–6099 Dove
78. 3900–4299 Pine
79. Farrell
80. Rock
81. 8400–8599 Ewart
82. Westview
83. 2600–2999 Pine
84. 3900–4699 Dove
85. Morris
86. 4700–5199 Dove
87. 8600–8799 Ewart
88. Heinz

PRACTICE II

DIRECTIONS: The next 88 questions constitute another practice exercise. Again, you should mark your answers on your answer sheet. Again, the time limit is THREE MIN-UTES. This time, however, you must NOT look at the boxes while answering the questions. You must rely on your memory in marking the box location of each item. This practice test will not be scored.

1. 5200–6099 Dove
2. 8600–8799 Ewart
3. Knight
4. 4300–4599 Pine
5. 3900–4299 Pine
6. Farrell
7. 8400–8599 Ewart
8. Hill
9. 2600–2999 Pine
10. 5200–6099 Dove
11. 3000–3299 Pine
12. Large
13. 8800–9199 Ewart
14. Heinz
15. 3400–3899 Dove
16. 3900–4299 Pine
17. Westview
18. 6100–6199 Dove
19. 8600–8799 Ewart
20. Fountain
21. Smith
22. Morris
23. 5200–6099 Dove
24. 9600–9899 Ewart
25. 3300–3899 Pine
26. 8400–8599 Ewart
27. Farrell
28. Rock
29. 4300–4599 Pine
30. Large
31. 3900–4699 Dove
32. 4700–5199 Dove
33. 9200–9599 Ewart
34. Knight
35. Hill
36. 2600–2999 Pine
37. 9600–9899 Ewart
38. Smith
39. 6100–6199 Dove
40. 3000–3299 Pine
41. 8600–8799 Ewart
42. 3900–4699 Dove
43. 9200–9599 Ewart
44. Rock
45. 3900–4299 Pine
46. 4700–5199 Dove
47. Morris
48. 8400–8599 Ewart
49. 3400–3899 Dove
50. Westview
51. Farrell
52. 2600–2999 Pine
53. 4300–4599 Pine
54. 5200–6099 Dove
55. 9200–9599 Ewart
56. Large
57. Knight
58. 6100–6199 Dove
59. 8800–9199 Ewart
60. 9600–9899 Ewart
61. Fountain
62. Hill
63. Heinz
64. 3300–3899 Pine
65. Smith
66. 4700–5199 Dove
67. 4300–4599 Pine
68. 5200–6099 Dove
69. 3000–3299 Pine
70. 8600–8799 Ewart
71. Rock
72. Farrell
73. 3400–3899 Dove
74. 4300–4599 Pine
75. 6100–6199 Dove
76. 9600–9899 Ewart
77. Smith
78. Knight
79. 3900–4699 Dove
80. 2600–2999 Pine
81. 8400–8599 Ewart
82. Large
83. Westview
84. 9200–9599 Ewart
85. 3900–4299 Pine
86. 4700–5199 Dove
87. Heinz
88. 5200–6099 Dove

PRACTICE III

DIRECTIONS: The names and addresses are repeated for you in the boxes below. Each name and each number span is in the same box in which you found it in the original set. You are now allowed FIVE MINUTES to study the locations again. Do your best to memorize the letter of the box in which each item is to be found. This is your last chance to see the boxes.

A	B	C	D	E
5200–6099 Dove Rock 9600–9899 Ewart Fountain 3000–3299 Pine	3900–4699 Dove Morris 8600–8799 Ewart Large 2600–2999 Pine	6100–6199 Dove Knight 8800–9199 Ewart Hill 3300–3899 Pine	4700–5199 Dove Heinz 8400–8599 Ewart Westview 4300–4599 Pine	3400–3899 Dove Farrell 9200–9599 Ewart Smith 3900–4299 Pine

DIRECTIONS: This is your last practice test. Mark the location of each of the 88 items on your answer sheet. You are allowed FIVE MINUTES to answer these questions. Do NOT look back at the boxes. This practice test will not be scored.

1. 4700–5199 Dove
2. 8800–9199 Ewart
3. Fountain
4. 3000–3299 Pine
5. 3900–4299 Pine
6. 3900–4699 Dove
7. Knight
8. Farrell
9. 9600–9899 Ewart
10. Westview
11. 8600–8799 Ewart
12. Hill
13. 4300–4599 Pine
14. Smith
15. Rock
16. 5200–6099 Dove
17. 3400–3899 Dove
18. 9600–9899 Ewart
19. 2600–2999 Pine
20. Large
21. Westview

22. Fountain
23. 3900–4699 Dove
24. 3000–3299 Pine
25. 3900–4299 Pine
26. 9200–9599 Ewart
27. Heinz
28. 6100–6199 Dove
29. 8400–8599 Ewart
30. 8800–9199 Ewart
31. Morris
32. Knight
33. Farrell
34. 3300–3899 Pine
35. 4700–5199 Dove
36. 8400–8599 Ewart
37. 3000–3299 Pine
38. 3400–3899 Dove
39. Large
40. Fountain
41. 3900–4699 Dove
42. 3000–3299 Pine

43. Westview
44. 8800–9199 Ewart
45. 4700–5199 Dove
46. Rock
47. 9600–9899 Ewart
48. 2600–2999 Pine
49. Large
50. Smith
51. 3300–3899 Pine
52. 9200–9599 Ewart
53. Fountain
54. 3400–3899 Dove
55. 5200–6099 Dove
56. Farrell
57. Hill
58. 8400–8599 Ewart
59. 3900–4299 Pine
60. Morris
61. 3400–3899 Dove
62. Heinz
63. 4300–4599 Pine
64. 9600–9899 Ewart
65. 8600–8799 Ewart

66. Knight
67. 4700–5199 Dove
68. 9200–9599 Ewart
69. 4300–4599 Pine
70. Farrell
71. 5200–6099 Dove
72. 3900–4299 Pine
73. 8800–9199 Ewart
74. Large
75. Heinz
76. 3000–3299 Pine
77. 6100–6199 Dove
78. Smith
79. 9600–9899 Ewart
80. Hill
81. 8400–8599 Ewart
82. Smith
83. 2600–2999 Pine
84. 4700–5199 Dove
85. Knight
86. 4300–4599 Pine
87. Fountain
88. 3900–4699 Dove

MEMORY FOR ADDRESSES TEST

TIME: 5 Minutes. 88 Questions.

DIRECTIONS: Mark your answers on the answer sheet in the section headed "MEMORY FOR ADDRESSES TEST." This test will be scored. You are NOT permitted to look at the boxes. Work from memory, as quickly and as accurately as you can. Correct answers are on page 250.

1. 8400–8599 Ewart
2. 3300–3899 Pine
3. 3400–3899 Dove
4. Fountain
5. 2600–2999 Pine
6. Large
7. Smith
8. 6100–6199 Dove
9. 9200–9599 Ewart
10. 5200–6099 Dove
11. 9600–9899 Ewart
12. 4300–4599 Pine
13. Westview
14. Heinz
15. 3900–4699 Dove
16. 3000–3299 Pine
17. 3900–4299 Pine
18. Rock
19. Knight
20. 4700–5199 Dove
21. 8600–8799 Ewart
22. 8800–9199 Ewart
23. Morris
24. Hill
25. Farrell
26. 8400–8599 Ewart
27. 3400–3899 Dove
28. Knight
29. 3000–3299 Pine
30. 6100–6199 Dove
31. Knight
32. Large

33. 5200–6099 Dove
34. 9200–9599 Ewart
35. 3900–4299 Pine
36. Westview
37. 4300–4599 Pine
38. 8800–9199 Ewart
39. Rock
40. Fountain
41. 2600–2999 Pine
42. 3900–4699 Dove
43. 9600–9899 Ewart
44. 3300–3899 Pine
45. Farrell
46. 4700–5199 Dove
47. 9600–9899 Ewart
48. 3300–3899 Pine
49. Westview
50. 2600–2999 Pine
51. 8400–8599 Ewart
52. 6100–6199 Dove
53. Morris
54. Large
55. 5200–6099 Dove
56. 9200–9599 Ewart
57. 3400–3899 Dove
58. 3000–3299 Pine
59. Hill
60. Heinz
61. 3900–4299 Pine
62. 3900–4699 Dove
63. Rock
64. Farrell

65. 8800–9199 Ewart
66. 4300–4599 Pine
67. 8600–8799 Ewart
68. Fountain
69. Knight
70. Smith
71. 8400–8599 Ewart
72. 3300–3899 Pine
73. 3400–3899 Dove
74. 9600–9899 Ewart
75. 2600–2999 Pine
76. Knight

77. Westview
78. 3900–4699 Dove
79. 9200–9599 Ewart
80. Heinz
81. 3900–4299 Pine
82. 3000–3299 Pine
83. Farrell
84. Rock
85. 5200–6099 Dove
86. 8800–9199 Ewart
87. Large
88. 3900–4299 Pine

END OF EXAM

ADDRESS CHECKING ERROR ANALYSIS CHART

Type of Error	Tally	Total Number
Number of addresses which were alike and you incorrectly marked "different"		
Number of addresses which were different and you incorrectly marked "alike"		
Number of addresses in which you missed a difference in NUMBERS		
Number of addresses in which you missed a difference in ABBREVIATIONS		
Number of addresses in which you missed a difference in NAMES		

SELF-EVALUATION CHART

Test	Excellent	Good	Average	Fair	Poor
Address Checking	80–95	65–79	50–64	35–49	1–34
Memory for Addresses	75–88	60–74	45–59	30–44	1–29

CORRECT ANSWERS FOR TENTH MODEL EXAM

ADDRESS CHECKING TEST

1. D	13. D	25. D	37. D	49. D	61. D	73. D	85. A
2. D	14. A	26. D	38. A	50. A	62. D	74. A	86. D
3. A	15. D	27. D	39. D	51. D	63. D	75. A	87. D
4. D	16. D	28. A	40. D	52. D	64. A	76. D	88. D
5. D	17. A	29. D	41. D	53. D	65. A	77. A	89. A
6. D	18. A	30. D	42. A	54. A	66. D	78. A	90. D
7. A	19. D	31. A	43. D	55. D	67. A	79. D	91. D
8. A	20. A	32. A	44. D	56. D	68. D	80. A	92. A
9. D	21. D	33. A	45. A	57. D	69. D	81. D	93. A
10. D	22. A	34. D	46. D	58. A	70. D	82. D	94. D
11. D	23. D	35. D	47. D	59. D	71. D	83. A	95. A
12. D	24. D	36. D	48. A	60. D	72. D	84. D	

MEMORY FOR ADDRESSES—PRACTICE I

1. B	12. D	23. C	34. B	45. B	56. C	67. C	78. E
2. D	13. B	24. E	35. B	46. E	57. B	68. A	79. E
3. A	14. C	25. B	36. B	47. C	58. A	69. A	80. A
4. C	15. B	26. A	37. D	48. E	59. D	70. D	81. D
5. E	16. C	27. C	38. E	49. C	60. A	71. B	82. D
6. E	17. B	28. E	39. A	50. D	61. E	72. C	83. B
7. A	18. D	29. D	40. C	51. C	62. E	73. C	84. B
8. A	19. A	30. D	41. D	52. E	63. B	74. E	85. B
9. D	20. E	31. A	42. A	53. B	64. C	75. C	86. D
10. E	21. E	32. E	43. D	54. C	65. A	76. E	87. B
11. D	22. B	33. A	44. A	55. B	66. A	77. A	88. D

MEMORY FOR
ADDRESSES—PRACTICE II

1. A	12. B	23. A	34. C	45. E	56. B	67. D	78. C
2. B	13. C	24. A	35. C	46. D	57. C	68. A	79. B
3. C	14. D	25. C	36. B	47. B	58. C	69. A	80. B
4. D	15. E	26. D	37. A	48. D	59. C	70. B	81. D
5. E	16. E	27. E	38. E	49. E	60. A	71. A	82. B
6. E	17. D	28. A	39. C	50. D	61. A	72. E	83. D
7. D	18. C	29. D	40. A	51. E	62. C	73. E	84. E
8. C	19. B	30. B	41. B	52. B	63. D	74. D	85. E
9. B	20. A	31. B	42. B	53. D	64. C	75. C	86. D
10. A	21. E	32. D	43. E	54. A	65. E	76. A	87. D
11. A	22. B	33. E	44. A	55. E	66. D	77. E	88. A

MEMORY FOR
ADDRESSES—PRACTICE III

1. D	12. C	23. B	34. C	45. D	56. E	67. D	78. E
2. C	13. D	24. A	35. D	46. A	57. C	68. E	79. A
3. A	14. E	25. E	36. D	47. A	58. D	69. D	80. C
4. A	15. A	26. E	37. A	48. B	59. E	70. E	81. D
5. E	16. A	27. D	38. E	49. B	60. B	71. A	82. E
6. B	17. E	28. C	39. B	50. E	61. E	72. E	83. B
7. C	18. A	29. D	40. A	51. C	62. D	73. C	84. D
8. E	19. B	30. C	41. B	52. E	63. D	74. B	85. C
9. A	20. B	31. B	42. A	53. A	64. A	75. D	86. D
10. D	21. D	32. C	43. D	54. E	65. B	76. A	87. A
11. B	22. A	33. E	44. C	55. A	66. C	77. C	88. B

MEMORY FOR ADDRESSES TEST

1. D	12. D	23. B	34. E	45. E	56. E	67. B	78. B
2. C	13. D	24. C	35. E	46. D	57. E	68. A	79. E
3. E	14. D	25. E	36. D	47. A	58. A	69. C	80. D
4. A	15. B	26. D	37. D	48. C	59. C	70. E	81. E
5. B	16. A	27. E	38. C	49. D	60. D	71. D	82. A
6. B	17. E	28. C	39. A	50. B	61. E	72. C	83. E
7. E	18. A	29. A	40. A	51. D	62. B	73. E	84. A
8. C	19. C	30. C	41. B	52. C	63. A	74. A	85. A
9. E	20. D	31. C	42. B	53. B	64. E	75. B	86. C
10. A	21. B	32. B	43. A	54. B	65. C	76. C	87. B
11. A	22. C	33. A	44. C	55. A	66. D	77. D	88. E

PART IV
Number Series Questions

HOW TO ANSWER
NUMBER SERIES
QUESTIONS

Number Series questions are a part of the Letter Sorting Machine Operator Exam. These questions measure your ability to think with numbers and to see the relationship between elements of a series.

The mathematics of number series questions is not usually difficult. Most problems involve simply adding, subtracting, multiplying or dividing. What these problems do require is concentration and the flexibility that will allow you to come up with a different method of solving the problem if your first try does not work.

WHAT ARE NUMBER SERIES?

Number Series questions consist of a row of numbers that follow some definite order and five answer choices containing two numbers each. Your job is to find out what order the row of numbers is following so that you can determine which of the five answer choices contains the two numbers that would come next if the series were continued.

Let's look at some simple number series to see how they work.

1. 1 2 3 4 5 6 7 . . . . (A) 1 2   (B) 5 6   (C) 8 9   (D) 4 5   (E) 7 8

The numbers in this series are increasing by 1. If the series were continued for two more numbers, it would read: 1 2 3 4 5 6 7 8 9. Therefore the correct answer is 8 and 9, and you should choose answer (C) for question 1.

2. 15 14 13 12 11 10 9 . . . (A) 2 1   (B) 17 16   (C) 8 9   (D) 8 7   (E) 9 8

The numbers in this series are decreasing by 1. If the series were continued for two more numbers, it would read: 15 14 13 12 11 10 9 8 7. Therefore the correct answer is 8 and 7, and you should choose answer (D) for question 2.

3. 20 20 21 21 22 22 23 . . . (A) 23 23   (B) 23 24   (C) 19 19   (D) 22 23   (E) 21 22

Each number in this series is repeated and then increased by 1. If the series were continued for two more numbers, it would read: 20 20 21 21 22 22 23 23 24. Therefore the correct answer is 23 and 24, and you should choose answer (B) for this question.

4. 17 3 17 4 17 5 17 . . . . . . (A) 6 17   (B) 6 7   (C) 17 6   (D) 5 6   (E) 17 7

This series is the number 17 separated by numbers increasing by 1, beginning with the number 3. If the series were continued for two more numbers, it would read: 17 3 17 4 17 5 17 6 17. Therefore the correct answer is 6 and 17, and you should choose answer (A).

5. 1 2 4 5 7 8 10 . . . (A) 11 12   (B) 12 14   (C) 10 13   (D) 12 13   (E) 11 13

The numbers in this series are increasing first by 1 (plus 1) and then by 2 (plus 2). If the series were continued for two more numbers, it would read: 1 2 4 5 7 8 10 (plus 1) *11* (plus 2) *13*. Therefore the correct answer is 11 and 13, and you should choose answer (E) for this question.

FINDING A PATTERN

There is a system with which to approach number series questions.

Step One: LOOK at the series. The pattern may be obvious just by looking at the numbers. Do you see the pattern in the following number series?

1. 1 2 3 1 2 3 1 . . . . . .

This series consists of the numbers 1 2 3 repeating themselves over and over. The next two numbers must be: 2 3.

2. 1 2 15 3 4 15 5 . . . .

The numbers in this series increase by 1 with the number 15 inserted between each series of two numbers. The next two numbers are: 6 15.

Here are five series questions which you should be able to answer by inspection. Mark the letter of the next two numbers in each series on the sample answer sheet.

Sample Answer Sheet

1 Ⓐ Ⓑ Ⓒ Ⓓ Ⓔ   2 Ⓐ Ⓑ Ⓒ Ⓓ Ⓔ   3 Ⓐ Ⓑ Ⓒ Ⓓ Ⓔ   4 Ⓐ Ⓑ Ⓒ Ⓓ Ⓔ   5 Ⓐ Ⓑ Ⓒ Ⓓ Ⓔ

---

1. 12 10 13 10 14 10 15 . . . (A) 15 10   (B) 10 15   (C) 10 16   (D) 10 10   (E) 15 16

2. 20 40 60 20 40 60 20 . . . (A) 20 40   (B) 40 60   (C) 60 40   (D) 60 20   (E) 60 40

3. 9 2 9 4 9 6 9 . . . . (A) 9 9   (B) 9 8   (C) 8 10   (D) 10 8   (E) 8 9

4. 5 8 5 8 5 8 5 . . . . (A) 8 5   (B) 5 8   (C) 5 5   (D) 5 6   (E) 8 8

5. 10 9 8 7 6 5 4 . . . . (A) 4 3   (B) 4 2   (C) 3 2   (D) 5 6   (E) 2 1

Answers

1. **(C)** The series is a simple +1 series with the number 10 inserted after each step of the series.
2. **(B)** The sequence 20 40 60 repeats itself over and over again.
3. **(E)** This is a simple +2 series with the number 9 appearing before each member of the series.
4. **(A)** In this series the sequence 5 8 repeats itself.
5. **(C)** Each number in this series is one less than the number before it. You can call this a −1 series.

Step Two: LISTEN to the series. Sometimes you can "hear" a pattern more easily than you can "see" it. If you do not immediately spot a pattern by looking at the series, try saying the numbers softly to yourself. Try accenting the printed numbers and whispering the missing numbers. Or try grouping the numbers within the series in twos or threes to see if a pattern emerges. Can you hear the pattern of the number series that follow?

1. 1 2 4 5 7 8 10 . . . .

   If you read the numbers aloud and whisper the missing numbers, you may be able to hear that the numbers in this series are increasing by 1 with every third number dropped out. Following this pattern, the next two numbers must be: 11 13.

2. 2 2 4 4 6 6 8 . . . .

   If you say this series aloud, you can probably hear that each number repeats itself and then increases by 2. The next two numbers must be: 8 10.

You may be able to answer the next five series questions by inspection. If you cannot, then try sounding them out.

Sample Answer Sheet

1 Ⓐ Ⓑ Ⓒ Ⓓ Ⓔ   2 Ⓐ Ⓑ Ⓒ Ⓓ Ⓔ   3 Ⓐ Ⓑ Ⓒ Ⓓ Ⓔ   4 Ⓐ Ⓑ Ⓒ Ⓓ Ⓔ   5 Ⓐ Ⓑ Ⓒ Ⓓ Ⓔ

---

1. 1 2 5 6 9 10 13 . . . . (A) 15 17   (B) 14 15   (C) 14 16   (D) 15 16   (E) 14 17

2. 2 3 4 3 4 5 4 . . . . (A) 4 3   (B) 3 5   (C) 5 6   (D) 3 2   (E) 5 4

3. 10 10 12 14 14 16 18 . . . (A) 18 20   (B) 20 20   (C) 20 22   (D) 18 22   (E) 18 18

4. 1 2 3 2 2 3 3 2 3 . . . (A) 2 3   (B) 3 2   (C) 3 4   (D) 4 2   (E) 4 3

5. 10 9 8 9 8 7 8 . . . . (A) 8 7   (B) 7 6   (C) 9 10   (D) 7 8   (E) 8 9

Answers:

1. **(E)** Read aloud (softly): 1 2   5 6   9 10   13
   whisper: 3 4   7 8   11 12

   The next number to read aloud is 14, to be followed by a whispered 15 16, and then aloud again 17.
2. **(C)** If you group the numbers into threes and read them aloud, accenting either the first or last number of each group, you should "feel" that each group of three begins and ends with a number one higher than the previous series. Read 2 3 4; 3 4 5; 4 5 6 or 2 3 4; 3 4 5; 4 5 6.
3. **(A)** Once more group into threes. This time be certain to accent the third number in each group in order to sense the rhythm and thereby the pattern of the series. 10 10 12; 14 14 16; 18 18 20 . . .
4. **(D)** In this series the rhythm emerges when you accent the first number in each group: 1 2 3; 2 2 3; 3 2 3.
5. **(B)** After you have seen a number of series of this type, you may very well be able to spot the pattern by inspection alone. If not, read aloud, group and read again.

Step Three: MARK THE DIFFERENCES between the numbers in the series. If you cannot see or hear the pattern of a series, the next step to take is marking the degree and direction of change between the numbers. Most series progress by either + (plus) or − (minus) or a combination of both directions, so first try marking your changes in terms of + and − . If you cannot make sense of a series in terms of + and − , try × (times) and ÷ (divided by). You may mark the changes between numbers right on your exam paper, but be sure to mark the letter of the answer on your answer sheet when you figure it out. Only your answer sheet will be scored. The exam booklet will be collected, but it will not be scored.

Try this next set of practice questions. If you cannot "see" or "hear" the pattern, mark the differences between the numbers to establish the pattern. Then continue the pattern to determine the next two numbers of the series.

Sample Answer Sheet

1 Ⓐ Ⓑ Ⓒ Ⓓ Ⓔ   2 Ⓐ Ⓑ Ⓒ Ⓓ Ⓔ   3 Ⓐ Ⓑ Ⓒ Ⓓ Ⓔ   4 Ⓐ Ⓑ Ⓒ Ⓓ Ⓔ   5 Ⓐ Ⓑ Ⓒ Ⓓ Ⓔ

---

1. 9 10 12 15 19 24 30 . . . (A) 35 40   (B) 36 42   (C) 30 36   (D) 30 37   (E) 37 45

2. 35 34 31 30 27 26 23 . . . (A) 22 19   (B) 22 20   (C) 23 22   (D) 20 19   (E) 20 17

3. 16 21 19 24 22 27 25 . . . (A) 28 30   (B) 30 28   (C) 29 24   (D) 30 27   (E) 26 29

4. 48 44 40 36 32 28 24 . . . (A) 22 20   (B) 24 22   (C) 23 22   (D) 20 18   (E) 20 16

5. 20 30 39 47 54 60 65 . . . (A) 70 75   (B) 68 70   (C) 69 72   (D) 66 67   (E) 68 71

Answers:

1. **(E)** $9 +^1 10 +^2 12 +^3 15 +^4 19 +^5 24 +^6 30 +^7 37 +^8 45$
2. **(A)** $35 -^1 34 -^3 31 -^1 30 -^3 27 -^1 26 -^3 23 -^1 22 -^3 19$
3. **(B)** $16 +^5 21 -^2 19 +^5 24 -^2 22 +^5 27 -^2 25 +^5 30 -^2 28$
4. **(E)** $48 -^4 40 -^4 36 -^4 32 -^4 28 -^4 24 -^4 20 -^4 16$
5. **(C)** $20 +^{10} 30 +^9 39 +^8 47 +^7 54 +^6 60 +^5 65 +^4 69 +^3 72$

Step Four: WATCH FOR REPEATED NUMBERS. Some number series problems contain a number that is repeated periodically throughout the series.

Example: 1 2 3 50 4 5 6 50 7 8 . . . .

The numbers in this series increase by 1 with the number 50 inserted after each group of three numbers. Continuing this pattern, the next two numbers must be: 9 50.

Other series contain repetitions of certain numbers within the series.

Example: 5 5 10 15 15 20 25 . . . .

The numbers in this series increase by 5 with every other term repeated. The next two numbers must be: 25 30.

In series that contain repeated numbers you must search a bit harder to spot both the pattern of the series and the pattern of the repeated numbers. Try the problems that follow for practice in finding repeated numbers.

Sample Answer Sheet

1 Ⓐ Ⓑ Ⓒ Ⓓ Ⓔ   2 Ⓐ Ⓑ Ⓒ Ⓓ Ⓔ   3 Ⓐ Ⓑ Ⓒ Ⓓ Ⓔ   4 Ⓐ Ⓑ Ⓒ Ⓓ Ⓔ   5 Ⓐ Ⓑ Ⓒ Ⓓ Ⓔ

---

1. 10 13 13 16 16 19 19 . . . (A) 19 19 (B) 19 22 (C) 22 22 (D) 22 25 (E) 22 24

2. 2 4 25 8 16 25 32 . . . . . . (A) 32 25 (B) 25 64 (C) 48 25 (D) 25 48 (E) 64 25

3. 80 80 75 75 70 70 65 . . . (A) 65 60 (B) 65 65 (C) 60 60 (D) 60 55 (E) 55 55

4. 35 35 32 30 30 27 25 . . . (A) 22 20 (B) 25 25 (C) 22 22 (D) 25 22 (E) 25 23

5. 76 70 12 65 61 12 58 . . . (A) 55 12 (B) 56 12 (C) 12 54 (D) 12 55 (E) 54 51

Answers:

r = repeat. 0 = extra number repeated periodically.

1. (C) $10 \overset{+3}{} 13 \ {}^r\ 13 \overset{+3}{} 16 \ {}^r\ 16 \overset{+3}{} 19 \ {}^r\ 19 \overset{+3}{} 22 \ {}^r\ 22$

2. (E) $2 \overset{\times 2}{} 4 \overset{\times 2}{} \boxed{25} \ 8 \overset{\times 2}{} 16 \overset{\times 2}{} \boxed{25} \ 32 \overset{\times 2}{} 64 \overset{\times 2}{} \boxed{25} \ \dots \ 128 \overset{\times 2}{}$

3. (A) $80 \ {}^r\ 80 \overset{-5}{} 75 \ {}^r\ 75 \overset{-5}{} 70 \ {}^r\ 70 \overset{-5}{} 65 \ {}^r\ 65 \overset{-5}{} 60$

4. (D) $35 \ {}^r\ 35 \overset{-3}{} 32 \overset{-2}{} 30 \ {}^r\ 30 \overset{-3}{} 27 \overset{-2}{} 25 \ {}^r\ 25 \overset{-3}{} 22$

5. (B) $76 \overset{-6}{} 70 \overset{-5}{} \boxed{12} \ 65 \overset{-4}{} 61 \overset{-3}{} \boxed{12} \ 58 \overset{-2}{} 56 \overset{-1}{} \boxed{12} \ \dots \ 55$

Step Five: CONSIDER TWO ALTERNATING SERIES. Sometimes a series problem contains two alternating series. Each of the two series follows a pattern, but they may not necessarily follow the same pattern. Both series may be increasing, both may be decreasing or one may be increasing and the other decreasing. Each series may progress one step at a time or one series may progress by two or three steps for each step of the other. The rate of increase or decrease may be the same for each series or it may be different for each one. The examples that follow illustrate some of the many variations possible in alternating series problems.

1. 30 2 28 4 26 6 24 . . . (A) 23 9   (B) 26 8   (C) 8 9   (D) 26 22   (E) 8 22

The first series starts with 30 and decreases by 2. The second series starts with 2 and increases by 2. The next two numbers must be 8 and 22, which is answer (E).

$$\overset{-2}{\frown} \quad \overset{-2}{\frown} \quad \overset{-2}{\frown} \quad \overset{-2}{\frown}$$
$$30 \quad 2 \quad 28 \quad 4 \quad 26 \quad 6 \quad 24 \quad 8 \quad 22$$
$$\underset{+2}{\smile} \quad \underset{+2}{\smile} \quad \underset{+2}{\smile}$$

2. 9 10 1 11 12 3 13 . . . . (A) 2 14   (B) 5 14   (C) 14 5   (D) 14 15   (E) 14 1

Here one series starts with 9 and increases by 1, and the other series starts with 1 and increases by 2. Note that the first series progresses two terms at a time while the second series progresses one term at a time. Continuing the pattern, the next two numbers must be 14 5, which is answer (C).

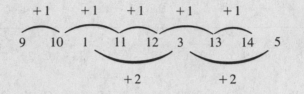

3. 8 8 1 10 10 4 12 . . . (A) 13 13 (B) 12 7 (C) 12 5 (D) 13 6 (E) 4 12

The first series starts with 8 and increases by 2 repeating each term. The second series starts with 1 and increases by 3 with each term given only once. The next two numbers must be 12 7, as in answer (B).

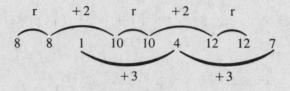

Look for alternating series in the practice problems that follow.

Sample Answer Sheet

1 Ⓐ Ⓑ Ⓒ Ⓓ Ⓔ   2 Ⓐ Ⓑ Ⓒ Ⓓ Ⓔ   3 Ⓐ Ⓑ Ⓒ Ⓓ Ⓔ   4 Ⓐ Ⓑ Ⓒ Ⓓ Ⓔ   5 Ⓐ Ⓑ Ⓒ Ⓓ Ⓔ

---

1. 38 15 32 17 27 19 23 . . . (A) 20 20   (B) 21 26   (C) 20 21   (D) 21 20   (E) 21 25

2. 1 20 3 19 5 18 7 . . . . . . (A) 8 9   (B) 8 17   (C) 17 10   (D) 17 9   (E) 9 18

3. 90 83 92 86 94 89 96 . . . (A) 92 98   (B) 98 100 (C) 90 99   (D) 98 92   (E) 98 99

4. 80 12 40 17 20 22 10 . . . (A) 25 15   (B) 15 25   (C) 24 5   (D) 25 5   (E) 27 5

5. 5 6 20 21 34 35 47 . . . (A) 48 49   (B) 48 59   (C) 48 36   (D) 36 48   (E) 48 55

Answers:

1. **(D)**

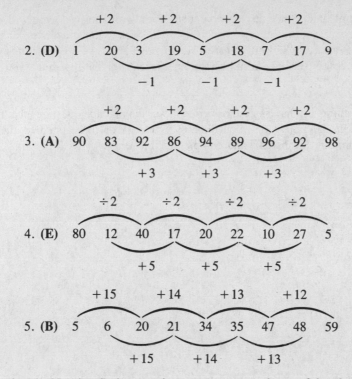

In answering the Number Series questions on your exam, be careful and methodical. You are allowed twenty minutes in which to answer twenty-four questions. That should be enough time. With study and practice, you should become skillful enough to handle any kind of number series question.

NUMBER SERIES TACTICS

1. Do first the questions that seem easiest to you. The questions are not necessarily arranged in order of difficulty, so answer quickly the questions which require little time and leave yourself extra time for the more difficult questions.

   When you skip a question, put a mark before the question number on the question sheet and SKIP ITS ANSWER SPACE. When you return to a question that you have skipped, be sure to mark its answer in the correct space. The time you spend checking to make sure that question and answer number are alike is time well spent.

2. Follow the procedures outlined in this chapter. First, look for an obvious pattern. Second, sound out the series; if necessary, group the numbers and sound out again. Third, write the direction and amount of change between numbers. If you still have not found the rule, look for two alternating series and for uncommon types of progressions.

   If you do any figuring on the question sheet, be sure to mark the letter of the correct answer on your answer sheet. All answers must be marked on the answer sheet.

3. If none of the answers given fits the rule you have figured out, try again. Try to figure out a rule that makes one of the five answers a correct one.

4. Do not spend too much time on any one question. If a question seems impossible, skip it and come back later. A fresh look will sometimes help you find the answer. If you still cannot figure out the answer, guess. There is no scoring penalty for a wrong answer on this part of your exam, so by all means guess.

5. Keep track of time. Since there is no penalty for a wrong answer, you will want to answer every question. Leave yourself time to go back to the questions you skipped to give them a second look. If you are a slow worker and have not quite finished this part, leave a few seconds to mark random answers for the questions you cannot reach.

Apply everything you have learned as you answer the practice questions that follow. Build up your skill. Do not worry about time as you work on these practice questions. Concentrate on finding the pattern and completing the series.

NUMBER SERIES PRACTICE QUESTIONS

SET 1

DIRECTIONS: Each number series question consists of a series of numbers which follows some definite order. The numbers progress from left to right according to some rule. One lettered pair of numbers comprises the next two numbers in the series. Study each series to try to find a pattern to the series and to figure out the rule which governs the progression. Choose the answer pair which continues the series according to the pattern established and mark its letter on your answer sheet. Correct answers and explanations are on page 262.

Sample Answer Sheet

1 Ⓐ Ⓑ Ⓒ Ⓓ Ⓔ	6 Ⓐ Ⓑ Ⓒ Ⓓ Ⓔ	11 Ⓐ Ⓑ Ⓒ Ⓓ Ⓔ	16 Ⓐ Ⓑ Ⓒ Ⓓ Ⓔ	21 Ⓐ Ⓑ Ⓒ Ⓓ Ⓔ
2 Ⓐ Ⓑ Ⓒ Ⓓ Ⓔ	7 Ⓐ Ⓑ Ⓒ Ⓓ Ⓔ	12 Ⓐ Ⓑ Ⓒ Ⓓ Ⓔ	17 Ⓐ Ⓑ Ⓒ Ⓓ Ⓔ	22 Ⓐ Ⓑ Ⓒ Ⓓ Ⓔ
3 Ⓐ Ⓑ Ⓒ Ⓓ Ⓔ	8 Ⓐ Ⓑ Ⓒ Ⓓ Ⓔ	13 Ⓐ Ⓑ Ⓒ Ⓓ Ⓔ	18 Ⓐ Ⓑ Ⓒ Ⓓ Ⓔ	23 Ⓐ Ⓑ Ⓒ Ⓓ Ⓔ
4 Ⓐ Ⓑ Ⓒ Ⓓ Ⓔ	9 Ⓐ Ⓑ Ⓒ Ⓓ Ⓔ	14 Ⓐ Ⓑ Ⓒ Ⓓ Ⓔ	19 Ⓐ Ⓑ Ⓒ Ⓓ Ⓔ	24 Ⓐ Ⓑ Ⓒ Ⓓ Ⓔ
5 Ⓐ Ⓑ Ⓒ Ⓓ Ⓔ	10 Ⓐ Ⓑ Ⓒ Ⓓ Ⓔ	15 Ⓐ Ⓑ Ⓒ Ⓓ Ⓔ	20 Ⓐ Ⓑ Ⓒ Ⓓ Ⓔ	

---

1. 12 26 15 26 18 26 21 . . . (A) 21 24 (B) 24 26 (C) 21 26 (D) 26 24 (E) 26 25

2. 72 67 69 64 66 61 63 . . . (A) 58 60 (B) 65 62 (C) 60 58 (D) 65 60 (E) 60 65

3. 81 10 29 81 10 29 81 . . . (A) 29 10 (B) 81 29 (C) 10 29 (D) 81 10 (E) 29 81

4. 91 91 90 88 85 81 76 . . . (A) 71 66 (B) 70 64 (C) 75 74 (D) 70 65 (E) 70 63

5. 22 44 29 37 36 30 43 . . . (A) 50 23 (B) 23 50 (C) 53 40 (D) 40 53 (E) 50 57

6. 0 1 1 0 2 2 0 . . . . (A) 0 0 (B) 0 3 (C) 3 3 (D) 3 4 (E) 2 3

7. 32 34 36 34 36 38 36 . . . (A) 34 32 (B) 36 34 (C) 36 38 (D) 38 40 (E) 38 36

8. 26 36 36 46 46 56 56 . . . (A) 66 66 (B) 56 66 (C) 57 57 (D) 46 56 (E) 26 66

9. 64 63 61 58 57 55 52 . . . (A) 51 50 (B) 52 49 (C) 50 58 (D) 50 47 (E) 51 49

10. 4 6 8 7 6 8 10 9 8 . . . . (A) 7 9 (B) 11 12 (C) 12 14 (D) 7 10 (E) 10 12

11. 57 57 52 47 47 42 37 . . . (A) 32 32 (B) 37 32 (C) 37 37 (D) 32 27 (E) 27 27

12. 13 26 14 25 16 23 19 . . . (A) 20 21 (B) 20 22 (C) 20 23 (D) 20 24 (E) 22 25

13. 15 27 39 51 63 75 87 . . . . (A) 97 112 (B) 99 111 (C) 88 99 (D) 89 99 (E) 90 99

14. 2 0 2 2 2 4 2 6 2 8 . . . . (A) 2 2   (B) 2 8   (C) 2 10   (D) 2 12   (E) 2 16

15. 19   18   18   17   17   17   16 . . . (A) 16 16 (B) 16 15 (C) 15 15 (D) 15 14 (E) 16 17

16. 55   53   44   51   49   44   47 . . . . (A) 45 43 (B) 46 45 (C) 46 44 (D) 44 44 (E) 45 44

17. 100   81   64   49   36   25   16 . . . (A) 8 4   (B) 8 2   (C) 9 5   (D) 9 4   (E) 9 3

18. 2   2   4   6   8   18   16 . . . . (A) 32 64 (B) 32 28 (C) 54 32 (D) 32 54 (E) 54 30

19. 47   43   52   48   57   53   62 . . . . (A) 58 54 (B) 67 58 (C) 71 67 (D) 58 67 (E) 49 58

20. 38   38   53   48   48   63   58 . . . . (A) 58 58 (B) 58 73 (C) 73 73 (D) 58 68 (E) 73 83

21. 12   14   16   13   15   17   14 . . . . (A) 17 15 (B) 15 18 (C) 17 19 (D) 15 16 (E) 16 18

22. 30   30   30   37   37   37   30 . . . (A) 30 30 (B) 30 37 (C) 37 37 (D) 37 30 (E) 31 31

23. 75   52   69   56   63   59   57 . . . (A) 58 62 (B) 55 65 (C) 51 61 (D) 61 51 (E) 63 55

24. 176   88   88   44   44   22   22 . . . (A) 22 11 (B) 11 11 (C) 11 10 (D) 11 5 (E) 22 10

CORRECT ANSWERS—SET 1

1. D	4. E	7. D	10. E	13. B	16. E	19. D	22. A
2. A	5. B	8. A	11. B	14. C	17. D	20. B	23. D
3. C	6. C	9. E	12. C	15. A	18. C	21. E	24. B

Explanations:

1. **(D)** A + 3 series with the number <u>26</u> between terms.

$$12 \overset{+3}{} \textcircled{26} 15 \overset{+3}{} \textcircled{26} 18 \overset{+3}{} \textcircled{26} 21 \overset{+3}{} \textcircled{26} 24$$

2. **(A)** You may read this as a −5, +2 series

$$72 \overset{-5}{} 67 \overset{+2}{} 69 \overset{-5}{} 64 \overset{+2}{} 66 \overset{-5}{} 61 \overset{+2}{} 63 \overset{-5}{} 58 \overset{+2}{} 60$$

or as two alternating −3 series

3. **(C)** By inspection or grouping, the sequence 81   10   29 repeats itself over and over.

4. **(E)** Write in the numbers for this one.

$$91 \overset{-0}{} 91 \overset{-1}{} 90 \overset{-2}{} 88 \overset{-3}{} 85 \overset{-4}{} 81 \overset{-5}{} 76 \overset{-6}{} 70 \overset{-7}{} 63$$

5. **(B)** Here we have two distinct alternating series.

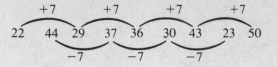

6. **(C)** The digit 0 intervenes after each repeating number of a simple $+1$ and repeat series.

$$\textcircled{0}\,1^r1\,{}^{+1}\textcircled{0}\,2^r2\,{}^{+1}\textcircled{0}\,3^r3$$

7. **(D)** Group the numbers into threes. Each succeeding group of three begins with a number two higher than the first number of the preceding group of three. Within each group the pattern is $+2$, $+2$.

8. **(A)** The pattern is $+10$, repeat the number; $+10$, repeat the number.

$$26\,{}^{+10}36^r36\,{}^{+10}46^r\,46\,{}^{+10}56^r56\,{}^{+10}66^r\,66$$

9. **(E)** The pattern is -1, -2, -3; -1, -2, -3 and so on. If you can't see it, write it in for yourself.

10. **(E)** Here the pattern is $+2$, $+2$, -1, -1; $+2$, $+2$, -1, -1.

$$4\,{}^{+2}6\,{}^{+2}8\,{}^{-1}7\,{}^{-1}6\,{}^{+2}8\,{}^{+2}10\,{}^{-1}9\,{}^{-1}8\,{}^{+2}10\,{}^{+2}12$$

The series which is given to you is a little bit longer than most to better assist you in establishing this extra long pattern.

11. **(B)** This is a -5 pattern with every other term repeated.

$$57^r57\,{}^{-5}52\,{}^{-5}47^r47\,{}^{-5}42\,{}^{-5}37^r37\,{}^{-5}\,32$$

12. **(C)** This series consists of two alternating series.

$$
\begin{array}{ccccccccc}
& \overset{+1}{\frown} & & \overset{+2}{\frown} & & \overset{+3}{\frown} & & \overset{+4}{\frown} & \\
13 & 26 & 14 & 25 & 16 & 23 & 19 & 20 & 23 \\
& & \underset{-1}{\smile} & & \underset{-2}{\smile} & & \underset{-3}{\smile} & &
\end{array}
$$

13. **(B)** This is a simple $+12$ series.

14. **(C)** Even with the extra length, you may have trouble with this one. You might have to change your approach a couple of times to figure it out.

$$2\,{}^{\times 0}0;\ 2\,{}^{\times 1}2;\ 2\,{}^{\times 2}4;\ 2\,{}^{\times 3}6;\ 2\,{}^{\times 4}8;\ 2\,{}^{\times 5}10$$

15. **(A)** Each number is repeated one time more than the number before it. <u>19</u> appears only once, <u>18</u> twice, <u>17</u> three times and, if the series were extended beyond the question, <u>16</u> would appear four times.

16. **(E)** This is a -2 series with the number 44 appearing after every two numbers of the series. You probably can see this by now without writing it out.

17. **(D)** The series consists of the squares of the numbers from two to ten in descending order.

18. **(C)** This is a tricky alternating series question.

$$\overset{\times 2}{\overgroup{2 \quad 2 \quad \underset{\times 3}{\undergroup{4 \quad 6}} \quad \overset{\times 2}{\overgroup{8 \quad 18}} \quad \underset{\times 3}{\undergroup{16 \quad 54}} \quad 32}}$$

2   2   4   6   8   18   16   54   32 (×2 pairs above: 2→4, 8→16, ... ; ×3 pairs below: 2→6, 6→18, 18→54)

19. **(D)** The progress of this series is −4, +9; −4, +9.

20. **(B)** This series is not really difficult, but you may have to write it out to see it.

$$38 \overset{r}{} 38 \overset{+15}{} 53 \overset{-5}{} 48 \overset{r}{} 48 \overset{+15}{} 63 \overset{-5}{} 58 \overset{r}{} 58 \overset{+15}{} 73$$

You may also see this as two alternating +10 series with the numbers ending in 8 repeated.

21. **(E)** Group into sets of three numbers. Each +2 mini-series begins one step up from the previous mini-series.

22. **(A)** By inspection you can see that this series is nothing more than the number <u>30</u> repeated three times and the number <u>37</u> repeated three times. Since you have no further clues, you must assume that the series continues with the number <u>30</u> repeated three times.

23. **(D)** Here are two alternating series.

75   52   69   56   63   59   57   61   51   (−6 above: 75→69, 69→63, 63→57, 57→51 ; +4, +3, +2 below: 52→56, 56→59, 59→61)

24. **(B)** The pattern is ÷2 and repeat the number; ÷2 and repeat the number.

$$176 \overset{\div 2}{} 88 \overset{r}{} 88 \overset{\div 2}{} 44 \overset{r}{} 44 \overset{\div 2}{} 22 \overset{r}{} 22 \overset{\div 2}{} 11 \overset{r}{} 11$$

NUMBER SERIES PRACTICE QUESTIONS

SET 2

DIRECTIONS: Each number series question consists of a series of numbers which follows some definite order. The numbers progress from left to right according to some rule. One lettered pair of numbers comprises the next two numbers in the series. Study each series to try to find a pattern to the series and to figure out the rule which governs the progression. Choose the answer pair which continues the series according to the pattern established and mark its letter on your answer sheet. Correct answers and explanations are on page 266.

Sample Answer Sheet

1 Ⓐ Ⓑ Ⓒ Ⓓ Ⓔ   6 Ⓐ Ⓑ Ⓒ Ⓓ Ⓔ   11 Ⓐ Ⓑ Ⓒ Ⓓ Ⓔ   16 Ⓐ Ⓑ Ⓒ Ⓓ Ⓔ   21 Ⓐ Ⓑ Ⓒ Ⓓ Ⓔ
2 Ⓐ Ⓑ Ⓒ Ⓓ Ⓔ   7 Ⓐ Ⓑ Ⓒ Ⓓ Ⓔ   12 Ⓐ Ⓑ Ⓒ Ⓓ Ⓔ   17 Ⓐ Ⓑ Ⓒ Ⓓ Ⓔ   22 Ⓐ Ⓑ Ⓒ Ⓓ Ⓔ
3 Ⓐ Ⓑ Ⓒ Ⓓ Ⓔ   8 Ⓐ Ⓑ Ⓒ Ⓓ Ⓔ   13 Ⓐ Ⓑ Ⓒ Ⓓ Ⓔ   18 Ⓐ Ⓑ Ⓒ Ⓓ Ⓔ   23 Ⓐ Ⓑ Ⓒ Ⓓ Ⓔ
4 Ⓐ Ⓑ Ⓒ Ⓓ Ⓔ   9 Ⓐ Ⓑ Ⓒ Ⓓ Ⓔ   14 Ⓐ Ⓑ Ⓒ Ⓓ Ⓔ   19 Ⓐ Ⓑ Ⓒ Ⓓ Ⓔ   24 Ⓐ Ⓑ Ⓒ Ⓓ Ⓔ
5 Ⓐ Ⓑ Ⓒ Ⓓ Ⓔ   10 Ⓐ Ⓑ Ⓒ Ⓓ Ⓔ   15 Ⓐ Ⓑ Ⓒ Ⓓ Ⓔ   20 Ⓐ Ⓑ Ⓒ Ⓓ Ⓔ

---

1. 5 21 8 19 11 17 14 . . . . . (A) 17 15 (B) 19 15 (C) 15 17 (D) 12 19 (E) 20 12

2. 2 4 12 8 16 12 32 . . . . . . (A) 64 12 (B) 32 12 (C) 12 32 (D) 12 64 (E) 16 12

3. 45 45 39 39 33 33 27 . . . (A) 21 21 (B) 27 27 (C) 27 22 (D) 21 27 (E) 27 21

4. 17 19 23 29 31 35 41 . . . (A) 48 52 (B) 43 47 (C) 49 59 (D) 44 48 (E) 47 55

5. 5 4 3 6 5 4 7 . . . . (A) 8 9 (B) 5 3 (C) 8 7 (D) 6 5 (E) 6 7

6. 64 63 60 55 48 39 28 . . . (A) 16 6 (B) 17 5 (C) 18 9 (D) 15 0 (E) 14 −2

7. 1 3 6 4 2 4 8 . . . . (A) 6 3 (B) 10 8 (C) 16 14 (D) 10 14 (E) 6 4

8. 74 69 54 64 59 54 54 . . . (A) 54 49 (B) 49 44 (C) 54 59 (D) 49 54 (E) 59 54

9. 21 66 25 70 29 74 33 . . . (A) 37 78 (B) 38 79 (C) 79 37 (D) 78 38 (E) 78 37

10. 35 37 39 37 39 41 39 . . . (A) 40 41 (B) 41 43 (C) 41 39 (D) 37 39 (E) 42 44

11. 75 32 83 12 75 32 83 . . . (A) 32 75 (B) 75 32 (C) 12 75 (D) 83 12 (E) 26 64

12. 12 13 15 16 19 20 24 . . . (A) 25 26 (B) 25 28 (C) 29 30 (D) 28 30 (E) 25 30

13. 46 39 39 34 34 31 31 . . . (A) 31   29 (B) 31   30 (C) 30   30 (D) 30   29 (E) 29   29

14. 4 6 9 11 14 16 19 . . . . . . (A) 21   24 (B) 22   25 (C) 20   22 (D) 21   23 (E) 22   24

15. 26 31 36 42 48 55 62 . . . (A) 70   78 (B) 69   70 (C) 70   72 (D) 66   72 (E) 68   74

16. 85 76 67 58 49 40 31 . . . (A) 24   18 (B) 29   20 (C) 21   12 (D) 23   15 (E) 22   13

17. 33 30 37 34 41 38 45 . . . (A) 39   48 (B) 48   46 (C) 52   41 (D) 42   49 (E) 49   42

18. 2 1 4 1 1 6 1 1 1 . . . (A) 12   1   (B) 1   12 (C) 1   1   (D) 1   8   (E) 8   1

19. 72 72 86 86 90 90 104 . . . (A) 104   114 (B) 104   118 (C) 104   104
(D) 104   112 (E) 104   108

20. 16 18 17 19 18 20 19 . . . (A) 21   20 (B) 20   21 (C) 21   19 (D) 22   21 (E) 22   20

21. 5 5 10 6 6 12 7 . . . . (A) 7   8   (B) 7   14 (C) 14   8   (D) 14   16 (E) 7   7

22. 25 32 31 28 35 34 31 . . . (A) 35   22 (B) 37   30 (C) 38   37 (D) 39   36 (E) 37   38

23. 8 9 10 10 11 12 12 . . . . . (A) 12   13 (B) 11   10 (C) 11   12 (D) 13   14 (E) 14   16

24. 5 87 10 81 30 76 120 72 . . . (A) 600   69 (B) 160   70 (C) 200   76
(D) 400   68 (E) 600   68

CORRECT ANSWERS—SET 2

1. C	4. B	7. A	10. B	13. C	16. E	19. E	22. C
2. A	5. D	8. D	11. C	14. A	17. D	20. A	23. D
3. E	6. D	9. E	12. E	15. A	18. E	21. B	24. A

Explanations:

1. **(C)** There are two alternating series here. One series increases at the rate of $+3$; the other decreases at the rate of -2.

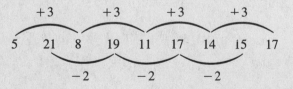

2. **(A)** This series increases at the rate of $\times 2$ with the number 12 repeated after each two members of the series.

3. **(E)** This is a -6 series in which each member of the series repeats itself.

$$45 \ ^r 45 -^6 39 \ ^r 39 -^6 33 \ ^r 33 -^6 27 \ ^r 27 -^6 21$$

4. **(B)** The pattern of increase is $+2$, $+4$, $+6$; $+2$, $+4$, $+6$; $+2$, $+4$, $+6$.

$$17 +^2 19 +^4 23 +^6 29 +^2 31 +^4 35 +^6 41 +^2 43 +^4 47$$

5. **(D)** Group the numbers into threes. Each succeeding group of three begins with a number one higher than that of the preceding group. Each group of three is a -1 series.

6. **(D)** The best way to find the pattern for this series is to write the amount of decrease between the terms of the series.

$$64 -^1 63 -^3 60 -^5 55 -^7 48 -^9 39 -^{11} 28 -^{13} 15 -^{15} 0$$

7. **(A)** It may take some trial and error to establish a pattern for this series. If you limit yourself to *plus* and *minus*, you cannot make sense out of it. However, if you expand the possibilities to *times* and *divided by,* you will eventually discover that the pattern is $+2$, $\times 2$, -2, $\div 2$; $+2$, $\times 2$, -2, $\div 2$.

$$1 +^2 3 \times^2 6 -^2 4 \div^2 2 +^2 4 \times^2 8 -^2 6 \div^2 3$$

8. **(D)** This is a -5 series with the number $\underline{54}$ separating each group of two terms. Don't be confused because one term in the series happens to be the number $\underline{54}$.

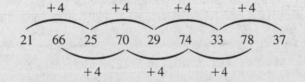

9. **(E)** There are two alternating $+4$ series.

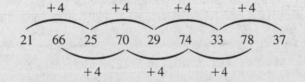

10. **(B)** This series can be interpreted in either of two ways. You may see $+2$, $+2$, -2; $+2$, $+2$, -2. Or you may see three-number miniseries with each miniseries increasing by 2, and each new miniseries beginning two numbers below the end of the previous series.

11. **(C)** The numbers bear no meaningful relationship to one another. The same miniseries of four unrelated numbers—75 32 83 12—repeats itself over and over.

12. **(E)** You will find the pattern of increase by writing in the differences between numbers. The pattern is $+1$, $+2$, $+1$, $+3$, $+1$, $+4$ and so on

$$12 +^1 13 +^2 15 +^1 16 +^3 19 +^1 20 +^4 24 +^1 25 +^5 30$$

13. **(C)** The numbers are decreasing first by -7, then by -5, -3 and -1. Each number is repeated before the subtraction is made.

$$46 -^7 39 \ ^r 39 -^5 34 \ ^r 34 -^3 31 \ ^r 31 -^1 30 \ ^r 30$$

14. **(A)** You may see this as two alternating series, one beginning with 4 and increasing by 5 and one beginning with 6 and increasing by 5. Or you may see it as a series that increases by $+2$, $+3$, $+2$, $+3$. . . .

15. **(A)** The progress of this series is $+5$, $+5$, $+6$, $+6$, $+7$, $+7$, $+8$, $+8$. . . .
16. **(E)** This is a simple -9 series.
17. **(D)** The pattern for this series is -3, $+7$, -3, $+7$.
18. **(E)** There are two distinct patterns. The first pattern is a simple $+2$ pattern. The alternate pattern consists of an increasing number of 1's.

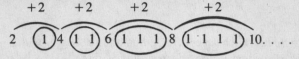

19. **(E)** The increase is at the alternating rate of $+14$, $+4$, $+14$, $+4$. Each number is repeated before it is increased.

$$72 \; ^r \; 72 +{}^{14}86 \; ^r \; 86 +{}^4 90 \; ^r \; 90 +{}^{14}104 \; ^r \; 104 +{}^4 108$$

20. **(A)** The pattern of this series is $+2$, -1, $+2$, -1, $+2$, -1.
21. **(B)** Grouping will help you continue this series. The pattern is somewhat unusual. The first two numbers are added to reach the third. The next group moves one up in counting order from the one before it.

$$5 + 5 = 10; \; 6 + 6 = 12; \; 7 + 7 = 14 \ldots .$$

22. **(C)** Write in the direction and amount of change between numbers to find that the pattern is: $+7$, -1, -3; $+7$, -1, -3.
23. **(D)** Again, grouping should help. Accent the third number in each group of three. Repeat the accented number as you begin the next group.

$$8 \quad 9 \quad 10; \quad 10 \quad 11 \quad 12; \quad 12 \quad 13 \quad 14; \quad 14 \ldots$$

24. **(A)** There are two alternating series, and both are somewhat difficult to figure out. The first series starts with 5 and increases by multiplication, first by 2, then 3, then 4, then 5. The second series starts with 87 and decreases first by 6, then by 5, then by 4, then by 3.

$$\overset{\times 2}{} \qquad \overset{\times 3}{} \qquad \overset{\times 4}{} \qquad \overset{\times 5}{}$$

$$5 \quad 87 \quad 10 \quad 81 \quad 30 \quad 76 \quad 120 \quad 72 \quad 600 \quad 69$$

$$\underset{-6}{} \qquad \underset{-5}{} \qquad \underset{-4}{} \qquad \underset{-3}{}$$

For practice with eight full-length model exams, purchase Arco's *Distribution Clerk, Machine*.